What Would It Take to Make an Ed School Great?

What Would It Take to Make an Ed School Great?

**VOICES FROM AN
UNFINISHED REVOLUTION**

JOHN SCHWILLE

MICHIGAN STATE UNIVERSITY PRESS
EAST LANSING, MICHIGAN

Michigan State University Press
East Lansing, Michigan 48823-5245

This publication was made possible through the generous support of the College of Education of Michigan State University.

Library of Congress Cataloging-in-Publication Data is available
ISBN 978-1-948314-13-8 (Paperback)
ISBN 978-1-948314-14-5 (PDF)
ISBN 978-1-948314-15-2 (ePub)
ISBN 978-1-948314-16-9 (Kindle)

Cover design by Peter Holm, Sterling Hill Productions

Visit Michigan State University Press at *www.msupress.org*

Contents

PART THREE. What Was So Revolutionary about All This?

Foreword

COURTNEY BELL

Education reform is disheartening. Most often, it does not work well or cannot be scaled effectively. Funding wanes. Political coalitions fracture. Founding reformers grow weary. And the promise of newer, untried reforms distracts. If you are even a casual student of school reform, you likely know the disappointment that accompanies this endeavor.

And yet, here you find yourself reading a book about teacher-education reform. Teacher education has been so remarkably resistant to reform that a private funder recently told me, "We've given up trying to change teacher education. It just can't be done under the current conditions."

But in this book Jack Schwille tells us a story about how a group of people did just that—they changed teacher education at Michigan State University (MSU), a preeminent land-grant university and one of the largest research-intensive institutions in the nation. This group of unlikely collaborators accomplished unprecedented change in secondary and elementary teacher-education programs that serve hundreds of preservice teachers yearly. In fairness, the group did not achieve all they set out to do. There were many failures. But over three decades they changed teacher education for themselves and hundreds of prospective teachers, teacher educators, and researchers.

Jack Schwille has a unique perspective on the unfinished revolution, one not yet shared in the literature. He was a faculty member at MSU throughout the timespan covered in this book, retiring in 2013 as an emeritus professor and assistant dean of international education. Yet Schwille was not a central actor in the reform, and he is not a teacher educator. While he knows many of the central actors personally and deeply, his account weaves that knowledge with an analysis of primary documents (internal memos, program reports, budgets, etc.), research articles written by MSU teacher educators and practicing teachers, and books. His account therefore blends aspects of both insider and outsider perspectives.

Even with a unique perspective on an important teacher-education reform, you might reasonably wonder what can be learned from reform in a single institution. Our country faces different challenges than it did when the Holmes Group issued its reports and *A Nation at Risk* was launched at MSU. COVID-19 caused new and profound human losses and exacerbated economic, racial, and political divides that were already large. What can we learn today from MSU's experience over the past three decades?

This question was especially relevant for me as I began to read the manuscript. I graduated from Michigan State University in 2004 with a PhD from the department that is arguably at the center of the reform—MSU's Department of Teacher Education. I taught one of the courses mentioned in the book and knew or came to know many of the faculty members that participated in the revolution. Some were on my dissertation committee. You might expect that as a doctoral student during the waning days of MSU's unfinished revolution, I would know much of this story. But I did not. And the intervening eighteen years of my own leadership, research, and professional teacher-education experiences have given me a different lens through which to regard the lessons in this book.

Schwille's account of the unfinished revolution is both heartbreaking and inspiring. The revolution at MSU involved hundreds of people across all four subjects—mathematics, English language arts, science, and social studies—in elementary and secondary programs. The revolution deliberately dismantled long-held power differentials between university staff and K–12 teachers, treated teaching and teacher education as serious intellectual pursuits worthy of study and training, and collaboratively enacted and investigated teaching and teacher-education practices that were groundbreaking for all involved.

The scholarship that can be traced back to the MSU revolution includes some of the most important contributions to the field in the last fifty years: the development of research on pedagogical content knowledge; the mentoring of novice teachers; the eliciting and reform-minded instruction of students' ideas (e.g., misconceptions, naive conceptions) in all four subject areas; and the development of a scholarship of teaching.

For leaders of the revolution—both K–12 teachers and teacher educators—the collaborative work engaged their hearts, minds, and bodies. Across time and actors, Schwille details multiple instances in which the researchers, teacher educators, and teachers undertook this exciting and consuming work together. Those descriptions include verbs such as invent, create, discuss, try, and collaborate, as well as the notions of "constant dialogue," "synergistic energy," and "webs of connections" that Schwille uses to characterize the collaborative work in professional development school partnerships. As I read, I could visualize the passion, intellectual engagement, and exhaustion embraced by so many. In my mind's eye, many participants were carrying out whole-body professional work at the edges of their understandings and capabilities. Some reported that the work was the highlight of their professional lives.

Given the scholarly and human impact of MSU's revolution, it is heartbreaking to read how routine aspects of school and university life—budgets, politics, tenure requirements, leadership turnover, etc.—intervened to truncate additional research contributions and wholistic professional work. It is heartbreaking to know the revolution remains unfinished. And as I consider the teacher education occurring at our current research-intensive institutions—increasingly siloed and filled with gifted scholars incentivized to prove their worth on metrics of the least publishable unit and most grants awarded—it seems unlikely that new revolutions will take hold in the medium-term future. That realization makes this story even more heartbreaking.

MSU's unfinished revolution made important progress on core challenges that we face today, such as the deep and abiding disconnect between research-intensive universities and K–12 schools; the effective mentoring of novice teachers; the development of novices' subject-matter knowledge in order to elicit, interpret, and support students' ideas; and the role of curriculum in teaching.

Schwille's story inspires us to return to these challenges and see them with fresh eyes, framed by the urgent need to address inequities exacerbated by COVID-19 and racial injustice.

It is especially inspiring to be reminded about the bodies of research on teachers' knowledge that can help us with today's core teaching challenges. MSU revolutionaries made significant progress in helping us understand the need to support novices around subject-matter knowledge. They documented what novices know and do not know, and the kind of skilled mentoring that is required to transform novices' knowledge and skills in ways that support connections to students' understandings. This can inspire us to connect those insights with contemporary insights around the need to support children's social and emotional learning and the importance of grounding classroom activities in the rich diversity of our students' identities and life experiences. The MSU story reminds us to consider the work of teaching and teacher education as both/and, with respect to subject matter and social-emotional support for students.

I offer one last reason for inspiration. As Americans, we often celebrate the lone individual who accomplishes—through their own brilliance, hard work, luck, or a combination of these elements—what others could not. At its core, MSU's unfinished revolution is a human story that demonstrates the power of a group of people, not an individual. The MSU revolution is about bright, hard-working, intellectually humble colleagues (like many of you reading this book) who joined forces to study and innovate around enduring problems in teacher education. Margaret Mead's oft-cited conviction comes to mind: "Never doubt that a small group of thoughtful, committed citizens can change the world. Indeed, it is the only thing that ever has." The unfinished revolution can inspire us to gather with other thoughtful, committed citizens to change teacher education for the current generation. We need only find one another—and begin.

Acknowledgments

One of my purposes in writing this book was to do justice to the people who did the work of the revolution and have made the MSU College of Education great. Therefore, this book is dedicated to the many people who made it possible.

- To the leaders who brought intellect, charisma, creativity, and doggedness to start the revolution in teaching and teacher education at MSU and keep it going, including (but not limited to) Judith Lanier, Joyce Putnam, Henrietta Barnes, Sharon Feiman-Nemser, Lee Shulman, Harry Judge, and Robert Floden.
- To the amphibious professors who demonstrated so much of what was revolutionary about the era: Deborah Ball, Magdalene Lampert, Dan Chazan, Kathy Roth, Suzanne Wilson, and David Wong.
- To the MSU and K–12 educators whose leadership brought revolutionary change to university-K–12 relations, including Tom Davis, Cookie Crutchfield, Sue York, Mike Lehman, Bruce Rochowiak, Charles Thompson, Doug Campbell, Cheryl Rosaen, Chris Wheeler, Perry Lanier, Jan Alleman, Jim Gallagher, and Tim Little; and to the MSU scholars and activists whose work was instrumental, at least for a time, in making the Holmes Group and the Michigan Partnership for New Education principal national centers of educational reform: Richard Elmore, Joyce Grant, Gary Sykes, and Jay Featherstone.
- To Doug Campbell, who joined me in saving the documents that made this book possible, and to the others who tolerated our packrat habits in spite of their distaste

for the lack of order that this entailed, saving speeches, memos and other fugitive literature he received during his years of devoted work on the MSU revolution.

- To the other leaders who, in the face of severe stress and extraordinary challenges, maintained and increased the overall quality, organizational soundness, financial viability, and exceptional spirit that characterized the College of Education: Gail Nutter, Carole Ames, Andrew Porter, Cass Book, Sonya Gunnings-Moton, Barbara Markle, David Cohen, Jere Brophy, and David Pearson.
- To Courtney Bell for being the perfect choice to write the foreword, and to Laura Holden who, as a graduate assistant, helped me start this project before I retired.
- To Chris Sovey for the support I needed to finish this book.
- To Bob Floden who, from start to finish, over a period of ten years, was my main supporter in the writing of this book, and who at the end gave me the editorial help I needed to greatly reduce the length of the book and without which I could not have finished it.
- And finally, to my spouse, Sharon Schwille, who devoted most of her career to the revolution and whose extraordinary qualities and achievements were my main motivation and inspiration for writing about this absorbing tale.

Introduction

In 2014 Elizabeth Green published a book in which chapter 3 was titled "The Spartan Tragedy." Had it been a more typical book, one might have imagined that it dealt with a sad saga in Spartan sports at Michigan State University (MSU)—football or basketball most likely. But that was not the case at all. The book was about newsworthy attempts to improve teaching in U.S. K–12 schools, and the chapter in question dealt with revolutionary reform efforts at MSU that took place in the 1980s and 1990s.

But was it a tragedy? What happened at MSU that could be so characterized? In my view, these developments could indeed be viewed as ending at least hyperbolically in tragedy. But they could also be seen in a much more positive light.

I hope it goes without saying, but perhaps it won't, that this book is my personal take on the ideas, events, and personalities that shook the MSU College of Education to the core, more visibly disruptive perhaps than any other school of education had experienced in the relatively short history of educational study as institutionalized in U.S. higher education. Others who experienced this period of reform and turbulence will no doubt have somewhat or completely different interpretations of what went on and even, in some cases though hopefully few, differences on matters of fact. Whatever the case, my hope is that this book will bring new life to the debate over whether teacher education in the United States and the nature of university-K–12 relations can be transformed in revolutionary ways, less subject to stultifying conventions and orthodoxy, to the benefit of all the nation's children.

This is thus a book that reexamines the era of the 1980s and early 1990s when MSU became a de facto center for education reform and much was learned as a result. Extremely ambitious agendas for reform of K–12 teaching and reform of teacher education were put on the national table under MSU leadership through two organizations created to move these agendas forward. One was the Holmes Group and the other the Michigan Partnership for New Education (MPNE). The Green book examines only a small part of these efforts, concentrating mainly on the work of Magdalene Lampert and Deborah Ball and their colleagues at Spartan Village Elementary School in East Lansing. It then moves on to other icons and venues of national reform.

Despite MSU's central role in this account, *What Would It Take to Make an Ed School Great?* is far from a straightforward institutional history, but rather a history of ideas, conveyed through the words of teachers and scholars responsible for what was revolutionary about this period. The lessons range from how to help aspiring teachers accept and embrace the intellectual rigors of teaching, to new understanding of what it takes to mentor novice teachers, to how universities and K–12 schools must fundamentally recast their relationships to create effective settings for teacher preparation and educational research. At the heart of the revolution was its insistence on treating teacher education, however low status it had been, with the respect due such a key lever in the future of schooling and the nation at large. Teaching was to be understood not as a low-level occupation that anyone could do, but as an intellectual challenge that can consume whole lifetimes—and that cannot be expected to come naturally with experience. Instead teaching must be taught.

In figuring out how to do this, the MSU revolution has left us with the following questions for schools of education attempting to become the best that they can be.

- What is the role of K–12 master teachers in university schools of education? Are they teaching alongside traditional faculty in teacher-education programs with the legitimacy and status associated with university appointments? Are they sought after as members of dissertation committees? Are they even full partners in doing research?
- What has happened to PDSs where university professors were assigned as a major part of their workload to these

K–12 schools to do collaborative research, dissemination, and teacher education and where the K–12 teachers have released time and other incentives to engage in research, mentor teacher-education students, and carry out professional development for other teachers?

- How many of the school and university staff who currently mentor prospective teachers during their periods of field experience and student teaching receive enough preparation for this role, are freed up from other responsibilities sufficiently, and are rewarded financially and in other ways for their mentoring?
- What has been put in place to ensure that the graduates of initial teacher preparation have a solid research-based understanding of how content or subject-matter knowledge must be transformed for purposes of teaching? How well do they understand variations in how pupils learn subject matter?
- Are the graduates of teacher education prepared to work closely with other teachers and parents as well as students?
- Are the graduates of teacher education prepared to open their teaching to observation and critical feedback from colleagues, administrators, and parents?
- How sophisticated, innovative, and effective is the use of technology in learning to teach?
- What evidence is there that teacher-education students have advanced in their acceptance, understanding, and ability to cope with the intellectual rigors that learning to teach ought to entail?

Revolutionary efforts at MSU have already been discussed in a substantial literature on what was and was not accomplished and learned during the revolution. Disregarding for the moment all the journal articles and dissertations based on MSU and affiliated schools, it is enough to mention a number of remarkable books. These include not only books on the work of Lampert and Ball, such as *Teaching, Multimedia, and Mathematics: Investigations of Real Practice* (1998), but also books on various theoretical issues and program developments in teacher education, such as *Teachers as Learners* (2012), a republication of groundbreaking articles by Sharon Feiman-Nemser, which cast so much new light on teacher preparation. And if we make an analogy to the period of the Enlightenment in which eighteenth-century philosophers prepared the way for the French revolution, then surely this role at MSU was played by Lee Shulman and the many essays he wrote, which are much cited in the chapters that follow in the present book. These essays have been ably edited by another leader of the revolution, Suzanne Wilson, and republished in 2004 under the title *The Wisdom of Practice: Essays on Teaching, Learning, and Learning to Teach*. Still another book, *Exploring Teaching: Reinventing an Introductory Course* (1992), edited by Sharon Feiman-Nemser and Helen Featherstone, focuses on the much worked-over course to introduce MSU students to what teaching is all about. Then there is a book with extraordinary insights into the history of "Team One," one of the MSU five-year teacher-education programs (Carroll et al., 2007b). It illustrates much of what the reform agendas called for. As explained in the introduction, it is "a book about our efforts as passionate, committed practitioners to develop a high-quality teacher education program in a large and bureaucratic university over the span of a decade" (1). It goes on to say that "the Team One story is about radical democratic change on a big scale" (9). As such, this book could almost stand alone in representing the whole attempted revolution, except that a great deal also took place outside this particular program.

For three additional and different perspectives, see the extraordinary account of what Dan Chazan learned as a university professor teaching lower-track algebra at Holt High School in a suburb of Lansing, Michigan (Chazan, 2000) and another book that deals with mathematics teaching at the same school during the revolutionary era when it was a professional development school (Chazan, Callis & Lehman, 2008); the latter is the best account of a single professional development school (PDS). Its significance for the history of the PDSs is somewhat hidden because the title focuses only on mathematics. The title of Gary Sykes's chapter in that book, "A Quiet Revolution? Reflecting on Mathematics Reform at Holt High School," better captures the significance of this publication. It even uses the metaphor of revolution that I have taken to characterize the whole argument of the present book. Finally, there is also the in-depth study by Sharon Schwille, titled *Never Give Up: An Experienced Teacher Overcomes Obstacles to Change* (2016), of how much an experienced, thoughtful teacher, even within the context of a PDS, had to struggle to transform her teaching to fit the aims of the revolutionary era.

In addition, capturing much of the whole gamut of the MSU reform efforts was a PhD thesis by Francesca Forzani (2011), written not at MSU but at the University of Michigan, Ann Arbor, a rival and dominant university that has rarely taken MSU so seriously. Forzani did a very thorough and solid study of what was done to reform teacher education at MSU, both locally through the university and nationally through the Holmes Group under the leadership of MSU dean Judith Lanier. Forzani's thesis gives a clear picture of how ambitious this effort was and how much more was attempted than was ultimately realized. It provides a brief intellectual history of the Holmes Group nationally as well as what was done at MSU to implement these goals and ideas. Forzani reports on most of the same events in the revolutionary era as the present book does, but she does not go into as much depth in the substance of what was learned about teaching and learning as a result of the revolution.

The difference between the voices cited in my book and those cited in the Forzani (2011) thesis can be easily seen by comparing the reference lists in these two works to see how much they are based on different scholars. Forzani's list includes but few of the MSU scholars who were important in the revolution. Only Deborah Ball and David Cohen are credited with numerous publications, and while Suzanne Wilson, Magdalene Lampert, and Lee Shulman each are shown with a number of publications, the number is fewer or (in Wilson's case) about the same as on my list. Kathleen Roth and Dan Chazan, who were among the most important voices of the revolution, are not listed as first authors of any publications on her list. Others who receive very little attention, compared to the number of publications in my reference list,

are Sharon Feiman-Nemser, Jere Brophy, Robert Floden, Susan
Florio-Ruane, Mary Kennedy, and Cheryl Rosaen.

My conclusions also differ from those of Forzani. While I argue
that the revolution was both a great success and a great failure,
Forzani puts more emphasis on its failures than its revolutionary
successes. One of her headings in her thesis designates the end
of the revolutionary era as the "fall of a house of cards" (306).
She points out that "the Holmes Group failed to enact most of
its goals. Ten years after the publication of *Tomorrow's Teachers*
(1986), the first Holmes report, the teacher-education curriculum in programs across the United States had changed little, few
universities supported PDSs or other close collaborations with
K–12 schools, and the traditional teacher licensure system was
intact" (10–11).

In discussing the lessons learned that bear on these issues,
this book draws on unpublished or obscurely published sources
that can add to our understanding of what was accomplished but
subsequently disregarded. These include articles or chapters in
less widely known publications, unpublished papers presented at
conferences, dissertations, research memos and notes, a mass of
documents from college files that Doug Campbell and I managed
to collect, plus other fugitive literature. These provide a grassroots
perspective that demonstrates in considerable depth how far the
revolution had progressed before it was pushed back and in part
abandoned, orthodoxy and adherence to dysfunctional university
norms having once again taken over. Although Forzani (2011)
covers the same period of reform in splendid and superbly written
detail, there is a critical difference between her dissertation and
this book. She pays tribute to the ambitious nature of the reform
and takes note of its achievements, but concentrating on the politics and step-by-step attempts to bring reform into practice, she
does not quite bring the achievements to life in the way this book
attempts to do, so that the reader can fully appreciate the radical
nature of much that was accomplished (if not always sustained)
and see how different they were from prevailing practices across
the nation. The Spartan tragedy was not so much the failure of
college faculty and administrators at MSU or the K–12 teachers

in the PDSs as it was that the MPNE, the State of Michigan, and the central MSU administration failed to provide the resources, incentives, and organizational support necessary to keep the revolution going and redress its shortcomings. In my view then, this book is necessary to do justice to the success of those who brought so much of their talents and energy to this revolution before being cut off not just in midstream but even further back toward the origin of this work.

Ironically, for a university that has abandoned so many of these revolutionary pretensions, MSU is still known as a national and international leader in teacher education. In fact, in the 2020 Shanghai worldwide rankings of universities, the MSU College of Education is ranked as the top education school in the world. Likewise, according to *U.S. News and World Report*, it has been listed as first in the nation for graduate programs in elementary and secondary education for every year since 1995, the year when the magazine first published these rankings. This book explains what it took for the college to attain this status.

Abbreviations

AAAS	American Association for the Advancement of Science
CBTE	competency-based teacher education
EEE	Excellence in Elementary Education
EES	Educational Extension Service
FTE	full-time equivalents
IEA	International Association for the Evaluation of Educational Achievement
IRT	Institute for Research on Teaching
MEAP	Michigan Educational Assessment Program
MP	Multiple Perspectives
MPNE	Michigan Partnership for New Education
MSU	Michigan State University
NAEP	National Assessment of Educational Progress
NCRTE	National Center for Research on Teacher Education
NCRTL	National Center for Research on Teacher Learning
NIE	National Institute of Education
PCK	pedagogical content knowledge
PDS	professional development school
PTO	Parent-Teacher Organization
STEP	Student Teacher Experimental Program
STS	science-technology-society
TE	teacher-education
TEC	Teacher Education Circle
TELT	Teacher Education and Learning to Teach
TIMSS	originally the Third International Mathematics and Science Study, now Trends in International Mathematics and Science Studies

TNE	Teachers for a New Era
TPCK/TPACK	technological pedagogical content knowledge
TTT	Training of Teachers of Teachers
ZPD	zone of proximal development

The Rise and Decline of MSU's Visionary Aspirations for a Revolution in Learning to Teach

Although together the books already mentioned cover much of what was done in the movement for teacher-education reform at MSU, there is no one book that captures adequately both what was (and was not) done and how revolutionary it was. Some of the most relevant publications were written mainly for specific audiences, such as mathematics educators. Others cover partial pieces of teacher education such as the book on the development of the initial course that all teacher-education students took to begin to understand teaching from a teacher's point of view (Feiman-Nemser & Featherstone, 1992). Others leave out much that should be taken into account. Across all the publications and in comparing teacher-education teams and PDSs, less attention is given to Flint, Michigan, including in particular both Team Three in the five-year teacher-education program and the associated PDS efforts.

If so much was learned and published, is there still a need for yet another book two decades after the height of the revolution? The reason is that much of the knowledge generated was, in spite of the publications mentioned above, disseminated in relatively limited ways and without being incorporated widely in continuous professional development for teachers, which research has proved necessary to profound improvements in educational practice. It is therefore time to remind researchers and practitioners of this and renew the institutional memories, which have sorely faded away even at MSU. Part One recapitulates what it took to organize this revolution as well as the resources brought to the table.

CHAPTER ONE

First Steps toward
Challenging the Old Regime

Early innovation in teacher education at Michigan State University (MSU) occurred in the 1960s and 1970s. During those years a movement for fundamental reform of MSU teacher-education (TE) programs was started by a small minority of faculty who stood out for their willingness to take risks and responsibility for initial changes. Under their leadership, relatively small experimental programs took shape alongside the large and very conventional mainstream program. A major breakthrough occurred in 1975 when the college won a national competition for a federally funded Institute for Research on Teaching, which launched the college on a path toward national research leadership and provided a basis for gradual transformation of the college. At the same time currents of hostility emerged between the reformers and an energized old guard that was highly critical of much that was done.

It was in the 1990s that the college was first recognized by *U.S. News and World Report* as a national leader in teacher education. But the college viewed itself as a leader in this field well before that, although ironically, faculty specialists in teacher education were not given a status commensurate with this claim. While it is hard to date the start of MSU's claim to leadership in teacher education, the history of teacher education at MSU goes back to the earliest years of the twentieth century (Barnes, 1989; Inzunza, 2002). Two of the early deans, Clifford Erickson (1953–62, later provost) and John Ivey (1962–70), were farsighted in their emphasis on university engagement in K–12 schools. According to an earlier historian of MSU teacher education, "Ivey envisaged the cooperative arrangements with schools as providing a clinic for research and instruction somewhat analogous to the clinical program in a medical school" (Victor Noll, quoted in Inzunza, 2002, 33).

Use of K–12 schools as sites for MSU students learning to teach began as early as 1918. The college also reportedly had an induction program by 1923, and by the 1930s the East Lansing school district agreed to pay the salaries of three full-time teachers so they could devote themselves to preservice teacher education. However, after a financial disagreement with East Lansing, it was not long before the college moved on to other districts. Following years of continued variation in student-teaching arrangements, an era of MSU large student-teaching centers around the state began in 1954 (Barnes, 1989).

But, according to Inzunza (2002), it was not until the 1960s that innovation in teacher education became so intense that it remained one of the defining characteristics of the college throughout the remainder of the twentieth century. The first major such innovation was known as the Student Teacher Experimental Program (STEP), an attempt to relieve a severe shortage of rural teachers due in large part to closure of one-room schools. Designed for the graduates of two-year colleges, STEP was a mixture of long-term field experience and MSU study. It started with a summer session in liberal arts, followed by a full year of experience in a K–12 classroom during which the students also took college courses. In addition to the summer sessions, students were engaged in a two-year internship (later one-year) with full teaching duties on reduced salaries (compared to those of regular teachers). In 1963 the program was opened to on-campus students as well as two-year college graduates. By 1966 eight centers and forty-four school districts participated, and by 1970 about three hundred students per year graduated from the Elementary Intern Program or EIP (as STEP was by then called), constituting about a quarter of all MSU elementary education graduates at the time (Inzunza, 2002; Barnes, 1989).

As important and successful as STEP (or EIP) was, it never by itself threatened to undermine or supplant the mainstream status quo in the MSU College of Education. It was only in the 1970s that it was joined by other new initiatives that very gradually became a revolutionary movement aiming to transform MSU teacher education as a whole. These new programs included Training of Teachers of Teachers (TTT), Teacher Corps, Excellence in Elementary Education (EEE), Secondary Education Pilot Program, and the competency-based teacher-education program known as POINTE. They all had innovative features, especially in field experience, some of which are still not standard practice throughout the nation today (Inzunza, 2002, 72–73).

The EEE program resulted from the merger of TTT and the Teacher Corps after TTT's federal funding ended in 1973. A key feature, a presage to the later revolutionary changes, was its innovative, expanded opportunities for field experience:

> The TTT program . . . [had] both prospective teachers and teacher educators out in the schools for significantly greater periods of time than is typically allocated. . . . [Teacher candidates] observed and assisted Lansing teachers in the first term of their freshman year. They subsequently worked in schools every week of every term throughout their undergraduate years. . . . MSU teacher educators working in the program also made continuous and regular school observations, visitations and demonstrations. (MSU-17, ca. 1976–77)

In the meantime, the Teacher Corps program, which was also operating in Lansing, was similarly focused on teacher preparation, only with a special emphasis on recruiting and preparing minority teaching personnel. These prospective teachers entered the program in their junior year but also had intensive school experience since their program required a half day in school every day throughout the academic year (MSU-17, ca. 1976–88). However, these additional efforts, in spite of their strengths, were relatively small scale and remained numerically marginal to the mainstream standard program that had more than one thousand students doing student teaching at the same time around the state (Forzani, 2011, 192). At that point there was little to indicate that slowly and incrementally these innovations would eventually develop and be transformed into the full-scale assault on the status quo that took place in the late 1980s and early 1990s (Inzunza, 2002).

The mainstream standard program remained conventional and—viewed from hindsight—decidedly mediocre. After Sharon Feiman-Nemser joined the MSU faculty in 1981 as a conceptual leader in the emerging movement, she strongly criticized such programs because they consisted largely of separate courses reflecting the knowledge of a few faculty members drawn from different departments—courses that were too disconnected to constitute a coherent program and that usually relied on a pedagogy not suited to the development of practicing teachers. In addition, she noted that relationships with K–12 schools and with subject-matter departments were generally limited and weak. The program was "without a set of organizing themes, without shared standards, without clear goals for student learning, there was no framework to guide program design or assessment" (Feiman-Nemser 2001/2012a, 112–13).

In a later book on the five-year program at MSU, the weaknesses of this earlier mainstream program were laid out in still more unvarnished, uncomplimentary detail:

> At Michigan State, the standard program, which preceded the reforms of 1992, featured a laundry list of separate certification courses offered in multiple sections and taught by an array of tenured faculty, graduate students and adjunct faculty assigned centrally by teacher education department administrators. What was taught in any particular section of a course depended largely on who happened to be teaching it. There was seldom any conceptual linkage between courses and little in the way of a deliberate sequence building from one course to another. Student teacher arrangements were organized by a separate office responsible for hundreds of individual placements in over one hundred school districts spread throughout Michigan. (Carroll & Donnelly, 2007, 33)

The Movement Finds a Visionary Leader

If one had to choose one symbolic event that was critical in setting this internal movement for reform in motion, it might well be when Judith Henderson (later and best known as Judith Lanier) in her first major assignment after joining the faculty in 1968 took charge of a huge educational psychology foundations course (ED 200, Individual and the School) then required of all teacher-education students at MSU. My examination of the course packets with assignments and readings for this course, prepared for student use from 1971 to 1975 (MSU-12) by Lanier and colleagues, already reveals her passionate engagement with the issues of teacher education that continued to preoccupy her for the rest of her career. In particular, she was adamant that teaching deserved to be treated as more important and more consequential than was generally the case. For example, in the 1974–75 edition she draws on her own experience to discuss the deficiencies she had found in many teacher-education courses, especially because they had little to do with the practice of teaching.

> When I was a prospective teacher in training . . . I began with several education courses that still make my mind and emotions reel with frustration and incredulity when I think about them. The first course [on human] development, [went only from] . . . pre-natal development [to] . . . activities of the two-year-old. The second course was called "Introduction to Directed Teaching" . . . [where we] discussed many interesting things, e.g., was boy scouting an important activity for kids. . . . The professor lectured to us about how we should not lecture and fed us many spurious sounding platitudes about "good teaching." . . . But we worked very hard at staying far away from any concept of teaching, that is, what it actually involved, what its purposes were, etc., as we could. (16)

In those years, the course was offered in the largest lecture space in Erickson Hall, as well as in small sections to which some forty teaching assistants were assigned. The MSU teacher-education program at the time was huge: if one counts not just the elementary-education students with majors in the college, but also secondary-education students in other colleges, the College of Education had some twelve thousand undergraduates attending class in lecture halls with room for as many as a thousand students at a time in courses ill-suited to developing the skills, dispositions, or even knowledge needed by practicing teachers.

Early on, with pressure from students to make the psychological foundations course more relevant to preparation of teachers, Lanier was chosen to respond. It was hoped that she could use to good advantage the videotapes of classroom teaching that she produced during her dissertation on what distinguished excellent teachers from mediocre or poor ones (Forzani, 2011, 179).

Although the ED 200 course may seem very dated since so much has changed in the assumptions, conceptions, terminology, etc. relied upon to teach teaching, what Lanier said at the time still foreshadowed the future. The pitfalls of learning from experience, the knowledge previously gained about teaching, and the importance of introducing teacher-education students to how different it is to look at teaching through a teacher's eyes continued to be analyzed in depth by Sharon Feiman-Nemser and others in MSU publications in the 1980s.

Information from Forzani's interviews with Lanier and others show still more clearly how important ED 200 was to her development and subsequent career. Forzani explains:

> As she directed The Individual and the School, Lanier began exercising emergent skill at bringing people together to study and to learn. She organized voluntary meetings and seminars among the numerous other section leaders for the course, for example, often to probe instructional problems and discuss readings and other materials. (2011, 179)

As an emerging leader, Lanier began to bring together colleagues who shared her ability and enthusiasm for trying new approaches. These included Henrietta Barnes who joined the faculty in 1972 after being one of Lanier's first doctoral students and who remained a key person in MSU teacher education right up to her retirement in 2000 as chair of the Department of Teacher Education. Barnes received all her degrees from MSU and made her mark early, earning the Teacher Scholar award for junior faculty in 1975.

Joyce Putnam was another of the reformers from that period who then served as coordinator of successive teacher-education programs of reform more or less continually from 1974 to 2002. In looking back, she recalled that beginning when she was first hired, Judy Lanier had encouraged her to innovate in all her teacher-education work. As a result, in talking about this experience, she said that never in her whole career did she do teacher education in a traditional way. Whenever and however she experimented, Judy's response was never to hold her back but to encourage her to go even further (personal communication, April 12, 2017).

In 1975, Lanier, with her growing reputation for leadership ability, was selected for an administrative position in the college as director of the School of Teacher Education. On paper she had responsibility for the whole of teacher education in the College of Education (if not in other colleges where prospective teachers also took required courses), but in fact she had little real authority over the fragmented program. Nevertheless, this did not stop her from agitating for the beginning of real and substantial change in teacher education at the time.

Lanier's Indictment of Teacher Education

Judy Lanier's most comprehensive and cogently argued critique and indictment of the existing system of teacher education in the United States appeared in the third edition of the *Handbook of Research on Teaching* (Lanier & Little, 1986). Lanier started this review of the literature by totally excluding what she considered the trivial findings of studies that demonstrated only that "teachers can learn all sorts of things when formally taught" (528). Instead her focus was on an overall multidisciplinary analysis of the problems of teacher education and figuring out why this "troubled field is apparently so difficult to change." The wide-ranging chapter was organized into sections on each of four commonplaces that the influential curriculum theorist Joseph Schwab had defined as essential to any comprehensive analysis of educational practice: studying (1) those who teach teachers, (2) the students of teaching, (3) the curriculum for teaching, and (4) the milieu or context of teacher education.[1]

According to Lanier's analysis of the first commonplace, finding and keeping academically strong and competent teachers of teachers had proved problematic, and yet there was little research on this problem, most of it done by academic scholars little engaged in the education of teachers.

She did find research on the students of teacher education but said it was "desultory in nature, poorly synthesized, and weakly criticized." The key finding from this research was that the preservice teacher population had become smaller and "composed of fewer academically talented and more academically weak students than heretofore." Lanier noted that this decline was influenced by the conditions of teaching, including "the low professional and public regard for serious investment in teaching and teacher education, [plus] a work environment that is generally lacking in intellectual stimulation and group norms that traditionally and increasingly reflect below-average ability and interest in academic pursuits" (545).

From the research on the curriculum of teacher education, Lanier concluded that the increasing number of career teachers in the K–12 work force demanded both liberal-professional and technical components to teacher education, meaning that there should be more emphasis on the liberal-professional than had been the norm. She called for teacher-education curricula that are "deep, scholarly, coherent and related to continuing a liberal education throughout one's period of professional teaching." She also concluded that the teacher-education curriculum should not be based on research alone, but must be rooted in "codification, preservation and transmission of the lore of successful practice" (555).

From research on the context of teacher education, Lanier concluded that higher education was not investing in teacher

---

1. I took a course on this with Schwab at the University of Chicago in 1963.

education at a level commensurate with talk of its importance. Teacher education was severely underfunded. Moreover, accountability for use of these resources was absent or nominal. Finally, K–12 schools were doing no better in this respect. In Lanier's view, the experience of K–12 teaching was mostly noneducative or even miseducative.

At the end of her chapter, Lanier bemoaned the overall "deintellectualization" of teacher education within a milieu that keeps things as they are. She concluded that "the picture in each domain repeats a pattern that reinforces the maintenance of teacher education as a marginal part of the university community, criticized for its lack of rigor, but discouraged from trying to be anything else" (565).

Much can still be learned about teacher education over thirty years later from a careful reading of this chapter. It made public the justification for Lanier's commitment to the revolution. Marginal improvements would not be sufficient. Revolutionary change was necessary to break through the interlocking parts of the failing system. This movement had already begun. This small start by Lanier, her supporters, and allies led directly to increasingly significant change throughout the 1970s, 1980s, and into the 1990s. From this small beginning, profound even revolutionary changes were proposed and launched in stages, with larger and larger scope and more and more radically ambitious objectives. Eventually, a grand vision emerged that can be characterized as three concentric circles of reform centered at MSU: (1) reform of teacher education at the local college and university level (in other words at MSU), (2) reform of teacher education at the state level in Michigan, and (3) reform of teacher education at the national level.

The Institute for Research on Teaching, Trojan Horse of the MSU Revolution

In 1975 MSU won a federal competition to establish and fund an Institute for Research on Teaching (IRT), based on the recommendations of a 1974 national conference on research on teaching. The objective of this conference was to develop an agenda for further research and thereby guide the federal National Institute of Education (NIE) in the funding of educational research at the national level. The conference took the form of a number of expert panels, each of which was assigned a different approach or perspective on research on teaching to consider.

Panel 6, chaired by Professor Lee Shulman of MSU, was charged with developing "an understanding of the mental life of teachers, a research-based conception of the cognitive processes that characterize that mental life, their antecedents and their consequences for teaching and student performance." According to the mandate for this panel, innovations in teacher practice are best understood as mediated through teacher minds and motives. Teachers combine information about their students and classes and from the literature on education with their own expectations, attitudes, beliefs, and purposes. All this becomes the basis for decision-making and judgments (Gage, 1975, 1).

To win the competition for a research institute based on the panel's findings, Judy Lanier and Lee Shulman teamed up as proposed codirectors. Shulman was a professor with a strong national reputation in educational psychology. He had done important work outside the College of Education at MSU in medical education. He and his colleagues had studied how doctors bring their knowledge and problem-solving to bear on the diagnosis of patients; their intent was to use this research to improve the preparation of primary care physicians. Subsequently, Shulman and Arthur Elstein (1975) brought this expertise to their work on educational research.

The proposal MSU submitted in the IRT competition reminded the reader that the request for proposals called for research on "the classroom teacher as a clinician—one who processes information in order to reach diagnostic judgments and make prescriptive decisions in response to individual students" (MSU-25, 1976, B-I-12). It also called attention to the relationship between the proposal and panel 6 of the NIE conference. It admitted that it was "no coincidence" that five of nine researchers on the panel were also associated with the MSU proposal. Although this could have raised suspicions that the proposal had an inside track to win, the proposal itself took a more positive stance in suggesting that this was evidence that the five investigators had a sustained, strong commitment to the proposed research program. Calling attention to the parallels between this research perspective and Shulman's previous research on the thinking of physicians in clinical settings, the proposal adds:

> Research of this kind calls for studying teachers as gifted practitioners capable of performances which typically our best theories are not yet capable of explaining, much less predicting or generating. This valuing of the "wisdom of the practitioner" is a significant feature of our approach to research on teaching. (Shulman & Lanier, 1977, 45)

At about the same time, Joe Schwab, the University of Chicago professor, emerged to play the role of éminence grise in the IRT. Schwab is one of the forty-seven iconic professors whose careers are encapsulated chapter by chapter in the book on University of Chicago history edited by Edward Shils for the university's centennial in 1992 (Shils, 1991). In the IRT he was nominated to play a central role in the intellectual forum whose purpose was to be "the substantive interrelating of Institute activities, not as an administrative or fiscal task, but as an on-going conceptual challenge" (MSU-25, 1976, B-V-8). The proposal also made a commitment to create a national invisible college for research on teaching, an endeavor eventually orchestrated by Jere Brophy for many years with an annual meeting at the American Educational Research Association.

At the time of the IRT competition, the request for proposals did not make the goal of revolutionizing teacher education explicit for the new institute. It was much more concerned with understanding and improving K–12. In fact, research on teacher education was not yet fully recognized at MSU or elsewhere as a separate field from research on teaching. But the intention to improve teacher education was never far from the minds of the revolutionary leaders at MSU. The proposal did discuss the relationship between the IRT agenda and teacher education. It promised to work to heal the gulf between teacher education and research on teaching. And some research and evaluation in teacher education was planned for the institute, which was organized as a series of small projects, each drawing on a mix of MSU faculty, new faculty, graduate students, and at least one half-time K–12 teacher hired as a "teacher collaborator." The initial projects dealt with processes of reading, teacher conceptions of reading, teacher decision-making in language arts and mathematics, classroom management, contextual influences on teaching, and theory development in the study of teacher decision-making (Forzani, 2011, 183). In explaining how this approach differed from the dominant process-product work of previous years, the IRT proposal stressed that "it is not merely doing which defines teaching. It is knowing what to do and when to do it that constitutes the clinical aspect of teaching and defines the features of teaching that serve as the subject matter for research on teaching as clinical work" (MSU-25, 1976, B-I-6).

But the importance of the IRT for teacher education went far beyond the few projects that dealt with teacher education. The institute proved to be a Trojan horse for the revolution because it brought substantial resources and new scholars into the college, giving the revolutionary vanguard the power they needed to begin to overcome resistance to change without having to be out front about their long-term and controversial revolutionary agenda.

With federal funds from the NIE and the funds that MSU was willing to put up in cost-sharing, initial efforts of the IRT focused heavily on the recruitment of new researchers and faculty. Unlike other education research and development centers funded by the federal government such as Wisconsin and Pittsburgh, all researchers in the IRT were to be jointly appointed in one of the regular departments of the College of Education so they could, simultaneously with their externally funded research, strengthen degree programs in teacher education and related areas. This recruitment net was cast wider and wider as it developed, but in the beginning the recruitment strategy consisted of a pragmatic attempt to jump-start the IRT as fast as possible, taking advantage of whatever research strengths could be found and quickly mobilized. However, while certain faculty members who were already in the College of Education at MSU played an important role in the institute, Lanier and Shulman were united in the belief that specialists in foundational areas, not just in the fields of educational psychology already dominant in educational research, but also philosophy of education, sociology of education, anthropology of education, and even social sciences outside education, could make a contribution to the research of the multidisciplinary IRT and to the development of new teacher-education programs. The resulting hires throughout the 1980s and beyond helped reinforce MSU's growing reputation for national leadership.

Lee Shulman captured the unorthodox nature of this recruitment at the very beginning of this era in a section aptly titled "What's a Nice Philosopher Like You Doing in a Place Like That" (Shulman, 1993, 438).This referred to the arrival, early in the revolution, of Bob Floden and Margret Buchmann, neither of whom had teacher-education experience, and both of whom were destined to play important roles in teacher education at MSU—Floden throughout the entire history covered by this volume and Buchmann until she left MSU in 1997. At Stanford University, Floden had completed a master's in statistics and a PhD in philosophy of education. Buchmann's degree was also in philosophy of education with a dissertation on Hegel under David Philipps. Shulman recalled:

> Bob Floden and Margret Buchmann arrived at Michigan State University from Stanford's gentle climate on a Christmas Eve when the temperature was barely at zero Fahrenheit and the wind-chill was well below that mark. They came to work in an organization that was a department neither of philosophy nor of educational foundations. Instead they would begin to teach and to conduct research in a department of teacher education and a newly founded Institute for Research on Teaching. The institute, whose direction I shared with Professor Judith Lanier, was founded on a number of premises. We believed that problems of education were far too complex to be addressed by members of any one discipline or

educational specialty. Inspired in part by Joseph Schwab's image of practical deliberation informed by a disciplined eclectic, we had begun to organize an institutional cloak of many disciplines, a place where psychologists, teacher educators, economists, anthropologists, linguists, political analysts, curriculum specialists, philosophers and practicing school teachers could work together on the study of teachers. (Shulman, 1993/2004, 438–40)

By the time the IRT had completed its first five-year cycle in 1981 and was at work on a continuation proposal for another five years, the proposal's authors could claim growing success on the core goals of the institute:

Research on teacher thinking has come a long way, both conceptually and empirically, since 1974. The metaphor of the teacher as clinical diagnostician and decision maker has been put into perspective (teachers certainly do make diagnostic-prescriptive judgments and decisions, but this constitutes only a small part of their professional activities). Descriptive studies of the mental lives of teachers in real school settings reveal the powerful influences of context, policy, habit, and curriculum on teacher thought and action. Teachers themselves have been brought more fully into every phase of the enterprise of research on teaching as research collaborators. The wisdom of practice has joined with the rigor of scientific inquiry to produce descriptions and explanations of life in classrooms that are credible and useful to both communities. (MSU-26, 1981, A-19)

Although the IRT was expected to lay the basis for improvement in teacher education at MSU and elsewhere, little in its research program focused directly on learning to teach. The main exception was the project "Knowledge Use in Learning to Teach." The project leader was Sharon Feiman-Nemser, working with faculty member Margret Buchmann, K–12 teacher and graduate student Deborah

Ball, and teacher collaborator Beth Lawrence from East Lansing High School. They followed seven preservice students though two years of preparation from 1982 to 1984. Thorough, holistic research on teacher-education institutions and programs had not yet gotten off the ground at MSU or elsewhere. Lanier in her 1986 chapter in the *Handbook of Research on Teaching* was still emphasizing the lack of qualitative studies of the TE curriculum and what TE students were learning. Key research questions in need of investigation included (1) what teacher educators teach; (2) how learning opportunities are structured; (3) what happens when TE students move from university classrooms to actual classrooms; and (4) how these experiences do or do not add up to effective preparation for teaching. These questions were at the heart of the Knowledge Use in Learning to Teach project and continued to drive teacher-education research at MSU through the next two decades.

IRT Conclusions about Teaching

The final report of the IRT released in 1986 is a good summary of the conclusions reached by the institute on the state of teaching in U.S. elementary schools, plus recommendations based on these conclusions and directions for further research (MSU-27). Its vision, very different from conventional views on the nature of teaching, can be briefly stated as follows: Students are not there just to learn facts and solve problems given to them. Teachers create situations in which students themselves organize information in new ways and formulate problems for themselves. This includes coming up with problems in mathematics, creative writing, and independent projects in diverse subjects. This form of teaching is particularly demanding for both students and teachers. For all this to work, teachers have to monitor closely what students are learning and the reasons for this success. This requires, in turn, that teachers be more knowledgeable about subject matter than teachers who stick to a traditional approach. But in fact, teacher education and associated courses in the arts and sciences have not been able to get TE students to this level.

By this time, IRT research had gone through major changes between the first five years and the second. According to the final report, the institute had moved away from "questions of classroom management and student discipline and toward questions of the role of metacognitive strategies in the teaching of reading, how teachers decide what mathematics to teach, how to take account of student misconceptions in the teaching of science, and how might the amount of writing instruction in elementary schools be increased" (MSU-27, 1986, 18). With these results, the research had begun to develop a better understanding of how teaching is similar across subject matters and how it is different (MSU-27, 1986, 18).

Conclusion

The MSU revolution developed slowly over a long period of time. It began in the 1960s and 1970s when a few faculty members developed small experimental programs on the margins of the mainstream program. It gained momentum with the federal funding of the Institute for Research on Teaching that began in 1976. Judith Lanier became the leader of this reform and used her positions to develop a comprehensive indictment of teacher education as it then existed.

The IRT's increasing reputation strengthened the revolutionary movement. In 1983 Terrell Bell, the U.S. secretary of education, came to MSU to give the IRT a certificate of excellence for its achievements. While in East Lansing, he released *A Nation at Risk* (USDE, 1983), the report of a commission he had appointed that became famous for launching the wave of educational reform that rolled through state and national levels in the following years. His visit signaled that MSU was moving beyond the IRT into a second generation of national leadership in the reform of teaching and teacher education.

CHAPTER TWO

Initial Moves toward
Overturning the Old Regime

Toward the end of the 1970s, MSU under Judith Lanier's leadership began to develop a new generation of teacher-education programs. The idea had emerged that MSU was a place where questioning, renewal, and evaluation of teacher-education programs would continue indefinitely in order·to improve the field and develop better leaders for teacher education. But since there was still disagreement among faculty members about what to emphasize in the new programs, the solution was to create four experimental programs, each going beyond what had been achieved in the 1970s, paving the way for even more comprehensive reform. Each of these programs focused on a particular theme, reflecting what faculty felt was most important in teacher education. This strategy not only allowed faculty and students to choose among the four options, but it also was a way of avoiding conflict among faculty with differing views.

Nevertheless, the attempt to establish these alternatives quickly ran into opposition from the old guard. On November 1, 1979, the faculty advisory committee for the Department of Elementary and Special Education sent a letter to Dean Keith Goldhammer expressing opposition to the development of these alternative programs.

Commonality and Difference
in the Alternative Programs

The four themes given priority in the programs were subject matter, student diversity, teacher decision-making, and formation of learning communities. In 1981 these alternatives were approved for piloting before being given definitive approval in 1983. One of the best sources of information on them is an IRT study contrasting the Academic Learning Program and the Decision Making Program (actually known as "Multiple Perspectives") (MSU-27, 1986, section I). The study did not include the other two experimental programs focusing on student diversity and learning communities.

The Academic Learning Program put its emphasis on theoretical and subject-matter knowledge of teaching. It developed as a primarily university-based program in which prospective teachers were expected to concentrate on how students think about subject matter as a basis for teaching for understanding. In taking this approach, student teachers were supposed to learn, for example, how to deal with student subject-matter misconceptions as major impediments. In contrast, the Decision Making Program took place mostly in elementary schools where the prospective teachers spent a good deal of time in classrooms—observing, assisting in, and teaching lessons. The program put much of its efforts into figuring out how to shape these field experiences. It used one elementary school for first-year field experiences and another for student teaching. University classes for the program were taught in the selected school, and in addition, the teacher-education students worked in most of the classrooms as assistants. The program had elaborate forms to complete in evaluating lessons taught by the prospective teachers. The MSU coordinator for this program spent much of her work time in the school, supervising and evaluating the MSU students (I18).

In contrast, students in the Academic Learning Program had much less field experience. They did have some specific course assignments to do in K–12 schools, but it was not until the student teaching quarter that the students had their first extended classroom experience. Instead students in the Academic Learning Program up to that point had concentrated on case studies of teaching and learning. The program expected adequate performance by the students during student teaching even though they had received much less practical preparation for this experience (I18–19).

Overall, the expectation in both programs was for students to apply what they had learned in university courses to classroom settings. In both cases, the difficulty of doing this was underestimated. There was very little explicit consideration of how they might apply their learning in practice. Another problem was that students in both programs generally formed a low opinion of the practicing teachers with whom they worked. The students tended to think that these practicing teachers were neither desirable models nor even sources of needed knowledge. Moreover, both programs promoted the idea that good teachers do not use textbooks. Instead the approach that was advocated for learning to teach was highly individualistic in that each novice was deemed able to figure out "what works" for him or herself, without relying on professional standards and guidelines to decide whether their practice in teaching was adequate and defensible (119–20).

Students in both programs were handicapped by limited subject-matter knowledge; some of them even confessed to active dislike of at least one subject. Curiously, however, neither program did much to develop subject-matter knowledge in depth. Even in Academic Learning with its subject-matter emphasis, the instructors tended to assume that their students already had an adequate grasp of subject matter. For example, when students were asked to critique textbooks in ways that required subject-matter knowledge, many tended to rely on memories of what they themselves had learned in school at the same grade level, and not on more in-depth knowledge that might have been acquired at the university (121–22).

The Decision Making Program went even further than Academic Learning in not emphasizing subject matter. It promoted a generic view of teaching as applicable to all subjects. Even though lesson planning was a major emphasis of the program, planning was taught without focusing on the specifics of subject matter and differences between subjects. Once when one of the students got stuck on a subject-matter issue, her supervisor told her not to focus so much on content and instead concentrate on management. This lack of attention to subject matter can be traced to the existing division of responsibility among university departments. Liberal arts departments were generally responsible for the subject-matter courses taken by prospective teachers, but the instructors in those departments did not deal specifically with the special knowledge it takes to teach those subject matters. Thus, since the education courses stressed generic methods and assumed sufficient subject-matter knowledge on the part of their students, the specific subject-matter knowledge needed for teaching tended to get left out altogether (122–24).

Reflecting the work going into creating curricula for these thematic programs, Tim Little contrasted the curricular autonomy faculty he previously enjoyed with the new press-to-mold curricula that reflected the overall program focus. He revealed that, "after some seven years teaching and thirteen years as a social studies methods professor," he had a clear personal idea of the content that should be included in a comprehensive elementary social studies methods course. However, the alternative programs required that courses that became part of their programs followed "its carefully and collectively developed thematic frame of reference," thus leaving less space for instructor autonomy (1984, 1).

Little was charged with developing two social studies education courses for the alternative programs, one for the Decision Making Program, the other for the program known as Learning Community. The latter was described in its documentation as a program that focuses on the

> need to promote personal and social responsibility among students. . . . Students in the Learning Community Program learn to create a sense of community in classrooms and schools. . . . Students in this program become aware of the many related communities of home, neighborhood, school, and the teaching profession; and the interactive impact these communities may have on classrooms and teaching. (quoted in Little, 1984, 3)

The Decision Making Program had a different set of central concerns. Little described this program as follows:

> Teachers are decision makers who must balance . . . competing demands on the school. . . . The emphasis in this program centers upon teacher decision making. Attention is given to decisions regarding instructional design,

instruction, individual differences, and group development. This program enables the student to comprehend
the forces that impinge on decisions, to make the difficult
decisions that must be made daily in the classrooms, and
to understand the consequences of those decisions. (4)

In Little's view, developing different courses for these two
programs required dealing with two different sources of pressure:
(1) pressures generated in K–12 schools, and (2) pressures created
by the differing themes of the alternative programs. The first set
of pressures, Little recalls, were easily resolved by meeting with
K–12 practicing teachers on the course designs. But resolving the
programmatic cross pressures was in his opinion more difficult.
"Each program had developed a different terminology and different ways of doing things. . . . [The instructor] had to try to bring
a better balance to the integration of subject matter and thematic
emphases" (4–6).

Little searched for scholarly work on community in the social
science literature that could be used in the Learning Community
course. He also drew on his extensive experience with law-related
education to emphasize concepts of reciprocal responsibility and
used associated instructional methods such as mock trials (7–8).

In the case of the Decision Making Program, Little concluded that
the social studies literature would provide a good basis for designing
the course around decision-making. He drew on different models of
drawing conclusions ranging from intuitive hunch and reliance on
authority to use of inductive and deductive logic (8–10).

This emphasis on teaching and learning about modes of reasoning to arrive at warranted conclusions became central to Little's
work on social studies and years later was his signal contribution
to the group of teachers he worked with at Holt High School in the
professional development school era (Little et al., 1995).

Although none of the four alternative programs were meant to
reach definitive states of reform, many of the faculty who signed
on at the time did not understand that these four programs would
not satisfy the dean for long, but were simply stepping-stones
toward more profound and all-encompassing reforms. Already in

the college proposal that won the IRT competition of 1976, it was clear that, at least in the eyes of Judith Lanier and her closest associates, reform as ultimately envisaged was a comprehensive and single program for all MSU teacher-education students (MSU-25, 1976, B-III-14).

Judith Lanier Becomes Dean

From 1976 to 1980 Judith Lanier was both codirector of the IRT and director of the School of Teacher Education. The former was an influential role in the emergence of new approaches to research on teaching, but the latter was far more limited than might appear. Although Lanier made known her strong views on the deficiencies and need for improvement in the quality and effectiveness of the college's teacher-education offerings, she was faced with much opposition and had but limited ways to overcome it, hemmed in by entrenched departments and faculty members set in their ways who had no desire to move in new directions. In fact, the School of Teacher Education existed largely on paper, and whatever influence Lanier was able to muster from this position was based largely on her own intelligence, charisma, and the power of her personality, plus limited support from Dean Goldhammer and his especially influential deputy (with name to match—Lee Dean). Lanier's influence was strong enough to make enemies, but not enough to ensure compliance with her ambitious aspirations. It was principally through the IRT and the possibilities it generated for recruitment of new faculty that a foundation was laid for further revolutionary change.

Establishment of the IRT was followed shortly by the tumultuous years of the early 1980s when a deep financial crisis at MSU thrust Judy Lanier into an unexpected deanship (Forzani, 2011, 193–94). It had not been in the cards for her to become dean when she did. Former dean Keith Goldhammer having retired in 1980, an acting dean was to be chosen from a list of seven college-level administrators. Lanier was asked and agreed to become the interim dean in July 1980. Initially she had no intention of being a candidate for the long-term dean's position. But the college and university were in the midst of a major financial crisis with the college initially facing a 14 percent cut in its base budget for fiscal year 1981–82 (Lanier memo, January 9, 1981). Although she had previously alienated much of the faculty who opposed her efforts to change and do more for teacher education, her actions as interim dean gained provisional support from much of this opposition.

As dean, Lanier seized upon this opportunity for institutional change, unprecedented reform, and the power to overcome strong internal opposition to her agenda. The resources of the IRT had added greatly to what could be mobilized from the ordinary power residing in the deanship at MSU (where at least since the John Hannah era administrators had been more powerful than in most peer universities). Also, from the moment she was selected, Lanier told the provost exactly what she thought whenever she judged the college shortchanged by the central administration, and she was quickly and surprisingly successful in extracting concessions from Lee Winder, provost at the time (Forzani, 2011, 192–93).

By April 1981, as part of the response to the financial crisis, under Lanier's leadership, college governance committees were discussing a major reorganization of the college. Most important for the revolution in teacher preparation was the creation of a new Department of Teacher Education. Before, responsibilities for teacher education had been fragmented among various units. The new organization concentrated the management of teacher education in the college mostly in one department (although not including courses offered to prospective teachers by the arts and sciences colleges). Given the dean's reform agenda, this concentration made it easier for the dean and dean's office to play a strong role in micromanaging this department. The creation of this new department, almost large enough to be a college in itself, brought together those who were already responsible for teacher-education programs at MSU, plus willing new recruits from educational psychology, subject-matter fields like math education, and a range of specialties not heretofore thought of as important to such a department, such as philosophy, anthropology, sociology, and economics of education. In the dean's mind, one of the main purposes of this amalgamation was to raise the status of teacher educators within the college as well as bring new multidisciplinary research insights to improve the programs. Thus, these recruits were hired, entirely or in part, to join the revolutionary vanguard in a struggle that was destined to continue at MSU for the rest of the 1980s and 1990s.

Aggressive efforts to recruit new faculty for the coming revolution had begun with the IRT and continued unabated. Using her consolidated power, Lanier was able in many cases to handpick new faculty members who showed both scholarly promise and a propensity to engage in reform. Since the 1980s were years of financial distress for schools of education across the nation, the schools at other universities generally lacked the vacancies to compete effectively with MSU for the best of available recruits. It was an extraordinary opportunity to get outstanding faculty to come to East Lansing even among those who would have preferred to live on the East or West Coasts.

The search for persons best suited to move the reform agenda forward continued until Judith Lanier stepped down as dean in 1992. Between 1976 and 1992, the college moved more than ninety persons into tenure-stream positions (not counting the physical education/exercise science department) (Inzunza, 2002).[1]

It was also during this period that Harry Judge, the former head of educational studies at Oxford, was enticed to come to East Lansing as a part-time faculty member and consultant. Judge was commissioned by the Ford Foundation in the early 1980s to study American graduate schools of education (Judge, 1982). In his book about this study, he characterized these schools on the one side as a few elite schools like Harvard, Stanford, and Chicago that modelled themselves on the arts and sciences and had little involvement in actual K–12 schools, as opposed to the majority of

---

1. These included such notables as Andy Anderson, Deborah Ball, Jere Brophy, Dan Chazan, Chris Clark, Dick Elmore, Fred Erickson, Helen Featherstone, Jay Featherstone, Sharon Feiman-Nemser, Bob Floden, Susan Florio, Mary Kennedy, Bill McDiarmid, Susan Melnick, Penny Peterson, Dick Prawat, Diana Pullin, Steve Raudenbush, Brian Rowan, Gary Sykes, Charles Thompson, Suzanne Wilson, Lauren Young, and in the greatest coup of all, getting David Cohen and Magdalene Lampert to leave Cambridge, Mass., for MSU, David to fill the college's first Hannah professorship, another prize that Lanier had wrested from the MSU central administration (Forzani, 2011, 211–12; Inzunza, 2002).

education schools that were much more engaged in K–12 but were not doing much credible research. Upon publication of his report, Judge was told that MSU was different with strengths in research as well as in relationships with K–12 schools. To find out more, he came to MSU, developed a strong relationship with Dean Lanier, and stayed involved in MSU reform efforts for years (Schwille, 2017, 209–13).

With this new departmental organization and faculty in place, Dean Lanier proceeded to strengthen the college and especially teacher education in various ways. She recruited other very strong college administrators and department chairs and gave external funding a big boost. In building on the success and reputation of the IRT, the MSU College of Education began to climb the status hierarchy of colleges at MSU, becoming recognized as more and more of an asset to the university. Its rank on the scale of external funding was closely watched and then celebrated when the college caught up for a time with the College of Engineering in amount of external funding.

As faculty capabilities increased, the college became increasingly identified with scholarly analysis of the problems and promise of teacher education. Sharon Feiman-Nemser, upon arriving at MSU in 1981, immediately joined with colleagues in the new department and IRT, becoming the author of a long series of articles to better conceptualize the work of teacher education and to guide program development.

Birth of the Holmes Group, a National Consortium of Universities to Spearhead Revolutionary Reform

It was always Judy Lanier's firmly held view that schools of education should take responsibility themselves for their own reform and not leave outsiders to force change upon them. In the draft for an undated speech,[2] Lanier's handwritten note captures her career-

---

2. Apparently delivered to an unidentified audience sometime in 1983–84.

long commitment to reform from within. She gives her reasons for thinking reform will happen and why it will happen. Identifying herself with those who think it will happen (she writes, "I think it will happen"), she gives two reasons for why it will happen: (1) "Because the public will likely not support our incompetence in teacher education much longer"; and (2) "Because people like you and me decide to make it happen." In the early 1980s, in seeking to make it happen, she began working with two other deans (John Palmer of the University of Wisconsin and Bob Koft of State University of New York–Albany) to develop an organization of universities committed to profound teacher-education reform. After much discussion, they decided to invite the deans of thirteen other well-regarded schools of education at research universities to join them in this endeavor. The group began formally in 1983, with over one hundred universities joining before the first meeting of the expanded group in January 1984 (Lanier, 2007, xvi; Case, Lanier, & Miskel, 1986).

According to Forzani's thorough analysis of the Holmes Group and how it developed, it was an unprecedented move:

> This was the first time that education school insiders in the United States had taken such a hard look at their own shortcomings and summoned the energy to embark on significant reform. The Holmes Group's vision for a vastly improved education system was bold and their approach courageous. (2011, 124)

The Holmes Group sought nothing less than the reinvention of teaching and teacher education, of the profession of teaching, and of the identity of faculty members in schools of education. Rather than focus on just one element of the problem or one institution or state, they tackled the entire enterprise, across the entire country (142–43).

The resulting consortium of education schools was named the Holmes Group in order to avoid too much identification with certain universities or individuals who were playing leading roles in the new organization. Instead as a tribute, it was named for

Henry Holmes, the head of teacher education at Harvard in the 1920s, who had tried but failed to bring about a major reform of teacher education at that time.

Over a decade from the mid-1980s to the mid-1990s, the Holmes Group developed its ideas and agenda in three major manifestos, *Tomorrow's Teachers* (1986), *Tomorrow's Schools* (1990), and *Tomorrow's Schools of Education* (1995) (see also Forzani, 2011, 133–43). The reports pulled no punches. Strongly critical of existing schools of education, they insisted that "action must replace inertia. The education school should cease to act as a silent agent in the preservation of the status quo" (Holmes Partnership, 2007, 203).

Lanier gave a revealing retrospective account on the production, release, and reception of the three reports when they were republished in 2007. According to her, even at the beginning, many deans were not themselves eager to take on this responsibility for reforming. In an early meeting, when they were discussing a draft set of standards for teacher education, this became clear:

> The Secretary of Education (Terrell Bell) was there, as were representatives of several major foundations—but the education deans began to back off. They explained why the standards wouldn't work at their institutions (not enough money, insufficient faculty interest, contradictory state policy requirements, and so on). As they were slipping away, Secretary Bell took the podium—and commenced to scold the deans for their lack of fortitude and commitment to improvement. Apparently he shamed them into submission, for shortly after he left the meeting they voted to support the effort and move ahead with the agenda. (Lanier, 2007, xiv–xv)

The first report, *Tomorrow's Teachers*, set out five major goals, elaborating on the extensive discussions that had taken place in meetings of the group: (1) making the education of teachers more intellectually solid; (2) taking differences in teachers' knowledge, skill, and dispositions into account in their education, certification, and work; (3) establishing new standards for entry to the profession of teaching, ones that are "professionally relevant and intellectually defensible"; (4) connecting schools and departments of education to K–12 schools; and (5) making schools better places for teachers to work and learn (Forzani, 2011, 127). The release of this report was a major media event. It was published in full by the *Chronicle of Higher Education*, beginning on the front page. According to Lanier, the response to it was in large part negative. "Even in its infancy, the Holmes Group had more enemies than friends in higher education and in the organizations represented by its members" (2007, xxi). One area of trouble was in treatment of teacher education in historically black institutions, which the report ignored. In response to this criticism, the consortium had to admit it had made a mistake in not attending to issues surrounding teacher preparation for African Americans.

The second report was, according to Lanier, less controversial than the first, in part because so much leeway was left to the universities in figuring out how to work with K–12 schools according to the principles laid out in the report. Nevertheless, according to a later book on teacher education at MSU, it proposed a radically new conception of teacher education, and one that was significantly different from "the technical and professionalized rhetoric" of the first Holmes report. Instead it called for "ambitious teaching for all children; and a concern for schools as caring, democratic communities." And in addition, it committed Holmes to the establishment of a new kind of K–12 school, called a "professional development school" (PDS), a school in which university and school educators would collaborate on education research, professional development for practicing teachers, and the clinical education of future teachers (Carroll et al., 2007a, 12–14).

David Labaree, the MSU house critic of the revolutionary movement, also emphasizes how different the second report was from the first, likewise seeing the first as the expression of technical knowledge of what works in education in contrast to the second, which bases its recommendations on a commitment to shared democratic values (1992). Labaree argues that the two reports are contradictory and irreconcilable as primary motivations for reform. But, in my view, his review is not convincing in this argument, claiming that the two reports are irreconcilable and not simply complementary. Contrary to Labaree's position, the ideas that democratic values can lead to not doing some of what technical knowledge suggests and that technical knowledge can call for not doing some of what democratic values might favor are not only not contradictory, but almost go without saying.

Of the entire Holmes Group agenda, perhaps the most far-reaching and revolutionary aspect was this vision of a school that would attempt to change the nature of university relations with K–12 schools, getting university faculty to work in K–12 schools on a regular basis while giving K–12 teachers a more important role in all aspects of teacher education and educational research at the university. The report rejected older measures, such as the "boutique" university lab school that served a limited set of stakeholders, or the use of K–12 schools merely for field experience in teacher-education programs. Instead, the PDS would be called upon to offer a revolution in instruction with radical changes in the work of the teachers and their university colleagues. The Holmes second report explained further that "the professional development school needs to be seen as the major focus of the university's threefold mission of preparing teachers and administrators, serving as the research and development arm of the profession, and providing direct service to schools; just as teaching hospitals assist in the training of physicians, conduct medical research, and provide high quality patient care" (Holmes Group, 1990, 81).

Writing the third Holmes Group report, *Tomorrow's Schools of Education*, proved much more difficult, taking far longer to reach agreement than for the first two reports. It was after all a case of the participants coming to grips with the shortcomings and weaknesses of their own universities and schools of education, and trying to get the Holmes Group to commit to a set of radical reforms. Lanier reports that the search for a consensus on this report was long and tiring, and never really worked. In her view, more and more faculty and administrators were looking for a way to return to the status quo. She notes that the deans who signed off on the report did so reluctantly, inasmuch as they "remembered and feared the fate of Henry Holmes" (Lanier, 2007, xv–xxiv).

The work on all three Holmes Group reports was spearheaded at MSU, which served as the headquarters of the Holmes Group from its inception until Lanier stepped down as president in the 1990s. This work reflected the contributions of prominent MSU faculty, such as Lauren Young, Gary Sykes, Dick Elmore, Jay Featherstone, David Cohen, Michael Sedlak, Dick Prawat, Henrietta Barnes, and Dean Lanier, with the participation of additional outside experts. In the words of Jay Featherstone, writing in the later book on MSU teacher education, it was revolutionary work: "In the air in East Lansing there was the hope of a new fusion of theory, research, and practice and a new set of partnerships with schools and teachers in the service of a new vision of teacher education" (Carroll et al., 2007a, 14). MSU's importance in Holmes reached a peak of prominence and visibility during a single year (1988) in the writing of *Tomorrow's Schools* when the Holmes Group repeatedly brought scholarly and activist national leaders together in East Lansing in six seminars to discuss (1) models of learning, models of teaching; (2) conceptions of teachers' work and the organization of schools; (3) diversity, equity, and the organization of schools; (4) family, community, and schooling; (5) conceptions of restructured schools; and (6) new models for the role and training of the leadership for tomorrow's schools (MSU-8, 1988; Holmes Group, 1990).

By the time the Holmes Group started work on the third report, the consortium was already showing signs of discouragement and weariness in facing up to the overwhelming challenges of what they had already proposed (Forzani, 2011, 141). Thus, as Forzani says, they deserved great credit for sticking with such a courageous and bold call for reform that would be so hard to achieve. Forzani summarized these challenges as follows:

> The authors of *Tomorrow's Schools of Education* antic-ipated that significant changes in the norms and expec-tations for faculty work would be required in order to bring the changes they sketched. They envisioned a "new breed of professor" who would need to "learn to walk the new walk, keeping one foot in the traditional scholarly community of the campus, where one must satisfy rigor-

ous canons and norms, and keeping the other foot in the public school." . . . In this vision, university-based faculty members would divide their time between university and PDS, sometimes co-teaching children, often mentoring both practicing and student teachers, and frequently testing hypotheses through PDS-based research projects. There would be greater numbers of clinical professors, who would be treated with respect within the university even while most of their work took place in the schools. To accomplish and support these new kinds of educationists, the authors urged the creation of new criteria for judging faculty work, including revisions to tenure, promotion and merit pay policies such that those policies would reward commitment to work with student teachers and in schools. (139–40)

While Forzani's thesis repeatedly expresses admiration of the Holmes Group for making such far-reaching and bold proposals, she was also acutely conscious of what she thought was lacking. In her view, the analysis of the problems and shortcomings of teacher education was convincing, but the solutions offered were vague and insufficient guides for implementation. The details were left to schools of education, together with K–12 educators, to work out, but as Forzani took pains to point out, the programs that Holmes criticized as totally inadequate were ones developed by these faculties in the first place. How can there be, she asked, sufficient confidence in the capacities of these schools and their faculties to develop solutions and programs that could truly meet the extremely ambitious goals of the Holmes Group?

Early on, David Cohen purportedly warned Lanier that the time, energy, and attention that a national organization would require would distract her from the work of reform on her own campus—work that would be all-consuming just on its own. According to later informants, Cohen suggested that instead of splitting her time between national, state, and local reform, Lanier devote herself entirely to MSU. This, he said, is what Johns Hopkins medicine had done in the early 1900s when "it set out to create a medical school that would combine research, teaching and patient care in a comprehensive university." The local reform at Hopkins was then intended to influence other medical schools, which it did. But Lanier refused to go that route; she felt she needed a national organization, if for no other reason than as a way of exerting pressure for change at MSU where inertia and resistance were fierce. In short, Lanier took on the goal of developing MSU as a prototype, but she also decided that she needed a powerful national organization in order to fight and win the internal battles that were anticipated. From this perspective, founding the Holmes Group could be seen as a strategy for achieving local reform rather than the other way around (Forzani, 2011, 144–46).

Conclusion

The 1980s laid further groundwork for the MSU revolution. Judy Lanier became dean and immediately began to use her greatly increased power to initiate profound change. A new, distinctive, and diverse Department of Teacher Education was created to replace the fragmentation, incoherence, and mediocre effects of the old organization. More new faculty were recruited with commitments, experience, and knowledge required for a college devoted to the local and national reform of K–12 teaching and learning as well as teacher education. A national consortium of deans in research universities with well-known schools of education was established to lay out the principles and establish an agenda for reform of the teaching career, for profoundly changing the relationships between higher education and K–12 in educational research and teacher preparation. The PDS era was about to begin, with more revolutionary intent at MSU than elsewhere. Schools of education were called upon to acknowledge their deficiencies and transform themselves accordingly

The Revolution Takes Shape in Teacher-Education Research and Program Development

Following the IRT and under the influence of the Holmes Group, the college's revolutionary efforts at the local level were increasingly focused, first, on programmatic research on teacher preparation and teacher learning and, second, on the creation of still another teacher-education program, but one that for the first time would include all the teacher-education students at MSU in a single reform-oriented, coherent set of learning opportunities.

Teacher-Education Research Acquires a Separate Identity and Distinct Capabilities

Organizationally, the IRT was but the first of the federally funded research centers at MSU to support the revolution. Following the IRT were the National Center for Research on Teacher Education (NCRTE, 1985–90), the National Center for Research on Teacher Learning (NCRTL, 1990–96), and the Center for the Learning and Teaching of Elementary Subjects (1987–92). The availability of federal funding for these national research centers proved critical to moving the revolution forward, and the lack of further federal funding for any such center became a major factor when the revolution lost its momentum.

Already during the IRT the improvement of teacher education was a top long-term priority for Judith Lanier even though it was not the main mission of the institute. To carve out a niche for this priority, she and others made a special effort to make sure that research on teacher education would be recognized as a separate and distinct field though related to research on teaching (defined as research on the practice of teaching by practitioners in K–12 classrooms, generally with a focus on what pupils were learning). Research on teacher education was concerned less with K–12 students than with what teacher-education students were learning and what they continued to learn as practicing teachers. Teacher-education research was therefore, in part, a branch of research on higher education with students who were adults not children. As time went on, this domain, once disentangled from research on teaching, became a centerpiece of the vision that Lanier came to share with a critical mass of MSU faculty members.

Once Sharon Feiman-Nemser was hired in 1981 in the hope of benefiting from her knowledge of teacher education and how to improve it, she was chosen to direct the one component of the IRT that dealt with research on teacher education. During the years that followed, she worked with Bob Floden, Margret Buchmann, and others to reconceptualize the field of teacher education in a series of papers. For example, Feiman-Nemser and Floden in their early papers criticized the notion then current that there were fixed stages in learning to teach (Feiman-Nemser & Floden, 1980, 1981) and at about the same time they started work on new conceptions of learning to teach. They also did a review of the cultures of teaching for the third edition of the *Handbook of Research on Teaching* (Feiman-Nemser & Floden, 1986).

With work of this sort in hand, already advanced in the early 1980s, MSU was ready when the U.S. National Institute of Education issued a request for proposals for a national center to conduct research on the education of teachers. The college took on the previously established federally funded center in the field that was then located at the University of Texas, Austin. The MSU position was critical of Texas for its concentration on a single line of research with teachers, namely, the Concerns-Based Adoption Model, which focused on the stages teachers go through when trying to adopt innovations (Hall, 1978). MSU won this competition. The new center was a strong signal to those involved that the identity of research on teacher education as an independent field had been firmly established.

The NCRTE was chosen for its proposal to do nationwide research on ten programs of teacher education with a focus on how they prepared students to teach mathematics and writing. This research was known as TELT, the Teacher Education and Learning to Teach study (MSU-37, 1991). The programs studied by TELT varied in important ways including the type of institution in which they were located. Five were preservice programs for students who intended to teach but had not yet taught. These programs ranged from one in a highly selective college to an open-enrollment one, from large public universities to a smaller private college, from a former normal school to institutions with other roots.[1]

The Elite College offered teacher education for relatively few students and minimal credit hours, all taken within the students' senior year whereas Normal State University graduated hundreds of teacher-education graduates each year in a more traditional teacher-education program. Its students, who were mostly from nearby rural areas, generally planned to return to nearby towns to teach. Urban University began as a historically black institution, but at the time of TELT it had become half black and half white. It was the most flexible program. Its students could take the required courses at any time in any sequence. These courses emphasized behavior management and behaviorist theory, although at the time of the study these ideas had become passé. Nevertheless, the behaviors that it stressed were still the ones established by the State of Virginia as ones graduates were expected to use. Research State University in Florida was, in contrast, distinguished by a faculty that was more cosmopolitan than either Urban University or Normal State. They made more use of the research literature and were relatively active in reform movements. Also in contrast to the other institutions, Research State offered a five-year program for elementary-education students and a fifth-year program for secondary-education students with completed bachelor's degrees in the subject they planned to teach.

1. Although initially not identified, the names were subsequently revealed in a publicly available source. Illinois State University, a former normal school with a large teacher-education program, was characterized by Kennedy (1998) as "Normal State University," Norfolk State University as "Urban University," the University of Florida as "Research State University," and Dartmouth College as "Elite College." The last preservice program studied by TELT was the Academic Learning Program, one of the four alternative programs at MSU, but not discussed in Kennedy (1998).

Three other programs studied were induction programs for first-year practicing teachers; two of these were offered as alternative routes that allowed persons who had completed a bachelor's degree without teacher certification to become certified to teach without taking university courses and after starting to teach full-time. One of these alternate route programs was the Teacher Trainee Program at the Los Angeles Unified School District, which provided secondary teacher certification for people with a bachelor's degree in the subject matter they were expected to teach and who were able to pass a general skills and subject-matter test. The other alternate route was created by the state of New Jersey to give on-the-job training to liberal arts graduates able to pass the National Teacher Examination and who had already found a teaching position. The third induction program was the Graduate Intern/Teacher Induction Program sponsored by the University of New Mexico and the Albuquerque Public Schools for graduates of a preservice program. All three of these programs provided mentors and seminars for novices engaged in full-time teaching.

The two in-service programs in TELT were also contrasts in organization. One was offered by a large prestigious private university (Teachers College Columbia). It focused on the teaching of writing and operated through local schools working with intact groups of teachers rather than enrolling teachers individually in continuing-education programs as was more commonly the case. University faculty visited schools to provide in-class coaching while offering summer institutes and other seminars. The other in-service project was a summer math experience for teachers at Mount Holyoke College.

TELT found that some of the programs studied were preoccupied with the management of children and classrooms, with little or no emphasis on learning more about specific aspects of subject matter. They concentrated their efforts on the management strategies considered most useful in efficiently organizing student work, orchestrating classroom life, and attempting to maximize learning, regardless of the subject matter. The generic strategies stressed in these programs included practical advice like telling students what they would be learning, how to assign readings and worksheets, how to prevent classes from becoming disorderly. As far as content was concerned, the management-oriented programs operated on the assumption that subject matter was to be taught, not in schools of education but in the other academic departments of a college or university, and that therefore the teacher-education programs could be limited to other aspects of teaching. In contrast, the reform-oriented programs in TELT put more emphasis on content than on pedagogy.

In the preservice sites, TELT collected data from a wide range of students: elementary teacher-education students, secondary mathematics teacher-education students, secondary English teacher-education students, mathematics majors, English majors, and at some sites, arts and sciences students majoring in other disciplines. This diversity of students allowed TELT to compare different groups—such as teacher-education majors versus arts and sciences majors—concerning their views about teaching and their knowledge and understanding of selected aspects of teaching. In addition, twelve students were selected at each site for more intensive data collection. Across the entire study, over 160 teachers or teacher candidates participated in the intensive interviews and observations. The longitudinal part of the study followed participants through the programs and into teaching.

Prospective and Practicing Teachers and Their Lack of Readiness for the Revolution in Teaching and Teacher Education

By the 1990s research on teaching and teacher education had provided revealing insights into the characteristics of prospective and practicing teachers. At the time of their report in 1995, Feiman-Nemser and Remillard described the typical American teacher as a Caucasian female, married with two children, teaching in a suburban elementary school. Teacher-education students were overwhelmingly female and white. The backgrounds of these teachers were often particularly limiting in respect to the people they had known growing up since they mostly came from small, homogeneous, lower-middle-class communities. The article adds that they "have been characterized as culturally insular with limited career horizons." A typical pattern was for them to attend college nearby and then return to their hometown and surrounding region to teach (6). Kennedy likewise concluded that "their exposure to students who are even marginally different from themselves is often close to nonexistent," meaning persons of a different race, ethnicity, or social class. Kennedy adds that "many teacher candidates had never considered that there might be learners who respond to school subjects differently than they themselves did" (1991, 7; see also Feiman-Nemser & Remillard, 1995, 6–7).

Feiman-Nemser and Remillard drew on research on feminist epistemology and on women's perceptions of the work of teaching to portray how women tended to think about themselves as learners and teachers. According to this report, preservice students choosing to become teachers were generally hard-working, serious, and mostly the products of school systems that rewarded passivity and obedience. Typically believing teachers and texts to be authoritative, they were consequently reluctant to question what their teacher-education instructors said.

> Seldom have they been encouraged to build their own knowledge or value their own ideas and questions. Disenfranchised as learners, they have achieved success by figuring out what the teacher wants and by doing it. ... Large numbers of women describe their college classes as stifling and disempowering, reminding them of their mental shortcomings. (1995, 7)

The research reported by Feiman-Nemser and Remillard (1995) also found that many preservice teachers, especially women, chose teaching not out of a desire to engage in academic pursuits, but because teaching was an outlet for nurturing and caring. According to a survey of elementary teacher-education students in the early 1980s, many viewed teaching as "an extended form of parenting" to be learned through experience, natural instincts, and intuitions.

Such students did not look to teacher education for intellectual challenges or research-based knowledge. To the extent that they lacked experience and confidence in their own intellectual abilities, it can be argued that they were unlikely to value these qualities in their students.

But finding other teacher-education students with the desired intellectual abilities had not proved feasible either. One reason can be found in what an NCRTL pamphlet (MSU-38, 1992) characterizes as a myth of teaching. This myth assumes "we can produce good teachers if we start with people who are smart and who have subject matter degrees, and then give them classroom management survival skills." The TELT study did research on programs based on this myth and found that "these programs did little more than help novices learn to survive in classrooms and fit into the local school setting. They did not improve teachers' ability to engage students with important substantive ideas in their classrooms and did not help teachers learn to examine their own instructional practices" (MSU-38, 1992, 5).

In general, then, teacher education has proved to be a weak intervention whose graduates do not, for the most part, change their views on teaching from what they were beforehand. They tend to teach as they were taught. Nevertheless, evidence indicates that powerful, innovative teacher education is possible and can affect how teachers think about subject matter, teaching, learning, and students (Feiman-Nemser & Remillard, 1995, 3; see also MSU-37, 1991). In one program studied by TELT, an intensive three-course sequence in mathematics content, followed by a course in methods of teaching mathematics, did have such an effect. The students were exposed to a new approach to teaching, both live and on video. They received support from university instructors and K–12 mentors to try out this approach themselves. Nevertheless, these students in general did not continue to teach in this way once graduated (MSU-37, 1991, 29).

According to NCRTL and NCRTE research, to have any hope of changing the beliefs and practices of prospective teachers in mathematics, teacher-education programs must deal explicitly with improvement of the content and pedagogy of this subject matter. Although the research indicated that university study does influence the way teachers think about what knowledge is and how to teach academic knowledge, this research also found that just requiring prospective teachers to major in mathematics was not going to make much difference (MSU-38, 1992).

What Makes Learning to Teach Well More Difficult than Generally Assumed

To move the revolution forward, research had to find out what makes learning to teach in reform-oriented ways so difficult and what to do about it. TELT made a lot of progress in that respect so that when NCRTE was recompeted in 1990 as a federally funded center for the study of "teacher learning," the TELT findings about the difficulties and obstacles in learning to teach became useful starting points for the agenda of the new center. These were articulated in a publication by Mary Kennedy (1991). Her brief account of the constraints, limitations, and shortcomings that the teaching profession and teacher-education programs had put in the path of both preservice and practicing teachers was especially instructive.

It was also during the NCRTL years that Feiman-Nemser and Remillard offered their comprehensive synthesis of what was known about learning to teach. Their report provided teacher educators with information the authors felt ought to influence the structure, content, and pedagogy of teacher education. They also called attention to major questions still not satisfactorily addressed, such as, "What does learning to teach entail? How is teacher learning similar to and different from other learning? What sort of teaching is being learned? What sort of teaching do we hope teachers will learn?" (1995, 1).

Even though they were conscious of the pitfalls and limitations of learning from experience, Feiman-Nemser and Remillard conceded that, no matter how much or what prospective teachers have learned during preservice preparation, learning to teach inevitably takes place mostly on the job. First-year teachers have two jobs: they teach and they learn to teach. But no one learns to teach in just one year. It takes a long time to develop routine instructional practices and gradually learn how to deal with all kinds of students. Only after five to seven years do teachers come to believe they really know how to teach (4).

According to the TELT findings, differences in the structure of teacher-education programs did not have much impact on how their graduates thought about what and how to teach. In such respects, alternative programs turned out not so very different from conventional university programs. The conceptual orientation of the program and the views of entering students were far more important than structure (MSU-38, 1992; MSU-37, 1991, 64–65).

Trying to overcome obstacles and defy resistance to reform movements is not likely to succeed unless directly challenged by more innovative programs. Accordingly, MSU researchers identified four conditions that are necessary if teacher education is to be effective in getting prospective teachers to adopt innovative practices: First, university instructors and K–12 mentors have to be able to show why the new practices are better than the conventional approaches. Second, the students have to see such practices in action. Third, they have to take part in such practices themselves. Fourth, they have to have on-site support and assistance to learn what it takes to put these approaches into practice (MSU-37, 1991, 68).

One of the conclusions drawn by Feiman-Nemser and Remillard (1995) and already emphasized in earlier MSU work on teacher education is that there is far more to learn than teachers can possibly master in periods of preservice preparation. And not enough is known about what is most important to include in this phase.

These findings informed planning for the NCRTL when it followed NCRTE and TELT. Instead of undertaking another comprehensive nationwide study or continuing to study students, faculty, and programs in TELT, the NCRTL returned to the more traditional model of a national research center in education by organizing its work in separate projects, all operating with a good deal of independence to address research questions deemed most important.

What It Took to Develop a Reform-Oriented Program for All the Hundreds of MSU Teacher-Education Students

Learning about learning to teach at MSU has been a gradual, incremental process of learning to take nothing for granted in teacher education. Earlier teacher-education programs left many issues for teacher-education students to figure out, if not completely on their own, at least without systematic perspective and guidance. Moreover, when they entered K–12 schools for field experience or as newly hired teachers, they often came to feel that what they had learned at the university was not practical and could be discarded. Their views continued to be based on what they already thought they knew about teaching and learning to teach—rooted in what has come to be called the apprenticeship of observation. Students were thinking that they understood teaching whereas research has shown they were often and in many ways misinformed about and unfamiliar with what many experts considered good teaching.

MSU spent the last three decades of the twentieth century developing teacher-preparation programs that increasingly took these considerations into account. At the local level, the four experimental MSU TE programs operating in the 1980s were a remarkable success for their time. Their reward was to be asked to start the whole process of program development again. Judy Lanier and her chief lieutenants judged that the time was right to develop a new teacher-preparation program to replace not just the experimental programs but also the mainstream standard program that was mediocre by comparison. As the revolution started to develop, this standard program, largely unchanged in spite of its deficiencies, became more and more of an embarrassment. But transforming this large program within the constraints and complexities of a public research and land-grant university in order to reflect the innovations and strengths of the four alternative programs and then make still more improvements was a daunting challenge that made many wonder if it could be done. It constituted an enormous bureaucratic challenge at a university where nearly all the colleges shared some responsibility for teacher education and where even

minor changes to programs and courses had to go up the hierarchy of governance from department to college to be approved
in all-university committees. Many faculty members were resistant simply because they were understandably so invested in the
courses that they had been teaching that they were unwilling to
make major changes.

Lanier, however, was not to be deterred, especially since the
Holmes Group that she had founded and headed was one of the
main impetuses for more comprehensive and in-depth reform of
the MSU programs. Forzani's (2011) thesis reports in detail on the
many steps it took to launch and implement this effort. Initially
as a first step, after informal consultations with faculty that began
in the mid-1980s, in May 1987, Dean Lanier appointed a twen-
ty-three-person task force that included such notable members
of the faculty as Susan Florio-Ruane, Michael Sedlak, Gary
Sykes, Andy Anderson, and others to make recommendations
for improvement of teacher education at MSU. After months of
deliberation, this task force recommended replacing the standard
as well as the four alternative programs, strengthening course
requirements for all course work and clinical experience, and
creating a full-year internship in year five of the program (MSU-
24, 1988).

From the perspective of one who later developed a contrasting program at the University of Michigan, Ann Arbor, Forzani
thought the 1988 report lacked specific details:

> Task force members were able to say little about the
> specific practices and skills prospective teachers should
> learn. Their ideas about "content-specific pedagogy" were
> undeveloped and there was no discussion about what
> novices should be able to do before receiving an initial
> license to practice. (2011, 207)

Regardless of criticisms and reservations, the 1988 task-force
report became a standard reference in the development of the new
program. The details of the new program were worked out as part
of a university-wide change in the academic year calendar from

three quarters to two semesters. Since this shift required revision of every university course, it was an opportunity to consider more radical program changes than had seemed possible before.

Forzani (2011) describes the three stages of change in the College of Education that then took place. In the first stage (spring 1989), Judy Lanier and Henrietta Barnes, the teacher-education department chair, invited representatives from each of MSU's colleges and departments where prospective students do their courses and majors to participate in "development teams" that were charged with examining and implementing the recommendations of the 1988 task force. Each team had faculty members from Education and also from at least two other fields—Team A from Natural Science and Agriculture; Team B from Arts and Letters and Communication Arts; and Team C from Social Science, Public Affairs, and Human Ecology.

The second stage, taking place over two and a half years, involved intensive, laborious meetings between College of Education leaders (especially Lanier and Barnes) and the development teams, deans of other MSU departments and colleges, university leaders, and many individual faculty members (Forzani, 2011, 215). At the same time, five working groups within the College of Education began to flesh out the program in more detail, especially the professional component for which the education faculty was directly responsible.

Progress was slow. Members recalled that there were endless meetings in the rush to produce course descriptions and syllabi without much leadership. One faculty member remembered thinking: "'what is this meeting supposed to be about?' . . . Sometimes the ball sort of gets rolling and people just don't even know where they're going" (quoted in Forzani, 2011, 220).

The third stage of the program development required completion of written program and course descriptions for approval by the university curriculum committees. One faculty member later described this process as hasty and carried out by just a few individuals. She explains that during the summer after a year of directionless discussions, "someone just sat down and wrote out the stuff, wrote out what these classes were going to be." Yet another faculty member recalled that a few very junior faculty members wrote most of the course descriptions for the new program themselves, with little direct input from others (quoted in Forzani, 2011, 220). Forzani suggests that many faculty members viewed this stage of the work as just bureaucratic, and therefore not worth their time or attention. Instructors were confident that they would have a good deal of freedom to teach what they wanted in the way they wanted, once the new program was implemented. The resulting plans received final approval by university governance in January 1992.

Criticism and skepticism surfaced throughout this process. MSU provost David Scott raised questions about the cost, feasibility, and financial burden of the new program. He also questioned the level of academic competence being assumed, concerned that education students might not be academically prepared to undertake the proposed advanced coursework in the disciplines. College of Education leaders were infuriated and insulted by these criticisms (Forzani, 2011, 216).

However, the prospects were daunting enough that Lanier even faced a short-lived revolt among the faculty members on whom she most relied to make the new program workable. One of the intended leaders of the new program characterized the first meeting as follows:

> We had sort of a revolt of the people doing the teacher certification program who just downed tools and said, "We won't be able to do all that, you know, we can't." . . . There we were, mutinying against the best dean in the history of the university, of world education, there was nobody as good who had better ideas. It was just totally tragic. (quoted in Forzani, 2011, 251)

The proposed program made one major concession by breaking with the Holmes Group recommendation to have all students, including those planning to teach elementary school, complete a college major outside the College of Education. Lanier believed the College of Education would be hurt politically and financially if it gave up its authority to grant undergraduate degrees. Although the Holmes Group report *Tomorrow's Teachers* had made the improvement of teachers' academic preparation a critically important goal, and the college's own task force report had called for a program that "should instill deep understanding of subject matter disciplines," the effort to do this was abandoned in the frustrating negotiations between the College of Education and MSU's disciplinary departments (217–18).

Still, extraordinary improvements were made (as documented, e.g., in Carroll et al., 2007b). Shortcomings notwithstanding, this long, difficult, and contentious development process culminated in implementation of a five-year teacher-preparation program, about which many had been skeptical and resistant, but still conforming in various respects to the recommendations of the Holmes Group. It included a full-year internship in K–12 schools, combined with postbaccalaureate university courses taken in the fifth year. Implementation was carried out by three design teams that involved almost all members of the teacher-education faculty, with leadership from the more recently hired faculty members, many of whom were inspired by Lanier and shared her vision for dramatically improved teacher education and had played a major role in the design of the program (Forzani, 2011, 212–14).

Revolution in Foundation Courses

In the MSU revolution, a social foundations course (TE 250), required of all teacher-education students and led by Chris Wheeler, was taught in some fifteen to twenty sections of twenty to twenty-five students in order for discussion to be the primary vehicle for instruction. Use of small sections, with no large groups, was judged necessary in a course that asked students to engage deeply and sincerely in issues of social inequality and inequity, confronting their own preconceptions and biases. According to Wheeler,

> Students need to develop an appreciation of the positive qualities that come from living in a heterogeneous soci-

ety and teaching in a heterogeneous school. . . . At its
core, TE250 aims at training students in the *analysis* of
[questions such as] how does inequality work its way into
schools? What effect does it have on school processes?
In what ways do schools exacerbate social inequality? In
what ways do they mitigate inequality? What characteristics of school knowledge and skills make learning easier
for some than others? (Wheeler, "What Is TE250 All
About?," May 23, 2005)

The course even included a service-learning requirement.
Although finding placements for such a large number of students
was onerous, the course had help from MSU's service-learning
office, which was happy to find such a requirement.

Although section instructors had some autonomy, quality
control and accountability were strongly embedded in the course
director's leadership. He selected the teaching assistants, and since
the course acquired a reputation as a stimulating and valuable way
to gain teaching experience, talented applicants were not in short
supply. His basis for being able to judge their performance was
well developed, based on professional development for instructors
each summer, weekly meetings with all graduate teaching assistants (optional for faculty instructors) during the academic year
(two hours each Friday), and regular classroom observations by
Wheeler of all teaching assistants (personal communication, April
13, 2020).

One of the summer workshops for instructors illustrates Wheeler's
approach to helping instructors achieve the course goals. A session
on unearned white privilege was facilitated by Khalel Hakim, an
independent-minded and charismatic African American doctoral
student. Then a new African American faculty member with a
Harvard PhD, Dorinda Carter, was in charge of another discussion of seven articles that participants had been instructed to read
before the workshop. Next there was a discussion of "normalcy" in
disability led by two other teaching assistants. After lunch, the workshop moved on to "social construction of gender and masculinity,"
and finally to theories of social reproduction (Bowles and Gintis,

Bourdieu, Bernstein, Willis, Giroux) and the challenge they pose to beliefs in social mobility.

To prepare for his classroom observations that year, Wheeler sent instructors a message on what he would be looking for:

> How is the classroom organized to facilitate student inter-action during the lesson, how does that happen? . . . What are the main ideas the instructor is trying to get across? . . . What evidence is there that students feel comfortable participating, asking questions, engaging in dialogue with the instructor or other students? . . . What evidence is there that students are "getting" the big ideas? (Wheeler memo, "Observation guidelines")

Team One, a Well-Documented
Part of the Revolution

After taking foundation courses in their first two years at MSU, the first cohort of students entered the new program in spring 1993. At first the program had three teams, each with both elementary and secondary education students. But after several years, faculty members specializing in secondary education became disen-chanted, and a secondary-only program was established as Team Four.

The evolution of one of these teams, over several years, is well documented by the Team One instructors who published a book about the work of their team (Carroll et al., 2007b). This book illustrates the general approach taken by each of the teams, with detail about the time and resources required to stay true to the principles of the revolution. When they entered the program in their junior year, students were expected to start learning to *think like a teacher*. To this end, the first junior-year course, TE 301, was meant to help students learn about children, childhood, and teachers' work. The next course in Team One, TE 302 called for a careful study of a single child. It was designed not as a course in educational psychology, but rather as a course that sought to "engage the student in a highly inductive, situated, local process of theory-*making*, rather than in illuminating, qualifying, or refuting a theory being studied" (Roosevelt, 2007, 120).

According to Dirck Roosevelt, who did so much to shape this course:

> Child study maps onto a larger vision of just and profes-sional teaching, for such teaching legitimizes itself—earns intellectual and moral authority—in part by practitioners' abilities to reason to and learn from individual children, large educational purposes, specific goals for learning, pedagogical decisions, and consequences or "outcomes." (2007, 132–33)

In the senior year in Team One, students were supposed to learn what it is "*to know like a teacher*—integrating subject-matter knowledge, curriculum, and pedagogy" (Carroll et al. 2007a, 20). One of the senior year courses was TE 402. It met four times a week for fifteen weeks to prepare prospective elementary teach-ers to teach mathematics and literacy. There were two instructors for each section of the course, one for math and one for literacy. Typically, each week the students met for one day on each subject area and then spent the other two days out in schools observing math and literacy instruction and working with small groups of individual children (Carroll et al., 2007a, 20; H. Featherstone, 2007, 74).

Administration of the new program was a big challenge. In Team One, there were typically four sections for each course. Turnover of instructors from one semester to the next was a big issue. The solution was to provide a small amount of faculty load time to the coordinators for each course:

> These people convened all the instructors for a particu-lar course before the semester began to develop common plans and similar syllabi. Instructors continued to meet regularly across the duration of the course to adjust plans, discuss individual student issues, and support each other's

teaching. In effect each course in the program conducted a parallel seminar on itself, by and for its instructors. (Carroll et al., 2007a, 20)

Twice a year in Team One there was also a team-wide retreat for all the instructors and other staff. Early on in the program, the retreat included a walking tour of each course, where the instructors for a given course prepared a presentation for the whole team, responding to the following questions:

- What, in essence, is the course about?
- How does the course connect with others in the program?
- To what extent does it build on what students already know or lay a foundation for what is to follow?
- How does the course begin? What are the key assignments?
- How is student learning assessed?
- What do students find particularly interesting or challenging? (23–24)

Then in the intern year, students got the opportunity "*to act like a teacher*—putting thinking, knowing and doing together in supervised practice" (Feiman-Nemser & Hartzler-Miller, 2007, 60–62). In Team One, to create a curriculum of learning tasks and activities for interns over the whole year, there were working groups organized around each of the three main standards: planning, instruction, and classroom learning community. The first phase of the internship (August–October) stood out for its importance to interns' learning as they watched how their cooperating teachers began the year with a new group of students: learning about their students; communicating expectations; putting in place norms, routines, and procedures; and working on long-range planning. Within the whole internship, there was a focus on the team standards, with the development of standards-based observation guides, planning frameworks, and rubrics for analyzing interns' lesson plans and units. Each year there was a faculty retreat to examine course syllabi or student work in relation to the standards (63).

As the revolution receded and the restoration took over, amid growing financial pressures, those responsible for the program were required to explain and justify the time and skill needed manage the five-year program, as the college as a whole was reducing the number of support staff. Team One's leaders recognized the intensive demands required to run their program. Seven of them "formed a steering committee that met every two weeks to provide intellectual leadership and continuity and to deal with the full range of administrative, financial, educational, psychological and institutional issues that arise in any enterprise focused on human improvement" (Carroll et al., 2007b, 6).

Conclusion

In further describing the challenges they faced, the editors of the Team One book gave a compelling account of its difficulties:

> Immersed for many decades in the difficult work of teacher preparation, we have learned that helping prospective teachers develop sophisticated understandings of subject-matter, students' thinking, and the creation and management of classroom learning communities—the whole, complex package—is hard, intellectually demanding work. We have seen that nourishing curiosity about children's ideas; mathematics, science, literature, and art; and the workings of the wider world as the cornerstone of professional development is relatively uncharted territory. We know that all too often we fail to accomplish all of our goals for our students. (Carroll et al., 2007b, 1)

However, despite its weaknesses, the five-year program proved to be the most enduring change of the revolutionary era. As

Forzani points out, in spite of all the difficulties, many faculty members found that participating in the development of the five-year program was a highly rewarding part of their career:

> Many of these individuals [faculty members] describe themselves in these years as being on a kind of professional "high." They were working directly on problems of education practice that had intrigued them for years, and they were receiving an unprecedented amount of support for it in a period when many other schools and colleges of education were closing their doors. They had been invited to redesign teacher education and to reinvent what it meant to be a professor of education and a practitioner of teacher education by a dean who cared deeply about teachers and teaching and was willing to devote herself to the cause of improving education in the United States. They were surrounded by co-workers who challenged and stimulated them on a daily basis, many of whom would remain their friends and colleagues for many years after the Holmes Group era. (Forzani, 2011, 248)

CHAPTER FOUR

Revolution in School–
University Relations during
the PDS Era at MSU

Of the entire Holmes Group agenda, perhaps the most far-reaching and revolutionary aspect was the attempt to change the nature of university relations with K–12 schools. To get university faculty more involved in K–12 schools on a regular basis while giving K–12 teachers a more important role in all aspects of teacher education and educational research, MSU created its first PDSs, as called for by the Holmes Group report Tomorrow's Schools. That report made the long-term and uncertain nature of this revolutionary intent as clear as could be:

> We're trying to develop something that's never been done in an organized way, here or in the rest of the world. We have to say in a reasonable tone of voice that we are just learning how to do this. We are inventing it as we go. This is a great new ambition in the history of the world. It will be hard and take a long time. (Holmes Group, 1990, 21)

The report goes on to clarify the time scale envisaged by saying that it will take three generations of teachers to achieve these goals.

This mission was reiterated in the 1987 MSU draft plan for its PDSs: "The best analogy to the PDSs may be the teaching hospital. Teaching hospitals offer the finest medical care available, while also conducting research and preparing medical professionals. Similarly, PDSs will offer children fine education, while conducting educational research that is based in and relevant to practice, and preparing education professionals in settings that encourage reflection and growth" (MSU-13, February 24 version, 6).

This chapter examines the institutional changes launched at

MSU to create and nurture such schools. It sets the stage for still more in-depth accounts of PDS work in the chapters that follow. Unlike the published literature, which gives but a partial picture by focusing mainly on a few of the MSU schools, mainly Holt High School and Spartan Village Elementary School, this chapter draws on other PDSs as well, specifically, the six schools that were the first MSU PDSs created in 1988–89: Averill and Kendon Elementary Schools in Lansing, Spartan Village Elementary School in East Lansing, Holt High School and Elliott Elementary School in Holt, and Holmes Middle School in Flint. It also deals with Otto Middle School in Lansing that was added the following year.

Expectations for these schools went far beyond being sites for giving prospective teachers better field experience, although in hindsight readers could be excused for seeing them that way, given the later retreat of the PDSs to this position. These PDSs were field laboratories in which teacher-education responsibilities and expectations were reorganized and studied in ways that had not been done before. But they were also on their way to becoming restructured schools in which K–12 teachers, university faculty, and doctoral students would do the research and development needed to embody the principles of the Holmes Group manifestoes, with a reach extending far beyond what was usual for teacher education at the time.

Holmes Group institutions were free to develop and implement their own versions of the PDS concept. The PDSs as they developed at MSU were only one possible variant and arguably a particularly demanding and more uniform version relative to PDSs in other universities (Book, 1996). At another extreme were the PDSs at Ohio State University, another institution where the Holmes Group initiative was taken especially seriously. In contrast to MSU, PDSs at Ohio State were notable for their diversity; some were not even single schools in the ordinary sense (Johnston et al., 2000).

One of the first detailed versions of the vision for PDSs at MSU is contained in a draft paper titled "Professional Development Schools," February 24, 1987 (MSU-13).[1] According to the draft,

1. No authors are listed, but the language and the argument are very closely associated with Judy Lanier and her closest associates. I have therefore assumed that the dean primarily, but probably others as well, had a hand in its writing.

the first objective of the PDS effort at MSU was to create six "professional practice sites" beginning with a few teachers and administrators and evolving over time into PDSs. This proviso is important given the later criticism that these schools did not begin with enough of a whole school buy-in.

The proposal enunciated a number of fundamental principles to live by in this restructuring of schools including, for example,

> *Collaborative and parity between schools and the university.* A PDS must exemplify in its structure and daily work, equal status and equal engagement of school and university faculty in the common tasks of professional education and research and development on teaching and learning. This principle requires a new form of organization between schools and universities, a restructuring of teachers' and administrators' work within schools, and a new structure of incentives and sanctions for university and school faculty. (MSU-13, Feb 24 1987 version, 2–3)

Awareness that MSU was embarking on a revolution can be found in a section of the proposal that deals with reworking the incentive system for faculty work in the College of Education and even to some extent the core subject-matter colleges at MSU who were responsible for so much of the teacher-education curriculum.

> Efforts succeed or falter in no small measure by the distribution of incentives, explicit and tacit. The present effort will inevitably disturb—in fact, will set out to rearrange—well-established incentive structures, with unpredictable but predictably troublesome results. Coping with the dislocations and arranging new structures that favor achievement of the new vision will be major challenges. (MSU-13, February 24, 1987 version, 17)

Although MSU education faculty already received credit for service and outreach, the meaning of these terms had been too loose to advance the cause of the revolution. In contrast, Lanier's position was that everything faculty do in a research university cannot just be routine performance of duties in teaching and outreach, but instead have to contribute to the advancement of knowledge in some way. The PDS proposal was consistent with her position when it spoke of the stringent demands to be made on the faculty: "We shall be asking faculty of the College of Education and some other colleges to re-orient their work, to carry out more of it out in the schools, and to participate in forms of research that are not yet widely understood or accepted in the profession." In K–12 "all up and down the line we shall be asking people to live their work lives differently, and we shall have to provide appropriate incentives and reduce disincentives to doing so" (MSU-13, February 24, 1987 version, 17). Unfortunately, the needed changes in incentives never came to pass. At most there was some reinterpretation of existing faculty policy in favor of PDS work.

Intentionally, no detailed plans were made at the beginning for how PDSs would be organized to implement this vision. Starting the PDSs cautiously with a small group of teachers on a tentative, experimental, and voluntary basis without immediately working out all the problems of restructuring was an intentional, reasoned strategy. Doing more in mapping out the design at the beginning, although advocated by later critics, was arguably not possible. It is true that MSU had been working on such changes for several years. New faculty had been hired with experience, capacity, and inclination to do school-site work. Exploratory projects had been launched with local schools and districts to help schools become agencies for professional development and more important partners in other work. Nevertheless, the early plans remained intentionally vague, not specific, and variable in response to the diversity of affiliated schools. In this sense, MSU was not so different from Ohio State after all.

> We propose to create PDSs in collaboration with practicing educators in several nearby school districts. Thus, we cannot specify precisely how these schools will be structured or how they will operate. We do, however,

have a general idea of the sorts of activities they will likely
undertake, albeit to different degrees and in different ways
across schools and districts. (MSU-13, February 24, 1987
version, 5, 14–15; June 11, 1987 version, 15)

The 1987 draft proposal went still further in explanation of why
detailed planning before launching was not needed or even desirable; to do otherwise could lead to "death by planning."

> Broad but graspable principles and vivid metaphors are
> probably preferable to extremely detailed plans as guides
> to change efforts. . . . Looked at under the microscope, a
> developmental effort consists of thousands of small deci-
> sions that can neither be anticipated nor controlled by the
> leadership. . . . So while leaders need to articulate goals
> and means clearly, they must also recognize the need for
> continuous discussion, reinterpretation, and restatement of
> goals and means in many different contexts as the project
> unfolds. This is obviously a delicate balancing act. For obvi-
> ous reasons, a shared vision must be achieved in each PDS
> during the development effort; it cannot simply be given
> at the outset. (MSU-13, February 24, 1987 version, 14–15)

The draft proposal goes so far as to say that imposing a design
would be "fantasy":

> The notion that a project can be planned in advance and
> implemented as planned has an almost irresistible appeal
> in a culture as rationalistic as ours. Yet to believe in the
> possibility of programmed planning and control is to
> engage in a "rational fantasy." It may seem logical, but it
> isn't realistic. Unanticipated—indeed, *unanticipatable*
> [*sic*]—obstacles arise, as do unanticipated opportunities.
> (MSU-13, February 24, 1987 version, 18)

At about the same time this draft plan was circulated in February
1987, MSU hired a new associate dean, Charles Thompson, to

organize and coordinate the PDS work. In June 1987 he informed colleagues that he had revised the earlier PDS plan, calling for reform from within and from without. In discussing calls from within, he gave attention to the four alternative teacher-education programs of the 1980s, which he said had reached the point where "their vision of what TE ought to be has outgrown the constraints imposed by schools as currently organized." He acknowledged the importance of the Holmes Group in guiding the college's reform agenda, but also cautioned: "We leave open the possibility—indeed the likelihood—that additional thought, planning, and experience will lead to significant shifts from the Holmes recommendations" (MSU-13, June 11, 1987 version, 11).

His proposal called for major institutional change not just in K–12 schools, but also in the College of Education itself, saying that its faculty would, in general, do much more work in K–12 schools with appropriate incentives for doing so. But the description of restructuring of the College of Education was even vaguer and more general than the proposed transformation of K–12 schools.

The following year, 1988, at about the time that the first MSU PDSs were created, Judy Lanier gave a speech to an Educational Testing Service conference in which she laid out much of her vision for what PDSs were to become:

> Holmes Group Universities are working with surrounding districts to create "professional development schools." These institutions, analogs of the teaching hospital in medicine, will be cooperatively staffed by district and university faculty and prospective teachers, on site for various field experiences or extended internships. . . .
>
> Professional development schools must emerge within the context of long-term partnerships between universities and school districts, with the goal being mutual change in both partners. These will not be short-term interventions by universities in the lives of children and teachers. They must become enduring new organizational arrangements devoted to mutual change. . . . They will blend research

and practice to the mutual benefit of both the schools and the universities. In a sense, the professional development schools will be centers of applied research, testing research understanding under real world conditions and using research to change our sense of what is achievable in the real world of schooling.

. . . Professional development schools, and other restructured institutions will expect and encourage teachers to assume a variety of responsibilities, both in the classroom and out, that are ordinarily not conceived as lying within current role boundaries. While not abandoning the classroom, some teachers would contribute to vital work in curriculum improvement, evaluation, and the education and induction of novice and continuing teachers. . . . Such an enrichment in the professional role of teachers would minimize the damaging effects of a flat career structure, help to halt the defection of ambitious and energetic teachers from schools, and allow schools to take advantage of thoughtful, skilled employees to the greatest extent possible.

The idea that the PDSs as described above would emulate laboratory schools of the past was firmly rejected due to the tendency of such schools to transform themselves into elite college preparatory schools serving the children of university faculty and other nearby professionals. At a meeting of the south-central section of the Holmes Group in April 1991, Dean Charles Corrigan of Texas A & M University explained how PDSs were intended to be different from the school–university partnerships in previous reforms of teacher education such as the Teacher Corps. According to him, a PDS, properly understood, would be neither school nor university. In his view, "the development of partnership between university and school is very complicated, because these are very different cultures. This must be discussed beforehand, and one or another of the groups has to give up something to make the new thing work. You have to create its own rules, roles, expectations and reward system and get the institutions who send people to

adjust." This, again according to Corrigan, meant that any education school establishing a PDS had to deal with the restructuring
of the school of education itself and that the reform of teacher
education had to take place simultaneously with the reform of
K–12 schools (Devaney, 1991, 17–18).

Likewise, as charter schools started to find their place in
Michigan and other states, the idea of charter schools serving
the goals of the Holmes Group was also firmly rejected, at least at
MSU. The PDS was to be a regular public school serving nonelite
populations and in the aggregate a nonselective cross section of
children, including a substantial number of children judged to be
at risk. In her speech at the second annual Holmes Group meeting
in January 1988 Lanier made it very clear that PDSs were not to
be located in the midst of advantaged surroundings and privileged
families:

> The professional development schools must be concen-
> trated in neighborhoods and communities with consid-
> erable numbers of children who represent the greatest
> challenge to a society that is not only highly developed
> scientifically and technologically but also true to its
> democratic heritage.

To launch the PDSs at MSU, the university used its existing
contacts with mid-Michigan schools in which teacher-education
students had been placed and college research and development
had taken place. Given development of the four alternative teacher-education programs, the closeness and intensity of these relationships was already exceptional. In spring 1987 the first step
was to identify six school districts as potential partners; four were
districts in which the College of Education was already working
on teacher education or research, namely, East Lansing, Haslett,
Holt, and Lansing. Some schools in these districts were already
notable for their willingness to work with the university. Spartan
Village, for example, already had teachers who taught daily within
this school but were also MSU tenure-stream faculty—referred
to in the remainder of this book as "amphibious professors." At

Elliott Elementary School in Holt, teachers were already reexam-
ining their thinking and practices in continuing discussion with
several MSU ethnographers. To this mix of four districts, Flint was
added, in part because of its large, low-income, minority population living under inner-city conditions. Battle Creek was sixth on
this list, but nothing came of this during the initial period of planning. Permission to approach selected schools with an invitation
to participate was negotiated with the teachers' union and district
administration in each case. It took nearly a year to establish sufficient trust to proceed with the teachers' union at state and district
levels.

In general, MSU and K–12 faculty active in the early PDSs
had strong subject-matter affiliations that led them to start with
subject-matter improvement projects; later when a critical mass
was achieved at the school, the participants began to think more
about the need for school-wide projects. PDSs that were launched
later did not have the same supply of MSU faculty and resources for
subject-matter improvement and so were inclined to start school-
wide projects instead. The mix of subject-matter and school-wide
projects remained an issue and varied throughout the PDS era,
with the inclination of some schools to go back to greater emphasis on subject matter after starting their first school-wide projects
(Campbell et al., 2000).

According to an October 1989 MSU report (MSU-18), fifty-
three MSU faculty and staff were assigned to work part-time in the
six original MSU PDSs. By September 1990, the number of K–12
teachers who had joined in the work in these PDSs, plus Otto
Middle School, had increased to the following numbers: Averill
Elementary in Lansing, fourteen teachers; Elliott Elementary in
Holt, eighteen; Holmes Middle School in Flint, seventeen; Holt
High School in Holt, twenty-five; Kendon Elementary in Lansing,
fourteen; Otto Middle School in Lansing, twelve; and Spartan
Village Elementary in East Lansing, fifteen, for a grand total of 115
(MSU-20, November 1990, appendix A).

Typically, the volunteer teachers in a new PDS spent months
getting to know one another and picking out issues of mutual
interest for possible projects. This was followed by formation of

project teams, typically a university faculty member and a handful of teachers. Early activities in a project usually included reading of relevant literature, discussion of readings, observation in one another's classrooms, and team teaching by school and university faculty. Governance was partially in the hands of the PDS coordination or steering committees of school and university faculty, but the extent to which these committees were empowered to make decisions varied substantially across schools and across time.

At Holmes Middle School in Flint, the formation of the PDS was different. According to informants, it was more top-down with the superintendent deciding to participate and the teachers' union being willing to support the effort from the beginning. Teachers in Flint were used to building administrators telling them what to do. Since the first PDS teachers in Flint were to some extent the chosen ones rather than real volunteers, suspicion from other teachers was more of a problem at the beginning than at other PDSs.

By July 1993 there were ten additional PDSs in various stages of development. At that point, over thirty MSU faculty members, about sixty graduate students, and four hundred K–12 teachers were working in the sixteen PDSs in seven school districts where the MSU faculty members were typically assigned for a quarter or more of their work week. The staff of these PDSs ranged from three to four university faculty and fifteen schoolteachers at one of the smaller schools to nine university faculty and forty-six school-teachers in the largest (Charles Thompson draft report, July 20, 1993).

The Settings in which the First MSU PDSs Were Established

MSU PDSs were by definition regular public schools with substantial numbers of at-risk students. Examination of the six original PDSs plus Otto Middle School (established the following year) shows how well these schools met the criteria. They are listed below in the order of the percent of their students eligible for free or reduced-cost lunch, which is very roughly a measure of the proportion of families from lower socioeconomic levels.[2]

Holmes Middle School, Flint (eligibility for subsidized lunch 59 percent in 1989–90, 75 percent in 1994–95)

Holmes Middle School was MSU's most ambitious effort to create a PDS within the most challenging of inner-city conditions in the city of Flint, Michigan, where white flight and a deteriorating economy had created a steady decline in school district enrollments over the previous twenty years. Holmes, when it became part of MSU's revolutionary efforts, had a 99 percent African American student population and a teaching staff divided about equally between whites and African Americans. Most of the students lived in households headed by a single female. In the surrounding neighborhoods, violence and other inner-city afflictions were common. Before the PDS became operational, many of the school's more academically oriented students had already transferred to magnet schools elsewhere since Holmes had no magnet program. Within the school, classroom teaching in the period before the PDS was generally very traditional, relying heavily on textbooks, worksheets, and teacher-centered instruction. Isolated in their classrooms, teachers did not collaborate among themselves while, at school level, decisions affecting teachers were made in top-down fashion.

2. All information in the following descriptions is from reports listed under "MSU and PDS Source Documents" in the references at the end of this volume: The most used report was MSU-33, but others drawn on included MSU-23, MSU-29, and MSU-35. The figures for subsidized (i.e., free or reduced-cost) lunches are from the 1989–90 EES reports (MSU-19 and MSU-20) and the 1994–95 MPNE report (MSU-33) except for Holt High School where the 13 percent for 1994–95 is from the 2008 book about Holt High School mathematics (Chazan, Callis & Lehman, 2008, 1). Although the 13 percent is based on the entire district enrollment, it should be sufficiently accurate for this ranking since Holt had only the one high school.

Spartan Village Elementary School, East Lansing (eligibility for subsidized lunch 69 percent in 1989–90, 65 percent in 1994–95)

This school is located in a university campus neighborhood for undergraduate and graduate, mostly married students, including those with school-age children. In 1995–96 250 K–5 students at the school came from over forty countries, speaking over thirty home languages. Many children were from single-parent households where the parent was earning a university degree. About a quarter were enrolled in English as a Second Language classes. The student body was highly transient. Typically Spartan Village students remained at the school for only a few years. Roughly one-third of the students transferred in or out of the school in 1995–96. Students even enrolled and withdrew in the same year. The limited income that these families received from their university work and other sources made 65 percent eligible for free or reduced-cost lunches in 1994–95.

Otto Middle School, Lansing (eligibility for subsidized lunch 48 percent in 1989–90, 56 percent in 1994–95)

Another MSU PDS was located on the north side of the city of Lansing. It served about 1,200 students in sixth, seventh, and eighth grades. According to Lansing sources, the school was in a "'depressed' area with 'inner-city' characteristics as compared with the Lansing Metropolitan Statistical Area overall" (MSU-35, 1996, 321). The area was one of the most racially and ethnically diverse areas of the city. The school itself was 50 percent white, 28 percent African American, 16 percent Latino, and 6 percent other. It, too, was relatively transient. In 1994–95 284 students transferred to other schools while 238 entered Otto during the year. In this area of the city 37 percent of the children under eighteen years old were below the poverty line and 15.6 percent of the adults were unemployed compared to 6.2 percent in the Lansing area overall. A third of the adults had less than a high school diploma. Parent participation in teacher conferences was low: 46 percent, 32 percent, 33 percent, and 40 percent in the four years from 1992–93 to 1995–96. Otto was designated as a "high needs" school because fewer than 50 percent of the students achieved satisfactory scores on the Michigan Educational Assessment Program. However, this changed when scores increased in fall 1995, resulting in its designation changing from unaccredited by the state to interim accredited status.

Kendon Elementary School, Lansing (eligibility for subsidized lunch 49 percent in 1989–90, 52 percent in 1994–95)

The Kendon PDS had about three hundred students and served three distinct communities within Lansing: Mill Pond, a nearby mobile home park; inner-city Lansing; and neighborhoods surrounding the school. By 1992–93 more than half the students were bused in from downtown Lansing and Mill Pond, thereby making the student population more transient and reflecting a situation in which more young families were moving into the school's feeder neighborhoods. The resulting student body was 70 percent Caucasian, 20 percent African American, 9 percent Latino, and 1 percent Asian American. In the PDS the school's fourteen full-time teachers were reportedly working with eight MSU faculty members and graduate students.

Averill Elementary School, Lansing (eligibility for subsidized lunch 25 percent in 1989–90, 32 percent in 1994–95)

Averill Elementary School in Lansing started PDS work under much more favorable conditions than at Holmes and other schools even though it was also an urban school. It had a generally receptive and very capable teaching staff, an extraordinary principal who knew how to support and facilitate this initiative, and not least, a long history of work on MSU teacher-education programs and special projects—in just the most recent example the school had completed nine years of participation in the Multiple Perspectives Program (aka Decision Making Program), one of the four alternative teacher-education programs of the 1980s. At the time of the revolution Averill was a school of some three hundred students in a neighborhood experiencing white flight. The neighborhood around Averill was changing from homogeneous middle and upper middle class to more heterogeneous low to middle class. In the 1980s and into the 1990s, the minority enrollment increased from 20 to 63 percent (MSU-35, 1996, 5). During these changes, however, the teaching staff remained relatively stable, and by 1995–96 toward the end of the most revolutionary period, Averill had distinguished itself and become the most requested school under the Lansing district's school-choice policy.

Elliott Elementary School, Holt (eligibility for subsidized lunch 19 percent in 1989–90, 25 percent in 1994–95)

Elliott Elementary in the Lansing suburb of Holt had a reputation of being a school with more diverse learning needs than other schools in the community and being a school in which it was difficult to teach. Although its students were relatively homogeneous in ethnic, racial, and linguistic terms (96 percent white in 1989–90), it was diverse in socioeconomic status. About half the students lived in homes with other than two biological parents. The percent of students eligible for free or reduced-cost lunch was about twice the average for the district.

Holt High School, Holt (eligibility for subsidized lunch 3 percent in 1989–90, est. 13 percent in 1994–95)

Holt High School was the only high school in a predominantly white Lansing suburban district with over five thousand students in its nine schools. In 1990–91 it had 924 students in grades 10–12; 94 percent were white, and almost all were proficient in English. About a third of students came from single-parent homes. In 1990–91 about 20 percent of its graduates went to four-year colleges and about 20 percent to community colleges.

Creating State-Level Support for Revolution

When the first MSU PDSs were created, the revolution was moving ahead at the local MSU level and through the Holmes Group at the national level, but at the state level there was an unmet need to mobilize sustainable support and financing for the PDSs and their outreach. Two models with demonstrated impact in the history of higher education were taken as inspiration for the hoped-for changes in school–university relations. One was, as mentioned above, the development of teaching hospitals that had been central to the history and work of medical schools.

The other was the Cooperative Extension Service (originally created to support agricultural extension work) that had played a historic role in developing mutually beneficial relationships between land-grant universities and their constituent farmers. The relevance of this history was made clear in the MSU plan of September 1990 in which the defects of prior attempts at dissemination in educational research were compared with what could be done with the planned work of an education counterpart to the teaching hospitals and the extension service.

> Research reports and other print materials, though important, will not be adequate. What if agriculture had relied on research reports to get the latest knowledge and know-how into practice on the nation's farms? Like agriculture, we need a network of people who are in close touch with the sources of new knowledge on the one hand and with the needs and situations of potential users on the other. People who can provide sustained face-to-face assistance. (MSU-21, 2)

The first arrangements explicitly designated for support of PDSs in this way were considerably more modest than the visions suggested by these two models. Nevertheless, the work quickly became difficult and complex; it took several different projects and organizations to launch the six original PDSs at MSU and to start moving ahead with others. The arrangements to do so were worked out during the pivotal 1988–89 and 1989–90 academic years.

The first was an Educational Extension Service (EES) inspired by the Department of Agriculture's Cooperative Extension Service. As a first step $250,000 were appropriated for this service by the Michigan legislature, through a collaborative initiative on the part of the MSU College of Education, the Middle Cities Education

Association, and the administration of Governor Jim Blanchard. With this authorization, the EES was founded in November 1988 to develop, demonstrate, and disseminate new approaches in Michigan to teaching and learning for K–12 students, especially at-risk students, preservice and continuing education of educators, and organization and management of schools. To do this, EES took responsibility for two sets of partnerships: direct partnerships between MSU and a small number of public schools "committed to using research-based knowledge for educational improvement"— that is, the PDSs; and partnerships between MSU and intermediate organizations devoted to broader dissemination of practical knowledge in education across the state (MSU-20, November 1990; MSU-21, September 1990; Thompson, 1988, 1989).

In 1989 another related MSU proposal was submitted under Dean Lanier's name to the Rockefeller Foundation titled "A Leadership Academy for Tomorrow's Schools" (November 28, 1989). It proposed to offer principals and other school leaders in the state an intensive, four-week program based on recent research on effective instruction and school management in urban settings, with follow-up support in their home schools to apply what they had learned.

At the same time cooperative relations were being forged between MSU, other Michigan research universities, and urban school districts. However, in order to start the leadership academies as early as summer 1990, it was most feasible to begin with only the school districts that were already working with MSU, that is, where MSU had started its PDSs. The primary targets in 1990 were Flint and Lansing districts with a work plan as follows: curriculum development for first leadership academy, winter–spring 1990; pilot and redesign of academy in summer 1990; formative and summative evaluation from spring through fall 1990. The primary staff for this academy project were Richard Elmore, Brian Rowan, Gary Sykes, Lauren Young, and Stuart Rankin, key figures charged with attending to organizational aspects of the revolution at MSU (Lanier, 1989).

State-Level Support Becomes
a Sword of Damocles

All this initial activity was shortly eclipsed by a much bigger coup that went public in December 1989. It was a deal engineered under the leadership of two persons: the billionaire philanthropist Alfred Taubman and Dean Judith Lanier of MSU. Given the urgent need for more money to support the growing PDS network in Michigan, Dean Lanier put her charisma and powers of persuasion into convincing Taubman, who was already well known for his large gifts to Harvard and the University of Michigan, Ann Arbor, to use some of his money not just for brick and mortar, but also for the improvement of what went on inside buildings, in other words, to commit himself to the improvement of K–12 teaching and learning in general and to the revolutionary agenda of the MSU College of Education in particular. Taubman was initially introduced to MSU through an organization that helps philanthropists find recipients to develop and implement what they desire to fund. Taubman wanted to fund professional military officers and mid-level managers to change careers and become K–12 teachers. Lanier instead gradually talked him into working with her in creating the Michigan Partnership for New Education (MPNE) as an organization with the funds and capability to work with universities, private business, the state government, and K–12 schools in transforming teaching, learning, and teacher education in Michigan, along the lines advocated by the Holmes Group.

In 1989–90, MPNE took shape, jointly founded not only by Taubman and Lanier, but also by the presidents of the three main Michigan research universities (MSU, the University of Michigan, and Wayne State University). A blue-ribbon board of directors with thirty-one members was established that included, among others, the governor, the president of the state AFL-CIO, the CEOs of some of the most important Michigan companies (specifically, Kmart, Upjohn, Ford Motor Company, and Dow), plus eight prominent K–12 teachers. This meant that the second concentric circle of reform (reform of teacher education at the state level) was off to an explosive start with promises of $48 million, the most funding of any such public-private partnership for educational reform in the nation at that time (MSU-23, November 1991; MSU-28, May 1991; Fendler, 2004). Averill Elementary School in Lansing, not a university or other more prestigious site, was selected as the venue in which MPNE went public for the first time on December 14, 1989. The partnership then increased greatly the number of staff members at its MSU headquarters. By September 1994, the annual MPNE plan identified thirty-five people on its staff (MSU-31, appendix D).

The three initiatives, EES, MPNE, and Rockefeller grant, more or less merged their efforts for a number of years. Over time, however, EES shifted to state-level dissemination of effective practices from the PDSs and other sources. It was no longer allowed to directly fund the work of individual PDSs. This meant that it moved farther away from the model of a land-grant university's agricultural extension service on which it was founded. As a result, the future of the PDSs was left still more in the hands of state agencies, politicians over which MSU had limited influence, and an MPNE that Taubman could dominate through the power of his purse. During the school year, none of these three funding agencies worked routinely and directly on a weekly basis with the students, teachers, or administrators in the PDSs. Instead their primary mode of intervention consisted of two-week PDS institutes and leadership academies, held mainly in the summer. The first institute took place at East Lansing High School in summer 1989, while the second in 1990 was at Holt Junior High. In these institutes, each of the emerging PDSs was represented by all or a substantial portion of the K–12 faculty members who had committed themselves to PDS work.

The purpose of the first summer institute was to develop shared understandings among PDS teams and dissemination partners of EES about new and promising educational practices. The first two days were devoted to introducing new perspectives on mathematics, science, writing, reading, cooperative learning, and school organization/management. Then each participant chose two of these areas to pursue in greater depth in the two three-day cycles next on the schedule. All this took place in morning sessions, while afternoons were devoted to elective sessions organized by volunteers in an effort to convince participants that they had contributions to make that had not been anticipated by the Holmes Group. Finally, in the late afternoons the PDS teams and dissemination partners spent time working on their own.

In 1990, the planners had to figure out how to do both the leadership academy and the second summer institute for PDSs in a three-week session. The first week's leadership academy had sessions focusing on family, community, and cultural influences for the four participating urban schools (Averill, Holmes, Kendon, and Otto). The following two weeks were devoted to a summer institute-leadership academy at Holt Junior High School for all PDS teams and dissemination partners. The Holmes Group's second report, *Tomorrow's Schools* (1990), served as the point of departure. Sessions stressed the need for empowering teachers and relying on their strategic planning committees.

As the years went by, the PDS institutes became shorter, declining from two weeks to one or two days. There was also less planning and leadership from MPNE staff. Beginning in fall 1992 the institutes were designed and implemented jointly by volunteer K–12 and university PDS staffs. Three institutes were held during the school year in 1992–93, each lasting just one day.

The first two annual summer PDS institutes have been well described by participants from Elliott Elementary School in Holt. Cheryl Rosaen and Elaine Hoekwater, an MSU faculty member and an Elliott teacher writing together in 1990, gave readers a good sense for what the institute felt like to participants:

> In many ways, the Summer Institute had the flavor of summer camp. The weather was warm, approximately 100 people spent nine full days together (sharing morning coffee, breaks, lunch and afternoon tea), people met old acquaintances and made new contacts, we drifted off to various activities in different configurations and subgroups to mingle with school and university faculty working in other PDS schools (during workshops and issue sessions), and got back together again almost each day to face our joint

> work as [individual school] planning teams. This variety of activity provided a range of experiences that stimulated and motivated, but also exhausted the participants. (145)

After the institute, the Elliott team spent more time that summer and fall firming up their plans for the three projects they finally settled on. They found this very difficult. For example:

> It was time for people to choose an area that was interesting but also feasible for their own work load and teaching situation. There were times when people felt like they were giving too much up to make one choice, and other times when they felt like making even one choice was overwhelming. People worried about whether they were focusing too narrowly by choosing one project, but yet knew they couldn't start with everything at once. Feelings were running high at this point, at a point when they are naturally high—the beginning of a new school year. (146)

At the second institute the following summer, the three Elliott project groups shared with other participants what they had learned and achieved during the year. They conceded that being a member of a PDS meant a lot of extra work and stress, but they were proud of what they had done and enthusiastic about the future. Most of their time at the second institute was spent planning for the next year. For their project focused on Literacy in Social Studies and Science, they decided that their focus would be on "teacher as researcher" and doing case studies of classroom teaching for understanding. To accomplish this ambitious agenda, teachers Hoekwater, Carol Ligett, and Barbara Lindquist planned to cut back their teaching to half-time with the rest spent studying their own practice. To help get these studies off the ground, MSU faculty members Roth and Rosaen agreed to do some teaching in Elliott as well, serving as models for how to examine one's own teaching from a researcher's perspective (see e.g., Roth & Rosaen, 1995).

The impresario for PDS institutes and other MPNE, EES, and PDS events that filled the summer calendar for a good number of years was Barbara Markle, who had joined MPNE in the early days after having been the first female deputy superintendent of public instruction in Michigan where she had leadership responsibility for Michigan's education reform initiatives. Born and educated in Michigan, she had become a high school teacher, counselor, secondary school principal, and central office administrator in Michigan's second largest school district before she moved on to the state's Department of Education. Later when MPNE changed direction, she left that organization and was brought into the college itself where, as director of K–12 outreach, she built on her incomparable experience and concentrated on relationships and collaboration with state government and K–12 districts, always with a strong emphasis on professional development and school reform.

Conclusion

Overall, in short order, during the years 1988–94, the MSU PDSs had been created, took root organizationally, engaged many K–12 teachers as well as MSU faculty and graduate students, transformed teaching and learning in a good number of classrooms, and looked forward to a long-term future of continual change and improvement. But that was not to be. The PDSs experienced continued success, but their viability was sapped over the next five years by negative changes in their support system, major reductions in funding, changes in leadership, and ultimately the loss of the revolutionary momentum and power that had been so carefully and strategically amassed over the preceding ten years.

CHAPTER FIVE

PDSs and Revolution under Siege

In July 1993, when the PDSs at MSU were in a state of high activity, nearly sixty-five MSU faculty members were working in sixteen PDSs in seven school districts. But the revolution was starting to run into trouble. According to Michael Fullan et al. (1998), in the years 1993–95 the Holmes Group was already experiencing doubts and loss of momentum. At MSU these years roughly coincided with coups at the top in which Judy Lanier was forced to give up her deanship and later, in 1994, was fired as president of MPNE, changes precipitated by a number of factors largely beyond her control.

Ironically, as the PDSs slipped toward crisis, an external evaluation of their work in 1995 brought back very positive results. But to little avail since their main funding agency and advocate, the MPNE, had been hijacked by hostile forces at the state level, and as a result funding from MPNE and through MPNE from the state started to wind down. In addition to these changes of direction at state and MPNE levels, the university was also under financial pressures that led it to push the colleges to find more income-generating activities—the antithesis of assuming a regular recurring responsibility for funding the PDSs. In coping with this crisis over the next five years, the PDSs, starved for funds, moved away from some of their revolutionary aspirations. In a nutshell, the effort to create permanent university–school partnerships in the form of a new type of schools was faced with the threat of going back to more traditional school–university relations. It was as if, after creation of community colleges in the United States during the twentieth century, the idea that they would become permanent institutions—at least most of them—had been abandoned as too difficult, costly, and incompatible with existing institutions, and as if, as a result, the community colleges had gradually become no more than collections of projects, undertaken for a limited number of years for specific purposes without institutionalization. Neither the teaching hospitals nor the Cooperative Extension Service, inspirations for the PDSs, had ever been forced into such limiting and temporary arrangements.

In truth, institutionalization of the PDS movement had never been stressed as much as it might have been. Making too much of the intent to establish a new type of permanent school would perhaps have been rejected out of hand as overly ambitious and unrealistic by universities and colleges alike if promoted prematurely. In fact, the information available to me indicates that the MSU central administration never bought solidly into the vision of creating College of Education equivalents of the teaching hospitals and Cooperative Extension Service. It is hard to find discussion of this in the annual reports from the Educational Extension Service (EES) and MPNE. The retrospective study at the end of the 1990s noted that there were those at school, district, and university levels who never really understood what the PDSs were supposed to be all about (MSU-16, July 2000). And most remarkably, what arguably was the most important step taken in this direction, the recruitment and deployment of amphibious professors to K–12 schools, was not routinely highlighted or even mentioned in the annual reports. And eventually when the amphibious professors stopped their K–12 teaching to undertake other pursuits, they were not replaced. In the case of Magdalene Lampert and Deborah Ball, poached by the education dean at the University of Michigan, Ann Arbor, MSU failed to respond in kind by hiring amphibious replacements.

Leadership of those truly committed to institutionalization of the PDSs was sidelined when Lanier was replaced first as dean of the college and then as president of MPNE and finally as head of the Holmes Group. The college had a new permanent dean, the MPNE moved into new hands, and Nancy Zimpher of Ohio State University became head of the Holmes Group. Zimpher in her earlier leadership at Ohio State had never bought into the idea that the PDS had to be a single school and was open to alternative arrangements. In short, each of these organizations moved away from the idea of a school–university partnership in the form of a permanent, new type of school. More interest was expressed in alternative organizational arrangements, especially cross-school networks.

Thus, in the Holmes Group, when it came time to issue its third report, *Tomorrow's Schools of Education* (1995), arriving at a consensus had become much more difficult than agreement on the earlier two reports. Although the report made clear that PDSs were more than a collection of projects and sites for TE field experience, planning for institutionalization after the report came out was virtually nonexistent. Essential questions were not addressed, for example, What could be done to get to the point where all PDS teachers could meet the qualifications for filling permanent positions in which they would divide their time between teaching children and the more university-oriented functions of the PDS (producing research, mentoring TE students, taking responsibility for outreach and dissemination)? Instead the PDSs—at least at MSU—were under pressure to move away from the revolution by making teacher education central and putting less emphasis on improvement of teaching and learning and solution of school-wide problems apart from teacher education.

Opposition Builds to Judy Lanier and the Revolution

As the 1990s went on, those responsible for each of the three concentric circles of reform began to opt out of or scale back on the original utopian vision. Lanier came under fire for attempting too much and making too little progress in implementation. Although working with Judy Lanier to fulfill a shared vision had been highly motivating to her allies and followers, at least at the beginning, her expectations proved to be virtually impossible to meet, partly because they were a response to dependence on MPNE funding. For example, in 1991 MPNE had set goals that were more than the college could reasonably be expected to accomplish. One such goal was to offer PDS experience to every teacher trained in Michigan. According to an MPNE calculation in 1991, it would take four hundred PDSs, spread among the participating universities, in seventy-four to one hundred school districts to meet this target. In each PDS there would need to be at least two full-time equivalents of university faculty to do the work (MSU-28, May 1991).

Although Lanier was brilliant and her talents prodigious, her shortcomings were telling as well. In addition to her insistence on goals others considered highly unrealistic, she was difficult to work with on a continuing basis. The work she demanded was grueling in each of the three circles, and after a few years, burnout and resentment of Lanier for all the demands she made as well as her intense criticism of those who did not meet her expectations took a big toll (Forzani, 2011, 242, 247, 322).

By late 1992, Alfred Taubman, who dominated the MPNE, had become dissatisfied with Lanier's overextended leadership, alarmed at what he perceived as insufficient progress and matters getting out of control. As recounted by Forzani (252), he complained to the MSU central administration, and Lanier was told to give up one of the three leadership roles that held the three concentric circles of reform together (head of the Holmes Group, head of MPNE, and dean of the college). She chose to step down as dean, thereby losing the authority she had over College of Education resources and playing into the hands of the opposition within the faculty. Although Lanier's longtime protégé and accomplished scholar Bob Floden was appointed interim dean and held that position for a year, he was the second choice of the search committee evaluating candidates for dean. Under the influence of representatives from the three departments disadvantaged by the dean during the revolution, the arithmetic within the search committee turned in favor of Lanier's opponents. The committee nominated Carole Ames, an educational psychologist and department chair at the University of Illinois, Urbana-Champaign, and a reputable scholar, but one who had virtually no teacher-education experience.

When Ames was installed in office in 1993, she and Lanier almost immediately became foes. Ames rejected out of hand the idea that the college should continue to take so much responsibility for the radical reforms pursued during the revolutionary era (Forzani, 2011, 308). Moreover, additional pressures early in the

Ames era made sustaining the PDSs even more difficult. Facing reductions in state support for the university, the central administration at MSU wanted colleges to undertake more income-generating activities in addition to outside grants. In the College of Education this meant, for example, development of online courses and other activities competing with the PDSs for faculty time.

In her first year as dean, Ames was asked by Provost (later president) Lou Anna Simon for a college vision statement. Her response was a carefully written and moderate argument in favor of a multiple-agenda college that included both her priorities (e.g., for educational technology, online education, policy studies) and continuing support for advances in teacher education and work in the PDSs.

A leadership retreat early in the Ames era on May 26–27, 1994, led by David Labaree (a dissident during Lanier's deanship) revealed much faculty support for the new dean's priorities but with reservations. In response to David Labaree's request for "suggestions about how to write a statement about the nature of our agendas as a College" (Labaree email, May 13, 1994), faculty wrote that they found Ames's memo too detailed and specific, preferring to stick to statements about the importance of the scholarly study of education in general. That was consistent with an earlier assertion of faculty autonomy voiced by a transition committee for the new five-year program, which saw fit to reaffirm the rights of faculty members to set their own research agendas and to retain their freedom in the design of courses and programs. At the beginning of Ames's deanship, the faculty were likewise resistant to specific expectations being set for PDS work.

The responses that Labaree received, including those from persons who had been prominent in pursuing the reform agenda of the Lanier era, are remarkable in rejecting or ignoring the college's role as a key agent of reform as this role had developed under the MPNE, including the work in PDSs. They had virtually nothing to say about how much had been learned by faculty and students from the college's engagement in the PDSs and its other work as a leader of educational reform. Thus began a period of what could be called increasing collective amnesia with respect to the scholarly achievements of the revolutionary era. Nevertheless, in spite of rejection of so much of what had brought the college to its position of national leadership, according to Forzani, the college "remained a vibrant place . . . with a genuine commitment to improving education practice and professional education for teachers" (2011, 313).

Draconian Cuts in PDS
Funding and Number of PDSs

Although the PDSs were making progress, there was no long-term commitment from state policy makers and politicians. So as leadership changed, new leaders did not begin with the assumption that PDS work should be a priority. Thus, the dynamic in the second concentric circle was similar to the first—displacement of the revolutionary leader and replacement by someone not committed to the revolution as it had taken shape. If Judy Lanier could be pushed aside as its relentlessly utopian, overly demanding, and inconveniently revolutionary president, MPNE would be free to assume a new identity, abandoning its support of the PDSs and opting instead to put all its eggs in the charter school movement (Fendler, 2004).

The revolution's position in MPNE had weakened early on when, after only one year, one of its three initial leaders, Jim Blanchard, the Democrat governor, was replaced on the MPNE board by the new Republican governor John Engler. Initially Engler expressed limited support for the PDSs but also skepticism about expansion of the investments. When he visited Holt High School, according to a school administrator quoted in the student newspaper, "the staff was impressed with his level of questioning and I feel he came away with a positive view of the work going on at Holt High School. [But] he was frustrated though, about how to replicate what is going on here at 300 schools across the state" (*Ramparts*, May 29, 1992).

This expectation turned out to be unwarranted. Instead of making PDSs a priority, Engler opted to support charter schools and choice in K–12 education, with a greater role for the private sector. Although MSU resisted any effort to shift toward charter schools, MPNE began to reshape itself, developing a strong relationship with the State Board of Education, the Michigan Department of Education, and the governor's office to play a key role in the creation, development, and support of charter schools (MSU-33, 1995, vol. 2, F-5, 9–12).

The result was a palace coup in September 1994, when Taubman took action to replace Judy Lanier at the top of MPNE with William Coats, a professor at Western Michigan University and former school superintendent. According to *Education Week* (September 14, 1994), the organization had decided to "downplay its role in fostering professional-development schools" because they were "too expensive to start up and maintain." It had concluded that funds from universities, foundations, corporations, and the state for this purpose were in danger of drying up and that its goal of greatly expanding the PDSs was unrealistic. Instead the partnership had decided to reduce its current number of funded PDSs from twenty-six to fewer than half that number. Coats soon said that he had decided that "neither the bulk of our current programs [PDSs] nor their expansion is sustainable for an extended period." Noting that MPNE was supporting PDSs at an average $137,500 per year, with a comparable cost share from participating Michigan universities, he declared that there was no way at that level to get possible funders to sustain the twenty-six PDSs that had been launched by the state's universities, not to speak of the hundreds of PDSs proposed for the long run. Nor, in Coats's opinion, did the universities and PDSs have the faculty members to do what had been planned (MSU-33, 1995), vol. 2, F-5, 1, 8).

Coats showed no sign of recognizing that universities could contribute anything special when collaborating with K–12 schools. Still, although Coats had shown himself to be a severe critic of the PDSs, he did not at this point advocate abandonment of the PDSs by the partnership, saying, "we should continue our involvement with PDSs, but on a smaller, well defined and better defined basis"—about ten schools in this early estimate (not just MSU but total for all MPNE partners) (MSU-33, 1995), vol. 2, F-5, 2).

In an April 18, 1994, memo to Provost Lou Anna Simon, Dean Ames discussed her view of the PDSs in light of this changing situation. This document was an early sign of possible decline in college support for the PDSs, suggesting that, in the dean's mind, PDSs no longer had to be understood as the transformation of a single school. Starting with a summary of the educational reform activities of the college in the Ames era, the·memo made clear not only that the PDSs were no longer as central to the college as they had been under Lanier, but also, in Ames's view, collaborative relationships with schools could take many different forms. "The PDSs offer us one unique opportunity for studying collaborations, for contributing to reform. . . . [But] no single map for collaboration or for participating in the ed reform agenda is adequate." Ames stated further that while the college was looking for a few PDSs performing a full set of its intended functions, it was "equally interested in studying alternative configurations such as collaborative networks across schools that may contribute in a very meaningful way to systemic change of the individual institutions, teacher preparation, or research and development."

How Much Could Each MSU PDS
Be Expected to Accomplish?

After sharp reductions in funding for the PDSs began in 1994–95, the question of how many PDSs the college could support became critical. Carole Ames, in spite of her reservations and worries, was far from giving up on the PDSs at this point. A memo of March 23, 1994, expressed her point of view. Noting that at this point the number of MSU PDSs had increased to seventeen, the memo cautioned: "Most of our PDSs . . . now exhibit only a few of the functional characteristics of a PDS as outlined in the first two Holmes reports." As the dean saw it, a fully realized PDS had to carry out a broad range of functions in coordinated fashion. But according to the memo, "combining all the functions in a single school seems to create a number of problems, conflicts and dilemmas."

Given the small number of schools and their capability at that time, MSU's PDSs were not able to accommodate all the university's teacher-preparation students. Even so, faculty resources and other PDS costs were still a problem. And yet MPNE wanted even more PDSs. Ames argued that it was time to take stock of what had been done and learned. She did not mince words in concluding "there must be a balance between thought and action; and while the [MPNE] is action-focused, the College must not sacrifice an inquiry focus in the apparent fervor to accomplish reform." Also, responding sharply to criticism from unnamed sources, she added: "We do not accept any accusation that we are *only* interested in research and reporting these findings to strictly an academic community."

In addition, the dean showed interest in finding ways to improve the productivity of the PDSs, including summer salary for MSU faculty to analyze data and write up results of their PDS work; more mentorship and support for faculty to undertake research in PDSs; a colloquium series for both work in progress and completed work, as well as a report series for the results of PDS research; and finally competition for college financial and other support of PDS research, requiring proposals that could pass rigorous screening by university and school-based peers.

In another undated memo written in 1994–95, Ames insisted that it was impossible to have a full complement of tenure-stream faculty at each of the current PDSs without jeopardizing on-campus instructional programs. "The faculty in the college have become acutely aware of the impossibility of providing additional faculty resources to the existing PDSs or assuming responsibility for the development of any additional PDSs." Instead she proposed changing to a three-tier model for reform. Although her proposal did not advance the revolutionary vision of establishing a permanent new type of school at all and did not call for any changes in the school of education itself, in other respects it stuck to the original vision. It was framed in terms of holding schools accountable for the number of PDS functions they fulfilled and limiting the PDS designation to a small number of fully functioning PDSs with a sufficient number of MSU and K–12 faculty committed to the work of the school.

In still another memo of July 12, 1994, Ames reported on her discussion with Judy Lanier about whether to reduce the number of PDSs by giving some of them another name. They could not agree on that since Judy had already discussed this issue with Taubman and they had stuck to the target for four hundred PDSs in Michigan. In fact, Lanier told Ames that MSU had to be willing to add one or more additional PDSs to its current number. Although Ames regarded this as an ultimatum, her response was to dig in her heels.

> I believe we have a good plan that brings/maintains integrity in the PDSs and that sets out a set of principles that will serve the TE program and our partnerships with schools. I think we need to pursue the plan and evaluate it—if it doesn't work then we need to revisit our plan. I am wondering whether if you agree with my unwillingness to say we will remain open the possibility of more PDSs. Quite frankly, I think we were on the verge last fall [1993] of everyone saying "get out of PDSs" and we are now at a point that we have restored a lot of confidence in the operation [apparently referring to PDS leaders Charles Thompson and Perry Lanier as well as other MSU PDS participants] and I believe we stand a very good chance of establishing sustainable models. I guess I am saying that I think it is time to draw the line in the sand.

During this period, as might be expected, relations between MPNE and MSU became steadily worse. By spring 1995 Ames called attention to this conflict when reporting on a meeting of Michigan deans of education attended by Coats and at which MPNE plans were discussed (memo from Ames to Thompson and P. Lanier, March 22, 1995). Ames said the reaction to MPNE and Coats at the meeting was hostile; the other deans found the MPNE representatives too top-down and heavy-handed. In particular, the deans opposed an evaluation plan that MPNE put forward, considering it too expansive and intrusive. Although nominally it was a plan for MPNE work, it was the deans' belief that all the work would fall on K–12 schools and university faculties.

PDS Funding Starts to Dry Up Precipitously

Funding for MSU's PDSs started on a shoestring in 1988 when the EES was established and received an initial state grant of $250,000 for the first PDSs. But not long afterward the MPNE was founded with initial promises of a great deal more funding to support PDSs not only at MSU but at any of the state's universities establishing PDSs. In the case of MSU, these promises were in large part fulfilled in the years up to 1994. Between 1988 and 1995 MPNE and state funding provided MSU more than $7 million for support of its PDSs with MSU contributing a similar amount in cost sharing (memo to PDS steering committee et al., October 16, 1995).

In 1993–94 when this funding was at a peak, MSU received more than $2 million from MPNE. Given this history, the expectation took hold that $150,000 was the "normal" average amount of annual funding required for each MSU PDS. In addition, the cost sharing expected of MSU was staggering. In 1993–94 it was about $1.7 million mostly in the form of donated time for faculty working in the PDSs. It was MSU policy not to use soft money for this. When a counterrevolution broke out in 1994 with the firing of Judy Lanier and the ascension of the charter school advocates under Coats, MPNE had already begun withdrawing support. Expectations for continued funding were further quashed in the draconian cuts of 1994, 1995, and 1996 (memo to PDS steering committee et al., October 16, 1995).

For example, a December 7, 1994, memo from Dean Ames to MSU provost Simon discussed the ongoing demands for cuts already that year, with the dean noting, "This is not an easy process mid-year." She pointed out that most of the budget was in personnel costs (temporary faculty, graduate assistants, coteachers, consultants under contract, and clerical staff at the schools) and as such, "we have agreed that where there are personnel commitments, they will be honored." In any case, it was impossible to take a 10 percent cut in PDSs at that point because some schools simply did not have enough flexibility in their budget midyear. The dean reminded Simon that the original request for the year had totaled $1,813,992 for schools and $232,070 for management and coordination. Initially, MPNE had expressed willingness to fund $1,770,000 and $100,000 respectively—which still amounted to a total cut of 8.2 percent. MPNE then called for another 10 percent cut from $1,870,000 to $1,683,000. This cut would have brought the total to less than the 1993 MPNE total of $1,780,000. In conclusion, Ames told the president: "I do not believe we can take any cut beyond the 10% (from initial agreement) if we can come up with that. To do more, we would have to cut personnel and cut so seriously the programs that the PDS effort would be jeopardized for the future."

Competition to Reduce
the Number of MSU PDSs

In 1994–95 and 1995–96 the sharp cuts continued. By the spring of 1995 MSU succumbed to the necessity of reducing the number of PDSs due to reduced funding. MPNE decided to reduce the number of MSU PDSs it would support from fourteen to between seven and ten. Therefore a process was set up to select the PDSs that would continue to receive MPNE funding over the next three years. A request for proposals was issued by MSU, and five to seven elementary and five to seven secondary schools were expected to respond. To evaluate proposals, two six-member panels were selected, one elementary, one secondary. Both MSU faculty and outsiders were included. After reading the proposals, they held a hearing for each school before presenting their rankings to the dean and PDS codirectors, who consulted with TE team leaders before submitting a slate of seven to ten PDSs to MPNE for advice and consent (Charles Thompson memos, April 5, 1995, and April 11, 1995).

Evidence of the dean's support for PDSs at this point can be seen in that plans were made for massive MSU cost sharing to continue even while the initial drastic cuts were made. An MPNE letter from Joyce Grant dated August 16, 1995, informed Perry Lanier that only $570,000 had been allocated by MPNE to MSU PDSs for 1995–96, that is, only 52 percent of what MPNE had previously planned to allocate for the year. This meant cuts of roughly 50 percent for each of the PDSs. On the cost-sharing side an MSU spreadsheet dated May 26, 1995, showed that the university still planned to contribute $600,023 plus $210,000 of fringe benefits to pay for MSU faculty time in PDSs in 1995–96. Of the thirty-seven tenure-stream faculty members listed, twenty-seven of the PDS assignments were for quarter time, plus three for more than that, and seven for less than quarter time. In addition, $209,620 was budgeted for additional college cost contributions: $90,000 for mentors of one hundred interns at $900 per intern, and $119,620 for other staff, travel, and supplies.

External Evaluation of MSU PDSs in 1995

In 1995, in addition to growing difficulties in its relationship with MPNE, the college faced internal university pressure to produce an evaluation to find out how effective the PDSs had been. In a memo to Charles Thompson (August 21, 1995), the dean confided that this pressure was coming from MSU president McPherson: "I believe that McPherson views that since I have been here, I have failed to come forward with an evaluation of the PDSs. I believe he is now fearful that MSU will be held up as reason for eliminating support for this effort—both from the Governor and MPNE." At the time the college was receiving an annual increment of $250,000 from the central administration for the PDS work, and reportedly since McPherson thought the whole endeavor was costing too much, he was considering taking it away. Ames was also worried that if she did not produce data showing good results for the PDSs, the college could lose central administration support in other areas as well.

In commenting further Charles Thompson gave his perspective on the MSU president's position at the time:

> McPherson is worried that the [MPNE] Partnership will use the lack of evaluation to scapegoat MSU publicly when they drop all funding for PDSs before long—probably in

the spring [1996]. So he wants info re "outcomes." I think that means improvements in student learning and teacher learning. We cannot deliver anything very convincing to the simpleminded on these points. That is, no achievement test score showing big gains nor the MEAP, nor any quantitative measures showing that interns in PDSs are vastly better prepared than interns elsewhere. McPherson also wants to know what "I am getting for my money"—the $250,000 the University put into the College's budget on a recurring basis with some (poorly defined) connection to the PDSs. The only other thing I know about McPherson's attitude is that, according to Carole [Ames], he is very impatient with the assertion that what he's getting for his money is the top-ranked teacher education program in America (according to *U.S. News and World Report*). He tells Carole that he wants the top-ranked program, but he wants it cheaper!

All this pressure again goes to show that the president and central administration had not reached the point of a long-term commitment to the revolution, in the sense of endeavoring to institutionalize the PDSs as the college's counterpart of teaching hospitals and extension service.

To carry out the 1995 evaluation, Harry Judge was named chair of a three-person panel. Judge was one of the best-informed persons to judge how well the MSU PDSs were doing in implementing the Holmes Group reforms for which he had been a principal consultant early on. Another person on this panel was Susan Moore Johnson, a faculty member at the Harvard Graduate School of Education, nationally known for her work on educational reform and school organization. The third panel member was Ruben Carriendo, who at the time was the assistant superintendent for research and evaluation in the San Diego (CA) Unified School District.

After visiting nine of the MSU PDSs, the panel issued its report, concluding that each site was "demonstrably involved in a collective and holistic enterprise," which consisted not of isolated innovations in single classrooms, but rather "sustained efforts to change and improve the culture and effectiveness of whole schools." Observing that such integrated achievements were rare, the review team agreed that "they had rarely, if ever, observed a set of schools in which teacher morale and active participation were higher, in which university involvement was more intense, in which pupil attitudes to learning were more positive." However, notwithstanding these very positive conclusions, the panel also took note of major shortcomings. In particular, it found that MSU's documentation of PDS work was inadequate in three areas: student learning outcomes, research production, and participation of PDS K–12 teachers in the college itself. Without complacency, the report stressed that "although the Review team knows of no university in which the faculty of the college of education is so deeply involved in the daily work of schools and in collaborative efforts to improve them, it does not follow that all is well or can safely be allowed to continue just as it is." The panel found instead that three strong criticisms of MSU's efforts were warranted: (1) the need to assure a much better match between what faculty members individually and personally wanted to achieve and the needs of the schools; (2) complaints of lack of transparency in how PDS workloads were computed and given credit in assigning and evaluating faculty work; (3) the simultaneous lack of credit toward tenure and promotion for PDS work, and feelings of some faculty that administrators were nevertheless favoring PDS work over non-PDS work (Judge, Johnson & Carriendo, 1995, 7–8; Forzani, 2011, 244). In this sense it was a case of "damned if you do and damned if you don't" as far as faculty making time for the PDSs was concerned.

The panel also took a strong position on the much-debated issue of how much research was being done in the PDSs and whether it was worth all the resources and effort put into this institutional change. According to the report,

> much solid and well-focused research and development
> ... has been effected in such fields as the teaching of math-
> ematics, science, social studies and literacy, and this has

been accomplished within a framework of school and university collaboration that makes it more likely that the outcomes of the research will be attended to by teachers and policymakers alike. Reports of much of this work have usefully found their way into a range of professional and learned journals, as well as presentations at national and regional conferences. Even if it is not always a simple matter to attribute such published work to a PDS origin, it is beyond doubt that much of it would not have seen the light of day but for the existence of this institutional innovation. [In fact], whenever a member of the review team expressed some doubts about the volume of such publications and presentations, the [K–12] teachers' response was quietly to leave the room only to return a few minutes later with a heavy bundle of such evidence. (Judge, Johnson & Carriendo, 1995, 11)

Another particularly telling anecdote bore directly on disagreements over whether the PDSs were receiving the credit they deserved. When new state guidelines for science assessment were announced, the president of MSU was told that these guidelines had in large part been developed within a PDS. Subsequent investigation showed this to be true. Nonetheless, the published guidelines gave no credit to the PDS, thus lending credence to the contention that the PDSs were not receiving all the credit they deserved (Judge, Johnson & Carriendo, 1995, 11; Forzani, 2011, 301).

When the panel compared quantitative data from a special survey of MSU PDS teachers with a 1991 survey of Michigan teachers in general, they found that even though teachers in PDSs reported worse student behavior than other teachers in the state, "teachers in PDS elementary schools report[ed] a more positive school climate, a very much higher level of involvement in professional development activity, and more ambitious teaching approaches and practices than teachers in other Michigan elementary schools" (Pallas, 1995). In general, the findings showed that PDS schools and teachers in the state were doing better than other schools and teachers.

In addition to this evaluation, 1995 was the year when the Holmes Group released its long-delayed third manifesto, *Tomorrow's Schools of Education*. It took a very strong stand on the importance of the PDSs to schools of education:

> The PDS is not, we repeat, IS NOT, just another project for the education school. It must be woven into the very fabric of the TSE, its many strands combining with those of the institution's other programs. Beginning small, the TSE must plan to increase eventually the number of such sites so that learning experiences for most TSE students can occur at a PDS. This suggests the need for careful planning for a lengthy future for what will be an integral and integrating part of the TSE. The education school may, in fact, have to trim the breadth of other outside involvements and researchers may have to submit to some restraints so that they focus more of their investigations through the PDS prism. (Holmes Group, 1995, 86)
>
> When nothing more than a school to which students are sent for their practice teaching automatically carries the designation PDS, the deepest and most radical intentions of this innovation fade away. (79)

Delayed because it had proved very difficult to get agreement on this document, the report immediately ran into strong criticism and never gained the traction of the previous two volumes. David Labaree, continuing as the most nationally vocal of the Holmes Group critics and dissidents within the college, moved quickly to disavow the report:

> I find that the report is both contradictory and counterproductive. Its populist rhetoric presents an anti-intellectual vision of the education school that hopelessly muddles the composite message of the three Holmes reports and substantially undermines the credibility of the Holmes Group as a voice for educational reform. At the same time, this vision sets out an agenda for education schools that,

if followed, would radically narrow their currently broad range of functions for American education, both instructionally and intellectually. The report would reduce instructional programs to the point that broad-based schools of education would effectively turn into schools of teacher education; and it would constrain the scope of intellectual activities to the point that academic research on education would devolve into industrial-style research and development, focusing on the production of educational technologies for schools. (Labaree, 1995, abstract)

How ironic that the MSU revolution was misconstrued in this way by someone hired in the effort to enrich teacher education with contributions from a variety of arts and science disciplines, especially since the revolution was later criticized by Deborah Ball and others for neglecting to focus on teaching beginning skills to prospective teachers.

The Elliott Parent-Teacher Organization Lobbies the Legislature to Fund PDSs

In a 1996 memo, Mary Kennedy, the influential MSU faculty member who had been director of the National Center for Research on Teacher Education, made a strong claim for PDS success, but also warned that this achievement was provisional, pending a lasting source of financial support:

We now know that it is possible to create a new kind of institution. These nine professional development schools are very close to what we had originally envisioned. We could not have achieved these outcomes without a long-term investment in organizational change. . . . But the system is still formative, and if we don't obtain dependable financial support, all of the development costs we have invested will be lost before we have had an opportunity to really capitalize on our investment in these schools. We are requesting a dependable base of financial support that will enable us to continue to develop these unique institutions. (Kennedy memo, September 19, 1996)

Unfortunately, the last best opportunity to obtain such support had passed. Earlier in 1996, remarkably, it was a Parent-Teacher Organization (PTO) in one of the PDSs that had taken the lead in directly appealing to the state legislature for the sort of support that had always sustained the agricultural extension service. This occurred at Elliott Elementary School in Holt. Elliott had recovered from a year of conflict in which the PDS had nearly fallen apart. And in fact, in the annual vote in May 1996 that was required by agreement with the teachers' union on whether to continue the PDS at Elliott, of the thirty-one surveys distributed to everyone working at Elliott, the results were "yes" to continue, fifteen; "no," zero; "not sure," two; left blank, two; not returned, twelve. Remarkably, there was no expressed opposition to the PDS continuing.

What was even more remarkable was the leadership that Elliott took in pushing for legislative funding. The March 1996 issue of the Elliott PTO newsletter made this clear:

> Elliott Elementary has participated with the Michigan State University PDS program for over five years. OUR teachers can't say enough about the benefits PDS has provided to OUR students, OUR intern teachers, and to OUR teachers themselves. *Unfortunately, funding for the Professional Development School is being discontinued next year.* The Elliott PTO is taking action to try and save this valuable program.

Doug Campbell, the MSU coordinator at Elliott, was one of the main leaders of the MSU PDS effort overall, based on his role as head documenter. On March 7, 1996, he wrote to many others active in PDSs urging them to contact legislators. He also sent a letter directly to state Senators John (Joe) Schwarz, Jon Cisky, and Don Koivisto on March 6, 1996:

As a member of the faculty of the College of Education at MSU, I have been working with teachers at Elliott Elementary School in Holt since 1985. Initially, MSU colleagues and I worked with only a few teachers in supporting their efforts to improve their practice, but with the advent of the PDS concept and associated funding from the state in 1989, we were able to involve many more teachers in ways we all feel has been very beneficial to them as professionals as well as to the education of their students.

The PTO invited legislators to visit the school. Lingg Brewer, the member of the Michigan House who represented Holt, was the first to visit at a PTO meeting on February 12, 1996. After this visit, he wrote to twenty other legislators on key committees and from districts with PDSs. "I have seen how this program has benefited the schools in my district, and believe this initiative to be a critical part of our mission to improve the overall quality of education, and sharpen the professional skills of teachers."

Unfortunately, additional funding was not given legislative priority. In past years the appropriation in support of MPNE—all activities including the PDSs of other universities, not just MSU—had been magnanimous: $5 million in fiscal year 1995, $5.3 million in fiscal year 1994, and $1.8 million in fiscal year 1993. The legislature had even appropriated $2 million for the PDSs in fiscal year 1996, but with the proviso that this be last year of state funding for the PDSs. Brewer acknowledged that this decision was based on the new charter school mission of MPNE.

One of the most influential legislators for education, Senator John Schwarz from Battle Creek, followed suit and made his own visit to Elliott the first week of March 1996. Schwarz was chair of the Senate Higher Education Committee, member of the K–12 appropriations subcommittee, and president pro tempore of the Senate. After his visit, he, too, was converted to the cause, but it was too late in the appropriations process to add an additional appropriation for the PDSs.

Schwarz did continue to express support of state funding for the PDSs and came out in favor of adding that in the next fiscal year.

In the meantime, the parents had done their best, as exemplified by the following letter from Brad Coombs to Perry Lanier on April 17, 1996:

> As a parent of one daughter who has now graduated from Elliott Elementary School in Holt, and another who next year will be entering the fourth grade there, I have witnessed firsthand the benefits my children have experienced as a result of Elliott's relationship with Michigan State, and specifically with PDS. At a recent Elliott PTO meeting, we learned that you had the dubious responsibility of overseeing financial cutbacks in this fine program. At that time, I know it was discussed that the PTO would voice their concern and support for its continuation, and if you have not already heard from our group, I am sure you soon will. Additionally, I wanted to take it upon myself to express my hope as a parent that there is something you can do to continue the wonderful impact that this program has had upon the impressionable lives of the hundreds of young people it has so positively affected at our school.

After 1995, the MSU faculty and administrators who remained committed to the PDSs moved forward as much as the greatly reduced resources and opposing forces permitted. For example, the 1996–97 work plan for Elliott described what they would do with a smaller number of PDS staff: the equivalent of two quarter-time assistantships, plus seven MSU interns. They planned a Science Connections and Inquiry project done with one section of the Science Methods course, TE 402, taught by MSU faculty member Kathy Roth coteaching science units to children with Elliott teachers and TE students. Emphasis was put on assigning prospective teachers to observe and participate in classrooms across a semester as part of a university methods course, developing assignments for juniors, seniors, and interns, and coteaching of the curriculum by school, university, and prospective teachers in classrooms associated with PDS projects. MSU faculty Roth and

Rosaen also were to continue working with Elliott mentor teachers to improve portions of TE 401 and TE 402 both in terms of field experiences and with Elliott teachers participating in on-campus courses to discuss their curricula, teaching, and assessment experience.

Response to Coats's Hijacking of MPNE

On October 15, 1995, Sue York, an MPNE board member and school administrator at Holt who had dealt with the PDSs almost from the beginning, sent a memo to other members of the board that was extremely critical of how MPNE management under Coats was dealing with the board. The memo expressed various concerns about how MPNE leadership had operated with respect to the board: control of information, minutes of meetings sent late or not at all or only to those who requested them, and violations of bylaws on advance notice of meetings and cancellation without notice. She charged that "the Partnership leadership has failed to keep the board informed of major events and issues concerning the Partnership, with the result that board members hear about critical Partnership actions through the news media." York alleged failure to comply with the constitution and bylaws of MPNE in that the president was appointed, not elected; failure to obtain board support through formal votes on major issues of substance; documents misrepresenting views of the board, for example, board support for charter schools; and dismissal of some board members in violation of bylaws. In short, "the intended role of the board in major decisions of policy, clearly stated in Article III.C of the Constitution, has not been achieved."

On December 4, 1995, further dissension within MPNE came to light: a press release was issued in the name of six educators who had resigned from the MPNE board. It was faxed from the state offices of the AFL-CIO. Their action was triggered by the signing of an agreement between MPNE and the State Board of Education on June 1 for the partnership to play a major role in encouraging the development of charter schools. According to the press release, most of the MPNE board members had learned of this agreement from the newspapers. The resigning members were critical of politicization of the partnership and the effort "to purge educators from the board," as well as the cost of maintaining the MPNE administrative structure, and the possible use of the partnership to circumvent the Michigan constitutional ban on public aid to religious schools. Attached to the press release was a statement from those who had resigned. It reminded readers of their very positive view of the board when it was founded five years earlier:

> It was a genuine coalition of K–12 education, higher education, business, labor and state government. The organization was dedicated [to] finding ways to improve education within the existing public school system, primarily through the creation of "Professional Development Schools." The Partnership board had an excellent mix with respect to political affiliation, gender, geography and ethnicity, and within K–12 education there was a strong mix of classroom teachers, administrators and school board members. We were all proud to be part of an undertaking designed to enrich and improve the lives of the children we teach.

But when Coats replaced Lanier, it all changed. According to those who resigned, within a year Coats "had completely changed the top leadership and the mission of the organization without consulting [the board]." In July 1995 all remaining educators were asked to resign. When instead they asked for a board meeting, it was held on October 16, 1995, but according to the opposition was "a travesty of the democratic process."

Dean Ames, increasingly disillusioned and opposed to MPNE, moved toward a divorce between the college and the partnership. Early in the restoration era in 1994–95, the MPNE dissolved its fiduciary relationship with MSU and moved its offices out of Erickson Hall and off campus to the Eyde Building in East Lansing in order to operate initially as a nonprofit organization (MSU-33, 1995, 1:11). The EES as well as the component responsible for the leadership academies was turned over to MSU. Then, in 1996, under Coats's leadership, the MPNE was dissolved and replaced with the Leona Group, a for-profit private corporation without aspirations to partner with higher education and devoted to ownership or management of charter schools (Fendler, 2004).

An Example of a Diminished but Still Active PDS

In the years following the failed Elliott-led effort to obtain state legislative funding in 1996, there continued to be much discussion and various plans for how to keep the PDSs going with greatly reduced funding. For example, in her April 6, 1998, memo the dean set new parameters for the PDS budgets in this time of sharply reduced resources, updating the plans for eight PDSs. Since by that time teacher education was more central to PDS work than it had been, this budget was based on the assumption each PDS would have seven to nine interns. This budget was enough to cover sixteen faculty at one-eighth time for eight PDSs, one quarter-time graduate assistant for each PDS, minigrant funds of $5,000 to be applied for, travel to the Holmes Partnership meeting, the possibility of a teacher-in-residence program, and summer salary for PDS coordinators of one to two months. This budget was not intended to pay for teacher released time, secretarial support in the schools, or other expenses that could be covered by the school. Little information is currently available to me on the actual budgets for each of the PDSs in the years after the MPNE and the state had withdrawn their financial support of MSU PDSs. But Elliott budgets for 1998–99, which I do have, give an order of magnitude idea of how much PDS external funding was available during those years. On August 24, 1998, Perry Lanier and Susan Melnick, the codirectors of MSU-affiliated PDSs, stated that it was not possible to fund any of the eight PDSs at the levels requested. What they proposed for Elliott instead was $23,166 from the MSU general fund (MSU's recurring state-funded hard money account), plus special grant funds of $5,805 and a request for school district funding of $18,200. In addition, MSU was planning to contribute $21,007 in faculty time.

After 1995, the surviving PDSs continued in diminished form. Since the MPNE annual reports were discontinued once MPNE had withdrawn from the PDS field, documentation was no longer so available in a form that could be tapped for this chapter. The Elliott PDS was an exception, producing annual reports through 1998–99 that are still available. These reports illustrate what Elliott was able to do with greatly reduced resources. In fact, according to the 1997–98 report, Elliott had begun to include "increasingly detailed and cumulative discussion of the progress and problems we have experienced in recent years in achieving implementation of the overarching, all-building unifying goals we articulate each year" (MSU-6, September 1998, 11; see also MSU-5, July 1997).

This 1997–98 report confessed that Elliott had once again failed to live up to the work plan's vision and rhetoric. But that year was also different since a new building principal, Francine Minnick, had brought stability to building leadership, achieving more "unity of purpose and coordination of effort." High priority was put on dealing with student behavior problems and developing what was called, not discipline policy but rather behavior policy. In summer 1998 a workgroup with some PDS resources met to develop a "behavior plan." In fall 1998 the introduction of this plan to students and parents went very well, whereas in the past inconsistent behavior expectations and consequences had, according to the report, undermined PDS work. Work on integrating school improvement goals and PDS goals also proved more successful than in the past. For example, a whole school effort on the school improvement goal of informational reading was touted as evidence of success, including summer work on organizing a new reading resources room. This all represented a "whole building commitment, commonness of purpose and participation in curriculum development that had been somewhat lacking in the past" (MSU-6, September 1998, 11–12).

According to the next annual report, 1998–99 was even more successful. The implementation of the behavior policy, according to consensus in the building, had led to a reduction in the number and severity of behavior problems. More emphasis was given to school-wide involvement and impact. In planning for 1999–2000, the following targets were suggested: (1) consistent building-wide "best teaching" strategies in informational reading, writing, technology, and socio-emotional development; (2) improved adult/child ratios through smaller class sizes, adult volunteers, and use of MSU students; (3) early interventions through a full-time counselor, coupled with preschool, special education, and use of social promotion; and (4) community involvement through parent education, high school and junior high volunteers, area businesses, etc. Teacher-education activities in 1999–2000 were planned to include Elliott teachers working with MSU instructors on how to use MSU seniors and interns as resources for pursuing school improvement goals and PDS project outcomes and designing and conducting MSU teacher-education courses for Team Two. Two MSU graduate assistants were anticipated to work on this and other PDS work at Elliott, especially the technology integration project (MSU-7, July 1999).

In spite of such positive developments, there was also much self-criticism at this point. The school's report at that time confessed that "to date, however, we have not adequately engaged district-level officials and organizations, have not linked teacher preparation well enough with professional development and school improvement, and have not organized networks that could make powerful professional development opportunities available to many of the teachers in partner schools." The vision of the EES seems by this point to have been lost.

Centering the PDSs on Teacher Education, Progress or Regress?

After the precipitous decline in funding had made the PDSs more dependent on the college's regular budget, Dean Ames made it clear that in her opinion, the PDSs needed to be reoriented to be more beneficial to the college and to make teacher education more central to their work. On the one hand, this could be seen as moving the revolution forward since a profound reform of teacher education had always been a central plank in its platform.

But if it meant that other PDS functions were less important and even expendable, then maybe it meant going backward toward the university using K–12 schools solely as sites for teacher-education field experience and for other purposes only on an ad hoc basis when called for by external funding.

At this point, PDSs were playing a critical role in the preparation of teachers. All the PDSs hosted fifth-year interns and also provided, in schools located close enough, field experience for juniors and seniors. But a number of schools did much more, including Averill, Elliott, Holmes Middle School, and Holt High School, as will be discussed elsewhere. Nevertheless, there was still concern that the PDSs were not sufficiently on board in the five-year program and could do more. In an email, Cheryl Rosaen on May 13, 1999, candidly gave her sense of how these issues were evolving: "I got the sense that Carole [Ames] is going to 'step into' the process this spring in some really direct ways. She feels it is essential for [teacher-preparation] team leaders to be part of the conversations about what PDS work will/should look like. It was very clear that she values the work at Elliott and other elementary PDSs and wants that work to continue."

Nonetheless, by the year 2000, the situation had further evolved and was coming to focus on how to bring the PDS era to a close with a transition to a new form of organization that would sustain some of the work in a different form. A memo from Tom Bird to college leaders on October 17, 2000, described the new plan as a "successor" to the PDSs. His view was that the earlier vision calling for empowerment of College of Education faculty and K–12 teachers within an organization of more equal status between schools and university had not been realized, that instead the PDSs had been "strongly shaped by a grantor-grantee relationship between the College/Partnership on the one hand and COE faculty/school personnel on the other." "To date," he continued, "we have not adequately engaged district level officials and organizations, have not linked teacher preparation well enough with professional development and school improvement, and have not organized networks that could make powerful professional opportunities available to many of the teachers in partner schools."

He described the emerging organizational framework as follows: "The College of Education has asked the Department of Teacher Education to lead in forming school–college partnerships in which teacher preparation is a central activity." This plan specified that "the placement and support of juniors, seniors and interns often will be the central element in the negotiation of a partnership." But the plan contained no assurance of adequate resources. Only $145,000 was to be set aside for these partnerships, a truly paltry sum relative to the aspirations involved and the earlier peak of financial support for the PDS MSU-39 draft plan, fostering school-university partnerships for teacher preparation, 2000–2001.

In March and May 2000, another proposal was drafted and revised by a subcommittee of the PDS steering committee to turn the PDSs into networks (MSU-40). On the basis of a retrospective study conducted by the school and university partners in 1999–2000, it was acknowledged that for eleven years the PDS and the five-year teacher-preparation program had been on separate tracks and that few innovations had spread to other schools and districts. This new proposal concluded that there was a need for a new institution, given that that the established principles "call for such profound changes that the PDS will need to devise for itself a different kind of organizational structure, supported over time by enduring alliances of all the institutions with a stake in better professional preparation for school faculty."

Notwithstanding these proposed changes, much of the original PDS concept did survive within the proposed network. It called for each of the four teacher-preparation teams in the five-year program to establish a formal partnership with a cluster of local schools, in which one of the schools would be designated as a leadership site. This site would still be called a PDS. In addition to offering the fifth-year internship, the PDS node of each cluster would continue to be expected to be a center of investigation into teaching and learning, teacher education, and related school-improvement issues.

But soon thereafter, a draft letter dated June 8, 2000, from PDS leaders Sue York, Sharon Feiman-Nemser, and Doug Campbell acknowledged that the term "professional development school" was likely to be given up: "The designation of any individual building as a PDS will not continue indefinitely." This statement implied that the vision of a new type of school embodying a revolution in school–university relations was being abandoned.

Conclusion

During the decade of revolutionary work with PDSs, those leading the work were unable to persuade funders—state, university, K–12 school districts—that PDS work should become an essential part of the educational system. As a result, when leadership changed, new leaders chose to support other approaches, such as charter schools. The Elliott-led campaign to secure legislative funding for the PDSs was the nearest MSU would come to keeping the PDSs going in the form inspired by the agricultural extension service. Although efforts to secure needed external funding for the PDSs continued, none was successful enough to keep the operation going. With the loss of support from MPNE, the college found no way to replace the loss of all that money. It reduced its financial support for the PDSs and eventually withdrew it altogether. As a result the PDSs could not continue to exist in the form and with the goals they had adopted. They were going back to the traditional basis of just being sites for the field experience of teacher-education students, plus one-off settings for whatever research projects the college could get funded whenever these projects required some sort of participation by K–12 schools. The hope that the PDSs would come to play a role in research comparable to the college itself was given up as well. The idea of transforming the PDSs into a thriving network of schools playing such a role never came to pass.

CHAPTER SIX

The Restoration at MSU

The most intense period of PDS activity at MSU took place from 1989 to 1995. With hindsight, it is obvious that a duration of six years was insufficient for the PDSs to become the institution to which the leaders aspired. In fact, from the beginning, the creation of the PDSs and associated innovations was cast as a long-term effort in which new institutions were being created over decades, not years. As Charles Thompson, the associate dean in charge of the PDSs, stated in 1990, responding to a question of whether MSU was already succeeding in the creation of PDSs: "Well, we're starting. This is not a two-year or even five-year undertaking" (Thompson, 1990, 7). Unfortunately, the long-term follow-through needed to prove the value and viability of the PDSs never took place.

It is important to remember that Judy Lanier never said the revolution was bound to succeed. To the contrary, she wrote in 1993: "Whether the title [professional development school] or Holmes Group lasts or not is unimportant. What is important is that the movement succeeds." In fact, one reason that the reform group was named after Henry Holmes was that he had tried to reform teacher education and had failed.

By the end of the century, the Holmes Group was indeed no longer a revolutionary force. In 1996, it had taken a huge step back from the revolutionary agenda, when it transformed itself from a select group of education schools into the Holmes Partnership, a large and unwieldy alliance of schools of education and giant education interest groups (e.g., American Association of Colleges of Teacher Education, National Education Association, National Board of Teaching Standards, American Association of School Administrators) (Holmes Partnership, ca. 1997). Nancy Zimpher, a prime mover of Holmes at Ohio State University, had become the president of Holmes, replacing Lanier. Adam Scrupski made a compelling case when discussing how the consortium had changed: "[Its] reasonable objective . . . fell prey to the ideology that has dominated academe since the late 1960s. What had been a rather exclusive group of teacher education units with a realizable agenda was, by 1997, hijacked into a merger on the national level with powerful education organizations" (Scrupski, 1999, 36).

The change in Holmes was not well received at MSU. Although MSU had been instrumental in founding Holmes and had served as its headquarters, Dean Ames decided to withdraw, arguing that MSU no longer received sufficient benefit from the substantial dues the organization required. In taking this action, MSU again signaled its abandonment of its pretensions to leadership in the reform of K–12 schools, returning to its place as a more traditional school of education. It was a move reminiscent of revolution and restoration in political history, 1688 in England and 1789 in France, periods in which revolutionaries, once they have done so much to dismantle the old regime, were beat back by their opponents and a restoration took place—but a restoration that was not just the old status quo.

At MSU orthodoxy returned in many respects, but as in political history, it was orthodoxy enhanced by the accomplishments of the revolution. Ames was not at all in favor of going all the way back to what the College of Education had been. Like Lanier, she was in favor of more research, higher quality research, and emphasis on quality of teaching within the college, but along the orthodox lines of other universities, like the University of Illinois from which she had come. As Forzani concluded, "What Carole Ames and the faculty rebuilt after Lanier left was a strong college, if a much more traditional one" (2011, 312).

As a new dean, Ames had immediately repudiated what she saw as a single-agenda college, preferring to develop multiple agendas and thus pleasing the three non-teacher-education departments. She did not want the college to be spending its limited resources on trying to bring about radical educational reform on a large scale outside the college at the state and national levels. From her perspective, with limited resources, rather than doing more than was likely to succeed, the college was better off informing the reform movement through its research while educating the leaders needed for reform to succeed.

In this new era, not only did the Holmes Group, MPNE, and the college cease to be forces for the fundamental large-scale reform of teaching, learning, and teacher education, but even the institutional memory of what had been achieved and what it took to bring about these achievements was somehow largely erased. By this point Judy Lanier was hardly ever mentioned at college functions or in collective discussions—or at least that's how I remember it. However, there was one notable exception. For the fiftieth anniversary of turning educational studies into a full-fledged college at MSU, Dean Ames and Associate Dean Cass Book encouraged the college's public relations director Victor Inzunza (2002) to write a history of the college. His approach was studiously neutral, outlining all the achievements during the last half century and not appearing to favor any of the contentious factions in the college.

Once they no longer held revolutionary roles in the college, Judy Lanier, Henrietta Barnes, and Joyce Putnam joined together in a sort of exile in Flint, working closely with district administrators as well as schools and teachers on further efforts at reform, building on what had already been achieved. This work was supported by a special Rockefeller grant. Their relations with Dean Ames were bad. The dean was especially aggravated that they refused to come to campus to teach courses—a university requirement.

Under the influence of these three, the four PDSs in Flint became a source of criticism of the five-year program. With this notable exception, however, most of the college faculty apparently found the restoration of orthodoxy welcome, necessary, and very successful. Indeed, if one accepts Dean Ames's premises that denied legitimacy to so much of the revolution, one must conclude that she was a dean of great excellence, completely devoted to more traditional notions of quality in research, teaching, and the selection of faculty. She was a skilled administrator with the financial acumen that could have made her exceptionally successful in business. She increased the proportion of first-rate faculty not just in teacher education, but throughout the college, and last but not least, kept the college's portfolio of external funding at an impressive level.

Within the college, the decline of revolutionary fervor and aspirations took effect in the college's reward system that, in fact, had never been sufficiently modified to support the radical reforms that had been launched (e.g., by giving more credit for work in the PDSs). Whatever adaptations had been made informally and unofficially in the Lanier era were quickly reversed under Ames. The traditional norms of research universities were reemphasized and strengthened. Collaborative as opposed to individual work on school reform and in the PDSs received little or no recognition in tenure and promotion decisions. Instead the college went further than ever before in enforcing criteria that emphasized publication by individual first authors, not coauthors, in highly respected peer-reviewed journals. In addition, there was at long last individualized insistence on evidence of quality teaching (Forzani, 2011, 311). The latter was one of Dean Ames's greatest contributions to the revolution and one in which she was able to move forward and go beyond what Lanier had been able to do.

In fact, attention to the quality of MSU teacher education as constituted in the five-year program was on the increase during this period. More attention was given to collecting evidence of quality in spite of reduced resources for quality assurance such as cuts in the number of times interns in the fifth year were observed by university personnel. It was a case of "doing more with less." Suzanne Wilson (2012) has documented much in this regard in her chapter titled "Doing Better: Musings on Teacher Education, Accountability, and Evidence." She gives specific examples of how closely the five-year program was monitored after she became TE department chair during the restoration era:

> Every day we respond to information we have received and interpreted. A doctoral student has to be removed from field instruction because he is not visiting an intern's classroom regularly enough and his feedback is neither frequent nor constructive. An instructor needs support in learning to teach her class better, her students are confused and feel like they are wasting their time. An intern needs to be moved to a different classroom because her collabo-

rating teacher is not providing her with sufficient opportunities to teach. (41) . . .

In the internship year itself, we have 500 students, 10 observations, 2 evaluations, which means that we have at least 6000 data points on the program's effectiveness. We also have the information we gather on their grades and grade point averages, used both to admit them to the program and to monitor their progress, which includes their performance in liberal studies, disciplinary majors and minors, and professional coursework. We're quite vigilant in watching our students' progress, an expensive enterprise. (45) . . .

We're constantly using data. . . . We have a well-articulated set of expectations for what they have to do in order to progress to that internship. As Department chair, I read the student evaluations (SIRS) for every course for every instructor for every term, as do the instructors for each class. Every faculty member who supervises a course with multiple sections also reads and reviews the SIRS for all instructors for whom they have supervisory responsibilities. (43)

Once *U.S. News and World Report* started ranking education programs in 1995, Ames did her best to keep and increase MSU's standing in the rankings. When the programs were first ranked, Ames had not been dean for long, and therefore the rankings were based on the achievements of the Lanier era. But the fact that MSU already ranked first for programs in elementary and secondary education set the stage for continued efforts to maintain the MSU edge. As pointed out above, Ames made quality of faculty her first priority throughout her eighteen years as dean, and under her management, the new five-year program of teacher education was implemented as planned. The fifth-year internship proved to be an outstanding success, while at the same time the dean turned to other departments, giving them more attention and resources, enabling more fields to move up in the rankings. By 2020 MSU had nine graduate fields ranked among the top twelve in the country. In traditional terms, the multiple-agenda college was a great success.

Ames's strengths were not, in fact, so different from those of Judy Lanier. For example, she continued to take full advantage of the dean's ability to influence faculty appointments. It was no longer a search for revolutionaries, but rather for the best qualified people to meet more traditional criteria, emphasizing exceptional records or promise in research and teaching. As far as I know, no faculty member in the college was ever hired during the Ames era without being scrutinized and making a case for themselves that was convincing to the dean. She hardly ever missed personally interviewing candidates to make sure they met what she judged to be the college's expectations. Thus, the college was able to continue to recruit some of the best of the crop of new PhDs nationwide, as well as established professors at other universities who were well known for their scholarly productivity (e.g., David Pearson, Michael Pressley, and Barbara Schneider). To do all this was a tall order since most of the college's faculty turned over during the Ames era.

As the revolutionary fervor abated, losing force and influence in East Lansing, the revolution took a new turn, not at MSU but at its rival in Ann Arbor. The leader in this development was none other than Deborah Ball, who after leaving MSU for the University of Michigan in 1996, continued as a leader in teacher education as well as becoming still more highly regarded for her work in mathematics education. By the time she became the dean of education at U of M, she was convinced that the Achilles heel of the revolution at MSU was its reliance on developing teacher judgment without expecting preservice students to achieve entry-level mastery of key teaching practices. She and her colleagues organized a project, known as Teaching Works, to identify these key practices, to develop training and assessment for students to be able to achieve the desired level of mastery, and to build a teacher-education curriculum based on these key practices. Colleges in other locations across the country were encouraged to join in this effort, but MSU did not accept this invitation.

A Flawed Attempt to Take
the Revolution to a New Level

At the beginning of the new century, the one big initiative in teacher education at MSU that could be seen as having the potential to carry the revolution forward was the Teachers for a New Era (TNE) project designed and funded by the Carnegie Corporation. MSU competed successfully to become one of the first four universities to be funded by this project to move teacher education to a new level. To get this award, universities had to commit to a university-wide initiative with a strong commitment from the central administration and responsibilities shared with arts and sciences colleges. Dan Fallon, the prime mover of the project at Carnegie, had picked the following problems to be addressed by the project as primary obstacles to improving the quality of teacher education (McDiarmid & Caprino, 2018, 1):

- Lack of evidence to demonstrate the effects of university-based teacher preparation on candidates' and graduates' classroom performance.
- The need to raise the status of teacher-preparation programs in higher education and to engage arts and sciences faculty more deeply in this work.
- Failure to engage K–12 schools and educators as full and equal partners in developing the classroom practices needed for the success of prospective and beginning teachers.

Among the other mandates of Carnegie was that direction of this project be located in the office of the president or chief academic officer of the institution, not in a school or department of education.

Insofar as moving teacher education to a new level, in my opinion, the design of TNE was fatally flawed from the beginning. Its three objectives could not be achieved in any profound lasting way without institutionalization, without lasting changes in norms, practices, and organization at participating universities. McDiarmid and Caprino, whose book took stock of this whole project, were of similar mind, pointing out that "institutional-ization requires a level of leadership commitment and stability to identify, allocate, and protect the resources required to make a position, program, or collaboration part of the organization's fabric" (2018, 168). Although the project was relatively well funded, Carnegie was in no position to undertake such deep and comprehensive change with only project funding.

In their book on the results of the project, McDiarmid and Caprino (2018) make clear that TNE, from the start, was based on assumptions that were problematic, minimizing obstacles and resistance stemming from state and local policies, the unwillingness of faculty to do what was needed, especially the arts and sciences faculty, and the difficulty of finding suitable K–12 schools as partners.

Much could have been learned about the flaws in the design of TNE if the lessons of the MSU revolution had been taken into account (as this book is attempting to do). McDiarmid and Caprino's (2018) book about the lessons of TNE mentions the Holmes Group as a precursor to TNE, but the description is brief and superficial. Almost nothing is said about the MSU revolution and what could have been learned from it. TNE might have, for example, learned from the overall lesson of the revolution that profound change in teacher education requires a multipronged comprehensive approach, not just a targeted, time-limited approach focusing on a few key factors. This was the argument Lanier made in such a compelling way in her 1986 chapter (Lanier and Little, 1986). The revolutionary experience that took place over the next dozen years or so in the three concentric circles of reform provided more than enough proof to this pudding. Instead TNE accepted constraints already boldly challenged by the MSU revolution. For instance, McDiarmid and Caprino (2018) warned against taking teaching hospitals as models for teacher education because teacher education is not well enough funded to do this. They did not acknowledge that more funding was an inherent part of the MSU revolution since profound change could not be achieved without it.

In spite of design flaws, TNE was successful in various respects in each of the three problem areas. According to McDiarmid and

Caprino (2018), it was work with arts and sciences faculties that had the most impact on improving teacher education at MSU, especially in mathematics education where gaps and problems (e.g., in statistics) were identified and new coursework was developed. The team working on science likewise made improvements in the introductory science courses taken by secondary-education students. In literacy, the TNE team did a longitudinal study of how teacher-education students thought about the teaching of literacy and, in addition, revised the elementary-teaching major in language arts. The social studies team also made such changes but not as much as in the other subject areas.

However, the question can be raised if these changes justified all the time and effort that, in collaboration with arts and sciences departments, was devoted to developing written standards for the subject-matter content to be learned by prospective teachers. The standards did not become engrained deeply enough in practice to guide the teaching and learning of prospective teachers at MSU in a sustained and profound way.

Earlier, in an excellent example of what it took to bring about effective collaboration between education and arts and sciences faculties to build pedagogical content knowledge, Peter Vinten-Johansen from the history department had worked with Bill McDiarmid from education. In their 2000 article aptly titled "A Catwalk across the Great Divide: Redesigning the History Teaching Methods Course," they ended with a confession what they had done was not yet sustainable at MSU in spite of the revolution. According to the authors,

> Such collaboration is fragile and vulnerable . . . because it is not institutionalized. For example, when McDiarmid left Michigan State University, Vinten-Johansen faced opposition to the course from teacher educators and prospective history teachers who thought it was too focused on subject matter. Without McDiarmid present to argue for the pedagogical benefits with his colleagues and to lend credibility in the classroom, the course was vulnerable. . . . In addition, when funding from the Provost to support cross-depart-

> mental planning and teaching expired, Vinten-Johansen
> had to justify to his department continued participation in
> a course for which his department receives no fiscal benefit
> or even student credit hours. (175–76)

This is just one example of how the MSU revolution demonstrates what would have to happen to ensure necessary institutionalization. The chapter by Feiman-Nemser and Hartzler-Miller in
the book on Team One is especially relevant because it explains
in some detail, in contrast to the implementation of the TNE
standards at MSU, what it took for that team's earlier standards to
become engrained in their program. The implementation of these
Team One standards was anything but a one-off, narrowly targeted
effort. Instead the standards were repeatedly studied and discussed
in all the relevant settings of the program, as the authors of this
chapter have explained:

> Some of this talk took place on the steering committee.
> . . . Some of it occurred in a weekly seminar for the intern-
> ship staff. . . . It also took place in a monthly study group
> with MSU liaisons and teacher representatives from each
> partnership school, in weekly school-based seminars with
> interns, and in our courses where students were introduced
> to the program standards. These professional conversations
> were all part of an effort to connect abstract statements
> about good teaching to the concrete practices of teachers,
> to form an organic link between teachers' own experience
> and teaching standards framed outside the experience.
> (Feiman-Nemser & Hartzler-Miller, 2007, 61–62)

Team One also developed standards-based observation guides,
planning frameworks, and rubrics for analyzing interns' lesson
plans and units. In addition, it also came up with a portfolio framework based on the standards and held a faculty retreat.

In working with K–12 schools, TNE again had some success,
especially in the induction of new teachers. In addition to offering online induction courses, it developed and experimented

with an induction model that proved successful, including in a matched comparison study in the Lansing schools. As described by McDiarmid and Caprino,

> The model incorporated several support activities including mentor study groups in which mentors and mentees met face-to-face or virtually to a discuss research on the program and learn new skills and approaches, theory-into-practice meetings that were offered in between-mentor study groups and provided opportunities for mentors to continue discussing their challenges with colleagues and coaches, and individual conferences in which LITIM coaches met with individual mentors to customize the support they receive. (2018, 8)

However, due to the lack of new teachers in Michigan, the bulk of MSU TNE induction activities were moved to Georgia, thereby foreclosing any possibility of institutionalizing induction as an integral part of MSU teacher education—if indeed there was any possibility of this in the first place (see also Carver, 2010; Nevins-Stanulis and Floden, 2009; Stanulis, Burrill & Ames, 2007; Wood & Stanulis, 2010).

Use of evidence was another area in which what TNE aimed for was necessary, but not sufficient to the desired improvement in the quality of teacher education. Data on pupil learning from the graduates of teacher education is important to know, but does not by itself provide sufficient insight into what it takes to improve programs. This is clear from MSU experience and, in particular, from Suzanne Wilson's discussion on how she kept track of the quality of MSU's program when she was department chair. Her conclusion was that

> our program and our faculty are, thus, in perpetual motion, and almost every activity is either catalyzed or informed by data and evidence. Accountability is everywhere: students are accountable to the program, instructors and field instructors are accountable to their

supervisors, everyone is accountable to the chair, the chair is accountable to the dean, the college and the program are accountable to the university and to the state. (2012, 44)

Being accountable, in Wilson's view, does not mean limiting oneself to a narrow set of quantitative measures.

The evidence-based movement has, in general, elevated quantifiable data and experimental designs over narrative and observational data, and this has led some teacher educators to reject calls for accountability based on the assumption that the only evidence that will be taken seriously is that which is quantifiable. But a narrow view of evidence is not a requirement of a commitment to evidence; in fact, many in the evidence-based medicine movement argue against the oversimplified interpretation that evidence only refers to data produced from experimental designs. . . . For [some] questions, one needs large-scale experiments. In teacher education, we need careful observations of our interns working in the classrooms of collaborating teachers, and we also need results of their performance on standardized tests. Ideally, we would have multiple methods of collecting data for each major outcome we care about so that we might triangulate across those different sources of inherently limited empirical evidence. To use my own example, the 6000 observations that we have of our interns in one given year are a mix of some Likert-scale ratings with a lot of observational notes and narratives, peppered with examples drawn from those observations. Similarly, instructors in courses write comments on papers, as well as assign grades. As part of the normal work of teacher education, we regularly produce evidence that is both qualitative and quantitative. There is no reason why we cannot use the full range of evidence we have available. (50–51)

But Wilson, characteristically, treats all this as unfinished and a work in progress. She acknowledges that more could be learned from the quantitative data gathered. She admits that although the collected data are used in reports, there is very little by way of faculty discussion of the data to assess the program's strengths and weaknesses. For example, the observational data are not used for program evaluation by asking, "What patterns do we see in what our interns can and cannot do?" (46). Likewise, there is no consideration of how well course grades correlate with performance in the internship. Instead, the emphasis is on assessing individual students or instructors, not on reaching conclusions about the effectiveness of the program in general. Wilson concludes that the potential of the data for program evaluation remains almost totally unrealized. But she credits the new Teacher Education Accreditation Council accreditation process for moving in the direction of program improvement in addition to assessment of individual outcomes.

"Creating a 'culture of evidence,'" she notes, "takes years and does not happen by directive from an administrator or a state department official" (54). Even so, she makes a convincing case that much can and should be done for quality control even without data on the performance of the K–12 pupils of TE graduates. In any case, in TNE it proved difficult to get appropriate data on the K–12 pupil achievement of MSU teacher-education graduates, even with help from the gigantic Promoting Rigorous Outcomes in Mathematics and Science Education project separately funded by National Science Foundation to gather data on K–12 achievement.

Partly as a result of these constraints, variation in what TE and K–12 students experienced was shown to have only very limited or no impact at MSU. However, TNE was able to show, to the surprise of some, that teacher-education students at MSU consistently outperformed students in other majors in campus courses (McDiarmid & Caprino, 2018, 77).

If more skepticism about the ability of TNE to bring the revolution were needed, one needs only to examine what Wilson (2012) had to say about the continuing resistance at MSU to implementing the teacher-education program as designed, implemented, and later ostensibly enhanced through standards set by TNE. She is frank in giving examples of deviation from and noncompliance with plans, saying that she discovered that field instructors in elementary schools had abandoned the observation form they were supposedly using and the ones in secondary school could not even agree on a common form across subjects. Some field instructors did not submit any of the information they were in theory accountable for. Teaching assistants and fixed-term faculty did not all use the syllabi and assignments developed and commonly did not use standard assessments and common rubrics created for the new accreditation process. They were quick to invoke academic freedom to justify their actions. In short, according to Wilson, there continued to be "widespread resistance to collective and public inquiry into the quality of our programs" (50).

Taking all this into account, in the end, TNE was largely a one-off project with the limitations and restrictions that such projects inevitably entail. It was successful, but not a game-changer. A one-off project does not a revolution make. McDiarmid and Caprino agree that "the goal of the TNE was . . . far more ambitious than changes at the 11 sites" (2018, 175). Limited in scope, funding, time, institutional commitment, devotion of staff, and contextual support, such projects were not enough to bring about sustained institutional change. TNE was at most a limited prototype of the change required, namely, a revolution in higher education in the preparation of teachers.

It was an era of second thoughts. In 2010 after the revolutionary fervor and vision at MSU had in large part dissipated, three influential members of the revolutionary vanguard at MSU (Gary Sykes, Tom Bird, and Mary Kennedy) published a paper in the *Journal of Teacher Education* titled "Teacher Education: Its Problems and Some Prospects." The paper is surprisingly pessimistic in its views on the prospects for reform. In a highly abstract analysis, the introduction characterizes teacher education's problems in developing teachers' occupational competence in several ways. One was in terms of characteristics of the occupation that had produced "a tilt toward continuity with and conservation of past practices that enjoy broad cultural legitimacy even as they fail to serve the emergent reform ideals of excellence and equity." The authors assert that the problems of teaching as an occupation "begin not with teacher preparation itself but in the enterprise it seeks to serve and develop" (466). They go on, however, to describe the state of teacher education in exceedingly negative terms:

> The field is filled with disagreements about proper methods for studying teaching and teacher education, rival conceptual schemes, an absence of shared vocabulary, a profusion of guidance resting on little systematic inquiry, and irresolvable arguments over the proper aims for instruction or of how to manage trade-offs among such aims. Findings from research do not offer strong support, based on rigorous designs, for any particular method; and no "signature pedagogy" has emerged, as compared with some other fields (e.g., the case method in law or hospital rounds in medicine. (467)

One might think that MSU having programmatically addressed all these problems for decades, that some reference would be made and discussed as to the merits and shortcomings of the MSU revolution in terms of what had been learned. But there is no specific mention of the MSU revolution at all, much less an analysis of what was learned. Instead there is an implicit admission of failure in an excerpt that sounds very much as if it refers to what was tried at MSU and, in the authors' eyes, failed:

> Teacher education cannot make good on fantastic claims to reform the practice of teaching and more grandly the institution of schooling, so it must orient around and project a mission that is both worthy and achievable. (473)

As a substitute for this sort of failure, the authors propose something that sounds more like the Ann Arbor agenda of teaching beginning teachers a limited set of "high leverage" skills, but without justifying their position with specific attribution to the Teaching Works project at the University of Michigan other than citation of certain articles connected to that university. In the end the article comes down on the side of aiming for modest, continuous improvement through communities of inquiry working on targeted aspects of larger programs.

Conclusion

The reader of the Sykes, Bird, and Kennedy article is left to ask: How can it be that nothing worth mentioning was learned from the extraordinary volume of research and work in schools at MSU in which these authors participated. As it stands, it is difficult to know from this article what is condemned and what is endorsed. Was the work of the amphibious professors too ambitious, or was it not? Was the approach to mathematics at Holt High School too ambitious? What level of understanding of carbon cycling was too much to aim for in high school science? How much can students in elementary school be expected to think like scientists? What moves in mentoring novice teachers were to be avoided as overly threatening to existing practice? Sykes, Bird, and Kennedy were well placed to address such questions. That they did not and left such consideration lacking, knowing where to draw the line between revolutionary change and starting with existing practice remains elusive.

Likewise, the short review essay by Floden (2015) on teacher preparation research to mark the fiftieth anniversary of the National Academy of Education pays no attention to learning from the MSU revolution even though he was throughout the revolutionary era one of its leaders. His only nod toward MSU was to acknowledge the importance of the Teacher Education and Development Study in Mathematics, the first international study of the learning outcomes of teacher education with nationally representative samples, a study in which MSU was the lead international center.

Struggles to Transform the Teaching and Learning of Subject Matter

Part 2 discusses the revolutionary efforts to improve both teaching of and learning to teach four school subject-matters in elementary, middle, and high school: mathematics, social studies, science, and writing. The distinctive contribution of this part to the overall book is to show how this work on teaching and learning of subject matter developed in diverse institutions and diverse locations and how this diversity made for a revolutionary impact. While each subject matter has its own story to tell, the telling draws on certain technical terms that, though not originating at Michigan State University, were used at MSU in ways that merit attention. These include "situated learning" or "situated knowledge," "conceptual change" theories, "cognitive apprenticeships," and "scaffolding." For a short discussion of these terms, based primarily on a synthesis of what was known about teacher learning as written by Feiman-Nemser and Remillard (1995), see the appendix.

Feiman-Nemser and Remillard (1995) warn against assuming that the terms "situated learning," "cognitive apprenticeship," and "assisted performance" apply only to teacher learning in actual school settings and not to other learning opportunities. These concepts can be applied to academic courses and education courses—any course that is criticized for being too theoretical and not practical. In such situations teachers are likely to struggle if they encounter concepts and ideas disconnected from meaningful contexts or if they work alone without the benefits of collaboration or modeling. Since teachers are more likely to develop usable knowledge if their learning is situated in practice, the study of cases provides one promising way to situate teacher learning in problems of practice when the learner is not immersed in field experience. Through analysis of cases, teachers can learn concepts in light of the way they are used and practice the kind of reasoning and problem solving that authentic teaching entails.

CHAPTER 7

The Assault on Old-School Thinking and Practice in Mathematics

Although the revolution at MSU took on all the school subject-matters, the most intensive assault on old-school thinking and practice was in mathematics. The multipronged nature of the revolution worked to reform the teaching and learning of subject matter by teacher-education students as well as K–12 pupils in multiple arenas—in research centers, preservice teacher-education programs, and the professional development schools (PDSs).

A key component of the substance of the revolution was the shift to curriculum and instruction that sought to improve student understanding of the subjects studied, rather than changing only superficial, behavioral responses to a restricted set of topics. The organizational revolution came in the substantial reliance on collaborations among teacher-education faculty, K–12 teachers, and education researchers. Fruitful collaboration required sustained work over time, in organizational settings that supported hybrid work spanning practice and research.

In particular, throughout the revolution federally funded research centers played a central role in reconceptualizing and transforming subject matter. These included the Institute for Research on Teaching (IRT, 1976–86), the National Center for Research on Teacher Education (NCRTE, 1985–90), the National Center for Research on Teacher Learning (1990–96), and the Center for the Learning and Teaching of Elementary Subjects (1987–92). The development of successive teacher-education programs, culminating in the five-year program of the 1990s, provided an opportunity to implement many of the new ideas including how to implement "teaching for understanding" as called for by the Holmes Group.

The PDSs, for their part, brought opportunities to extend the revolution in subject-matter teaching and learning into the heart of K–12 schools, especially those with challenging numbers of at-risk children.

This revolution in mathematics was all about relentless questioning of self and others, and trying to find the answers through mathematical reasoning in discussion. The culture of teaching that developed at the Holt High School PDS made this clear. At Holt, according to the book on mathematics at the school, "teachers are invited, even expected, to question everything, including their own understandings of mathematics and the sense their students are making of it. This questioning could be described not as doubting, but as a sort of wondering" (Simonson, 2008b, 228).

This emphasis on questioning can be seen in the work of Sandra Crespo, an MSU faculty member in mathematics education who worked on a research agenda in line with the revolution long after the overall revolution had largely run out of steam. For example, in a paper with Cynthia Nicol (Crespo & Nicol, 2006), she continued the work on what sense students make of division by zero. This paper provides a splendid summary of the skeptical spirit that guided the teaching and learning in the multiple settings discussed in this chapter.

The article reports on an intervention in which teacher-education students were asked to analyze division by zero as an instance of teacher responsibility to respond to K–12 student errors. These students were drawn from two different TE programs, one at MSU in a course taught by Crespo and the other at the University of British Columbia taught by Nicol. Before the intervention there was misunderstanding among these participants not only of division by zero, but also of division in general and what it takes to justify and explain such operations in mathematics.

Initially, few could explain why division by zero is not possible. About a third of the students concluded that division by zero equals zero. Challenged to explain their answers, students were more likely to use rule-based approaches to explanation rather than reasoned answers based on their own sense-making. The paper includes the following as one of the rules given by students:

"You cannot do 0 ÷ 5 because one of the rules in division is that you have to put the larger number first." According to the authors, "rule-bound explanations are problematic because they stifle and discourage mathematical sense making and understanding." Responses judged unacceptable for any student of mathematics and especially for prospective teachers included the response "you can't divide by nothing," or resorting to the authority of teacher, textbook, or calculator as a sufficient reason to justify a response. After the intervention, however, student explanation became more conceptually based than rule bound. Only two students continued to say that division by zero equals zero (89–93).

In order to give a more holistic account of what the revolution attempted to do in the transformation of school mathematics, the rest of this chapter expands on this initial illustration and documents the relentless questioning of mathematics through the various arenas in which it took place.

Research and Development in Mathematics Education on Campus

School mathematics was a natural focus of concern and work in MSU's educational research centers because of the widespread dissatisfaction with the state of mathematics in schools among professional educators and the public alike. Each of the centers added to the collection of facts and the body of informed opinion showing how deplorable the state of mathematics teaching and learning was. The NCRTE reported that fewer than two out of ten TE students could do a correct diagram of a simple proportions problem by the end of their program (McDiarmid, 1989). Similarly, when asked about 1¼ divided by ½, just three of ten prospective teachers were able to choose an appropriate representation. The rest showed a lack of understanding of division (Ball, 1988). In fact, it was the opinion of mathematics educators in NCRTE that mathematics was the weakest part of the elementary school curriculum even though science and social studies were held by others to be in even worse shape (Schram et al., 1988).

Earlier the IRT, in moving MSU to a new level of prominence in educational research, had a project on K–12 general mathematics that aimed "to identify the reasons why these courses tend to be unpleasant and ineffective for both teachers and students and to develop methods of improving their effectiveness" (MSU-27, 1986, 37). It concluded that the practices shown to be effective in ninth-grade general math classes are the same as ones found effective in other math classes. But such practices had generally not been used. Students and teachers in these classes still needed to get away from their obsession with computation and learning of procedures, and instead engage at conceptual levels, talk more mathematics, focus on strategies to solve problems not just get the right answer, and use more appropriate mathematical terminology while taking advantage of concrete, meaningful models and graphic representations. Although a widespread opinion held that this approach was bound to undermine computational skill, the final 1986 IRT report on the project contended that this approach actually improves computational performance while "a steady diet of drill and practice" does not (MSU-27, 39).

The NCRTE also gave mathematics a good deal of attention. Previous research on teacher education had tended to ignore the specifics of different subject-matters. In contrast, the NCRTE was concerned not only with mathematics as taught in K–12 but also "ideas about what it means to do and to know mathematics, what counts as legitimate mathematical thinking or activity, how answers may be verified or conjectures proved; . . . uses and origins of mathematics and about the relationships between school mathematics, everyday mathematics and mathematics as it is practiced in the disciplines." Teachers must be able to go beyond saying whether an answer is correct or not; they have to deal with underlying meanings and connections (MSU-37, 1991, 21).

In following up on these views, the NCRTE launched major studies of teaching practice in K–12 as well as teacher education. It used interviews and questionnaires to find out what a teacher does in deciding what to teach, planning to teach, choosing representations of subject matter for use in class, and assessing student learning.

The most ambitious attempt of the NCRTE to get an empirical fix on the questions raised was a national longitudinal survey over time of nine teacher-education programs: four preservice, two in-service, and three induction. It took a strong interest in how students were prepared to teach mathematics and what it meant to teach mathematics "well." It investigated the question of how students in these programs were responding to ideas that challenged more traditional ways of teaching mathematics.

As these students were followed longitudinally over the course of their programs, there was little increase in understanding of mathematics. When interviewed, only 17 percent of the graduating elementary-education students were able to analyze and explain the division of fractions in a meaningful way (MSU-37, 1991, 27). One reason for these dismal results is not hard to find. Of the programs that prepared elementary teachers, only one put much emphasis on mathematics. The other programs required but one term of mathematics content and one of mathematics methods. Moreover, the coverage of these courses was unpredictable in the sense that it was determined by whoever taught them. Only in the one program that emphasized mathematics did the results show promise. "The teacher candidates . . . displayed dramatic changes in their conceptions of mathematics, of themselves, and of mathematics pedagogy." (MSU-37, 29) Even so, later research showed that these students who had shown such promise in their thinking still taught in traditional ways (see Wilcox et al., 1991). With results like those, the NCRTE concluded in its final report that the usual two-course sequence was inadequate and that both mathematics pedagogy and mathematics content had to have more emphasis. However, according to NCRTE, getting students to major in mathematics, as some had suggested, would not make much of a difference (MSU-37, 1991, 31).

Other center research looked in more detail and depth at teacher-education issues. Floden, McDiarmid, and Wiemers investigated three elementary mathematics methods courses. They found that none of the instructors was taking responsibility to help their students increase their knowledge of mathematics content:

While one of them knows that mathematics is not just a given set of rules, his course does not include discussions of topics or problems that would involve students in thinking about how to produce or judge mathematical conjectures. These instructors assume limited responsibility for helping prospective teachers learn the subject matter knowledge sketched in the National Council of Teachers of Mathematics (NCTM) standards. Instead, they assume that students already have sufficient knowledge of subject matter. (1990, 7)

To show that these instructors were wrong and that prospective teachers need to and can learn mathematical content in math methods courses, Deborah Ball (1988) wrote "Unlearning to Teach Mathematics," a constructivist perspective on teachers' preservice learning. She notes that preservice students bring with them many misleading ideas about mathematics, such as the following: most mathematical ideas have to always be expressed with symbols; teaching procedures for solving problems is the way to teach mathematics; teachers do not have to know much math to teach it well to students in the early grades; and young children are not able to think about complicated mathematical ideas.

Ball chose to counter these ideas, not just in math methods, but in the first exploratory course on teaching required of all elementary teacher-education students at MSU. She developed a two-week unit on permutations in order to "challenge what entering teacher candidates know about mathematics and how it is taught and learned." Since many students might never have encountered permutations before, Ball could assume that they would be engaging "truly as learners." During this unit, "the prospective teachers first learn about permutations themselves, then watch a teacher explore the concept and finally try their hand at helping someone else (adult or child) learn about permutations" (40–42).

In search of a sense of awe on the part of the students, Ball starts by explaining that if one were to consider all the different seating arrangements for a class of twenty-five students, the resulting number would be so gigantic that if seats were changed every ten seconds, it would take almost five quintillion years to try out all the different arrangements.

For homework, when Ball encouraged the students "to explain and justify their solutions, . . . alternative approaches always emerge, to many students' complete astonishment. Gradually over two class periods, most students figure out the pattern by induction and develop some understanding of the concept of permutations" (42).

To deal with deficiencies in mathematics preparation, a new three-course sequence of mathematics was piloted in one of the four alternative programs, the Academic Learning Program, with the cohort that entered in 1987 and graduated in 1989. These courses focused on numbers and number theory, geometry, and probability-statistics with an innovative emphasis on conceptual understanding and problem-solving that was entirely different from the way the students had typically been taught in K–12.

An article reporting on an analysis of the first course described "what had changed in student understanding of mathematics content, mathematics learning, and how mathematics is taught." It noted that the ability of teachers to teach more conceptually was limited by their own lack of mathematics knowledge, since as K–12 students, they were "taught procedures and algorithms to manipulate numbers and symbols without understanding the meaning of symbolic representations or the meaning of mathematical processes" (Schram et al., 1988, 1–2).

This course began with an experience very different from what the students were used to. They were asked to brainstorm the following problem:

> In a certain high school there were 1000 students and 1000 lockers. Each year for homecoming the students lined up in alphabetical order and performed the following ritual: The first student opened every locker. The second student went to every second locker and closed it. The third student went to every third locker and changed it (i.e., if the locker was open, he closed it; if it was closed, he opened it). In a similar manner, the fourth, fifth, sixth,

> . . . student changed every fourth, fifth, sixth, . . . locker.
> After all 1000 students had passed by the lockers, which
> lockers were open? (Schram et al., 1988, 7)

This problem was the beginning of a new routine in which problems were used consistently to introduce mathematical concepts.
Students worked with multiple representations in small groups "to
explore, conjecture, and validate solutions for the problem situation" (8). They were expected to validate their conjectures with
convincing arguments, to make connections with other mathematical ideas, and to try to generalize their solutions.

In conclusion, the authors remind the reader that a ten-week
course cannot completely transform traditional views of mathematics teaching and learning. Nevertheless, this course had been
notable in challenging the students' views about what it means
to know mathematics. At the beginning they thought knowing
mathematics meant knowing appropriate procedures or formulas and getting the right answer. By the end of the course most
of the students were questioning their traditional views; they
were no longer satisfied with just searching for the right answer
or algorithm. Many for the first time understood why the rules
and procedures they had memorized worked. They questioned
whether the old routine was effective and accepted the ways in
which this course was different. And yet they did not rethink how
to begin to teach arithmetic through mastery of basic number
facts. Computational skills were to be learned first before problem-solving. Problem-solving was viewed as a separate topic.
In short, conceptual understanding and problem-solving were
deemed good for the teacher-education students themselves, but
not needed for students in the early grades as they started to learn
the basics. If students were having difficulty, the prospective teachers still planned to provide drill and practice as had been custom-
ary. As far as using what they had learned with children in the
early grades, they doubted that they could do so, especially since
parents, other teachers, and administrators were likely to be advocates of a traditional approach.

The Value of Research on One's Own Practice

In the book *Teaching Problems and the Problems of Teaching*, published by Yale University Press, the amphibious professor Magdalene Lampert (2001) shared her deep knowledge and experience in teaching fifth-grade mathematics. She reports in great depth and exceptional detail on the research she did on her own practice over a single year. She reveals what it means to teach by "engaging [her] students with the big ideas of the discipline as they work on problems and discuss the reasonableness of their strategies and solutions" (1). The result is a tour de force that stands as a monument to the whole revolutionary effort.

In the fourteen chapters of this book, Lampert first discusses how she set up the room and her schedule while establishing a classroom culture and teaching the students how to study. She then devotes three chapters (5, 6, and 7) to a single lesson. Then she goes on to show how she manages to link different lessons (chapter 8) and how she makes sure she covers the curriculum (chapter 9). Next in chapter 10 Lampert moves into the moral sphere: the teaching of intellectual courage, intellectual honesty, and self-restraint. In Lampert's view, teachers are only successful if their students come to regard themselves as the kind of people who pursue knowledge and skills by reading, observing, and researching, who pay attention, go over challenging parts, and memorize rules and facts that they will use repeatedly (48–49).

Especially illuminating are the three chapters on the teaching of a single lesson that Lampert taught toward the end of September. One was titled "Teaching while Preparing for a Lesson" (chapter 5), the second "Teaching while Students Work Independently" (chapter 6), and the third "Teaching while Leading a Whole Class Discussion" (chapter 7). It took a total of seventy-eight pages for Lampert to describe and analyze this lesson! She does admit that her microscopic approach to these chapters is "at times tedious and complex. But it reveals that each word and gesture the teacher uses has the potential to support the study of mathematics for all students or not" (144).

In this lesson, beginning on September 28, Lampert was ready to go from how to compute two-digit multiplication to knowing when and how to use multiplication to solve problems. The lesson was one she had thought a lot about; she had to get the class thinking about counting by groups. To do this, she had to consider individual students: What were the symbols, diagrams, and words that would get their attention and get them to think? How could she do this without the distraction of irrelevant computational difficulties?

> Both my analysis of the mathematics and my review of the students' performance on the paper-and-pencil pretest suggest that the difference in the mathematical ideas that need to be activated to correctly perform the procedure for a multiplication like "4 x 34" and the ideas that would support performing the procedure for a multiplication like "23 x 46" (both of which appeared on the test) is significant for this class. . . . I need to create a work environment where they can recognize what multiplication would mean in the problems they are trying to solve, and examine various approaches to carrying out this operation on large numbers. I need to provide them with an opportunity to take numbers apart into their components and then recombine them in ways that are mathematically legitimate and make sense to them so that they can study the constraints of the system. (117–18)

At a certain point she drafted a statement of the day to go with the problem. Modified to put on the board, it appeared as follows:

a. ☐ groups of 12 = 10 groups of 6
b. 30 groups of 2 = ☐ groups of 4
c. ☐ groups of 7 = ☐ groups of 21

Lampert was confident that the students could figure out that they had to fill in these boxes and was hopeful that they would realize that whatever they put in the boxes needed to "balance" the equations. She made the equations purposefully ambiguous in terms of what mathematical operation to use. Thinking about what approaches the students might take, she took note of what they could be learning in terms of number patterns and relationships, how multiplication relates to division, and their use of the times tables for digits 12, 6, 2, 4. Her discussion of the third equation is indicative of the depth and subtlety of this planning:

> I included the third [equation], with its new and some-what more challenging content, because the backgrounds and talents of the students in my class were quite varied. Almost a third of them had come from a different school, and I had not been able to get much information about what experiences and capacities they had brought to my class. I wanted to provide everyone with something to study that would be productive of worthwhile learning. I anticipated that some students would use this part of the assignment to investigate multiplication and others would use it to move into the domains of functions or fractions. Because [in equation c] the number of units in a group is an odd number (groups of 7 or 21 instead of groups of 2 or 4 or 6 or 12), more and somewhat different mathematics gets on the table. Although there are boxes on both sides of the equation, the numbers that go in those boxes have a relationship to one another. One is a "function of the other." A student working on this problem might begin to study ordered pairs of solutions as a special case of patterns and relationships. (107)

In the next chapter (6) Lampert deals with the first part of the lesson as she actually taught it. She makes clear that even though the students are largely working on their own, this is still an example of real teaching. As the students work by themselves and she observes, she also figures out what she needs to do in whole-class instruction at the end of the lesson. In this way, even a lecture could be modified based on what she observes the students doing and thinking as they work through the problems.

She also discussed using this time to work with individual students through interventions big, "as when I spend five minutes or so with my attention directed to one idea with one student," and small, "as when I simply place my body a certain way or point to a particular spot on a notebook page in a way that catches a student's attention" (122). But even when focused on a single individual, Lampert remains very much aware of the rest of the class:

> What I am able to do with individuals depends on my doing another piece of work simultaneously: assessing how things are going in the surrounding area. I assess the tenor of the whole class from moment to moment, and I also consider the disposition and activity level of the students sitting adjacent to the one I want to work with. This simultaneous assessment of individuals and the environment is necessary because I am teaching *efficacy, civility, and structure* as well as mathematics. (122, emphasis added)

In her third chapter on this lesson, Lampert has more to say about how she used the time for whole-class instruction. As she walked around the room, she saw that Richard, a student discussed briefly in another chapter, had written something questionable in his notebook. Although he was a student who found it hard to answer questions, Lampert still asked him about it. She explains why his participation was so important even though not easy for him:

> Through all the events I have described, my job is to teach Richard (and everyone else) that he (and anyone else) who speaks publicly in class is responsible for reasoning through a piece of mathematics. This element of my practice is so fundamental to teaching students to engage in mathematical work that it leads me into dangerous social territory, where Richard's self-image and his standing with his peers is at stake. . . . Although it might have been temporarily more comfortable for him to be "let off the hook," the consequences of doing that would interfere

with his capacity to study mathematics through engaging with problems. (159)

In this chapter, Lampert added that participation had been a big concern for her for this class at this point in the year, and especially since she lacked all the information she needed about students in order to make the most of her instruction. After the class, she reviewed in her mind what the class had not done and what mathematics they had not considered. She confessed to herself that she had not interacted with all the students that she had wanted to participate (177).

Mathematics for All at Holt High School PDS

Although the mathematics education research at the university and the experimental teacher-education programs were important, the most far-reaching attempts to implement a new approach to mathematics took place in the PDSs, and in the most consequential form at Holt High School, which took the implementation of mathematics *for all* to heart. As MSU instructor Bill Rosenthal told it, "6 April 1995 was the day on which Holt secondary mathematics and MSU secondary mathematics were forever united in teacher-educational matrimony. It was on this day that Sandy Callis visited MSU to tell the story of Holt algebra 1. From Sandy, our [MSU] students hear that mathematics can have a story-line written by the teachers who teach it" (2008, 72). Through collaboration and accountability, these educators reshaped their expectations for teaching as they all became curriculum writers, researchers, and mathematicians as well as teachers.

The work of Holt High School mathematics teachers, MSU colleagues, MSU students, and high school students is reported in *Embracing Reason: Egalitarian Ideals and the Teaching of High School Mathematics* (Chazan, Callis & Lehman, 2008). This book, which revisits twelve years of collaborative work in the Holt High mathematics department, is "about high school mathematics teaching, and an egalitarian ideal, not about particular instructional practices" (xxii). It tells of collective growth and empowerment. Writing a commentary chapter, MSU faculty member Gary Sykes (the sole outside author) gives the Holt teachers much credit for tackling such a thorough reform without being forced to (Sykes, 2008, 342). He even used the revolution metaphor in his title—"A Quiet Revolution?" He argued that the Holt teachers were not so much driven by demographic or external factors as by idealism.

The Organization of Mathematics at Holt High School for K–12 Secondary Students and for MSU Teacher-Education Students

As in most American high schools, mathematics already played an important role at Holt High School in pre-PDS days, but it became much more important as the Holt High School PDS developed. In 1989–90 there were twenty sections of math taught in the nine hundred-student high school with a teaching staff in the mathematics department of about four full-time equivalents (FTE). In the early 1990s, the mathematics faculty was teaching only about half the student population whereas at the end of the decade about 90 percent of all students were enrolled in mathematics courses. The percentage of students taking more advanced math had also increased. Across the 1990s, the teaching of arithmetic was discontinued (with the exception of a very few students given exemptions) and the number of sections of algebra 1 declined because most students took the first algebra course in eighth or ninth grade at the junior high school. Enrollments in Advanced Placement calculus grew from thirty-six students in 1992–93 to seventy-five in 2000–1. By 2000–1 the high school had 1,143 total students, 41 sections of math, and 8 FTE mathematics teachers (Chazan, Callis & Lehman, 2008, 110–21).

Initial PDS work at Holt High concentrated on student learning in lower-track classes, with special emphasis on the high failure rates in algebra and pre-algebra. When at the beginning of the PDS, the math teachers started rethinking the math curriculum, up to one-third of algebra 1 students failed and only 50 percent went on to geometry. To address this problem with pre-algebra, an MSU faculty member suggested that this course be eliminated, allowing all students to enter algebra 1. Some thought this change would increase failure rates. It did not (114–15).

Teacher education was also very important at Holt High School (Chazan, Callis, & Lehman, 2008, chap. 11). Teachers at Holt worked hard for consistency between what the MSU secondary mathematics program called for and their own beliefs and practices. During this era MSU juniors in teacher education were spending two hours a week in Holt or other affiliated schools for one semester; seniors spent four hours a week both semesters; the fifth-year interns spent four to five days per week for the whole school year. Secondary-education interns received six credits per semester for this field experience and, in addition, were required to enroll in two three-credit university courses each semester. At Holt, at the beginning of the year, the interns were initially given primary responsibility for one section of their mentor teacher's load. Later in the fall, two more sections were added to their workload, and then for ten weeks in the spring their teaching responsibilities increased to four sections (171).

Since Holt had such an excellent reputation for this teacher-education work, it is not surprising that openings in the math department tended to be filled by MSU graduates who had been interns at Holt. By 2007, seven of the teachers hired in the math department had done their internships at Holt, five with Mike Lehman (Kelly & Huhn, 2008, 201)

All Students Can Learn Mathematics

As a department leader, Mike Lehman articulated the school's commitment to mathematics for all: "We [in the Holt math department] have come to believe that instead of mathematics being for those who are gifted with the ability to do math, it is for all students" (Chazan, Callis & Lehman, 2008, 187). This change in attitude required a complicated shift toward the "adoption of teaching practices that helped teachers see strengths in students traditionally perceived as weak" (188). As Lehman explains, it took professional development tailored to the existing situation to bring about this shift.

> We have changed the lower-track curriculum, while increasing the number of students taking higher-track

math. The latter development resulted both from the elimination of some lower-track coursework and from some changed attitudes on the part of the teaching staff. . . . Many changes in our classroom practices have sprung from this shift in thinking. We now encourage more discussions around the math we teach. We listen more carefully to students and try to focus our teaching around their questions instead of around the next concept in the sequence. We have learned to develop concepts around situations that the students can understand and work with, instead of around symbol manipulation. (2008a, 199–200)

Even in a math department known for its gifted teachers of mathematics, Lehman stood out. He has written about how he came to be so actively engaged and noted for his work in the PDS:

I have taught high school mathematics for eighteen years [starting in 1977]. About six years ago, I started to re-think my teaching. I wanted my students to be able to do more than just give back what I told them. I felt students in algebra II and pre-calculus should be able to do more than apply what they had learned to situations similar to those we did in class. I wanted them to develop a deeper understanding of the mathematics I was teaching. My goal was for them to be able to take the mathematics taught and apply it to a wide range of situations. However, I was not sure what this type of student understanding looked like. I did not know if I could recognize it if I saw it. So I continued to explore my teaching. I learned a little about cooperative learning at a PDS institute. It sounded pretty good, and I thought it would be easy to use, so I set out to implement it in my classroom. I soon found out it wasn't so easy. I had a lot of group work going on but nothing I would call cooperative learning—unless you count one student doing the first four or five problems and then cooperatively giving them to the rest of the group in

exchange for the rest of the problems. My naiveté led me
to see that there was more to cooperative learning than I
thought. (Lehman, 2008b, 16)

Lehman's response was to get resources from MSU, join a study
group, read research, discuss theories, and share practices—all of
which helped him get students to do better. To know how well
students were doing, he had to pay attention to assessment. He first
asked students to write about the problems they were assigned, to
explain how they solved the problems and why that was the way
to go. For example, he asked students how they knew whether a
graph represented a function or not. Although this gave him a
sense for what students understood, it was not possible to read 150
explanations per day. Asking for shorter answers was helpful, but
the problem remained that students found ways to avoid coming
up with their own ideas. They repeated what other students said,
or they asked the teacher ahead of time and took notes on explanations they could use later to satisfy the teacher.

Finally, to deal with these problems, starting in 1991, Lehman
turned to oral examinations as discussed in his (2008b) chapter on assessment (and earlier in Lehman, 1991). Students were
given six problems they could use to prepare ahead of time, working in groups. Then they took an oral exam of ninety minutes
in front of three adult judges from the school and community.
Each student had to discuss one of the problems, without knowing which one it would be in advance. Passing required students
to discuss the strategies they used, including terminology, and
why they chose that approach and what gave them confidence
their answer was correct. As a result, students took the exam
very seriously whereas before they had been more or less satisfied not to do well. Doing well in front of the three judges and
other students in the group was important to them. They began
putting pressure on each other, and the teacher was forced to
keep this from getting out of hand.

This approach had many advantages. Students who were not
good at paper and pencil tests had another way to show what they
knew. Students could see for themselves what they did and did not

understand, especially since they got written feedback from three different judges.

Over time these oral assessments became increasingly important to the department. Alumni were coming back from college and talking about how much the preparation and taking of such exams had helped them. Nevertheless, giving such exams was hard on the teachers. In January 2000, for example, they were faced with finding 98 judges to examine a total of 290 students in algebra 1, geometry, algebra 2, honors precalculus, and honors discrete mathematics (Lehman, 2008b, 16–21).

Functions-Based Approach to Algebra

In light of what he had learned from teaching in the PDS, the amphibious professor Dan Chazan and Holt teacher Sandy Callis took the lead in revamping the teaching of algebra at Holt toward a functions-based curriculum (Chazan, Callis & Lehman, 2008).

> Rather than organize school algebra around the continued study of numbers and concentrate on a long list of symbolic manipulations, this approach organizes introductory algebra experiences around functions, their representations and operations on functions. (246)
>
> The intent is to have students see x's and y's as ways of communicating about relationships between quantities. . . . In this sort of approach, instead of first meeting x as an unknown number as is commonly done in most introductory algebra courses, x's and y's are introduced to students as variables, and expressions are introduced as calculation procedures that express relationships between input and output quantities. (27)

In the lower-track algebra course taught by Chazan and his colleague Sandra Callis, students were organized in pairs to do a yearlong project to look for activities that would illustrate the function-based approach. Each pair visited a workplace in the local community four times a year to collect this data. These visits were opportunities to learn about the workplace and the work done there. Afterward, the students were expected to write a report answering specific questions about the mathematical activities embedded in the work they had examined, such as the following:

- What quantities are measured or counted by the people interviewed?
- Why is it important to measure or count these quantities?
- What quantities are computed or calculated?
- Are there ever different ways to compute the same thing?
- What graphs, charts, or tables are used?
- What kinds of comparison are made with computed quantities?
- Why are these comparisons important? (Chazan & Callis, 2008, 81–83)

The Importance of Talking Mathematics

In sharp contrast to the typical American high school, Holt became more and more a place that fostered and valued conversations about mathematics—conversations among teachers, among students, and between teachers and students. Such conversations about mathematics among instructors, not to speak of students, were reportedly rare or nonexistent in other districts whereas at Holt they had become addictive (Huhn et al., 2008, 258–59). Discussions among teachers were about important though often impromptu issues, varying in length from a few minutes to over an hour. "While the [National Council of Teachers of Mathematics] Standards make much of students debating their *differing* constructions and conjectures, they contain no hint of the importance of what our colleague (and MSU graduate student) Whitney Johnson deliciously calls 'arguing with the mathematicians'" (Rosenthal, 2008, 72). According to the teacher Kellie Huhn,

> before teaching, I thought mathematical power meant the ability to perform certain algorithms, to compute using previously memorized formulas and to do what the teacher

said to do. . . . After teaching for a year, I was thinking more about students; I defined a mathematically powerful student as one who would investigate mathematical topics using appropriate strategies, who would make conjectures, and who would explain why certain mathematical statements were true. (Huhn & Schnepp, 2008, 156)

Teacher Tom Almeida reported that what he encountered when he first came to Holt was eye-opening: "I've had lengthy discussions with MSU interns since I've been at HHS. Most of these conversations were centered on teaching and learning, which benefitted everyone involved. . . . As I read this piece [Simonson and Rosenthal, 2008], I couldn't help thinking how well it describes what I love about my job at Holt—people sharing and helping each other to be better teachers." Tom goes on to say that as a teacher at Holt, he had thought more about math and how it relates to everything else than he had in the previous ten years even though earlier he had earned a bachelor's degree in pure mathematics, together with a teaching certificate. His undergrad years (not at MSU) were so very different:

> I'm saddened now, looking back, that we missed out on so much. During my student teaching, I interacted with one collaborating teacher and one university supervisor. . . . It felt very disconnected. Now that I've seen real collegial interaction, I'm amazed that I spent so much time and money to get so little out of my experience. (Almeida & Carmody, 2008, 168–69)
>
> After five years of [studying] mathematics at the collegiate level, I finally figured out my own perceptions after two months of actually teaching it from the "question everything from all sides" approach. I had never questioned anything before. (238)

Changes in Marty Schnepp's Teaching

The teacher who experienced the most dramatic and in-depth change while at Holt was Marty Schnepp. In his case a detailed account of his experience is available not only in his own words in the Holt book on high school mathematics (Schnepp, 2008), but in more depth in a dissertation by Jan Simonson, where she gathered data from three classes, taught in 1993, 1995, and 1996. Her dissertation is a valuable independent account of the dramatic changes Schnepp went through as he gained more experience in teaching high school mathematics (Gormas-Simonson, 1998; see also Simonson, 2008a, 2008b).

For the first five years of Marty's teaching, he stuck closely to the text. For him, at that time, an effective teacher was one who gave clear explanations of what was in the textbook. If done well, he thought, this would enable the teacher to be responsive to whatever students had to say. In the first lesson analyzed by Simonson, before Marty returned to Holt, students were asked to find the value of an unknown x or y in a linear equation. Students learned how to do a certain set of problems, whether presented by text or teacher; then they practiced until they could consistently get the right answer. Marty wanted them to think about the procedures and not become alienated as they might if abstract notions of functions were introduced too early (Simonson, 2008a, 95–96; 2008b).

Marty began to take a different approach once he started to coteach with Sandy Callis back at Holt. The unknown quantity x was treated, not as a specific unknown quantity, but rather as an independent variable whose changes in value affect the outcome or dependent variable y. Students had to think about what happens to y as x changes. Schnepp himself writes about how much he had changed. He goes back to his experience in MSU's undergraduate teacher-preparation program when he was challenged by new theories of learning. He recalls having read Jean Piaget and others as an introduction to constructivist learning theory, which then pervaded all his courses. He remembers: "So omnipresent was this view of learning that there was a tendency to take it for granted and not give it due consideration. Thus constructivist ideas were established in my subconscious, but a firm grasp of them remained out of reach for some time because of my inexperience and inattention" (Schnepp, 2008, 319–20).

As a teacher-education student in a science-education methods course, Marty had learned about a related conceptual change model in which curriculum units began with exercises intended to help students articulate their preexisting conceptions of what they were supposed to study. They then did experiments posing empirical challenges to these conceptions, and finally the teacher explained the concept in correct terms. It was an approach intended to force students to restructure and realign their personal understanding with accepted academic knowledge:

> This approach felt right when used in the Physics courses I taught during my first few years after college. . . . [But it] did not feel right in my math classes. To start a unit on circular functions, following an example of another teacher, I would ask students to make a table of values for sine and cosine functions using calculator outputs, graph the ordered pairs and describe any patterns or relationships they observed. The conceptual change model did not work because students only made observations regarding the graphs. There were no real conceptions to change. All I could do was to forge ahead with the prescribed skills, giving names like period to characteristics they observed like the repeating pattern of outputs, and explain what I knew of the sine function. Not realizing what was going wrong, but seeing misconceptions forming after I had shown students how to do problems, I began to simply lecture first, and then challenge their interpretations of what I said. This was the pattern of instruction I settled into for the first three or four years of my career. (320)

After Marty had moved back to Holt in his fourth year of teaching, he found the Holt teachers and their MSU colleagues were very deliberate and explicit in designing opportunities for students to link their understanding of mathematics to previous experiences. When Marty team-taught with Callis, it was his first time experiencing mathematics teaching so directly based on constructivist theories of how people learn. But Marty, who had become deeply reflective, found the approach problematic: "As I came to understand constructivist learning theory as being distinct from other ways of viewing knowledge transfer to students, I began to see contradictions among the things I was asking students to do, the goals I held for the lessons I planned, and what students were able to do as a result of my lessons" (321).

In later writing, Marty gave two examples of what was problematic. First, misconceptions are only an issue if students have some sort of conception to begin with. In mathematics, Marty found that students often did not have any prior conception, even an intuitive one. Second, when asked to do a concept map to represent their prior ideas, students simply memorized and reproduced Marty's map. As a result Marty changed his approach and gave the students activities to help them form the conceptions in the first place and on which they could then build. All this led to much soul searching on Marty's part:

> After the first few times I saw kids explore math objects, looking for and articulating generalizations, and seeking proof when asked to determine if their conjectures were true in all cases, some cases, etc., I began to wrestle with feelings of concern, embarrassment, excitement, anger, fear, and more. I felt embarrassed at how disengaged I had been as a student in my math classes, and how disengaged many of my students had been allowed to be while earning solid grades by simply memorizing and practicing procedures from lectures and tests. Anger crept into the picture for me when for a time my knowledge of math felt insufficient to attend to ideas and issues that arose when kids' inquiries raised questions I had not seen before. Anger was also a direct result of never having experienced courses that required me to stand on my own, using my own intellect and creativity. In my coursework in high school, undergraduate, and graduate school, I never saw mathematics as an endeavor where people seek to explore, ask questions, make assertions, and seek arguments to verify the validity of those ideas. It was about learning

preset ideas, memorizing theorems, and on occasion reproducing proofs that were shown in class. So a strong student was one who could reproduce instructed material. (Huhn & Schnepp, 2008, 157)

By the time Marty wrote about his transformation, his teaching practice was very different. Once he realized that the discipline of mathematics itself could be viewed as the result of "quasi-empirical social processes," he became much more open to basing his teaching on student discovery:

I often use computer-driven mechanical devices, for example, toy cars or a bicycle rider that will move in relation to function rules and graphs that can be manipulated to alter the motion. . . . Although the contexts I select must be amenable to my students, the questions I pose are ones for which students have been taught no previous algorithm for answering. Reasonable progress must be possible with previously known math. Early in the year, students are typically arranged in groups, presented with a context and asked questions. They discuss their ideas. I listen. I want to hear students formulate arguments, refute arguments, support arguments, and raise new questions. Students write, discuss, calculate and make presentations, all the while defining and refining terminology. New math grows out of the discussion of students' attempts to work toward answers to my questions and others that arise as they work. (Schnepp, 2008, 317–18, 326)

Aristotle Returns to Stir Up Debate at Holt High School

In Whitney Johnson, the Holt PDS benefitted from an MSU doctoral student who was exceptionally ready to challenge her own mathematical thinking and that of others in the manner that was becoming a part of the PDS culture. Writing about her own experience as an undergrad math major, she described herself as a survivor of bad mathematics teaching. She recalled how bad it was—the demeanor of her professors, their lack of patience, their lectures, and their lack of interest in what Johnson thought about the math she was studying. All of this she suffered with apparent conformity, while inwardly she was not at all happy at how they expected her to learn (Johnson, 2008, 284).

In contrast, once Johnson had become a teacher educator herself, she wanted her teacher-education students to question their mathematics knowledge. She wanted them to realize how much they had taken at face value, as opposed to what they were able to prove for themselves. To foster their skeptical stance, she took her students two thousand years back to the mathematics of Aristotle. Her section in the 2008 Holt book is titled "Lines and Points: Aristotle vs. Modern Math." His mathematics of points and lines is difficult for today's prospective teachers because it contradicts what they learned in school and college and what they expect to continue to teach as teachers. According to what they were taught, the set of real numbers is composed of infinitely many individual numbers, and the continuous number line is made up of infinitely many individual, dimensionless, and indivisible points. Reading Aristotle, students discover that he did not see it that way.

Johnson decided that in order to create the challenge she was looking for, she would assign a part of Aristotle's *Metaphysics* she had read for a course she had previously taken. She explains: "For me the article brought to the forefront of my thinking the relationship between the real numbers, the real line, and the nature of the real-number system." Knowing that Aristotle's writing is dense, Johnson expected preservice teacher-education students to have to struggle with it, a struggle that she thought would lead her students to think hard about the relationship between points and lines and the nature of the real-number system. Once they found out that Aristotle did not think of lines as made out of points, Johnson hoped they would begin to question their own mathematical knowledge (288–89).

When faced with this discussion, the MSU students majoring in mathematics education had come from a course in analysis that marked a big shift in how mathematics was taught. It was the first course in which they focused on proving theorems, not solving

problems. Earlier in calculus it was still a struggle to learn procedures, but in analysis for the most part there were no more procedures to learn. This change gave the students and their instructors
the feeling that for the first time the students were beginning to
study mathematics in a serious and authentic way. In analysis,
students learn, for example, that "the real numbers are uncountable
which suggests that they cannot be put in any order that would
allow them to be counted off (put in a one-to-one relationship
with the counting numbers)." It was then that the students might
ask themselves how the points on a number line can be ordered,
but uncountable (285, 289).

Johnson gave this Aristotle assignment to three different cohorts
of MSU seniors. When asked to summarize Aristotle's argument,
the 1999–2000 cohort had a hard time. Finding the text and argument difficult to understand, they responded negatively. Even so,
they participated actively in discussion with little direction from
Johnson. In this discussion, "they moved in and out of the text
using some examples that were mathematical and some that were
not. It was not long before they began to question the nature of the
numbers on the real line. The students arrived at the notion that
Aristotle is arguing that lines are not composed of points and also
that this is the opposite to what they have been taught" (288–90).

Laura was one of the students who found Aristotle confusing:
"I wasn't sure what the terms meant, let alone the purpose of the
article." "I remember that we did not all have the same definitions
in mind even for simple things like points and lines. And the fact
that we were all about to graduate with math degrees felt discon-
certing." In contrast, Craig was another student who, although he
responded with surprise, was more positive:

> I remember just that it was cool that we have a room full
> of math majors that couldn't agree on some of the most
> basic cornerstones of math. I was immediately struck with
> how exciting that concept could be, because when I began
> the teacher prep program, I intended to teach history, my
> minor, because I wanted to have debates and discussions
> in my class. This was the first time anything like that had

happened to me about mathematics. It wasn't just an argument about what was right; people were engaging in intellectual dialogue about math, and it didn't seem we could come to a reasoned consensus about anything. (quoted in Johnson, 2008, 296)

Craig went on to say that many of his classmates were angry and frustrated, and some even withdrew from the discussion. He remembered their frustration when Johnson would not give them the answer.

Conclusion

The MSU effort to transform the teaching and learning of mathematics during the revolution showed richness and promise. For there to be any hope of success in such a venture, a multipronged effort is required, in this case bringing together experimental work by research centers, newly designed and redesigned teacher-education programs, and settings in which K–12 teachers and university personnel all bring their distinctive capabilities and participate on an equal footing. This history, though brief, allows us to argue that transformation takes multiple forms, including research tightly linked to practice, school-based approaches to teacher education that are nonetheless closely connected to a university, and a new type of school devoted to revolutionary changes in teaching and learning, a school that is neither fish (belonging solely to K–12) nor fowl (belonging solely to the university). In contrast, individual and less coordinated projects, often initiated by individuals and small, somewhat isolated groups in the field with limited time frames, are surely much less likely to have revolutionary results when so much of what goes on around them continues much the same as before.

CHAPTER EIGHT

From Mindless to Meaningful in the Teaching of Social Studies

A key component of the substance of the revolution was the shift to curriculum and instruction that sought to improve student understanding of the subjects studied, rather than changing only superficial, behavioral responses to a restricted set of topics. The organizational revolution came in the substantial reliance on collaborations among teacher-education faculty, K–12 teachers, and education researchers. Fruitful collaboration required sustained work over time, in organizational settings that supported hybrid work spanning practice and research. Just as in the subject area of mathematics, a key feature of the revolution in social studies teaching was a shift toward curriculum and instruction that eschewed superficial coverage of many topics to focus on deep understanding of core ideas. And, once again, the revolution was supported by sustained, long-term collaborations among teacher educators, classroom teachers, and education researchers.

Trite Goals Make for Trite Content

MSU faculty members Jere Brophy and Jan Alleman, in their two decades of partnership, took the lead in a series of papers critiquing the state of social studies education in the United States. "Too often, the content developed is inherently trite or is developed in ways that do not promote progress toward significant social education goals. Triteness is often embodied in the goals themselves." As an example of this, they discuss the study of family size in the early grades. "First graders are already well aware that families differ in size, so what is the point of making this a major goal? Even worse, what is the point of following up such instruction with exercises requiring students to classify families as either 'big' or 'small'?" (Brophy & Alleman, 1993, 29).

As an alternative they propose to go more deeply into family size, asking why families differ in size, learning about variation in family size and roles across cultures and across time. As students mature, the students "might learn, for example, that a major effect of industrialization is the reduction of the extended family's role as a functional economic unit, which precipitates a shift from an extended family to a nuclear family as the typical household unit" (27). Turning family size into more conceptually based content is a way of putting the familiar in a larger perspective, which in turn helps students appreciate the trade-offs required by various economic systems and lifestyles.

Brophy and Alleman go on to address the shortcomings of social studies textbooks at the time. These textbooks, they point out, featured

> broad but shallow coverage of a great range of topics and skills. Lacking coherence, they are experienced as parades of disconnected facts and isolated skills exercises. . . . If teachers use the textbooks and provided ancillary mate-rials, and if they follow the manuals' lesson development instructions, the result will be a reading/recitation/seat-work curriculum geared toward memorizing discon-nected knowledge and practicing isolated skills. . . . Acting on the assumption that the series has been developed by experts far more knowledgeable about social education purposes and goals than they are, such teachers tend to concentrate on the procedural mechanics of implementa-tion when planning lessons and activities, without giving much thought to their purposes or how they might fit into the larger social education program. (27)

One fourth-grade social studies manual reviewed by Alleman and Brophy (1991, 306) suggested that students write research papers on coal. The manual discussed the mechanics of research-ing the topic and writing the paper, but it had little to say about the nature of social-education goals or social studies understanding. It did not note, for example, that humans have unlimited wants and limited resources; nor did it discuss issues such as conservation of natural resources or development of alternative sources of energy. Consequently, the social-education value of this assignment is minimal and its cost-effectiveness questionable because of all the time required to obtain, read, organize, write, and finally make presentations to the class.

> Role-play is another frequent basis for activities that are inherently limited in social education value or too time consuming to be cost-effective. For example, one unit on families we came across called for students to dress in costumes, play musical instruments, and participate in a parade as a means of illustrating how families celebrate. On the following day, they were to write about the event. This series of activities offers tie-ins with humanities and physical education and provides a stimulus for language arts work, but it lacks significant social education content. (306)

Brophy and Alleman believe these deficiencies have important causal consequences for children and adults. To them, the failure to focus on more significant learning goals has resulted in "symptoms ranging from student boredom and dislike of social studies to low achievement test scores to civic participation problems such as low voter turnouts and sluggish census returns" (27).

Alleman and Brophy remind the reader that a curriculum is not an end in itself, but the means of accomplishing major educational goals—goals that have to do with the knowledge, skills, attitudes, values, and dispositions that students are expected to develop. A curriculum is best designed when it is driven by these goals in the choice of content, representation of content, selection of questions to ask, patterns of classroom interaction, productive assignments, and methods of assessment (Brophy & Alleman, 1993).

The Deceptive Appeal of
Integrating Subject Matters

Although the integration of subject matters was strongly advocated during the MSU revolution, Brophy and Alleman, to say the least, were not convinced. Too often, they point out, so-called integration activities have disrupted the coherence of social studies. These activities are better described as "an intrusion" or "invasion" than integration with social studies. Worthwhile integration, in their view, means accomplishing significant curricular goals in two or more subjects simultaneously. A positive example might be teaching ecology with content from both science and social studies. The problem with integration occurs, not when it is natural, but rather when integration is pursued for integration's sake (Alleman & Brophy, 1991).

Combining knowledge from a content area like social studies with assignments from a skills area in language arts can be productive, provided that both content areas are given attention and students are assessed on skills in both content areas. Writing book reports, for example, together with the study of the lives of leaders of the American Revolution can be a way of achieving goals in both subjects.

MSU faculty member Kathy Roth, noted for her work in both science and social studies, made a major contribution to this discussion of integration. Writing for the widely circulated American Federation of Teachers union publication *American Educator*, she discussed her first-hand experience with integration of subject matters (Roth, 1994). Roth began by taking note of the desire for more integration in K–12 teaching, but as a teacher, researcher, and teacher educator continuing to teach fifth grade, she confessed to being uneasy with this trend. She wanted to know why "integration" is featured so prominently in national and state reform documents. Where is the evidence that integrated teaching produces meaningful learning? She was interested in what sort of integrated teaching is most powerful and meaningful for children. In conclusion, he urged educators to be more cautious.

Roth goes on to discuss the integrated teaching she did as a fifth-grade teacher in a PDS. She belonged to a group of teachers captivated by the notion they could use integration to mark the five hundredth anniversary of the "discovery" of America. They planned a year-long unit to bring science and social studies together around this 1492 theme, organized around such questions as "How has the land changed since 1492? How might it change in the next 500 years? How have people changed since 1492?" (46). Answering these questions would involve social studies concepts (diversity, adaptation, perspective, interdependency, social conflict, and change) as well as science concepts (diversity of species, ecosystems, interdependence, adaptations, evidence, and change).

To begin, the class focused on the diversity of Native American cultures five hundred years ago. In small groups, they learned about the lives of the Sioux, the Pacific Northwest Indians, the Pueblo, or the Aztecs, including change through time. This study of Native American cultures was linked to the study of diversity of species and adaptations in science, in which students examined the ecosystems in which the Native Americans lived. They learned about diversity and interdependence of life in the desert (for the Pueblos), the plains (Sioux), ocean (Pacific Northwest), and forested regions (Aztecs).

Among the questions raised by the teachers at the beginning were "Are there more different species in the desert, the rain forest, the plains, or the ocean? Does it matter if there are a lot of different species in an ecosystem? Why should we in Michigan care if species in these distant ecosystems are endangered?" (46). Then, by moving on to the question of "how plants get their food," the teachers planned to use science to explain the social world by examining what happened when plants from different parts of the world were exchanged. They intended to trace potatoes from the Incas in the Andes to Europe and the later potato famine, a phenomenon that could in turn serve to explain Irish immigration to the United States in the nineteenth century.

Although the teachers remained fascinated by all these connections, in Roth's candidly expressed view, the course was a failure. Many of the goals set by the team were never met. Three months into the school year, the team concluded that the interdisciplinary approach was not enabling students to learn important concepts as well as hoped, especially those in science. Roth recalled:

> As a science teacher, I was frustrated with the constraints placed on the science by the needs of the social studies concepts. Yes, diversity and interdependence are powerful concepts both in science and in social studies. And it made sense to begin by defining and exploring the diversity of Native-American cultures and environments. From a scientific perspective, however, this was a difficult starting place for the fifth graders. Without understanding ideas about plants as producers, food chains, cycling of matter and flow of energy in ecosystems, it was difficult for the students to do more than collect facts about plants, animals, and their habitats (and they paid attention mostly to the animals). Students were not developing meaningful ideas about diversity and interdependence in a biological sense. . . .
>
> We called this unit integrated science/social studies, but it really felt like social studies. If you asked me what science my students had learned at the end of this three month period, I would have to say it was limited to a basic descriptive level. Students could describe plants and animals that lived in the particular area their group worked on, but they could not go beyond these descriptions to explain interactions among species and the importance of diversity in ecosystems. They could not explain human impact on these ecosystems over the last 500 years except in quite superficial ways. The students did not develop meaningful understanding of ecosystems and interactions in ecosystems, nor did they wrestle with and construct ideas about why it would matter that there are many different kinds of species in an environment. (46–47)

Roth compared what the students were learning in the 1492 unit with what she had taught the year before. Much had been lost. A year earlier she had engaged students in thinking simultaneously about the nature of science and the concept of adaptation. The question addressed was similar to the one posed a year later, namely, are there more different kinds of species in Michigan or in the desert? Without the constraints of the interdisciplinary unit, the class could deal with this question on its own terms. The students could make predictions and give reasons for why one area would have more diversity than another. In this way, students were able to experience the nature of scientific inquiry, by which Roth meant having a scientific way of thinking, gathering evidence, and formulating a scientific argument.

This content led naturally to the study of photosynthesis, how plants get their food. But the difference between learning a year earlier and during the 1492 unit had become so dramatic that Roth abandoned the integrated approach that had been planned. Instead she chose to focus on simply teaching the biology of plants. She wanted the students to acquire more sophisticated and interconnected understandings of plants and to be able to use scientific ways of thinking. She did not want this teaching to be compromised by the need to fit within an interdisciplinary framework.

As a result, Roth came to believe that it is very difficult to teach in an interdisciplinary, integrated way without distorting or diminishing one of the disciplines involved. In contrast to those who believe it is necessary to view the world more holistically and to erase disciplinary boundaries, Roth took the position that understanding is best developed by helping students develop various disciplinary lenses with which they can examine the world.

Searching for a Better Way at
the Holt High School PDS

Although much of this chapter is based on the work and publications of Brophy, Alleman, and Roth, it would not do to give the impression that they were responsible for all the social studies improvement work of the revolution. Various PDSs had social studies projects carried out in collaboration with MSU faculty and doctoral students. An especially important and long-lasting one took place at Holt High School where MSU social studies educator Tim Little spent years working with K–12 teachers at the high school on better ways of teaching social studies. Instead of limiting themselves to a course on current events, they opted for a course that concentrated on teaching systematic reasoning skills to acquire concepts and skills from social sciences, history, and science and to develop strategies for learning about and analyzing global issues. To help others learn from what they had done, they published a book titled *A Handbook for Teaching Global Studies: The Holt High School Experience* (Little et al., 1995; see also MSU-15, Fall 1997).

The book begins, after comparing various approaches to global studies, by explaining why the Holt team chose a problem-solving and decision-making approach as the best way to accommodate multiple worldviews.

> An approach to global studies that adopts a rigid value-embodied conservative or reformist perspective . . . seems contrary to the process of students developing as independent, competent decision-makers and problem-solvers. A multiple perspectives approach allows the student . . . to examine his or her own values and decide what position he or she takes on an issue, and equally important, why. (Little et al., 1995, 12)

Finding suitable learning materials was a problem. The teachers rejected most textbooks, and they felt that students' reading skills were not sufficient for them to use primary source materials. They ultimately decided on the Opposing Viewpoints series from Greenhaven Press, which provided a unit on global warming with six different points of view. Students also read assignments from *Newsweek*, *Atlantic*, and *Scientific American*. They viewed a daily fifteen-minute news summary on CNN, with instructions to take notes, discuss, and answer key questions. In short, the course took the position that "it is vital that students learn to view issues, whether global, national, or personal, as capable of being defined in more than one way" (13–14).

Initially, three Holt teachers and one MSU faculty person designed the course over one semester. In the course of this semester, students were expected to take more and more responsibility for their own learning. "The course was designed to move students from carrying out teacher conceptualized, organized and directed projects to operating with ever-increasing intellectual independence. Similarly, the role of the staff shifted from that of exercising near total control over the instructional process toward that of a 'coaching' stance in the classroom" (17).

This shift in teacher control occurred over the span of three units. The first unit on global warming was teacher controlled. Each day a teacher took responsibility to select the topic and orchestrate the direction students were to take. This meant defining and framing issues to be studied, selecting materials, assigning daily activities, and evaluating student achievement. In the second unit, on the future of the automobile industry, students were to take more responsibility to frame the issues, organize their research, interpret the data, and formulate policy options that could be supported by the data. Finally, as originally planned, the third unit was to be turned more completely over to the students to select a topic, decide on an approach, and then carry it out.

In its first iteration, the second topic was carried out pretty much as planned. Although teachers had chosen the automobile industry as the overall topic, the students selected specific issues to address, such as buy American vs. free trade or the quality gap between U.S. and foreign cars. But students had trouble gathering data and were unable to maintain a focus on the chosen issues. They were unable to get away from a U.S. perspective in order to examine the Japanese economy from the viewpoint of the Japanese. Given this failure with the second unit, the teachers did not attempt to implement the third unit as autonomously as planned.

According to the authors, they then let the pendulum swing too far back toward teacher control. For two semesters, there were no student designed or codesigned units. They stuck to the approach that worked out for the first unit, emphasizing serious study of international affairs, especially unfolding developments in Somalia and Bosnia.

Although the global studies staff felt they were getting at important global issues with good understanding on the part of the students, they were nonetheless troubled:

> Motivated students and good scores on evaluation did not make up for the fact that the classes were not getting much practice at independently defining unit issues, forming good research questions, or developing infor-mation processing skills. Furthermore, . . . we tended to focus on economic, political, and scientific dimensions of world relationships; a cross-cultural treatment of the arts and humanities continued to receive inadequate attention in our course. (20)

At last, the pendulum did begin to swing back. Though the first unit topic continued to be teacher selected and directed, in the second unit, even though it was still teacher directed, the focal topic was chosen from those identified by students. Once topics were chosen, students could select the countries and key questions to be addressed. It is not clear whether a totally student constructed and directed unit would have worked at all in this one semester course.

Assessments for the course were also new, diverse, and chal-lenging. Early on, students had to create a bogus text with at least four of the logic errors considered in the course so they could be discussed in class. After each unit, students had to write position papers that were then graded on the students' ability to articulate and defend their position. In addition, the student research teams were orally examined on their policy positions by teachers, build-ing administrators, and MSU personnel. Debates were also held after each unit.

Still another challenge for the course was the inclusion of mildly disabled students. In the preceding three semesters of the course, one-fourth of the students were either special education (mostly learning disabled, but with some emotionally impaired) or other-wise considered at risk. The literature on such students shows that they often get no social studies at all, and if they do, it consists of memorizing facts, not critical thinking. In Holt a special-education teacher joined the team to work on the problems of such students. And the other teachers took care to engage at various times with all the students, not just the ones perceived as most able.

Searching for a Better Way in the Work of Alleman and Brophy

As in other subject matters, research on subject-matter improvement in social studies took place at MSU within the federally funded national research centers. Jere Brophy (1990) proposed a framework for research on social studies in the Elementary Subjects Center. After describing historical trends and current issues in elementary social studies, he concluded that the higher-order goals of social studies were basically the same as other subjects (conceptual understanding, critical thinking, and inquiry) even though these goals tended to be hidden under long lists of discrete skills. But, in addition, values, dispositions, and self-actualization goals were more central in social studies than in other areas.

In an article by Brophy and VanSledright (1993) on the responses of seven exemplary elementary schoolteachers to open-ended questions about social studies, the teachers agreed that the social studies curriculum in elementary school was thin, trite, and redundant but did not want to eliminate or reduce instruction on families, neighborhoods, and communities. Instead they wanted to teach this content more effectively and in comparison to past and present cultures. In response, much of what Brophy and Alleman did subsequently was a search for new approaches to social studies in the early grades.

Toward the end of this era, Brophy, Alleman, and a teacher with whom they collaborated intensively analyzed in detail that teacher's teaching of social studies (Brophy, Alleman & Knighton, 2009). They had wanted to find social studies classrooms where powerful social studies teaching was taking place and they could draw lessons for teacher education. By "powerful" they meant a curriculum aiming at important social understandings and social efficiency goals: integrative and transdisciplinary within social science across time and space; bringing together knowledge, beliefs, values, and dispositions to act. This sort of social studies is necessarily values based and aimed at the common good, but well supported by scholarly work, as called for in a position statement of the National Council for Social Studies (1993). Initially, Alleman and Brophy had trouble finding the teachers who taught such a powerful social studies curriculum.

As a stopgap, the two professors began to do the teaching themselves—forty-five-minute social studies lessons in K–12 classrooms. But this did not go well. Alleman did the teaching, but she was not familiar with the context and was not able to select the content as much as she wanted. Going back to regular teachers willing to try new practices, they found that the "teachers lacked experience with curricula based on big ideas and resources of most potential—drifting away from big ideas into facts, side issues and activities unconnected with major goals." To do better, Alleman and Brophy then began designing their own units on "cultural universals," producing nine units on food, clothing, shelter, communication, transportation, family living, childhood, money, and government (6).

It was in this phase that they discovered the teacher they had been looking for. Barbara Knighton was known to be "warm, nurturant, and sensitive to the needs and interests of her students, but also concerned about developing their knowledge and skills, and systematic in her efforts to do so" (6). From the perspective of Alleman and Brophy, the class was ideal for this research because the school was midrange in socioeconomic status, as well as racially and ethnically diverse.

The Alleman, Brophy, and Knighton team went on to pilot the units that had been designed, teaching each one for forty-five minutes per day for three weeks. Knighton taught the units, two per year, one in fall and one in spring, while Alleman tape-recorded and took notes on each one. Afterward, the three discussed what went well and what did not, taking into account Knighton's ability to maintain a positive climate, introduce new content, and respond effectively when students could not answer her questions. For example, when teaching about housing, with help from her collaborators, she found that students had little knowledge of the mechanisms that provide houses with water, heat, light, and other utilities. They generally knew that water was piped into their homes, but did not know how it got there or where it came from (7–9, 19; see also Brophy & Alleman, 2003).

Teaching social studies to young children in this way is especially challenging. Not only do the children have little prior knowledge, but much of what they do know is tacit and distorted with misconceptions. Telling stories with characters in which the content to be learned is embodied is one good way to deal with this. According to the authors,

> studies of children's historical learning indicate that much of what they retain about history is organized within narrative structures, usually compressions of larger trends into stories that focus around goal-oriented activities or conflicts involving a few key figures. . . . Stories are opportunities to introduce basic concepts and principles of disciplines, e.g. geography, economics, political science, sociology, and anthropology. (Brophy, Alleman & Knighton, 2009, 38–39)

Barbara Knighton proved to be a master of storytelling. She told stories to introduce new topics, including stories from her own life and from her students' lives—their family histories and experience with the local job market. She was able to work all this into the big ideas shaping the knowledge domains with which she was dealing. These stories were simplified accounts, sticking closely to the main ideas without unnecessary detail or vocabulary. Thus, "what appears to be spontaneous and informal story telling is actually a carefully prepared narrative intended to establish a content base which consists of a network of information structured around big ideas" (57).

The Brophy and VanSledright book on *Teaching and Learning History in Elementary School* (1997) further summarizes the style and effectiveness of this teacher; it is a reminder of the continued influence of process-product research as well as constructivism in the MSU revolution.

[Knighton] exemplified virtually all of the personal qualities and general teaching strategies that process-outcome
research has identified as correlates of student achievement
gain. . . . She was extraordinarily good at establishing her
classroom as a learning environment in which students
spend most of their time engaged in ongoing academic
activities. She presented information with enthusiasm
during presentations and structured it around main ideas
that were emphasized during presentations and followed
up using key word cards, story maps, study guides, and
related techniques for engaging students in meaningful
learning of connected content rather than rote memorizing of isolated facts. She used an active teaching approach
in which much classroom time was spent in whole-class
lessons and teacher-student discourse rather than in silent
work on assignments; she made sure that students knew
what to do and how to do it before releasing them to work
independently.

[Her] teaching also exemplified many features of teaching school subjects for understanding and knowledge use.
. . . She limited her breadth of coverage in order to develop
limited content around a few key ideas; she emphasized
the relationships and connections between these ideas;
she provided students with frequent opportunities to
actively process information that capitalized on naturally
occurring opportunities for students to communicate or
apply the history content that they were learning. (68–69)

Research on Children's Knowledge and Thinking as a Basis for Social Studies

For additional research to improve instruction, Brophy and
Alleman did a major work on what children in the early grades
know and think about cultural universals. Titled *Children's
Thinking about Cultural Universals* (2006), the book they wrote on

this research was intended as a basis for an alternative social studies curriculum in grades 1–3. The two researchers initially focused
on ninety-six students from a middle/working-class suburb. To
provide contrasts across communities when needed, follow-ups
were conducted in two other areas, one urban and one rural.

Brophy and Alleman believed that cultural universals could be
the basis for improved social studies teaching because (1) these
universals represent so much of everyday life, social organization, and community activity, and (2) what children already know
about these universals can be built upon—helping children learn
how the social system works, how and why it got that way, how and
why it varies across locations and cultures, and what difference this
makes for personal, social, and civic decision-making. But to do
this, a pedagogy to connect with prior experience, engage students
in building new knowledge, and correct misconceptions requires
data on what children know and think. Very little of this research
on cultural universals had been done. Alleman and Brophy were
able to fill this gap with interviews made possible by the fact that
K–3 children are old enough to respond to interview questions as
long as the questions focus on familiar experiences, not abstract,
remote, or hypothetical content.

The book discusses a host of specific findings about the nature
of each universal, its history, and its geographical and cultural
diversity. Children knew more about physical appearances than
underlying nature and more about finished products than what it
took to make those products. They knew little about other cultures
or changes in U.S. society and culture over time, and what they
did know was distorted by prejudice and lack of empathy. "A
major implication for curriculum and instruction is to make sure
that what is taught about other cultures is presented in ways that
encourage students to empathize with the people being studied
and thus appreciate their activities as intelligent adaptations to
time and place (rather than stupid, weird, etc.)" (ch. 1, e-book).

A striking example of this was found in the ignorance, misconceptions, and negativity of the suburban children interviewed
toward farm families. Their images of farm life were almost entirely
negative, for example: "Farm families have to work most of the

time, must endure unpleasant smells, must live in small houses that often lack amenities found elsewhere, and generally don't have much fun and 'don't know how to live like real people do.'" Some of the students interviewed even believed that farm children have not gone to school and are illiterate. Brophy and Alleman conclude that the suburban children need to know that farm children are much more similar to than different from themselves (ch. 7, e-book).

Given that the authors uncovered so much by way of ignorance, misconceptions, and neglect of children's thinking, it is remarkable to see how positive and optimistic they are about the possibilities for improvement. The book therefore exemplifies the fact that revolutions like the one at MSU require positive, even utopian visions of improvements to be made. But in the case of Alleman and Brophy, like that of Kathy Roth, these visions are carefully couched in practical, not unrealistic or utopian terms.

Their chapter on what students know and can learn about government is a particularly good example: "We believe that units on government for primary grade students can do a much better job of helping the students understand why governments are needed and what they do for their people. We recommend developing such instruction around the basic idea that governments provide important infrastructure and services that societies need but that are too big in scope, expense, and so on, for individuals or families to provide for themselves." And they conclude: "Such instruction would delineate a much richer picture of public sector activities than most children possess now, and likely would be of more interest and use to them than some of the more abstract notions often emphasized in lessons on government (e.g. how a bill becomes a law)" (ch. 8, e-book).

For example, one of the assignments recommended by Brophy and Alleman is a photo essay on a typical day in the life of one of the students in the class that would underscore the role of government in providing or supporting these activities. Examples of what students might include in their photos are wearing fire-resistant pajamas manufactured under government regulation, using running water supplied by local government, putting on clothes inspected for quality and safety as required by the government, or eating a breakfast of foods likewise inspected (ch. 8, e-book).

Brophy and Alleman were not able to do the large-scale studies found in other chapters when it came to the cultural universals of money and childhood, but they did complete smaller studies. Consideration of childhood led them to a major conclusion about the role of schooling: "It appears that the home, the media, and the culture generally make children very aware of the hedonistic and materialistic aspects of development toward adulthood, but it is mainly up to the school to nurture their awareness of the personal, social, and civic responsibility aspects" (ch. 11, e-book).

As Alleman and Brophy continued the research that led to their book, they also developed instructional units for each of nine universals (Alleman & Brophy, 2001–3). The units followed a common pattern: (1) begin with a cultural universal as experienced in the contemporary United States, (2) show how that universal developed over time, (3) examine variation across places and cultures, (4) illustrate with physical examples, classroom visitors, field trips, and children's literature, (5) include enjoyable assignments for families to do to gain additional insight into the universal, and (6) engage students in discussions of what all this means for personal, social, and civic decision-making.

Conclusion

This is a chapter about the importance of goals and how they are implemented. Goals can be trite, insignificant, undermining the whole concept of teaching for understanding. Or they can be the means of making teaching and learning powerful, but only if practices in teaching and learning are continually examined to see if the goals are taken seriously and to figure out what this means for practice. Increasingly, during the MSU revolution, the trend was to speak of teaching "big ideas," and predictably the term soon became a cliché. Brophy, Alleman, and Knighton (2009), however, were careful to articulate what this means in terms of establishing goals. They explained that big ideas are midrange between broad areas like transportation and particular matters of fact. They generally take the form of concepts, generalizations, principles, or causal explanations. These big ideas are embedded within networks of knowledge and connected to other big ideas. Big ideas give rise to worthwhile applications; trivial facts do not. If this is not clear, the authors suggested, readers should try to design "worthwhile activities based on information about the states' flags, songs, birds, etc." Examples they give of big ideas include "that geography affects how you meet your needs; that people are more alike than different; and that people make choices based on personal preferences, economic resources, local availability of potential options, climate, etc." (59).

Taking this approach to social studies is not easy. Social studies practice can be far from realizing major social-education goals, but much could be and was done as part of the MSU revolution to change that. In general, according to the authors cited, children are capable of much greater understanding than they are typically given credit for, and likewise, schools can do much more to foster personal, social, and civic responsibility than is usually done.

CHAPTER NINE

From Mindless to Meaningful in the Teaching of Science

Some of the earliest revolutionary changes in curriculum and instruction arose in science teaching, an area where the weaknesses in common practice were documented in international research led by MSU scholars. A press for teaching science for conceptual understanding came from faculty hired before the revolution got under way and accelerated as research in psychology and education made the cognitive shift. Faculty at MSU and in K–12 schools who studied their own efforts to orient teaching toward student understanding contributed to the revolutions in curriculum, instruction, and teacher education.

A Revolutionary Verdict Calling Science Teaching a Failure

In a 1991 article MSU faculty member Charles W. (Andy) Anderson declared that science education in the United States is a failure. Noting that this failure was neither recent nor absolute, he explained that at the time of his article, evidence of this failure had become more definitive than ever before. Elaborating, he said:

> A lot of science teaching is dull and meaningless stuff—an amalgam of boring lectures, cookbook "experiments," and worksheets or written work. Textbooks are for the most part poorly written and overloaded with technical vocabulary. Even what we normally call "good" science teaching generally fails to engage students deeply enough to help them achieve a meaningful understanding of science. (5)

Anderson drew attention to exceptions to this pattern, finding teachers whose students were engaged in meaningful science learning. For example, he described a unit on photosynthesis taught to seventh graders. The main point of the lesson was that plants make their own food, a point that many students found hard to believe and accept.

But for the most part the literature has documented the inadequacies of science education. In a study of students' ability to select correct definitions for biological and physical terms, there was no improvement at all between seventh and eleventh grades, even though most students had taken several science courses in between (Yager & Yager, 1985). Anderson (1991) cited other research showing that only 48 percent of American adults knew both that the earth revolves around the sun, rather than the other way around, and that it takes a year to do so. International research had also found that in the 1988 IEA international assessment,[1] the United States ranked ninth in physics, eleventh in chemistry, and thirteenth in biology (the last of the thirteen countries ranked in the latter assessment).

MSU's Role in International Studies
of What Is Learned in Science

MSU played a key role in a number of international studies cited in calls for a revolution in schooling. The famous report *A Nation at Risk* (USDE, 1983), which relied heavily on international studies in its call for reform, was released in person at MSU by the U.S. secretary of education. Although MSU also played a role in international studies of civic education and teacher education, it is best known for the IEA TIMSS (originally the Third International Mathematics and Science Study, now Trends in International Mathematics and Science Studies) (Schmidt et al., 2020).

---

1. IEA = International Association for the Evaluation of Educational Achievement, a consortium of research institutions and government agencies that has carried out cross-national studies since the 1960s.

As TIMSS began, a new era in comparative education research was taking shape, leading toward large-scale studies, which had much higher levels of government interest and funding than had previously been the case. Under the leadership of MSU's Bill Schmidt and others, a meeting of the IEA consortium in Beijing in 1990 endorsed proposals from the George H. W. Bush administration to do an unprecedented joint study of mathematics and science and a repeat study later that decade. All this was intended to measure progress, not toward agreed-upon international goals, but instead toward the ethnocentric U.S. national goal of being first in science and mathematics by the year 2000. This was an aspirational, unachievable goal, but still through TIMSS it had a long and lasting impact on educational research (Schwille, 2017, 53–57).

The Beijing agreements and what followed cleared the way for MSU to become a key center for TIMSS, collaborating first with the University of British Columbia and then with Boston College (which has remained the main international hub for TIMSS). Under Schmidt's leadership, MSU took on three important responsibilities for the original 1995 TIMSS. First, it became the center for an unprecedented, in-depth curriculum analysis, based on content analysis of over six hundred science and mathematics textbooks and about five hundred curriculum documents from nearly fifty countries (Schmidt et al., 2001). Second, MSU was funded to do classroom observational research for the design of TIMSS, conducting one hundred classroom observations in mathematics and science in France, Japan, Norway, Spain, Switzerland, and the United States (Schmidt et al., 2002). Third, Schmidt became the U.S. national research coordinator for TIMSS (working with the National Center for Education Statistics) and took the lead in producing the TIMSS national report for the United States (Schmidt, McKnight & Raizen, 1997).

The importance of TIMSS in its original 1995 version would be hard to overestimate. From release of the first results, the study attracted enormous attention. Schmidt went on to work closely with key federal and state education policy makers, including governors and important business CEOs. In a single year, 2000–1, Schmidt gave thirty-eight speeches in twelve states on implications of TIMSS with audiences ranging from state school boards in Illinois and Idaho, to the Pennsylvania Science Teachers Association and the City Club of Cleveland. He was also widely featured on broadcast media, including C-Span, CNN, NPR, and ABC's *Primetime Live*. In a 1997 speech to the Michigan legislature, President Bill Clinton thanked MSU and Schmidt for the TIMSS work (Schwille, 2017, 46).

But the most damning assessment of U.S. performance to come out of TIMSS can arguably be found in another report by former MSU faculty member Kathleen Roth (Roth & Garnier, 2007) on the TIMSS science video study in five countries. This report is a discussion of how science education in the United States had fallen short of what to teach for understanding required and of how other countries had done better. Thus, while not part of the MSU revolution per se, the TIMSS video report is illustrative not only of Roth's importance, but of how international research advanced the revolution at MSU and elsewhere.

The video study focused on teaching practices in the United States and in four countries that outperformed the United States in science achievement on the 1999 TIMSS: the Czech Republic, Japan, Australia, and the Netherlands. A random sample of one hundred eighth-grade science lessons in each of the five countries was videotaped to capture science content and science teaching practices within each country. The United States was seen to be the worst in both teaching and learning. "Although each country had its own approach, all of the higher-achieving countries had strategies for engaging students with core science ideas—that is, their science lessons focused on content. In U.S. lessons, content played a less central role, and sometimes no role at all; instead, lessons were usually built around engaging students in a variety of activities" (Roth & Garnier, 2007, 16).

Those U.S. "activities" were a mix of practical, hands-on activities, independent seatwork (including reading and writing), and whole-class discussions—activities much less common in the other countries. Content in the United States, if included at all, was typically presented as collections of discrete facts, definitions, and algorithms rather than as a connected set of ideas. Unlike

teachers in Australia and Japan, U.S. teachers did not use activities to develop content ideas in a coherent and challenging way for
students, but rather chose them because students would find them
fun or engaging. The following illustrates this absence of content.

> One teacher spent the first 10 minutes of class talking
> about an upcoming "teamwork-building" field trip,
> collecting permission slips for the field trip, reading over
> an assignment about teamwork related to the field trip, and
> discussing the schedule for the launching of the students'
> rockets the following week. The teacher then directed
> students to get out their rockets and their directions for
> building rockets. For the next 25 minutes, the students
> worked individually on building the rockets, consulting
> with the teacher and their peers as needed for help. The
> lesson ended with a five-minute clean-up period. During
> the entire lesson, there was no mention of a single science
> content idea related to the rocket-building process. (20)

In short, this research revealed striking differences between
countries in the science taught in middle schools. All the higher-achieving countries in the video study worked with high content
standards and content-focused instructional patterns.

> In Australia and Japan, for example, teachers carefully
> and thoughtfully developed just one or two science ideas
> across a lesson, presenting the ideas in a logical, coher-
> ent sequence. . . . In the Czech Republic, teachers some-
> times presented content conceptually and sometimes by
> introducing many facts, theories, and terms related to a
> given topic. But [they] . . . held their students to high stan-
> dards for mastering challenging, often theoretical content
> through frequent oral reviews, assessments, and public
> student work. (21)

The Japanese teachers went furthest in developing a limited
number of important concepts:

A typical Japanese lesson used an inductive, inquiry-oriented approach, focusing on just one or two main ideas that were developed in depth and supported with data, phenomena, and visual representations. Thus, students had opportunities to work independently on hands-on, practical science activities that were preceded and followed by discussions that helped them link these activities to science ideas.

For example, one lesson on the videotape developed a single big idea—*a change of matter from one form to another is not always a change of state* (for example solid to liquid or liquid to gas). The teacher began the lesson by asking students what kind of gas they thought was produced in the previous lesson, when they had heated sodium bicarbonate. The teacher wrote the students' ideas on the board and stated what the lesson would investigate: What kind of change occurred when the gas was produced?

The students then worked in small groups to heat the sodium bicarbonate, test for carbon dioxide, and write conclusions. After this activity, the class discussed the lesson question. The students also conducted additional experiments to support their conclusion, discussing the results of each experiment in turn. The teacher then summarized the main idea, telling the class that their work provided evidence that some type of reaction other than a change of state had taken place and that tomorrow they would continue to examine examples of such reactions. (18)

At the end of this report, Roth said that to follow up on this research, she had begun working with colleagues in ways inspired by these international comparisons. In lesson planning, she asked U.S. teachers to think more explicitly about how to set up and follow up each activity in the lesson, making sure the focus was on science ideas and not just on activities or procedures. Analysis of videos of science teaching and related student work also played an important role in helping teachers do this work.

Too Much Coverage Is Mindless

While still an MSU faculty member during the revolution, Roth authored other important articles about the deplorable state of science education and what might be done about it (e.g. Roth, 1989a). In particular, her paper titled "Conceptual Understanding and Higher Level Thinking in the Elementary Science Curriculum: Three Perspectives" begins with a very revealing and formative experience that Roth had when she was a K–12 teacher:

> At a fall open house in 1975, I explained to the parents of my middle school science students that one of my goals for the year was to help the students learn how to "think scientifically." After my presentation, one of the parents came up to me and asked, "Do you really think that you can teach someone how to think scientifically?" That question triggered a whole set of questions for me about the purposes of teaching science: Is teaching children to "think scientifically" a realistic outcome of elementary and middle school science instruction? Or was that just rhetoric that sounded good when communicating with parents? And what did I mean by "scientific thinking"? What is the nature of scientific thinking for the goals on my list: To help students appreciate the beauties and complexities of the natural world, to help students develop more independence in their learning, to teach students basic concepts in the life sciences. How did these goals relate to the goal of teaching for scientific thinking? And how did all of these goals match with what I was actually doing as a teacher? Which of these goals were the most important, and which could be achieved in meaningful ways while working with a group of 26 students for two–three hours per week across a school year? (1989b, 1)

Subsequently, Roth explored these questions further in her teaching in K–12 classrooms and teacher education as well as in her research. She concluded that it is possible to teach young children to think scientifically, but only by overcoming difficult challenges and complexities. For example, she found the long list of goal statements compiled by experts for science education completely unrealistic if the overall goal is to "teach for understanding."

To Roth, such expansive lists of goals were baffling. She had many questions that called for answers:

> How could a teacher possibly work toward all of these goals in meaningful ways? In compiling these lists, how did the experts expect teachers to handle the contradictions between the far-reaching goals and local constraints of classrooms? Did they expect teachers to pick and choose from this list in order to deal with a few of the goals in meaningful ways? Or did the experts define "understanding" of concepts and of science thinking (process) skills in ways that would allow teachers to claim success when students were merely *exposed* to opportunities to understand concepts and to think scientifically? (2)

Also problematic was the fact that most of these lists of objectives specified what scientifically literate adults should know, not children. What instead should a first or fifth grader know? What could it mean for such children to "know the major concepts, hypotheses, and theories of science" or to "use science thinking process skills" (9)?

MSU researchers saw that in both science and social studies, the problem of mindless activities and assignments had become even worse with the movement for reform. The critique of current textbooks and practices in science by Roth is similar to that of Alleman and Brophy in social studies, stressing the problem of trivialized teaching, with too many goals, too much superficial coverage, too many activities not well understood, precluding any depth of understanding.

The guidelines and position statements offered by experts failed to give schools and teachers a focused, manageable vision of what they might accomplish in teaching elementary school. As a result, according to Roth, science teaching in elementary school, if offered at all, was primarily textbook reading, recitation, memorization, using worksheets that emphasized learning of facts and vocabulary, not higher-order thinking. In following up, the main concern of teachers, in their questioning, was simply to see if students could come up with the right answer (see, e.g., Roth, Anderson & Smith, 1987).

The textbooks themselves were not organized for meaningful teaching and learning.

> Instead, their factual approach to science is generally organized around discrete topics (such as fossils, plants, rocks, weather, electricity, ecology, magnets, light, etc.). ... In the texts there is little or no attempt to make explicit conceptual connections among the topics addressed at a given grade level. Topics are arranged in a K–6 scope based again on a "sampling of science topics" strategy. (Roth, 1989b, 21, 23)

To work her way out of such dilemmas, Roth examined literature to answer such questions as the following: What do different experts mean by "scientific thinking"? "What does it mean to teach for conceptual understanding and higher level thinking in elementary science? How feasible is it to achieve such outcomes in elementary classrooms?" (3) She saw that the desired outcomes of elementary school science instruction are rooted in three different perspectives, each endorsed by different groups of science educators, educational researchers, and scientists: (1) a conceptual change perspective, (2) an inquiry perspective, and (3) a science-technology-society (STS) perspective. All three perspectives were committed to the teaching of science content (facts, concepts, generalizations, theories), processes of scientific thinking (predicting, hypothesis making, observing, inferring, etc.), and development of scientific attitudes. All three also emphasized that higher-order scientific thinking is critical. But these three perspectives also differed in important ways.

The Conceptual Change Approach

Roth contrasts the three visions with current practices, exploring why the practices were so different from the visions. In reflecting on her own teaching in a fifth-grade classroom, she pointed out that her own enthusiasm for a conceptual change perspective stemmed primarily from its potential impact on student learning. As she saw it, the conceptual change perspective is primarily concerned with how students learn and what students understand. The other two perspectives, according to Roth, are too much focused on what scientists, not elementary school students, know and are able to do. Textbooks appeared to pick and choose from the three perspectives. But Roth saw this eclectic approach as a mistake, because it did not build conceptual understanding with insight into the nature of scientific thinking.

In Roth's view, the primary goal of science education is to help students "develop meaningful, conceptual understanding of science and its ways of describing, explaining, predicting, and controlling natural phenomena" (59). She maintains that scientific knowledge is meaningful only if it helps learners make sense of the world they live in, and only if integrated with the personal knowledge and experience of the learner, with rich connections among concepts and facts, organized around ideas that have explanatory power. Science education has to change the intuitive, everyday ways students have for explaining the world, making the modifications called for by scientific thinking.

Simple ignorance is not the heart of this problem, because students come to class with ideas that conflict with the scientific explanations. They "know," for example, that plants need food, and they think that plants get their food the same way people do—by taking it in from outside their body. In other words, the roots of plants get food from the soil. That contradicts the scientific understanding of how plants carry out photosynthesis, using light to make food. In interpreting textbooks and what their teacher says, students tend to rely on their personal theories even if inconsistent with scientific understanding.

Inquiry and STS Perspectives

For comparison, Roth (1989b) discusses both the inquiry and the STS approaches in depth. Those approaches go back to science education in the 1950s and 1960s, when science educators and the scientists concerned with science education focused mostly on the processes of science—the ways of thinking that scientists use to do their work. At the time, much was done to identify these ways and to transform them into curricular objectives, which were to be taught hierarchically, starting with the concrete and leading to the abstract.

Roth recalls that this inquiry approach became dominant in the reform movement of the 1960s and 1970s. But it failed to meet its goals and by the 1980s had split into the three perspectives. In 1983, MSU faculty members Roth, Smith, and Anderson wrote about their experience using inquiry, one of the three perspectives They concluded that their students had failed to develop any real under-standing of the science involved in spite of having spent weeks experimenting, graphing, and discussing their research. Although much of this activity proved to be fun for the students, in the end all this emphasis on processes, together with the measuring and recording of data they had to do, became tiring and frustrating. As Rachel, one of the students, explained: "I don't know why we kept measuring those plants. I mean it was fun for a while, but I already [knew] that plants need light and now I know it again" (Roth 1989b, 44).

Roth concluded that this was an example of science activities and processes becoming ends in themselves. Rachel learned to do obser-vations and record them carefully, not in order to better understand the phenomenon, but just because "that's what you do in science" (44). Rachel's classmates came up with many different explanations of why plants need light, but they never discussed which explana-tions make the most scientific sense. After eight weeks of measur-ing, observing, and discussing plants, Rachel was left with no better understanding than she had had at the beginning.

From Roth's point of view, the conceptual change perspec-tive is better not only because it was richer, but also because it avoided too much emphasis on either process or content. Taking this approach led her fifth-grade students to become more eager and able to ask good questions, to puzzle over things, and to put their ideas together in making better sense of the world. The other approaches might seem fun, appealing to students, but liking or not liking is not what matters most. Instead desired outcomes are the result of getting to know what it really means to understand something and finding out what a good, scientific explanation entails. Roth noted that what she had learned about the conceptual change approach was based on and confirmed by her own teaching and research experience:

> The work that my colleagues and I have done at Michigan State University over the last seven years has involved observation and analysis of both teachers and middle grade students. . . . Our assessments of the effects of instruction typically included multiple sources of evidence: classroom observations of instructional units, teacher interviews, student pre- and posttests, student interviews, and focused observations and analyses of target students and their work.
>
> The most important generalization is that conceptual change instruction that engages students in integrating their own conceptions with scientific explanations and that actively involves students in using scientific knowledge to describe, predict, explain and control their world can have a significant impact on student learning. (86)

In general, however, most teachers are not prepared to teach in the way Roth recommends; most have limited understanding of science to begin with, and any courses they have taken in science are unlikely to have been what was needed.

> The science courses teachers take are typically taught in didactic, authoritative ways emphasizing detailed knowledge of specialized abstract cycles, formulas, structures, and principles rather than functional understandings of

how these cycles, formulas, structures, and principles can explain everyday phenomena in children's (and adults'!) experiences (how plants get their food, how and why we sweat, why we can see through some objects and not others, why it snows, why bicycles rust, why it's easier to ride a bike uphill in "low gear," etc.). (109)

The Teaching of Photosynthesis from the Three Perspectives

To further illustrate the differences and similarities among the three perspectives, Roth (1989b) discusses how a unit on photosynthesis and food for plants could be taught differently in fifth grade according to each of these paradigms. In the inquiry example, Roth describes three activities that served as the focus of the lessons, taught without a textbook. First, the students germinated and measured the growth of different seed parts in order to show that germinating seeds get their food from the seeds. Next, the students planted grass seed, keeping some in the dark, some in the light, in order to show that plants need light to grow. Third, the students planted, germinated, grew, and measured bean plants to see how the plants were doing under different conditions: with and without light, with and without the food contained in the seeds. At the end, the students were supposed to be able to use the concepts of photosynthesis to explain their observations. But the results were disappointing; only 11 percent of the students changed their ideas as intended (93–96).

In contrast, when learning about photosynthesis from an STS perspective, the study of photosynthesis is needed in order to understand the scientific and technological problems facing society. Since Roth (1989b) did not have an actual example of teaching photosynthesis from an STS perspective to use, she discusses a hypothetical case. For example, one way to illustrate this would be to examine the effects of deforestation and industrialization in producing a greenhouse effect. The class could work with scientific concepts to get a grip on the severity of this problem and what might be done about it. The result would be student design of activities to take action in this case (97).

Third, Roth discussed teaching photosynthesis from a conceptual change perspective. To understand photosynthesis better, they must change their commonsense approach to understanding the world, but as already mentioned, abandoning misconceptions and old habits of thought is hard (see Roth & Anderson, 1987). In this approach, Roth used curriculum materials she had developed. They were designed to get students to change their minds about how plants get food. The teaching methods got students and teachers to raise good questions and to show respect for what others were saying and learning. All needed to be engaged in generating, defending, and debating predictions and explanations, whether in pairs, small groups, or whole-class discussions.

At the beginning of the unit students were asked to write and talk about definitions of the word "food." Roth and Anderson note that although this word is rarely used with much precision by anyone, biologists are more consistent in its usage than others are. Biologists use the word to refer to "organic compounds with high-energy molecular bonds that organisms can use for growth and metabolism" (1987, I-3). Other substances, such as water, oxygen, and minerals, are not considered food. Nevertheless, many students in Roth's class continued to argue that water is food for plants even as others pointed out that there is no energy in it (Roth, 1989b, 101).

This distinction between food and nonfood is what makes the statement "plants make their own food" so critical for scientific understanding. Photosynthesis is the only bridge in the earth's environment by which inorganic matter can be changed into organic matter. All the organic compounds that make up the bodies of living things are derived from a single source: the glucose produced during photosynthesis. Students will not understand this point if they do not know that the food resulting from photosynthesis is different in critical respects from other nutrients such as water or minerals (Roth & Anderson, 1987, I-3).

The Science of Climate Change

The efforts of scholars in science education to make science more meaningful and understandable for students and ex-students continued after the MSU revolution lost most of its coherence and momentum. Encouraging examples of this continued work can be found in more recent work by researchers at MSU. One of the most important is responding to the need to educate children and adults about the processes and threats of climate change. To do this in matters so consequential for the future of humanity would be a major revolution in itself. This revolution could take place if students understand that the primary cause of global climate change is imbalance in the cycling of carbon. In an article by Mohan, Chen, and Anderson (2009) the authors reported on what students understand about climate change in terms of how much they have learned about carbon cycling. It is a story about how learners from upper elementary grades through high school develop understandings of the biochemical processes that transform carbon in socio-ecological systems at multiple scales of magnitude (see also Jin & Anderson, 2012).

Such learning progressions are guided in part by societal expectations (as embodied in science standards) about what we want high school and college students to understand about science when they graduate. But currently many students do not meet the standards they are supposed to reach, for example, in understanding of climate change. This understanding will make a big difference if we want to know whether and how young people will respond to scientific evidence as they assume diverse roles as consumers, workers, voters, and advocates. We have to ask whether the American public is being asked to consider profound changes in their lifestyles on the basis of scientific arguments that according to research data, they do not understand.

For instance, Al Gore and the Intergovernmental Panel on Climate Change received the Nobel Peace Prize for reports and presentations to promote public understanding of the science behind climate change. But the Mohan, Chen, and Anderson article points out that for too many students, these reports are incomprehensible. To meet this challenge, the authors defined levels of understanding and designed curriculum to move students up through the levels (2009, 676, 694, and abstract).

Although in natural ecosystems, the processes that generate and oxidize organic carbon are roughly in balance, humans have been upsetting this balance by extracting carbon as biomass and fossil fuel, oxidizing carbon from these sources in order to support human lifestyles, and returning the resulting carbon dioxide to the atmosphere. Knowledge of these processes and the ability to trace carbon compounds through them have become central to being able to understand our environment and the human systems that are dependent on it.

The study's authors spent three years studying what students in grades 4–12 know about carbon cycling and finding out what progression they had experienced in getting to the level of understanding that they had reached. Written assessments of student thinking were developed, focused on what happens to matter during carbon-transforming processes. An exemplar workbook was developed to distinguish between qualitatively different patterns of student response. After ordering responses from least to most sophisticated, exemplar responses were used to identify four levels of achievement. These levels of achievement can be described as follows: Students at level one describe changes in both living and nonliving things simply as natural tendencies in which living things grow, die, and decay while nonliving things burn or change in other ways. Students at this level do not understand principles of conservation in either solids or liquids. In their minds, materials can completely disappear. Students describe all this in everyday language, and there is no mention of cycles.

At level two, students are more concerned with principles of conservation in liquids and solids, but much less so in the case of gases (even though in contrast to level one they have come to see gases as real materials). These students also have begun to recognize that matter can be broken down into smaller parts that, even when not visible to the naked eye, are nonetheless essential to understanding what is being observed. Mostly the transformations of matter that students at this level recognize are from solids and liquids to other solids and liquids or from one gas to another. Students at this level can also describe living things in terms of organs and their functions: lungs are for breathing, intestines are for digestion, etc. Thus, eating is a matter of food moving through organs. They do not try to trace what happens to the atoms in this process. In the eyes of students, materials can turn into energy. In fact, at this level students tend to use the concept "energy" incorrectly to explain the disappearance of solids and liquids. Weight loss in animals happens, the article explains, when fat is turned into energy. Level two students start to recognize cycles. Their stories often include inputs and outputs of materials, but these inputs and outputs are limited to those that are visible, plus a few specific gases. Vaguely described solid matter, often identified simply as "nutrients," also cycles between organisms, according to these students. Level three students (who are found mostly in high school or higher) are able to use many words of scientific vocabulary when they speak of cellular processes such as respiration and photosynthesis. But, although they recognize the importance of tracing matter and energy, they cannot do so successfully. They are able to identify some inputs and outputs, and in addition add energy to their accounts of the food chain and combustion. But they make mistakes, describing cycles that are similar to those of level two students. Photosynthesis captures energy from sunlight and converts it to chemical potential energy stored in organic compounds. Energy, however, is an abstract and difficult concept for most students. Students must appreciate the critical importance photosynthesis plays in changing energy from sunlight into a form that is usable by living things (Roth & Anderson, 1987). Examples of mistakes they make include energy getting used up and disappearing.

Level four students are able to account for changes in organisms as cellular work that follows chemical rules. These students understand that accounts of carbon transformation are not complete or accurate unless all matter and energy are conserved, whether in an individual process or in the system as a whole. They know that carbon dioxide is the primary contributor to plant mass, and that plant cells engage in complex processes producing complex molecules. Level four understandings recognize that photosynthesis and combustion are important because they determine the location of carbon atoms in the environment.

Research has shown that among nonscience majors at college level, if they are taught from a scientific perspective to trace matter and energy, more of them can reach level four than when they are engaged in less directed, less active learning. According to Parker, de los Santos, and Anderson:

> Understanding of carbon cycling depicted as Level 4 understanding . . . is essential for our high school graduates to engage as informed citizens in discussion of global climate change and to make informed and responsible decisions. They will need to connect everyday events, news items, and knowledge of the global carbon cycle using conservation of matter and energy. (2015, 236)

Unfortunately, learning progression research shows that many high school students as well as much of the public remain at level two. Only 10 percent of high school students reach level four understanding (Mohan, Chen & Anderson, 2009; Jin & Anderson, 2012). Even level three understanding is not sufficient to analyze the consequences of decisions made regarding atmospheric carbon.

Conclusion

The story of science education in the revolution at MSU is a matter of great consequence. In the face of science denial (Darner, 2019), the future of humanity may depend upon the outcomes of science education, as investigated and pioneered at MSU and other like institutions. Much has been learned and is known about the science education that is necessary, but at the same time little has been achieved. Nothing more need be said in terms of assessing the value of what has been attempted by MSU science educators, their K–12 collaborators, and colleagues around the world—one step in finding out whether this revolution is likely to continue at the magnitude and in ways needed to be sufficiently effective.

CHAPTER TEN

The Difficulties of Teaching Teachers and Students to Write Meaningfully

Although the MSU revolution was an assault on old ways of thinking and doing in the teaching of subject matter, for each subject there were different obstacles and resistance to better teaching and learning and in some ways different views on what constitutes teaching for understanding. The case of writing is especially instructive when it comes to these differences. MSU research hauled the teaching of writing out of the shadows of misguided practice and even total neglect, bringing it into the limelight where it remained throughout the revolution.

Already in the early years, IRT research had started with the question "Why is it so difficult to teach writing?" At the time writing was "relatively invisible in the school curriculum"; it did not have the status of a regular subject. In short, there tended to be no explicit writing curricula, few materials for the teaching of writing, and no time regularly set aside in the school day for instruction in writing (MSU-27, 1986, C1, C8).

For five years, the IRT project known as the Written Literacy Forum worked with practicing teachers on transformation of theory into practice in writing instruction, the nature of schools and classrooms as sites for writing instruction, and how teachers think about writing and the teaching of writing. When researchers examined the relation between theory and practice in the teaching of writing, it was, according to the IRT final report, "an educative and humbling experience" for the researchers, who came to realize that "research and theory play only modest roles in improving and sustaining good practice" (C2). The researchers had erroneously assumed that there was a well-developed body of research on the teaching of writing, that this research was well suited to providing solutions to the problems of teaching writing in school, that researchers were in a position to tell teachers how to make best use of this research, and that teachers would readily change their teaching once research had shown the way. Instead researchers concluded that "even good teachers are not eager to make dramatic and labor-intensive changes in their ways of teaching writing and they are not looking to the research community for solutions to well defined problems of practice" (C4). As a result, the researchers were forced to study these unwarranted assumptions in order to arrive at a more realistic understanding of the challenges of teaching writing in schools.

After five years of work, the researchers concluded:

> Writing is not a private mental process that can be parsed into a series of inevitable steps. Writing is a set of tools for communication available to members of a culture. Learning to write depends on cultural membership and participation in institutions where writing is defined and used. In our culture, the school is the institution most responsible for teaching writing to the young. The history, social functions, and normative order of schools are powerful forces shaping the writing that is taught and learned there. (C4)

Understood in this light, the teaching of writing had proved to be especially difficult for teachers. It was not like other subjects; there was little or no curriculum development. Moreover, for the teachers it became even more difficult as they gained more experience. According to the IRT final report "surprisingly, experienced teachers tell us that teaching writing becomes more difficult each year, because their experiences lead them to see and risk more possibilities for themselves and their students. Writing, like music, permits of endless variations on infinite themes." Thus planning for writing instruction is hard, teaching it in the classroom is uncomfortable due to the many uncertainties involved, and giving feedback to student work is still more challenging since the teacher finds him- or herself "in the conflicting roles of audience, consultant, editor and evaluator." Writing for school can also be emotional for both teachers and students, given that it can be a personal form of self-expression, subject to criticism and misinterpretation (C10–C11).

Basically, the IRT researchers concluded that the teaching of writing had been a poor fit with the typical teacher's sense of self and what teachers make of teaching more generally:

> Teaching is basically an oral profession and few teachers are confident, competent and reflective writers. They are often discouraged by their own experience in writing as students. In contrast to such memories of writing perceived as inadequate, teachers tend to think about and talk about writing as an art. Not being artists themselves, they may overemphasize the role of natural ability and inspiration in good writing and feeling these qualities cannot be taught, thus relieving the teacher of much of the responsibility for student success in writing. (C12)

By the end of this research, the researchers were skeptical and cautious in the use of research to improve the teaching of writing. Instead they concluded that research would be valuable only in giving teachers a conceptual understanding of writing that could help them frame and solve their own problems. Nevertheless, the stage had been set for a more ambitious, more systematic study of the teaching of writing in the national teacher-education research center at MSU founded in 1985.

Writing as a Focus for MSU's National Center for Research on Teacher Education

When it came to planning and writing a proposal for the national competition for a federally funded National Center for Research on Teacher Education (NCRTE), one of the central questions for the writers of the MSU proposal was how to approach and cast the subject-matter-specific aspects of teacher education. Following up on the work of the IRT, the proposal took the position that it was not productive to study teacher education in a nonspecific subject-matter way, in what amounted to a generic approach as had been done in the past. But if subject matter was to be central and the research done one subject at a time, which subjects should be chosen? The proposers decided to focus on two subjects, mathematics, which was no surprise, and writing, which was indeed a surprise, given the characteristics discussed above.

Writing was chosen because students are universally expected to learn how to write in both elementary and secondary school and because of a recent revolutionary change in the way experts thought it should be taught. In the nineteenth century writing was taught as codified conventions of punctuation, grammar, and language usage. By the 1960s this approach had been shown to be ineffective, and emphasis shifted to strategies "for organizing one's thoughts and communicating those thoughts to others" (Kennedy, 1998, 7–12).

In the 1960s, National Assessment of Educational Progress (NAEP) assessment had found that nationally, student ability to write was unsatisfactory. The NAEP findings suggested that the traditional skills-based approach to teaching writing had interfered with the ability to write longer, more elaborate forms of text. To produce extended text the writer has to negotiate "between the content, the imagined audience, the genres and conventions [s/he] needs to work within, and the impact [s/he] wants to have. Writing, then, is an iterative problem-solving process" (MSU-36, 1990, 35). Thus a *process* approach emerged that focused on the writing cycle of drafting, revising, and seeking advice from others. In addition, a *conceptual* approach was developed in which the teacher teaches concepts that help organize and represent ideas, such as genre, metaphor, chronology, etc. The teacher's role should never be limited to teaching conventions, and instead to encourage revision, making sure the writing task is meaningful to students and that it has real purpose, not just an exercise in schoolwork. But these desires for teaching strategies and avoiding cut-and-dried prescriptions are difficult to implement. Students can take their teachers' point of view as prescriptive even when that is not intended (Kennedy, 1998, 8–12).

Mary Kennedy, former director of the NCRTE, aptly illustrates these differences when discussing the writing of paragraphs:

> Paragraphs are central to writing, and every student should learn about them. But what exactly should they learn? They could learn a set of prescriptions like these: make sure you indent the paragraph by five typed spaces or by one finger knuckle and make sure the paragraph has at least three sentences. Or they could learn some concepts, such as "main idea," "supporting details," and "transitions." Or they could learn how to use paragraphs strategically to accomplish their purposes. (11)

In other words, strategies can lead to violation of prescriptive norms. But in K–12 prospective teachers have had an "apprenticeship of observation" in which the prescriptive approach had most likely been taught with little or no attention to the changes in what experts thought about the teaching of writing. According to the NCRTE research, teaching prescriptions was valued because it reinforced the authority of teachers in the classroom. Kennedy makes this point as follows:

> School is an event in which teachers make children do things that are often tedious, but it is the teacher's job to set the rules and the student's job to comply. The strength and resilience of their concern about prescriptions, then, derives at least partly from its association with ideas about classroom management and ideas about maintaining authority in the classroom. (18–19)

Differences in What Teacher-Education Programs Do in the Teaching of Writing

In order for teachers to learn to write about complex arguments, NCRTE researchers took the position that they need to understand the nature of writing, what the process of good writing is like, about the importance of continual revision and the struggle to clarify ideas. Students learn the conventions of writing better when they have a purpose of their own that they are seriously trying to achieve. Unfortunately, good writers do not necessarily make good teachers of writing. Explicit knowledge of how to become a good writer is necessary. Good writers may not have that knowledge at the tip of their tongues; tacit knowledge is not enough. With only tacit knowledge, good writers will be unable to verbalize what they need to say in giving good feedback to students learning to write (Kennedy, 1998, chap. 1).

The NCRTE in its nationwide Teacher Education and Learning to Teach (TELT) study of ten different teacher-education programs examined what these programs were doing in attempting to teach prospective or in-service teachers how to teach writing. The differences they found were substantial in distinguishing the process from the prescriptive approach to the teaching of writing. The programs varied in the amount and intensity of attention paid to writing as a subject as well as the pedagogical approach to the teaching of writing. These programs ranged from one in-service program in which practicing teachers participated in several all-day workshops on writing while receiving professional development throughout the year, to programs that had little or nothing to offer in terms of learning about writing or how to teach writing. Preservice programs typically did offer language arts courses that dealt with the pedagogy of generative writing, but lacked attention to the nature of writing per se (MSU-36, 1990, 41–42).

When it came to the teaching of writing, the programs also differed in program coherence.

> The most coherent program we observed was the in-service program, where faculty agreed with one another and espoused a coherent, interrelated set of ideas about writing and teaching writing. This program view included the belief that writing should communicate to an audience for a particular purpose; that writing is a process of drafting, revision, editing and publishing; and that classrooms

should be structured to facilitate writing for real purposes
and audiences through the use of writing conferences
with the teacher and with peers. (41–42)

None of the other programs had this degree of coherence although
several others gave some emphasis to this same approach.
Programs that took a generic approach to teaching without regard
for differences in subject matter gave no attention specific to the
teaching of writing.

To investigate these differences, the TELT study collected data
on the various aspects of what teachers need to know to teach
writing. In an interview, respondents had to tell how they would
respond to a student text with errors (MSU-36, 1990). They were
asked simply: "How would you respond to this piece of student
writing [uncorrected for errors]?"

Dophins are really not fish. Other fish have
gill to breath in air and blow out again.
Dophins are like other big, big water animals they
at other small water animal
The ocen is the only place that Dophins can live.
The reason that the Dophins can only live in the ocen is
          because the Dophins have to live in salt water. Dophins
          are somewhat relaled to sharks and whales. There are
          only one kind of Dophins. There are very few places that
          have Dophins. Matter of fact there are only two places
          that have dophins.
The two places that have Dophins are the coast of Maine and
          Alaska are the only two places that have Dophins. The
          Dophins can weigh up to three tons. In 1963 a man was
          killed by a Dophin.
The Dophins name was Julie. The way they tell is the markins
          on the Dophins tale. (Kennedy, 1998, fig. 5.1, 112; cf.
          slight variation in wording in MSU-37, 1991)

In responding to this text, the interviewees had to say what they
thought was most needed to improve the text and were judged on

whether they were open to students having their own perspective as opposed to just satisfying the teacher. This task showed that the prospective teachers in general were not ready to give up the prescriptive approach they had learned in previous schooling in order to give the students more responsibility for what they write (MSU-37, 1991, 40).

Differences between programs in the teaching of writing made for a difference in outcomes. The teachers in traditional management-oriented programs became even more concerned about prescriptions by the end of their program than they had been at the start, while teachers in reform-oriented programs became less concerned about prescriptions and instead put more emphasis on student strategies and purposes. Even when programs had a strong, coherent approach to writing and the teaching of writing, the implementation of this reform in changes to classroom practice proved difficult (Kennedy, 1998, 21; MSU-36, 1990, 43–44).

Two programs that were particularly successful in teaching writing combined a process approach to teaching writing with intensive assistance in the classroom to help students implement the approach. The study found that these two programs actually changed teachers' beliefs about writing and their approaches for how to teach writing. The interview and observation data indicated that the in-service program in particular had a high impact on teacher practices. The professional development specialists in this program emphasized a structure of mini-lessons, conferences with students, and sessions in which the purpose was to share experiences (MSU-36, 1990, 43).

Structure vs. Freedom in Learning to Write

In addition to the TELT study, research on the improvement of writing instruction for K–12 and teacher-education students continued on the MSU campus. Some of this research was qualitative and ethnographic, inspired by the seminal research of Susan Florio-Ruane and her collaborators. Some was reflective of emerging concerns in educational psychology (Raphael, Englert &

Kirschner, 1988; Raphael, Kirschner & Englert, 1988; Englert et al., 1988). It is instructive to compare the emphasis on structure in the research on expository writing produced by the latter movement with the greater freedom called for by those who championed writing workshops for K–12 students.

In resolving this tension between freedom and structure in the teaching of writing, one group of MSU researchers was primarily concerned with teaching upper-elementary and middle-school students explicitly about different text structures. Students in these grades were not likely to benefit so much from exercising their imagination and creativity in writing as had been the case in the early grades. NAEP results at the time showed that among children in the upper grades of elementary school, progress in writing tended to decline as students advanced in school. MSU researchers thought it was time for a more disciplined, proactive approach to expository writing. Two important papers at the height of the MSU revolution showed how much had been learned from research that took that perspective.

In the first of their studies, Raphael and Kirschner (1985) explored the effects of teaching students about comparison/contrast text structure. Students were given seven hours of instruction over a period of six weeks. In the first lesson, they were faced with the situation in which they had to buy a puppy. Having hypothetically gone to a pet store, they found two puppies. To learn about the comparison/contrast structure, students were asked to think of questions to ask the store owner about the two animals. Then they did two additional lessons in which they read comparison/contrast passages and discussed what was being compared.

A second study showed that this method of instruction did improve recall and produced better organized and more relevant summaries, with better use of key words and phrases. However, these student writings were judged insufficiently interesting, that is, they lacked "voice" and were not the sort of papers for which the researchers were aiming. These shortcomings were not surprising given that the assignments were artificial exercises, not tied to the purposes of the student writers.

To put their processes of expository writing into practice, the MSU researchers (Raphael, Englert, & Kirschner, 1988, 9–10) designed "think-sheets" to lead students step-by-step through the writing of an expository paper. These sheets provided questions, prompts, formats, and other guidance on how to think their way through the paper. The first think-sheet, for example, asked the authors to think about four aspects of planning a paper: subject, audience, purpose, and form. They were also asked to make clear why they were doing this writing—just saying they were doing an assignment was not an acceptable response (see also Raphael, Kirschner & Englert, 1988b).

It is important to note that even though these researchers focused on the effects of text structure on quality of writing, they were nonetheless opposed to the teacher exercising too much control over what the students wrote. Instead the teacher was responsible for encouraging independence by transferring responsibility for self-regulation to the students. As the students developed self-awareness in thinking about their purposes and the nature of the audience, they tended to talk to themselves about what they were writing. This inner dialogue of talking to oneself was regarded as especially important (Raphael, Englert & Kirschner, 1988a, 10–11).

Writing is thus a socially mediated ability that develops slowly over a long period of time and in interaction with a more mature learner. The teacher "scaffolds" learning by simplifying the task, clarifying its structure, linking subprocesses to the larger task at hand, and providing guidance with rules and procedures. Scaffolding might include questioning to bring out information the student already knows but has not brought to the task at hand. It can also mean coaching and leading a discussion with a student who is otherwise unable to bring a critical perspective to his or her writing. The overall idea is to get the novice to gradually internalize these rules, procedures, and guidance until instruction is no longer needed (Raphael, Kirschner & Englert, 1988, 793).

The students in this experiment were given assignments in both fall and spring to write a paper comparing and contrasting two people, places, or things. They were supposed to convey information they considered important and interesting to an audience consisting of the student's best friend. Here are two examples of what students produced. Matthew, the author of the first piece, had not received any instruction on text structure. Note that the piece is copied here without correction of errors.

> Mcdonalds is a big place it even has a playground for the kids. That's probably why the kids gobble up their food and run outside. The father gets up grab the kid by the hair and says were are you going? He say swallow your food. So theirs a point that Mcdonald is a good place for the kids. Well the only thing I like is the bag mac and the strawberry shake. The other place I'm comparing is burgerking. Burgerking is a place that has the whopper. That's what I like. The end. (Raphael, Kirschner & Englert, 1988a, 13)

Although Matthew tried to compare these two restaurants, he did not do it very well. The beginning of his piece tells about the effect of the playground at McDonald's on the behavior of the children and their father. But when writing about the second restaurant, Matthew fails to stick with parallel characteristics. He mentions his favorite food at both restaurants, but does not make the comparison explicit.

The second paper is by a student who has been taught about text structures. It also compares two restaurants:

> I am going to compare and contrast Burger King and McDonalds. The first thing I'm going to compare/contrast them on is there service. These two restaurants are similar in many ways. One is the checkers are very nice. They always say have a nice day. But there also different. Burger King has propted [prompter] service. It takes them about a minute to get my food ready but at Mcdonalds it took them 30 minutes to get my food ready. The second thing I'm going to compare and contrast them on is there food selection. There selection is alike in many ways. One is they both have breakfast, lunch, dinner selection and they

both have a wide selection but Burger King has a wider selection than Mcdonalds. (14)

This paper is much more explicit about comparison. The author selects characteristics to compare. His reliance on text structure resulted in his being better able to organize and convey information in writing.

Freedom in Writing Workshops, Promise and Peril?

The writing workshop is another approach to the teaching of writing. In her work at the Elliott PDS, MSU faculty member and researcher Cheryl Rosaen discusses her research on writing workshops in two key papers. One was coauthored with Elliott K–12 teacher Barbara Lindquist who collaborated with Rosaen in creating and using writing workshops over the course of a whole year for a class of forty-seven fifth-grade students. The other paper, coauthored with Kathleen Roth, contrasted two approaches to the teaching of writing, one using writing workshops taught by Rosaen and Lindquist and another in which Roth herself taught writing using the content of a particular subject-matter—in this case science (Rosaen & Lindquist, 1992; Roth & Rosaen, 1995).

The teacher's responsibility in writing workshops is to create a setting for students to write regularly, share this writing with others, get feedback and help in revision, and celebrate finished work. These workshops are based on the assumption that students will take ownership of these tasks only if they get to make the same decisions that accomplished writers make, that is, by choosing their own topics, purposes, forms, audience, and time frames for crafting and publishing their work. In this setting, writers learn from practice and become proficient by exercising control over writing decisions. The teacher's role is limited to helping students learn how to manage the writing process and to improve what they have written, mainly through writing conferences, opportunities to share what they write, and mini-lessons to address specific challenges. The writing takes a variety of forms, including journal writing, personal narratives, fiction, poetry, biographies, memoirs, and letters. In all cases, the teacher's assistance is focused on helping the authors realize their own intentions instead of depending too much on others for guidance on what and how to write (Roth & Rosaen, 1995, 298).

In reporting on their experience with a writers' workshop, Rosaen and Lindquist started the project with a rough idea of what they wanted to do and then reworked the image as they went along in order to put it into practice. Doing that took a lot of time and patience. The two teachers moved cautiously, experimenting with different ways for the students to realize their own intentions. Both teachers spent hours exploring literature to find models to work with and to learn what they needed to know to inspire young writers. They kept in mind the requirements of the overall curriculum, especially in social studies, as well as what they needed to do to get students engaged in writing about the issues they encountered in other subject matters and to think about the audience for their writing.

As their analysis and observation continued, the teachers settled on multiple aspects of student writing to assess, such as "ownership and commitment to writing tasks, using a variety of resources in writing projects, asking questions to clarify thinking, participating in a variety of activities to stimulate thinking, engaging in purposeful editing, engaging in writing as an on-going process, increasing control over multiple aspects of the writing process" (Rosaen & Lindquist, 1992, 21–24).

Rosaen and Lindquist selected seventeen target students (from forty-seven in the class) to monitor more closely across the year. As they analyzed student written work, interviews, and class participation, they discussed critical points at which the development of students as writers changed dramatically. At these points, the students either suddenly became aware of their beliefs and assumptions about what it means to be a writer or they changed what they did as writers. One such incident occurred when, three months into the workshop, Billy, a "school-smart kid," was still having trouble thinking up topics on his own. But one day, since he especially liked adventure stories, Rosaen suggested he write one. At first Billy thought he couldn't, but later that same day he said, "I'm ready to become an adventure writer now." He went on to write the story and "published" it for the school library (37–38).

On another occasion Rosaen wrote about a satisfying writing conference with a student, discussing what had happened at the conference, why she said what she did, and whether her actions had been appropriate:

> I sat down with a kid named Casey, who I think has written nothing yet that he's invested in. . . . [He just been think-ing,] blah, "I'll write anything down." [and] not having any fun. So today he was looking at this pop-up haunted house book that I had brought in for a lesson with the haunted house writing and he said, "Can I make a pop- up book like this." . . . So I said, "Well, let's look at the writing on the page and what it means to write a book like this." So I had him do a couple of the pages and we talked about what's at the bottom and so forth, and how he could make a dummy copy of the book first and plan out what would be on the next page and what would be at the bottom and then start making his book. Now I think he finally has a piece that he's working on that he might really care about. (29–30, citing an interview by Rosaen)

Over time, the two teachers shifted from prescribing what to do during the whole writing time, that is, from deciding what and when to write or discuss, to just giving mini-lessons on various topics like poetry to help students make their own decisions. The writing conferences also changed from just checking on whether students were keeping up with assignments and spelling out what they needed to do to the more difficult teaching task of helping students make good on their own goals for writing. The more structured units had served to clarify and support particular aspects of writing, but they had also limited the decisions that students were allowed to make. As a result, when students took more control, they became more enthusiastic about writing. But they still didn't want to pay close attention to the quality of their writing. According to the teachers, "we were almost too successful. We ran into resistance to our instructional input and support. They didn't want mini-lessons. They wanted to 'write, write, write.' Didn't worry about quality, just ginned out page after page of unrevised text" (14–15, 31, 35).

Once the year was over, Rosaen and Lindquist summed up what they had learned about imposing structure versus letting go:

> When should teachers take an active role in facilitating the way group norms develop and when should they stand back and wait for naturally occurring opportunities to reflect with their students about the way people interact? We do not think there are clear-cut answers to these questions either. During the initiation phase of our curriculum, for example, we could see that some students began to flourish immediately in a more open environment while others floundered over how to use their new rights and responsibilities productively. We debated as to how much we should "interfere" in the naturally occurring process as students encountered new ways to interact about their writing.
>
> . . . As the year progressed we . . . noticed that some students did not follow through on the revision ideas we discussed the day before in a writing conference; that they were not necessarily motivated to improve their pieces, especially when their friend's piece did not require further attention and theirs did. (36–37)

As Rosaen worked on developing the knowledge and skills she needed in teaching a writers' workshop with fifth graders, she noticed that it influenced the way she approached planning and teaching her language arts methods course at the university. She noted, for example, that a university requirement of giving the preservice students a course syllabus with assignments, grading procedures, and readings already chosen in advance worked against developing the norms these students needed to promote with children in elementary classrooms. Rosaen was beginning to think of her preservice students as developing writers as well as developing teachers.

Timothy Lensmire's doctoral dissertation at MSU dealt with his own practice in teaching writing workshops (Lensmire, 1991). The book he wrote afterward, *Powerful Writing, Responsible Teaching*, brought many new insights to the attention of scholars and practitioners (Lensmire, 2000). Even though Lensmire's experience in designing and conducting writing workshops was with very young children in third grade when they might be thought to need much guidance, he went much further than Rosaen and Lindquist in stressing the need for freedom for young authors. And then as if this were not provocative enough, he framed this experience in the distinctive context of his passionate interest in the literary traditions of Russia and eastern Europe—a far cry from what the students were writing. One reason for this apparently exotic approach was to counter what Lensmire found too prosaic and pragmatic in writing workshops as typically practiced with children and to emphasize aspects, both positive and negative, of writing workshops that in his opinion had not been given enough attention before. He compared writing workshops to the fanciful atmosphere of medieval carnivals in the work of Mikhail Bakhtin and described the teacher metaphorically as a Dostoevskian novelist who creates a novel in the form of a classroom.

For Lensmire, featuring the workshop teacher as novelist makes clear how much power teachers retain in spite of the freedom given students to create their own narratives. "Rather than being antithetical to student freedom, teacher power is necessary to assure it." Novelists in general have the power to create and control their characters, and to write them "into roles within a larger creative design that determines who they are, how they act, what they will be." These roles are different from those offered in traditional classrooms. In writing workshops, the students exert control over the topics, purposes, audiences, and processes of the writing they choose to do. They do not, however, escape from or transcend the teacher-as-novelist's plan, nor are they really free of the larger context of schooling. Student freedom, such as it is, is part of the plan put in place by a teacher exercising power even though the power may be "pursued with different means and toward a different end" (32–33, 47–48).

Lensmire is no Pollyanna. He describes a case in which students decide to use their writing to make textual attacks on other students. Should teachers who see their task as just assisting students to improve how they write therefore help students with hateful or hostile writing to make their attacks more effective? (48).

Even though the opportunity to conference and share their work with classmates was positive for Lensmire's third graders, it created problems when children were choosy about their associates, working only with their friends and enforcing gender boundaries. Children also put differentiation and hierarchy in their stories. The result was that, as Lensmire was quick to admit, while he tried to make the workshop a safe place for all his students, the context that freed them to pursue their own interests can produce "denials of development, culture, and power, it may actually trap students in history, rather than help them struggle with and against it" (50).

Lensmire's analysis shows that teaching in a writing workshop is far harder than often thought: "As we make workshops into sites of serious moral and political deliberation—as teacher and student questions and reflections focus attention (and sometimes criticism) on meanings and values held dear by workshop participants—the work of the writing workshop becomes more meaningful and more difficult, riskier." These difficulties and risks cannot just be left to students to resolve in a show of respect for the freedom they have been allowed. Workshop teachers have to use their power and responsibility on behalf of the students (53).

Toward the end of the chapter on teacher as novelist, Lensmire admits to doubts about his Dostoevskian analogy: the teacher may be a novelist, but are the students really Dostoevskian characters? "I am undecided as to how well Dostoevsky's characters listen to and learn from one another. . . . If Dostoevsky's characters don't listen well and don't learn much, then they are not great examples of our hopes for students" (52). This realization leads Lensmire in his next chapter to develop an alternative conception of student voice.

Conclusion

Changes in the teaching of writing, it could be argued, were the revolution's most remarkable subject-matter achievement. MSU scholars and their K–12 collaborators took a neglected area of student learning where students, if they learned anything, were being taught grammar, punctuation, and language usage, but not how to write. It was an area without regular subject-matter status, without developed curricula, materials, pedagogy, and so on. The revolution brought it into the open with new understandings of what was involved, why it was so difficult to teach writing, why it became harder for teachers with more experience, how well different approaches worked, and in general, how much structure to impose and how much freedom to allow as students learned to write. The overriding question was to what extent students would become authentic authors, making their own decisions about topics, purpose, audience, genre, etc. During the revolutionary era, all this was investigated and elucidated in contrasting forms and ways. Students were learning to write with considerable autonomy in exercising freedom over what they wrote while becoming increasingly aware of and able to confront constraints, obstacles, dilemmas, and injustices over which they had but limited control.

What Was So Revolutionary about All This?

The focus of Part 3 is to demonstrate what was so revolutionary about not only what was accomplished in regard to teaching and teacher education at Michigan State University (MSU), but also what was attempted but not accomplished. It aims to show that the metaphor of revolution is not as overblown as one might suspect. While what was written during this period did not always sound revolutionary from the way that, for example, standards were discussed or a new jargon was used, there are many documents that make clear how much was innovative and unprecedented.

Common to all aspects of this attempted revolutionary change was a trend in which the responsibilities of teacher educators, their students, and cooperating K–12 teachers became less a matter of individualistic assumptions, premises, ideas, approaches, and responsibilities and more a matter of explicit collective decision-making than they had been. Change meant taking less for granted as nonproblematic, with more insistence on teacher educators and other responsible authorities reaching agreement on what preservice students are expected to learn, what learning opportunities are required to achieve this learning, what teacher educators themselves are expected and required to do, and the implications of all this for the involvement of K–12 schools and practicing teachers. As long as taking so much for granted was more prevalent, it had largely been the responsibility of individual students on their own, with little guidance, to draw together (and in part disregard) the strands of what they learned in subject-matter courses, pedagogy courses, foundation courses, and field experience. To be sure, much was still left outside the explicit domain, as Forzani's (2011) thesis has shown, but enough had been done to give credibility to the revolutionary nature of what was attempted as well as to bolster MSU's claim to exceptionalism.

The following chapters examine the arguments and the achievements that became the basis for this claim to exceptionalism. During the revolution, there was a shift from a behaviorist perspective on teaching and teacher education to a much more ambitious emphasis on teacher cognition and judgment, and the belief that teachers could not be simply trained in the usual sense of the word but had to develop the judgment to recognize and deal with the intellectual challenges of the moment in teaching. Doing this together, collectively and not just as a matter of individual teacher choice and action, was also crucial. Relations between K–12 schools and university schools of education would have to be transformed through the creation of professional development schools capable of putting into practice visions of improved teaching and learning outcomes for both pupils and preservice teachers). Under these conditions the understanding of what K–12 teachers, university teacher educators, and researchers could be expected to do would radically change with a blending of these roles in this new era of school–university relations. Changes in teaching would be justified and made possible, in part, by discoveries of what pupils think about their experiences and challenges, creating individual bodies of ideas, explanations, and conclusions of which their teachers were often totally unaware. Becoming aware and knowledgeable of such revolutionary developments made it clear that better mentoring of all those who were new to their roles in this system would be required. Mentoring could no longer be taken for granted by assuming that good teachers necessarily make good mentors. As knowledge of these revolutionary developments became more and more critical for all those in the system, the position of those who claimed that subject-matter knowledge alone could be sufficient preparation for teaching, a position that had never been strong at MSU, was further undermined. Under the influence of Lee Shulman, the opposition between subject matter and content could be shown to be a false dichotomy, recognizing that more advanced forms of subject-matter knowledge would necessarily include knowledge of pedagogy as well. The use of instructional materials and technology were also not much investigated as long as teacher-education students were left to learn so much on their own, making choices among available resources and technology without much preparation or guidance. But gradually, explicit research and preparation in the use of these resources took a more prominent place in the revolutionary agenda, and technology tools were developed to allow more in-depth investigation of teaching practice outside as well as inside the K–12 classroom. Finally, a new source of revolutionary intent emerged in Ann Arbor, the development of a practice-based curriculum of teacher education, tempering the judgment-based approach that had been so dominant at MSU.

CHAPTER ELEVEN

Teaching as Intellectual Challenge and a Matter of Professional Judgment

The revolutionary change in thinking about what elementary and secondary school teaching entails was not unique to MSU. It is dealt with extensively in the literature, where it is discussed as the "cognitive shift" away from a behavioristic approach based on behavioral objectives, competencies, and the like. During the period most influenced by the famous behaviorist B. F. Skinner and behaviorist psychology, the thinking of teachers was not regarded as a legitimate field of inquiry. Talk of thinking was taboo as far as serving as a vehicle of scientific inquiry for such purposes as the improvement of teaching and learning. But as cognitive science began to challenge the hold of behaviorism on such issues, this new trend was soon influencing research on teaching and teacher education. It was a trend firmly implanted at MSU upon the establishment of the Institute for Research on Teaching (IRT) in 1975. Shulman himself pronounced the death of behaviorism in educational research as follows: "The traditional behaviorism is nearly dead in psychology because of its theoretical and methodological limitations, and educational researchers might as well pull the plug on its respirator in our own field" (Shulman, 1974, 110).

In a 1988 essay he added:

> I am increasingly aware of the fact that the work we did in TAP [Teacher Assessment Project at Stanford] and the ways in which the teaching portfolio evolved there are really part of a continuing critique of theories of teaching. For me this critique first found concrete formulation in the creation of the Institute for Research on Teaching at Michigan State University. In 1975, when we created

the Institute, we designed it as a powerful argument against the prevailing views of teaching as skilled behavior—the process-product conception of teaching that clearly reigned at that time. We argued that teaching was a form of thought and judgment, that it was the act of an autonomous agent engaged in creating opportunities for students and adapting all kinds of goals and materials to the conditions of the moment and the students being taught. Therefore, we contended, an utterly new paradigm of research was needed for studying teaching, one that was much more cognitive and much more focused on the ideographic components of teaching, uniquely local. (Shulman, 1988/2004, 385)

It is easy to say that teaching is complicated intellectual work, but for people who are disinclined to believe this, it is hard to convince them that this can be true. A shift in teaching was needed from the more straightforward, clearcut aims of a behavioral perspective to the emphasis on teacher thinking, judgment, dilemmas, etc. Specific examples of this can be drawn from the work of MSU faculty and affiliated K–12 teachers who took this seriously and whose grappling with challenging intellectual issues is a documented part of their teaching. At the heart of this MSU revolution was an unrelenting attack on the myths that led people to believe that K–12 (especially elementary school) teaching was relatively easy to learn, an unchallenging career compared to other careers like law and medicine.

Teaching Is Impossible, the Most Complex of Human Activities

From Dewey's perspective, teaching was said to be "complicated intellectual work"—even impossible in some ways to exercise with complete confidence and mastery. In 1983 Lee Shulman wrote: "Teaching is impossible. If we simply add together all that is expected of a typical teacher and take note of the circumstances under which those activities are to be carried out, the sum makes greater demands than any individual can possibly fulfill" (Shulman, 1983/2004, 151).

Earlier research to answer the question, "What should teachers be able to do?" had reinforced the opposing and misleading impression that teaching is relatively straightforward. From this perspective teaching was understood as technical problem-solving in which teachers applied known methods to accomplish predetermined goals. In other words, teaching was a matter of planning lessons, arranging the classroom environment, presenting content. But the picture that emerged from actual classroom research during the period in question was very different. Classrooms were seen as complex, unpredictable, and multidimensional (Feiman-Nemser & Remillard, 1995, 17).

It was therefore up to teacher-education programs to debunk these prevalent myths and misconceptions about learning to teach being relatively easy and straightforward. Feiman-Nemser and Remillard (1995) called on teacher educators to question and test such commonsense theories as "Anyone can teach," "If you know your subject, you can teach it," "Teachers are born, not made," and "Everything you need to know about teaching can be learned on the job." Research does not support these views, and yet prospective and practicing teachers have not been inclined to challenge them.

Later in his 1997/2004 essay, Shulman asserted:

> The more time I spend in classrooms with teachers—talking with them, observing, watching videotapes, talking some more, reflecting on my own teaching—the more I peel off layer upon layer of incredible complexity. After some 30 years of doing such work, I have concluded that classroom teaching—particularly at the elementary and secondary levels—is perhaps the most complex, most challenging, and most demanding, subtle, nuanced and frightening activity that our species has ever invented. In fact, when I compared the complexity of teaching with that of a much more highly rewarded profession, "doing medicine," I concluded that the only time medicine even approaches

the complexity of an average day of classroom teaching is in an emergency room during a national disaster. (504)

Navigating the Complexities of Teaching

According to the Teacher Education and Learning to Teach (TELT) study, teachers at all stages of their careers were not inclined to value research challenging their beliefs. When asked how helpful a number of listed activities would be in learning to teach, the highest percentage in all groups of teachers was for "gaining more teaching experience." Moreover, the closer other activities were to actual teaching, the more they were valued by teachers at all levels (MSU-37, 1991, 70).

Experience was valued, in part, due to the belief that "since there is no one best way of teaching, you have to find what works for you." About 75 percent of all teachers in the National Center for Research on Teacher Education (NCRTE) TELT study at every career stage agreed with that statement. This revealing finding can be understood in three ways, all of which are plausible and not mutually exclusive. One is that this finding demonstrates the strongly individualistic nature of teaching in U.S. culture in contrast to other countries that put more emphasis on uniformity of practice. Second, the respondents could have been stressing the context-specific nature of teaching and the fact that what the teacher confronts in any one situation may differ from what generalized prescriptions may call for. And third, the statement gives teachers a reason to oppose general standards of good teaching even if adopted by public authorities or professional communities (71).

Research has also shown that the beliefs of prospective teachers about teaching are contradictory in some respects. For example, on the one hand, prospective teachers generally believe that they should be fair to all students, and that this means they should treat all students the same. But at the same time, they claim that each child is unique and deserves a school experience tailored to his or her particular needs. This tension between treating students as individuals and treating all students alike constitutes a major obstacle to dealing appropriately with race, social class, or other social inequities especially when limited experience and exposure to stereotypes influence what prospective teachers think of different groups. In one study, the researchers found that many preservice students did rely on ethnic or cultural stereotypes in judging their students' behavior and in adjusting their expectations as a result (Kennedy, 1991, 15).

The programs studied in TELT did try to enhance the understanding that prospective teachers have of learners different from themselves. But these attempts often proved counterproductive. These programs offered courses that consisted only in transmission of knowledge about what students from different cultures are like, how diverse students learn, and what alternative pedagogies can be used in such cases. But the views of prospective teachers rarely changed after taking these courses, they continued to assume that all students would respond to school subjects in the same way that they and their peers had done in their own K–12 years. The TELT researchers concluded that instead of just giving prospective teachers knowledge of other cultures, these prospective teachers had to come to understand the limitations of their own life experiences, to realize that not all students are as ready or unready, willing or unwilling to participate actively in class as they had been (14).

As understood at MSU, therefore, teaching calls for careful balancing of multiple concerns about understanding of subject matter, diverse learners, and the teacher role in facilitating learning. Teachers are responsible, in particular situations, for interpreting classroom events as they occur, making sound pedagogical decisions, and judging the outcomes of these decisions. They have to get off-task students back on track, redirect students heading in the wrong direction, and so forth. There are no fixed rules on how to do this (17).

It is by weighing the *momentary* importance of their many intentions that teachers construct their practices. At any given moment, one intention may become a more prominent concern in the teacher's reasoning. Across different situations, different patterns of intentions will emerge, and across time, different intentions may become more or less important in general. Often teachers criticized their decisions upon viewing the videotape, for the viewing allowed them to see things differently than they had appeared at the time. . . . Teachers frequently face conflicting intentions, so that they are forced to choose which will take precedence in a given situation. (Kennedy, 2005, ch. 2, e-book)

Even when teachers appeared to have a good grasp of the content, they were still frequently nonplussed by students' unexpected ideas. . . . There were also many whose understanding of both subject matter and students' understanding of the subject matter appeared to be quite elaborated, and yet they were stymied about how to respond adequately to students' enthusiastic but off-script ideas. One lesson for reformers might be to provide professional development that addresses ways of responding when students produce unexpected ideas. This is a nuts-and-bolts problem that teachers routinely face but that tends to get relatively little attention in reform literature. (ch. 9, e-book)

In a well-known study Lampert (1985) argued that teachers never get to solve teaching problems in any definitive sense, but instead navigate among competing goals and make moment-to-moment decisions about what to do in particular situations. The role of teacher educators is to help prospective and novice teachers learn how to think on their feet and to respond adequately to an ever-changing classroom situation.

Learning from the Study of History

Although not shared by all the advocates of the revolution, the development and elaboration of an understanding of teaching as an intellectual challenge became a priority and the focus of much research and program development at MSU. This development took the position that a liberal education, including a wide range of disciplines and the history of ideas, could do much to inform the theories and the practice of clinical judgment by teachers, teacher educators, and researchers. However in 1989, McDiarmid suggested that not much was known about what prospective teachers learn from the study of liberal arts and what had become known was not very encouraging:

> Students' encounters with the disciplines in liberal arts courses help shape their notions about the nature of the subject matter, their disposition to think about and find out more about ideas in a given field, as well as their concepts of how a given topic is best taught and learned. Imagine the difference between prospective teachers who experience history as an argument about what happened in the past and why, and those who encounter history as what is represented in a textbook. And yet, with [few exceptions], researchers tend to ignore what college students construct of the knowledge they encounter, focusing instead on . . . instructional issues, such as the relative advantages of lecture or discussion approaches to teaching. . . . As a result, far too little is known about what prospective teachers learn from their college study of specific disciplines. (5–6)

In this vein, MSU historian Vinten-Johansen and McDiarmid did a further study of whether having to write historical narratives influenced student understandings of history. In a history seminar intended to get students to go through various phases of research and writing systematically, these authors encountered an unexpected paradox. Orally, students did develop better skills for analyzing primary and secondary sources. This included identifying the thesis of an author, the structure of arguments made, and associated flaws. The students also acquired increased understanding of the habits of mind and methods used by historians (1997, 36). According to the authors, "When speaking, students are much more willing to take intellectual risks such as spinning out nascent theories or explanations, more adept at mustering support for their theories, and more analytical about the ideas and interpretations of others" (39). But, surprisingly, they did not put these capabilities to use in their written narratives. "Once they had formulated initial thesis statements, most seemed unwilling to do what good historians and detectives must do: step back from each draft, assess it critically and dispassionately, and, if necessary, rethink their 'case' and supporting evidence" (36). Instead they reverted to their earlier habits for writing term papers with the least fuss and bother. Their goal was simply to get the paper done, not to incorporate the insights acquired in class. According to Vinten-Johansen and McDiarmid, instructors faced with this dilemma would do well to find other ways to capitalize on the more sophisticated abilities that the students demonstrated when engaged in classroom discourse.

The Wisdom of Practice, Facing Up
to Its Neglect in Research

Among other things, the trend toward study of the complexities of teaching resulted in newfound respect for the knowledge that practicing teachers had gained in the classroom, as contrasted with the knowledge brought to teaching by formal research and highly regarded outside experts. The MSU revolution took the position that competent, experienced teachers had valuable knowledge needed to improve education that researchers outside the classroom could not be expected to know. It therefore became important to distinguish between researcher thinking and teacher thinking, and to value both. The phrase "wisdom of practice" came into vogue to characterize the knowhow and expertise of teachers. Judy Lanier in her speech at the second national Holmes Group meeting in January 1988 explained this development in these terms:

Certainly, a robust basic research effort is necessary to
create fundamentally new insights and understandings.
But a substantial new effort to examine educational practice through the eyes of the intelligent, reflective practitioner and to carry out disciplined inquiry from this point
of view is also required. Expert teachers know a great deal
that researchers do not know, but much of their knowledge is simply not codified and therefore goes untapped.

In light of this realization, practicing teachers were hired to work
on research in the IRT, bought out half-time from their K–12
teaching duties.

This valuing of the wisdom of practice actually goes back *before*
the emergence of cognitive science and the rise of research on
teacher thinking. As Lee Shulman (1990/2004) pointed out, its roots
are in the Aristotelian distinction between theory and practice. In
exploring this distinction at MSU, Shulman drew on his own roots
in the strong Aristotelian influence at the University of Chicago
where he got his undergraduate and PhD degrees. Shulman owed
much to the famous University of Chicago professor of science
and education Joe Schwab who as a visiting professor was highly
influential in the development of the IRT. According to Shulman,
"this extraordinary scholar and pedagogue shaped those he taught
in a profound and unforgettable manner. He was . . . a Deweyan in
the Aristotelian and Thomistic environment which existed in parts
of the University of Chicago when Robert Hutchins was president"
(Shulman, 1991/2004, 453).

In discussing the importance of the distinction between theory
and practice and the different understandings that researchers and
teachers bring to this distinction, Shulman explained:

One of the reasons that judgment is such an essential
component of clinical work is because theoretical knowledge is generally knowledge of what is true universally. It
is true in general and for the most part. It is knowledge
of regularities and of patterns. It is an invaluable simpli-
fication of a world whose many variations would be far

too burdensome to store in memory with all its detail and individuality. Yet the world of practice is beset by just those particularities, born of the workings of chance. To put it in Aristotelian terms, theories are about *essence*, practice is about *accident*, and the only way to get from there to here is via the exercise of *judgment*. (Shulman, 1998/2004, 534)

Did Suzanne Teach Today?

Suzanne Wilson, one of Shulman's PhD students at Stanford who became an MSU professor, provides her own vivid illustrations of the uncertainty and the nearly ineffable difficulties of teaching. In her essay in a book about the introductory course required of all teacher-education students at MSU, she discusses the variation in her pedagogy: "Sometimes I do a lot of talking, sometimes I am but one voice among many, sometimes I say nothing at all" (Wilson, 1992, 131).

> Whatever the lesson, whatever I teach, uppermost in my mind is making students think hard about teaching: how and why and when it works, what it means, who is in control. One of the ways I try to get inside those ideas is to sometimes end class with a question, "Did Suzanne teach today?" (138)

The answers are diverse and reflect the students' ingrained beliefs that teaching is telling, so how could Wilson be teaching when she did not say anything and even avoided taking a position.

> They know it's a trick. On days when I have the strongest voice, the answer is clear. Of course I taught. On days when we see videotapes and answer questions in small groups, I probably taught because I provided the videotapes and the questions. On the days I am mute, there's

> less agreement. . . . They know I'm the official instructor of
> the course, the university says so. Does that make me the
> teacher? . . . Did teaching go on because there was learn-
> ing? But they wrote nothing in their notebooks. What
> exactly did they learn? (138)

Rosemary, one of Wilson's students, struck a chord by writing
about her experience as a child learning the twenty-third psalm
by heart, but not understanding what it meant, and concludes
that her understanding of teaching is similar in being familiar at
the surface but without understanding what is underneath. But,
Wilson cautions, this is only a beginning (144).

> Sometimes I get depressed when I realize that I'm moving
> on to another group, another overgrown garden that I
> have 10 weeks to prune and weed and water. Who is going
> to continue to help my Joes and Rosemarys think about
> their assumptions? One term is little time in comparison
> to a lifetime of pedestrian teaching and a future in schools
> that leave little room for the creative and critical think-
> ing that good teaching requires. I'm worried too about
> the liberal arts and sciences classes (as well as some of the
> teacher education courses) that my students are going to
> take in which instructors often model teaching that reaf-
> firms all of the assumptions they have built up over their
> years of school experience. (145)

Seven Years of Struggle to Change Teaching

Sharon Schwille's study (2016) focused on one teacher (known as
Courtney in the thesis) who confronted challenges in teaching
that she found nearly impossible to meet. This book reveals that
she struggled for seven years before she succeeded in changing her
teaching from a teacher-centered, knowledge-transmission model
to an approach where students assumed more responsibility for

their learning. Initially, this new approach was unfamiliar, strange, and difficult for the educators and students at her school.

According to Courtney, "'We found we could talk about learning community and cooperative groups . . . but we didn't get it. . . . It didn't feel right. . . . It was very uncomfortable'" (14). Only at the end of these years of struggle did Courtney realize there was no end to learning how to teach. Once she understood that teaching is complex intellectual work, she knew she would "always be a learner, always striving to change her practice some way or other" (23).

The alternative programs of the 1980s and the subsequent five-year program considered teaching as an intellectual challenge for which rote learning, recipes for what teachers should do, and field experience without close mentoring were problematic. Team One in the five-year program characterized this change of perspective and how it came about in this way:

> Immersed for many decades in the difficult work of teacher preparation, we have learned that helping prospective teachers develop sophisticated understandings of subject-matter, students' thinking, and the creation and management of classroom learning communities—the whole complex package—is hard, intellectually demanding work. We know that all too often we fail to accomplish all of our goals for our students. (Carroll et al., 2007b, 1)

Revolutionary Leaders and Their Views on Teaching and Teacher Education

During its revolutionary years, MSU was fortunate in finding faculty and doctoral students with interests and skills to carry out the difficult changes. Lee Shulman, while still at MSU (until 1983), played a role analogous to the philosophers of the French Enlightenment in the eighteenth century who prepared the way for the French Revolution. He drew widely, as discussed above, on intellectual history while synthesizing such ideas with an emerging research agenda and his own consummate mastery of teaching. For Shulman, ideas about the wisdom of practice were a natural extension of his earlier research on clinical diagnosis and decision-making in medicine, which had been applied to medical education (Shulman, 1987/2004a).

Judy Lanier, the main instigator of the revolution, for her part, filled a role that brings to mind the image of a revolutionary commander organizing her troops to scale the ramparts and break through the defenses of the status quo. She brought to the revolution her acute ideas about the failures and shortcomings of existing teacher education while progressively inventing organizational vehicles to clear the field for radical reform. She strongly advocated a view of teaching that emphasized its intellectual challenges and the need to develop teacher judgment. For example, in a speech titled "Changing What We Teach and How We Teach It," she took note of how difficult this was to put into practice:

> I think schools do not cast teaching as intellectual work. The way most schools currently structure teachers' work runs counter to what you're asking them to do for others. When you seek to move to the new pedagogy and the new learning for understanding, it becomes an even greater problem.

In her later address to the second national meeting of the Holmes Group, January 29–31, 1988, she had still more to say about this challenge:

> We do not yet know everything about how to provide clinical education that is richly intellectual as well as genuinely practical, but we do know some things. We know more and more about mentorship in teacher education, and what we know holds promise for tapping the knowledge of our best experienced teachers and providing new teachers with access to it. . . . And we are finding out more about other dimensions of teacher education as we in the Holmes institutions make the education of teachers a field

of serious intellectual endeavor rather than a cash cow providing resources to underwrite the costs of serious intellectual endeavor elsewhere in the university.

Sharon Feiman-Nemser was another scholar who played a big role in shaping the revolution. When she was recruited to come to MSU from the University of Chicago in 1981, she fit neatly into a niche between Shulman and Lanier. Although the latter two did much to adapt MSU thinking and practice to the cognitive shift and corollary developments, the person with the most influence on what this meant for teacher education was Feiman-Nemser. Like Shulman, she had knowledge and a deep appreciation of relevant intellectual history. She was, in fact, the most devoted Deweyan of the revolutionary vanguard:

> For me, Dewey's essay [on theory and practice] was a raft in the sea of competency-based teacher education. It offered a view of teachers as practical intellectuals, students of subject matter and children's thinking who learn from experience, including their own experience as learners. It underscored a vision of liberal/professional TE that contrasted sharply with the narrow, technical views of teaching and teacher training associated with competency-based teacher education. (Feiman-Nemser 2012, 12)

As the last quotation suggests, in spite of Feiman-Nemser's strongly intellectual bent, her thinking also focused pragmatically on the specific practices and programs of teacher education, building in new ways on the foundations laid by Shulman and others. It was her conceptualizations that captured big ideas about teacher education and embodied them in a language that she and others could use to institute radically different practices and organization as well as perspectives (see Feiman-Nemser, 1983/2012, 1990/2012). The terms that she invested with new meaning, including for example "teacher learning" and "guided practice," were a response to limitations and misconceptions in the way people generally thought about and used the term "teacher education."

In rethinking teacher education, Feiman-Nemser had a perfectionistic tendency to revisit, agonize over, and continue to refine ideas in ways that initially made it difficult for her to get her exceptional ideas and original insights into print. But in her early years at MSU, she solved this problem by forging mutually beneficial and productive partnerships with Bob Floden and Margret Buchmann (e.g., Feiman-Nemser & Buchmann, 1985/2012, 1986/2012, 1987/2012; Feiman-Nemser & Floden, 1980, 1981, 1986; Floden & Feiman-Nemser, 1981).

Floden earned his bachelor's degree in philosophy with honors from Princeton, his master's in statistics from Stanford, and his PhD in philosophy of education and evaluation from Stanford in the mid-1970s, after which he came immediately to MSU as senior researcher in the newly established IRT. He has been with the university ever since. His exceptionally lucid and insightful mind, background in philosophy and statistics, ability to quickly master the latest trends in educational research, and facility in writing enabled him to collaborate effectively in getting many ideas of his collaborators as well as himself published in ways capable of influencing the national discourse. He proved exceedingly loyal to the college and became one of its top leaders and contributors to its national reputation from the 1980s on to his service as dean of the college from 2016 to 2021.

Margret Buchmann also completed her PhD at Stanford, working with Denis Phillips, a philosopher of education who encouraged her continued study in the general history of thought, which led her to do a dissertation on Hegel. When she arrived at MSU in 1977 as the German-born-and-raised spouse of Floden, she had no experience as an elementary or secondary teacher, no immersion of any kind in K–12 American education, and no record of achievement in teacher education. But to my mind, she was the best-educated faculty member in the college and the most capable of original thought (though she herself denied that originality was possible in the fields with which she was concerned). With this unusual background, she quickly became an accomplished scholar, qualifying first for a tenure-stream position and then quickly moving up the professorial ranks to full professor. Along the way, she and Feiman-Nemser bonded in friendship with a working relationship in which they both brought their strengths together in highly regarded articles on teacher education.

Jay Featherstone, who came from a career in education journalism, writing for *The New Republic* and other periodicals, could be regarded as the prophet of the MSU revolution, articulating a vision of education in a stirring and inspiring way. After joining the MSU faculty in 1987 he became not only an inimitable spokesperson for the purposes and means of teacher education at MSU, but also a grassroots leader to make it happen in the Team One version of the five-year program. Looking back, he characterized most of his writings as follows:

> None were written for insiders, experts, or academics. All aim for clear prose that can do justice to the intricate and even mysterious nature of teaching and learning, or such tangled topics as school desegregation. I have struggled over the years to conjure up that necessary, possibly mythical, character, Virginia Woolf's "common reader." Education is a vitally important, rich, and lively topic—perhaps the most important of all for any democracy—surely it deserves sustained coverage and conversation it rarely receives. (Featherstone, Featherstone & Featherstone, 2003, xv)

No one was more remarkable in bringing intellectual talents to the study of teaching and teacher education than David Cohen, who together with Magdalene Lampert came in 1986 to occupy the college's first Hannah Chair. Shortly after his much-regretted passing in September 2020, Suzanne Wilson wrote on Facebook about what he had brought to their collaboration and her development:

> When we first met, we worked on a sprawling research project that took more than 10 years for me to write a book about, with an unparalleled group of graduate students and faculty. It was David—and that project—that persuaded me to stay at MSU. We taught together, wrote

together, read together. Whenever he would give me feedback on something, he'd hand the paper back to me, no
ink to speak of, save for one question on page 20 or 14
or 37. After thinking about the question for a couple of
weeks, I'd usually have a thoroughly new way of seeing
what I was trying to do in the paper. Then we would talk.

I learned a lot about teaching from him; David was
consumed by a seminar when he was teaching one, with his
students, with the ideas, with what he was learning along
the way. He was fearless about trying something new, and
endlessly interested in understanding his students and their
lives. His thinking and writing were, of course, extraordinary. . . . His understanding of context was dazzling, and
he understood classroom teachers in cultural, intellectual, political, social, historical, and economic currents
that were broad and deep. His take on reforms was often
depressing, but he never gave up faith in teachers: We all
just had to understand in more depth what it would take to
create circumstances that would let them fly.

Bringing Ethnography to the Study of Teaching

Another diverse source of ideas and insights that could be applied
to teacher thinking came from colleagues in the field of anthropology of education in the guise of classroom and teaching
ethnographies. Relatively new to the college, this field was one
of the benefits that accrued when MSU began to recruit from a
wide range of specialties in order to shed new light on teaching
and teacher education. In this case it was Susan Florio-Ruane,
Fred Erickson, and Doug Campbell who called upon researchers
to examine teaching, as much as possible, through the eyes and
understandings of the participants.

One of Lee Shulman's essays makes clear how important he
considered this new approach for research on teaching. The
heading he gave to this development is revealing: "And then we
discovered context and culture." He goes on to explain:

> During the second year of the IRT, we began to bring anthropologists into the picture. They addressed a totally new set of issues, methodologically, conceptually, and ideologically. . . . They formulated different questions, conceptualized utterly distinctive programs, and conducted research in the interests of other parties. With the coming of the ethnographers, we added context and culture to a picture that had previously included only cognition and behavior. (1992/2004, 373–74)

Susan Florio and Frederick Erickson worked closely together to establish the importance and credibility of this newly introduced discipline. Florio also established new approaches to the study of literacy education, conducted in part with Chris Clark, an educational psychologist in the IRT (e.g., Florio & Clark, 1980, 1982). Many MSU doctoral students chose ethnographic approaches for their dissertations, while teacher-education students were introduced to ethnographic methods as a way of understanding what teachers and students were thinking and attempting to do in classrooms.

Erickson (2017) tells of the eclectic and unusual set of diverse experiences with which he began his career, including advanced study of anthropology, ethnomusicology in a context of African American music, volunteering with inner-city youth in Chicago, and eventually embarking on an urban education PhD program at Northwestern. His interest in interethnic communication led to a lifetime of research on inequality of life chances that has challenged the deficit narratives stigmatizing minority youth, the nature of gatekeeping in educational trajectories, and the dominance of "social physics" in educational research.

Erickson had studied ethnographic research in graduate school but did his first classroom ethnography only in 1978, working with Susan Florio and other doctoral students on her Harvard dissertation study (1978) that examined children's communications and interactions in kindergarten as compared with their homes in an Italian American neighborhood in Boston. After Florio came to MSU as a new faculty member, this dissertation quickly became a classic both in teaching methods of ethnography and in bringing new understandings to classrooms.

The introduction of ethnography at MSU came at a seminal time when Erickson and his students were progressively distancing themselves from the approach taken in the classics of ethnography. Erickson no longer aspired to be a Bronisław Malinowski of education in the tradition that he had criticized as follows:

> The incipient tendency in Western academia toward Platonism leads us to privilege the abstract over the concrete and thus to valorize the clearer-than-life analytic narrative over the messiness of actual, situated practice by human agents. Too much ethnography lacks the contradiction, irony, and nuance of the actual conduct of everyday life—the gritty and grotty stuff that great novels show us. (Erickson, 2006, 241)

But even though he wanted to correct this bias, he reports difficulty doing so because he had not yet personally experienced the "weight" of the experiences that teachers and students bring to the classroom. Instead his head was still that of a classic ethnographer in the sense that ethnography is experienced "as if it were effortless, taking place in a universe from which social gravity is absent. What is left out is the weight of history and of immediate material circumstances, the prestructured constraints that people face when they are actually working in the world" (243).

In 1982, after four years of doing fieldwork in classrooms, he admits, "I still didn't 'get it'—what the work of teaching felt like. Like Malinowski I had pitched my tent next to the houses of the village. But I hadn't been doing the work of daily living in the village. To be sure I was doing 'fieldwork' yellow note pad and all— but it did not include sharing in the teacher's daily work" (245).

It was only later that year while working at Elliott Elementary School, the school destined to become a professional development school (PDS), that a revelation brought home to him how much he had been missing the weight bearing on students and teachers.

He had spent the day with Alex, a student who was confounded by an assignment he had been given. Students in the class had been asked to pick an animal and then write a few paragraphs about the animal's life. Alex initially chose to write about a lynx, concentrating on the question "How does the lynx get its food." But he was stymied and could not finish. Erickson tried to help him. To Erickson, experiencing Alex's difficulties and burdens became a revelation that changed the course of his career.

> That morning I picked up my end of a pedagogical log. Never before as an observer had I felt the kind of weight that a child like Alex must have presented to an elementary school teacher. Nor had I had a way of feeling something like the weight that Alex must have been feeling as he struggled with that kind of a writing task. No wonder many teachers avoid students like Alex. . . . In my experience of engagement in the action with Alex, I gained a sense of social gravity in such a scene that my earlier fieldwork and descriptive reporting—done from a less participating stance—had not allowed me to learn. (246)

Experiences of this sort led Erickson to stop being a disengaged ethnographer and create instead an action research approach to ethnography. This change came to a head in a project in which Erickson, Doug Campbell, and Richard Navarro came to Elliott at least once a week to observe and meet with three early-grade teachers. After doing this from October to February, Erickson reached another important turning point in his disillusionment with nonintervention. It occurred when the second-grade teacher and Erickson spent a difficult morning with the bottom reading group. Erickson felt that the experience did not offer what the students had been promised—a place where it was safe to make mistakes. Although Erickson was afraid of offending the teacher, he told her about his feelings, and within a few weeks she had totally reorganized her reading program, asking low-skill readers to dictate their own stories to her and the other students. Erickson realized he had crossed an important line. "I decided that I wasn't

going to do any more of the kind of distanced observing that I had
done before, but rather would work more and more collaboratively
with teachers" (239). It was another change that altered the course
of his career.

From such experiences he concluded:

> In studying side by side it is possible to develop honest
> accounts of social and cultural production and reproduc-
> tion, which do not make the work of workers look weight-
> less, but which do not portray them as totally determined
> either. Social gravity is present in teachers' and students'
> work in schools. It does not make inevitable the imme-
> diate and long term consequences of that work. We
> need ethnography of education which can show us both
> the social gravity in the daily practices of teaching and
> learning in classrooms and the opportunities for socially
> progressive or regressive choice that resides in it, opportu-
> nities for accomplishing social justice or injustice locally.
> These are challenges which present themselves continu-
> ally to teachers and students in the course of their every-
> day work together. (255)

I, myself, was fortunate to team teach with Erickson in a social
foundations course for undergraduate teacher education. It seemed
to me that through much repeated analysis of the videotapes he
had made, he could practically read the minds of participants
simply by paying close attention to their verbal and nonverbal
language. To understand how this was possible, one needs to read
articles based on his analyses where language is broken down not
only by choice of vocabulary and syntax, but by all the other variation in talk that he took into account, including intonation, stress,
cadence, timing, hesitation, midcourse speech corrections, etc.

This concern with finding a middle way between determinism
and free will continued to be crucial to Erickson throughout his
career. In his capstone book (2004), he demonstrated the importance of analysis of local conversations for a critical understanding of social theories and their treatment of agency or freedom of

action. The book sheds much light on social interaction in classrooms. Erickson is critical of various social theories for their failure to accommodate the "wiggle room" between the deterministic and the voluntary that he finds across the board in the study of conversation.

Although while at MSU Erickson was another of the acknowledged intellectual leaders in the college, he remained in his own mind something of an outsider. In the 2017 retrospective account of his career, Erickson recalls leaving with a sour view of plans for the PDS, seeing it not as the vision explored in my present book, but rather a top-down attempt to sell questionable recommendations for what works to teachers. He never felt that his ideas, his approach, his unrivalled intellectual virtuosity had quite the reach and influence they deserved, especially in the project studying interactions between MSU scholars and K–12 teacher in one PDS. Nevertheless, he thought a better understanding of those interactions would be an important step toward the revolution in university-K–12 relations.

While anthropological methods played some role in revolutionary research, the older and more established approaches to research on teaching, the process-product school of thought, was still much in evidence, especially in the national Invisible College for Research on Teaching, which the IRT and Jere Brophy, in particular, were charged with organizing and leading in an annual meeting.

Continued Intellectual Leadership

Once the IRT era was over, it was people like Magdalene Lampert, Deborah Ball, Suzanne Wilson, Cheryl Rosaen, and Kathy Roth who went on to create and fill new roles of intellectual leadership in the study of teaching and teacher education. They did pioneering research on their own teaching to reveal, make visible, and thereby build a knowledge base of what was intellectually important and special about the knowledge that they had acquired and brought to bear on their practice, including in particular the intellectual insights that could be generated in serious discussion with their very young K–12 pupils.

Mary Kennedy was another leader of the revolution who remained and kept making scholarly contributions after revolutionary sentiments waned. She was recruited in 1985 to manage the newly founded MSU NCRTE. She continued in the same role for the subsequent National Center for Research on Teacher Learning. She demonstrated her scholarly strengths in a seminal book on the component of the Teacher Education and Learning to Teach study that dealt with preparing students to teach writing (Kennedy, 1998). But perhaps most surprisingly, in 2005 she published her last and singular major project, a book that can be regarded as an extension, expansion, and consolidation of the IRT efforts to understand the wisdom of practice and examine the implications for the reform of teaching. It was titled *Inside Teaching: How Classroom Life Undermines Reform* and was based, like much previous IRT research, on extensive interviews with teachers and observation of their practices. It is characteristic of her writing in being systematic, thorough, and bringing new insight to the matters discussed.

Notably, Kennedy took seriously the possibility that reformers' agendas may be too unrealistic to be put into practice:

> Reform ideals are not well suited to the realities of classroom life. Many reformers advocate relatively complex lessons, involving group activities and numerous materials and props, using pedagogies called "progressive," "discovery," or "constructivist." Even if these ideas are based on sound learning theories, they may actually increase the likelihood of distractions in the classroom, thus defeating their own purposes." (73%)

Biographical information on selected MSU faculty members in the revolutionary period reveals still more about the range and depth of their intellectual interests and backgrounds. The interests of Magdalene Lampert in the history of mathematics, of Deborah Ball in advanced number theory, of Dan Chazan in critiques of mathematical certainty by mathematicians and others, of Suzanne Wilson in the history of American education and its context in the development of American democracy, of Sharon Feiman-Nemser in understanding Dewey the philosopher, of Bob Floden in the philosophical underpinnings of educational research, of Margret Buchmann in the history of ideas more generally, and of Jay Featherstone in the significance of poetry are cases in point.

Lampert and Ball are especially clear in linking what might seem esoteric to the issues they faced in classroom teaching. Lampert writes that "the academic domain of mathematical epistemology and its esoteric disputes seem far from the realm of schools and teaching and learning at the time I was studying them. . . . But now looking back, I recognize in those disputes the foundations of my ability to entertain many of the ideas that are central to contemporary educational reform" (Lampert, 1998, 3).

Deborah Ball, in reflecting on her first years of teaching, especially the two years she spent teaching second grade in a multigrade teaching team, tells of how she first encountered teaching as intellectual work: "I experimented, adapted, and analyzed the results of my efforts. It was intellectually challenging and interesting. Somehow I had managed not to discover that most people, including many teachers, did not consider teaching intellectual work. Approaching it as a process of inquiry and examination in and from practice, I found a steady stream of complex practical challenges as I tried to engage students in class" (1998, 13).

In those years science was a central subject-matter challenge for her. She started her teaching with four sections of science for which she was not prepared. But it was the teaching of mathematics more than science that most shaped her future as a teacher. It led her toward the study of more mathematics—pure mathematics. Ball recalls beginning to take mathematics courses at MSU while teaching full-time at Spartan Village Elementary School in East Lansing, embracing a subject with which she had had almost no acquaintance as an undergraduate herself:

> Listening to my students' comments, and trying to understand their solutions, I felt pressed to delve deeply into

the mathematical ideas myself. I found I enjoyed this a lot and often was personally quite consumed with a problem or an idea. . . . Over the next few years, beginning with one elementary algebra course, I took the entire calculus sequence, and then number theory.

It was in number theory that I fell in love with mathematics. . . . I loved the content—divisibility, primes, congruences—and I loved working on proofs. . . . And I felt a kind of intellectual passion similar to my passions for language and text, teaching and learning, inequity and analysis. I saw how mathematics might entail hunches and intuitions, conjectures and arguments, experiments and reasoning. I began to think explicitly about knowledge—its nature, where it comes from, what it means to "know" different sorts of things.

I also remember realizing how these ideas immediately affected what I could see and hear in my first-grade students' ideas, as well as how I read the teacher's guide for the mathematics curriculum. For example, one day I was teaching a lesson on area to my first graders. We were using ½-inch-square graph paper to calculate approximately the area of a set of irregular regions. One of the children had an insight that we should go get some of the "very small graph paper that the fifth graders use" so that we could get closer to the "right numbers" for the shapes' areas. My work in calculus has helped me hear this student's idea as an intuition about limits. I never could have heard this in a child's talk before. (15–16, paragraphs reordered)

When Joe Schwab was brought to the IRT at MSU as a visiting professor by Lee Shulman and Judy Lanier, he became a catalyst in legitimizing and validating the links between K–12 teaching and the history of thought. Schwab is one of forty-seven iconic professors at the University of Chicago whose careers were documented in a book edited by the eccentric sociologist Edward Shils for the centennial of the University of Chicago in 1992 (Shils, 1991). Lee

Shulman wrote the chapter on Schwab. In this chapter, Shulman brings to life the seminars that Schwab, helping to launch the revolution, meticulously planned and conducted at MSU with a multidisciplinary group of professors, graduate students, and K–12 teachers in the early years of the revolution.

> The seminar met for two hours at the end of the afternoon, three days a week. It was exceedingly rare for anyone to miss a meeting. Using his ubiquitous cigarette as a combination pointer, conducting baton and general pedagogical prosthesis, Schwab led the seminar through a series of readings designed to lay bare their disciplinary or professional premises. (Shulman, 1991/2004, 465)

The readings included Genesis from the Bible, a William Faulkner short story, Aristotle on the elements of biological knowledge, and William Harvey on circulation of the blood. As Shulman recalls:

> Thus did Schwab continue his lifelong quest to cure his students, whatever their ages or stations in life, of the malady that some came to call the "hardening of the categories." As with all students who experienced his mastery of Socratic pedagogy, no member of that seminar would ever forget the experience. (Shulman, 1991/2004, 430; see also Forzani 2011, 184)

Conclusion

Unfortunately, as the years went by, the intellectual interest and effort that had been directed at improving teacher education institutionally in a holistic way at MSU faded as the college gave priority to building silos of subject-matter specialists preoccupied with the teaching and learning of mathematics, literacy, science, and social studies as well as recruiting heavily among those whose primary interest was in critical theory—therefore doing little to develop or even maintain the earlier revolutionary agenda. The intent was still revolutionary but in a different way, and the effect in many respects was to reaffirm earlier, more orthodox university practices, showing a lack of concern for much of the revolutionary agenda.

CHAPTER TWELVE

Collaboration as Never Before

From a naive perspective it may seem strange that K–12 teachers and teacher educators in the United States have had such
a hard time working together that collaboration could seem
revolutionary. But in fact, based on the MSU experience in the
1960s and 1970s, extreme collaboration became one of the most
noted and exceptional features of MSU. Throughout the 1980s
and 1990s and to a lesser extent until today, interviews with
prospective faculty have taken care to point this out and find
out if candidates are comfortable with this emphasis and willing·
to engage with other faculty and to facilitate collaborative work
among students in ways that their experience at other universities
would not lead them to expect. In the gradual development of this
collaborative ethos at MSU with all its meetings in which everyone spent a great deal of time discussing and resolving issues
they were facing, collaboration was emphasized at different levels
and among different categories of people, most notably among
K–12 students, among K–12 teachers, among teacher educators, between universities and K–12 schools, between university
teacher educators and K–12 teachers, between researchers and
K–12 teachers, among researchers of different disciplines and
methodologies, and among two or more of these categories.

Hitherto, extreme individualism had been the norm. It was a
problem made famous in Lortie's (1975) analysis of teaching as an
occupation. That book was influential in fostering an era in which
American essays and studies of teaching described this culture of
individualism and isolation as inherent to elementary and secondary school teaching in general, ignoring the fact that teaching in
Japan and China was already much more collaborative in nature.
It took the revolutionary movement at MSU to show in just one
institution what had to be done to reverse the dysfunctional problem of isolation and fragmentation in multiple and decisive ways.

In a speech to the 1988 Educational Testing Service Invitational Conference, Dean Judith Lanier spoke about the individualism of teaching and teacher learning as a major problem and collaboration as a necessary response:

> As Linda Darling-Hammond so memorably captured the traditional relationship of teachers to their professional knowledge, "You get it for yourself, figure it out for yourself, and keep it to yourself." This pattern aggravates already difficult problems of practice and leadership in schools . . . it must be broken.

This individualistic culture was not limited to K–12. It was even more the case in higher education. University faculty prided themselves on the relative autonomy they enjoyed. They often took satisfaction in their freedom to refuse to collaborate or to collaborate very selectively with colleagues on various tasks, assignments, projects, or programs. As a result when teacher education was no longer the mission of the more close-knit and coordinated normal schools of the past, excessive fragmentation became a major problem, especially in research universities. Specialists in subject matter, specialists in how to teach particular subjects, specialists in the foundations of education, and staff responsible for organizing the field experience of prospective teachers would make decisions and carry out their duties on their own or only with colleagues in the same niche. If the revolution were to succeed, progress had to be made in taking a more collaborative and coherent approach.

Most revolutionary of all in challenging the isolation and individualistic norms of educators was the growing intensity and importance of collaboration between MSU scholars (faculty and students) and their counterparts in K–12 schools. The more typical short-term "collaboration" in which the university sought assistance from K–12 teachers in order to do one-off research and prepare teacher-education students to teach was no longer viewed as sufficient. In fact, the unequal relationships in such collaboration were increasingly looked upon with suspicion and considered not only not optimally effective but also not justifiable in an ethical sense. The long and short of it was that the revolution at MSU could be achieved only if MSU faculty members, graduate students, and prospective teachers were regularly present and continuously engaged in K–12 schools, treating K–12 teachers as equal in status to university faculty.

Shulman justified the need for, indeed the necessity of, collaboration:

> We render individual experiential learning into "community property" when we transform those lessons from personal experience into a literature of shared narratives. Such connections between theoretical principles and practical narratives, between the universal and the accidental, forge professional knowledge. Such knowledge cannot be developed and sustained adequately by individuals experiencing and reflecting in isolation, however. No professional can function well in isolation. Professionals require membership in a community. (1998/2004, 536; see also Shulman, 1997/2004)

Obstacles to Collaboration between Researchers and K–12 Teachers

Since the revolutionary movement could not be successful if new forms of collaboration were confined to the university itself, it was critical to understand the obstacles to collaboration within affiliated K–12 schools and between the schools and the university. Susan Florio-Ruane drew on her work in her IRT project (the Written Literacy Forum) to describe some of these obstacles:

> Until quite a few years ago, I worked with teachers chiefly in two ways as I researched their practice. Trained as an ethnographer, I knew teachers as informants on classroom life. From that experience, I learned the value of inviting the collaboration of teachers in framing research

questions and in collecting and occasionally analyzing classroom data. Typically, however, these close working relationships changed or ended when, like my anthropologist forebears, I left the field to write the reports of my research.

Mentioning that I left the field to write research reports may seem trivial. There is, after all, a division of labor in education whereby teachers teach and researchers theorize about teaching and learning. But . . . leaving teachers out of the deliberative and expressive phases of research may not only create communication gaps between teachers and researchers, but also may limit the quality and usefulness of educational research. (Florio-Ruane, 1986, 1)

For this project, conversation, not the more formal conventions of research, became the chosen way for researchers to deal with the challenges they had encountered in working with teachers. They had tried before to understand and represent teacher ways of understanding, but they had failed in important respects. It was not the sort of misunderstanding that could be fixed by translating research reports into less technical language. Instead, the participants focused for a time on telling one another stories of what they knew about the teaching of writing. Initially, these conversations were awkward, but gradually as the group read and wrote together, they learned how to converse better.

Soon this process began to change the production of both oral and written accounts of their research. With teachers as coauthors, progress reports and academic articles no longer dominated the group's reporting. In time, this led the forum to clarify the audiences and purposes to be addressed in their reporting. They were then better able to think about what the audiences already knew, what these audiences would be interested in, and what the audience could contribute to interpretation of the forum's work. In so doing, the writing became "more vivid, evocative and immediate" and "less constrained by rules of formal argumentation" (18–19).

Among the kinds of texts we prepared to share research were simulation games, letters, autobiographies and other personal narratives, and displays of artifacts of children's writing. Most of these texts were open-ended and allowed their audiences to "complete the story." Even in oral presentations, forum teachers rejected formal presentations to their colleagues. Instead, they created roundtable formats that blended written materials with some oral presentations and considerable discussion. (19)

The forum participants learned that stories were by no means extraneous to research reports, but were instead "central to a valid portrayal of teachers' work."

Once we began conversations with one another, we learned a great deal more about the processes of teaching and learning writing in school than any of us could have learned in isolation. Insights came from looking at data together and talking about what was there, what was missing, what we had represented, and what we had failed to capture in our reports. That effort productively blurred distinctions between talk and writing, research and practical knowledge, inquiry and teacher education. (24; see also Florio-Ruane, 1990)

IRT Invention of Teacher-Collaborator Role

Early in the revolution with the establishment of the IRT in 1976, collaboration between K–12 teachers and university researchers spiked when practicing K–12 teachers were hired half-time as *teacher-collaborators* to work in Erickson Hall, serving as much as possible as equal members of IRT research teams, while continuing to be responsible for teaching with assistance from substitutes in their regular classrooms. Annette Weinshank, a teacher at Otto

Middle School in Lansing, one of the original teacher-collaborators, explains the novelty and appeal of this new role as she understood it: "We seven and the other teachers who came on board
had a chance of a lifetime. We wrote papers, went to conferences,
published technical reports and published in refereed journals. It
was an astonishingly productive environment" (quoted in Inzunza,
2002, 61).

According to one of the codirectors of the IRT, Andy Porter
(1987, 148–51), the IRT typically had four K–12 classroom teachers on staff at any one time, usually for a three-year assignment,
working with one or more of the approximately thirty professors
assigned to the IRT for part of their time. It would have been
better to have more, but the cost to MSU was exorbitant. MSU
paid all the costs, about $20,000 per year per teacher for half-
time assignments. School districts arguably should have paid
some of the costs reflecting the benefits accruing to them, but
they did not.

A letter from the codirectors of the IRT to the MSU director of
contract and grant administration in 1988 provided a profile of
the work and accomplishments of each of the nine teachers who
served as teacher collaborators from 1981 to 1986. Linda Alford, a
teacher at Haslett Middle School, was one of these, working on the
Content Determinants project to study what influences teachers'
content decisions in elementary school mathematics:

> As a member of that research team, she made contribu-
> tions in all phases of the research process (e.g., design
> of interviews and surveys, conducting interviews, docu-
> menting state policies) She was instrumental in helping
> the project team formulate research questions in ways that
> have direct bearing upon practice. Her understanding
> of teachers and teaching was of great value in designing
> appropriate instrumentation for the project's empirical
> work. Her greatest contributions to the project, however,
> were in the analysis and interpretation of research results.
> She pressed for dissemination of project work to practi-
> tioners and, during the last four years, averaged ten major

presentations of Content Determinants work per year to national, state and regional audiences.

Unfortunately, this teacher-collaborator role was the first of the revolution's major achievements to fall by the wayside. After IRT funding ended in 1986, MSU could no longer afford this practice in spite of its undeniable contributions to the improvement of educational research.

The Development of Collaboration in Teacher-Education Programs

In what other ways did this extraordinary emphasis on educators working together come about? It emerged from various sources. One was the development of experimental teacher-education programs in the 1970s and 1980s. They attracted faculty members who were willing to engage with other volunteer colleagues in working not in isolation, but together in the design and execution of new practices. They were members of teams that were much more present in K–12 schools than had previously been the case or was still the case in the fragmented mainstream program.

In the 1980s, as new faculty were hired with the predispositions and qualifications needed for this revolutionary work, they brought with them experience working to free teachers from the isolation and limitations of the status quo. The work of open education advocates, earlier reformers like John Dewey, Lucy Sprague Mitchell at the Bank Street School in New York, and Pat Carini at the Prospect School in Vermont, as well as contemporaries like Deborah Meier in New York and Ted Sizer in New England, became more and more important in influencing the thinking of the revolutionary vanguard at MSU and gave still more credibility to the work of collaboration (Carroll et al., 2007a, 17–19).

Once the five-year program was in place, Team One provided the best documented account of collaborative practices in teacher education. Carroll et al. contains many examples:

We developed a team structure whereby we assigned a small amount of faculty time to course coordinators. These people convened all the instructors for a particular course before the semester began to develop common plans and similar syllabi. Instructors continued to meet regularly across the duration of the course to adjust plans, discuss individual student issues, and support each other's teaching. In effect, each course in the program conducted a parallel seminar on itself, by and for its instructors. This structure was particularly helpful in mentoring doctoral students as they gained experience as teacher educators. (2007a, 20)

The following chapter elaborates:

It was a new experience for students used to contending with the faceless bureaucracy of a forty-thousand-student university to be treated reasonably and responsively and to be provided with explanations for policies and procedures and multiple opportunities for raising questions. (Carroll & Donnelly, 2007, 35)

School liaisons—positions most often filled by graduate students or retired teachers—were another essential feature of collaboration in Team One:

In addition to mentoring a group of interns in a school, liaisons served as bridges from the team to schools, getting to know important figures in the school community, building an ongoing and deepening connection. In the inevitable crisis, they usually knew whom to talk to. (Carroll et al., 2007a, 29)

When Team One developed standards for the program, this process proved to be another excellent example of the importance of collaboration within the program. Feiman-Nemser and Hartzler-Miller recall the process in this way:

Most significant for Team One was the summer working group that we set up with collaborating teachers from our partner schools. I remember meeting several mornings with a group of teachers, MSU staff and doctoral students to introduce the idea of teaching standards; share personal images of good teaching; and think together about what graduates of our five-year program should know, care about, and be able to do. We wanted to familiarize our school-based colleagues with national standards-setting efforts and create a sense that, by participating in this local work, they were joining a larger conversation about good teaching, and helping to enhance the teaching profession. (2007, 55)

David Carroll has described his intensive use of collaborative practices to improve the mentoring of teacher-education students. The complexities of this are strikingly pictured in his portrayal of a single meeting:

Twenty-five educators are seated around a ring of tables. The cross-school liaison group includes teacher representatives (teacher liaisons) from twelve schools, each of which is hosting five or six MSU teacher interns, plus Team One university liaisons and faculty leaders. Around the table are individuals with considerable teacher education experience . . . plus others relatively new to mentoring and even teaching. (2007, 181)

Then Carroll goes into far more detail in discussing a cross-school liaison study group from various Team One schools that came together to learn from what Carroll had done earlier with a study group from one of the schools (known as Capitol School) in which teachers had worked together to develop their practice as mentors. The cross-school group started with a number of video clips. The first was a video of a fifth-year intern teaching that had served as the first artifact for the original Capitol study group to discuss what they could learn from that video about mentoring. Additional videos of the Capitol study group discussing the artifact under Carroll's leadership, together with the original intern video, were then all used at the cross-school liaison session. The discussions of all these videos allowed participants to revisit the earlier discussions at the Capitol study group as well as to offer new observations that had not been made before, including mentor moves that might have been made but were not.

This intensive culture and practice of collaboration that worked for the Team One faculty, who were on the whole self-selected and voluntarily involved, did not transfer easily to the whole college and its departments. Throughout the most revolutionary period, relations between the favored teacher-education department and the remaining three departments (administration, exercise science, and educational psychology-special education) were problematic and at times hostile. And even within the very diverse and multidisciplinary Department of Teacher Education, achieving real collaboration and common ground on the reform of teacher education was no easy mission. Moreover, it is important to note that all this emphasis on collaboration did not mean that college decisions were generally made in a participatory, democratic manner. Under Judy Lanier as dean, the college never developed a consensual democratic culture emphasizing faculty governance. She and her closest collaborators managed to keep control of the most important decisions (Labaree, 1995; Forzani, 2011, 243–44)

Collaboration as It Developed in the PDSs

As the discussion of Florio-Ruane and the Written Literacy Forum project indicates, collaboration between researchers and K–12 teachers originally took place at MSU without any major organizational institutional changes other than establishment of the IRT. But the subsequent establishment and development of PDSs made it possible to take this school–university collaboration to a new level that was intended to take on, if possible, whole schools and within these schools teams of teachers and teams of students working together in ways that had not been possible before.

Under the leadership of Fred Erickson and other ethnographers brought in to diversify and enrich teacher education, one of the earliest and most significant efforts to achieve a more radical and egalitarian collaboration started at Elliott Elementary School in Holt, a suburb of Lansing. This effort got off the ground before the Holmes Group reports were published and before the MSU PDSs were established. Doug Campbell captured much of what was complex and subtle about this project:

> For three and a half years, I have been participating in a project involving teachers, building principals, and university researchers in collaborative activity designed to implement and study an approach to staff development that engages participants in reflection and dialogue grounded in respect for teachers' knowledge and modeled on the nonjudgmental and nonintervening features of ethnographic inquiry. . . . Contradictions and role dilemmas encountered in this project will be highlighted through my account of how the practitioners came to suspect a "hidden agenda" lurking behind the researchers' avowed commitments to a teacher-defined and teacher-directed approach to professional growth.
>
> Even though the project has largely succeeded in fostering significant changes in the teachers' and principals' thinking, practices, and self-esteem, it must be seen in the context of the difficulties, dilemmas, and misperceptions actually involved in attempting to relate research as a process of inquiry (rather than as a body of established results) to the needs and concerns of practitioners. (1988, 99)

At Holt High School, still another PDS, participants described the intense collaborative activity of the school's mathematics group as follows:

> As part of the community of educators within a Professional Development School, we had a very rich opportunity for

discussion about important issues concerning teaching and learning mathematics. For example, we each participated weekly in seminars consisting of mathematics teachers, guidance counselors, university professors and education doctoral students where current reform initiatives in mathematics education were discussed. The group became known as the Math Study Group as discussions centered on questions such as what it means to teach mathematics for understanding and what the *Standards* suggest about changing mathematics teaching and learning in today's classrooms. ([Lehman, Wilson & Geist, ca. 1990–91], 1–2)

The study of how one teacher experienced this change toward more collaboration is analyzed in detail in a book by Sharon Schwille (2016). In fall 1989, when schools were first establishing PDSs in collaboration with the university, Courtney (the teacher studied by S. Schwille) expected that the PDS would turn out to be just another set of "plug-in pieces." But what she experienced was extraordinarily different. The university participants at Courtney's school proposed a much more comprehensive and coordinated approach of working in more egalitarian ways to formulate problems to study and issues to explore. Then that same year, when the first summer institute brought PDS participants from different schools together, Courtney and other teachers experienced the pleasant shock of being treated for the first time as professionals who had much to contribute to educational reform efforts (34, 37).

Best Examples

While many examples of collaboration across traditional roles and challenging traditional norms and markers could be given, I have selected two that best illustrate what was done. One is the word picture painted by MSU professor Jay Featherstone, which captures better than any other the nature and ethos of this collaboration as it reached its peak in the revolutionary era:

> For a time, the corridors of Erickson Hall [the MSU educa-
> tion building] hummed with conversations that bounced
> back and forth from research to actual classrooms, from
> the theory to Monday's class. The early days of profes-
> sional development schools and research aimed at practice
> showed how research in the setting of a teacher education
> program partnered with schools can play an immensely
> fertile role in catalyzing ideas, energy and people in class-
> rooms. The researchers were in constant dialogue with the
> practitioners in school and the teacher education program.
> Many played the role of both researcher and practitioner.
> A program with researchers in schools that are also sites
> for teacher education gains synergistic energy. People and
> resources and networks begin to overlap, creating new
> village-like webs of connections. More people on both
> sides of the school-university divide become *amphibious*,
> at home in both worlds. Work in one seasons work in
> another. (J. Featherstone, 2007, 216)

The second example takes the form of a most amazing and memorable collaboration between two faculty members who had followed very different career paths in specialties unlikely to coop-erate intensively—Jere Brophy and Jan Alleman. Brophy, it could be argued, was the college's most famous professor, at least after the departure of Lee Shulman. He was an educational psychologist, a prolific scholar, researcher, and writer whose textbooks on educa-tional psychology were widely used across the nation and whose journal articles were likewise widely cited. Alleman was a social studies educator with a deep commitment to teaching teacher-ed-ucation students in unconventional, creative ways. She and Brophy first got together after MSU got a grant for a new federal center for the improvement of teaching elementary school subjects (mathe-matics, literacy, science, social studies, and fine arts).

At the start, the center had a problem. MSU had no one with enough of a reputation for prolific and highly valued research publication in social studies education. Brophy, despite a lack of experience in social studies education, decided to fill this gap

himself, and in an unexpected move he and Alleman decided to
work together since Alleman could bring to this partnership experience and knowledge about social studies education that Brophy
lacked. It turned out to be a wondrous and productive strategy. When Brophy died unexpectedly and prematurely in 2009,
Alleman (2009) wrote a heartfelt memoir about their relationship,
revealing how intense and productive it was. It is worth quoting
here at length:

> I had the rare and rich opportunity to collaborate with
> Jere for more than 20 years, and over that time he became
> my best friend and my intellectual soulmate. Our profes-
> sional journey together was a labor of love and filled with
> enormous positive energy as we explored theoretical and
> practical possibilities for teaching and learning elementary
> social studies. . . . Our secret for success stemmed from the
> fact that we approached all our research as learners, coming
> from different spaces and places, but with a shared sense of
> curiosity and infectious desire for excellence. Jere brought
> to the collaboration a naiveté as a learner that caused you
> to open up to him in amazing ways and he would push you
> to come up with examples that made you think creatively
> and more deeply. His mind was always on task. When we
> all met to discuss our work, we would interact for several
> hours, up to the point that [our teacher-collaborator] Barb
> and I had exhausted every last brain cell, but Jere seemed
> to reproduce them as we went. . . .
>
> Jere and I have met almost daily over the years. Most
> of our meetings started with an update on family, the
> political theme of the day, and sports, and then we spent
> quality time on our writing and research. Additionally, I
> never taught a class without popping into Jere's office for
> my informal debriefing. He would ask the most amazing
> questions in challenging ways. When I would describe
> one of my out-of-the-box strategies, he would ask my
> favorite questions, "What did you take out?" and "What
> evidence is there that it matched the goal?" I would joke

with him that he was the best coach in the world, and I did not have to pay a cent.

We never parted without a plan for our next session. I would come to his office with my Franklin Planner and he would pull out his version of a Blackberry from his shirt pocket, a simple mini-sheet of white paper. His "calendar" was not a representative artifact of his accomplishments. He did not spend much time writing about what he was going to do, he just did it.

Among my fondest memories is the day that he was going to observe me teaching for the very first time in an elementary classroom. He was going to be taking notes and recording me. I was on my way to the school in Haslett; and about a mile from the site, I pulled over to the side of the road and brought my car to a screeching halt. I said to myself, "My gosh, what have I gotten myself into? The world-renowned guru of motivation, the process-product mastermind, the expert on classroom management was going to watch me teach." I took a few deep breaths and said to myself, "It is too late to turn back." While worried that I had blown my cover of knowing what I was doing, things continued to work out. He gave me specific praise for my instruction that morning. His continued support and faith in me and my work allowed me to flourish. Not long ago, wearing the jacket that I wore on that memorable morning, I shared the story with him. I said, "That jacket will always be in my closet. It represents such powerful messages and gifts you gave to me."

In short, odd couple that they might appear from a traditional education school perspective—a famous nationally and internationally known educational psychologist who for years was not required to teach at all, even at the university, and a teacher educator in social studies with unorthodox ideas who was completely devoted to teaching both practicing and prospective teachers—it was Jan Alleman and Jere Brophy who best epitomized the collaboration across fields in research and practice to which the revolutionary era aspired. In general, however, collaboration in the revolutionary era did not remain as strong over time as in the case of Alleman and Brophy.

Conclusion

As the revolution faded, so did many examples of extraordinary collaboration detailed in this chapter. It proved impossible to maintain collaboration in its many forms at a peak level. The sad commentary of one of the early IRT teacher collaborators, Annette Weinshank, when she returned to full-time K–12 teaching, is more typical:

> Inside my classroom, it was as if the IRT had never existed. I had changed so much that my job no longer fit me. I had acquired new knowledge and skills that I wanted to apply in my classroom and school district; yet there was no accepted, institutionally sanctioned way for me to do that. I tried to make my own way. . . . But a funny thing happened as the years passed and my vita expanded: my continuing effort to integrate research and teaching remained in the category of personal idiosyncrasy.
>
> On the one hand, my school district has not stood in the way of what it considers to be my personal professional-development pursuits; neither has it seen fit to investigate with me the promise, implicit in my work of synthesizing practice and research in the interest of improved student achievement. (quoted in Porter, 1987, 151)

In the university itself insofar as tenure, promotion, and merit pay were concerned, collaboration never became the plus that it had been during the revolutionary era. In fact, it remained a minus in the sense that other things being equal, a publication written as a sole author was regarded as superior to one with multiple authors. In the restoration era, collaboration could receive the recognition it deserved only if it was carried out as an official load assignment for administration or coordination of the work of other faculty or students. And even then recognition was limited in comparison with other factors deemed more important in promotion and tenure. Ordinary voluntary collaboration among faculty tended to be no longer considered better in principle than working on one's own.

CHAPTER THIRTEEN

Revolutionary Synergy within the PDSs

The PDSs started out with the intent—at least in the eyes of the revolutionary vanguard—of developing a completely new type of school for school–university collaboration. A powerful coalition was organized in support of this mission, but implementation began in a very small way with volunteer teachers and selected MSU faculty. In spite of their modest beginnings and before their premature demise, the MSU PDSs were able to move toward a full realization of their mission in manifold ways. Although they began with narrow classroom-based, subject-matter improvement, the work evolved toward more school-wide engagement in which the whole staff could work together in changing the nature of their school.

Regardless of the funding difficulties that threatened their very existence, extraordinary work continued to be accomplished in the PDSs. The following account contrasts five of the original PDSs that were most notable in realizing the PDS vision: Holmes Middle School in Flint, Holt High School and Elliott Elementary School in Holt, Spartan Village Elementary School in East Lansing, and Averill Elementary School in Lansing.

Holmes Middle School in Flint

Holmes Middle School was MSU's most ambitious effort to create a PDS within the most challenging of inner-city conditions, in the city of Flint, which suffered deeply from white flight and a deteriorating economy, resulting in steady declines in school district enrollments. In response to the social effects of these conditions, the PDS put particular emphasis on working with disengaged students, fostering better attitudes, defining and operationalizing the concept of learning community, and developing constructive relationships with parents and community actors.

For the most part, all this was new. Within Holmes, classroom teaching in the period before the PDS was generally very traditional, relying heavily on textbooks, worksheets, and teacher-centered instruction. Isolated in their classrooms, teachers did not collaborate among themselves while, at school level, decisions affecting teachers were made in top-down fashion (Sykes et al., 1995, 15).

None of this was easy to change. Putnam and Schwille (2020) tell of the complicated negotiations that were necessary before MSU involvement in the district could even begin. A formal agreement was required if MSU was to be intensely involved, as planned, on a daily basis. Diverse stakeholders took part in these negotiations: school district superintendent, teachers' union president, school board president and board, associate superintendent as well as university deans, department chairs, and faculty leaders in the MSU College of Education. Notably absent, however, were those at Holmes who would have to carry the ball and do the daily work: the teachers and school-level administrators. None of these had a voice in the choice of which of four middle schools in the urban district were to become PDSs. As might be expected, teachers when first informed about the PDS plans were skeptical, even resistant, as expressed by one of the informants in Putnam and Schwille:

> There was an announcement that people from the university were coming to a staff meeting to talk to us about "something." The "something" was not explained. At the staff meeting we teachers kept looking at each other. We were wondering, "What is that university person saying? What does she want? Tick tock, time is wasting. Is this more work? We have got things to do. We don't have time for this." . . . I thought I was a good teacher already. I read in my area; I was concerned about kids. That university person would be "here today and gone tomorrow." We teachers all thought, "This too shall pass." (2020, 50)

Notwithstanding this not very auspicious start, PDS work at Holmes began in the winter of 1989 with a large number of participants: twenty Holmes teachers, nine administrators, seventeen MSU faculty and graduate students, nine elementary-education MSU teacher candidates. Several subject-matter groups were formed. Throughout the PDS era, the most active Holmes subject-matter group was in mathematics. The most dynamic of this study group's efforts got off the ground in the spring of 1990 when a special education teacher who had been participating in a PDS activity in literacy told an MSU mathematics educator that she wanted help in learning how to teach fractions better to students with learning disabilities. Over time, the group developed ways to provide opportunities for students with learning disabilities to investigate powerful mathematical ideas (Wilcox & Wagner, 1994).

Two other PDS study groups, literacy and social studies, were less active but had successes to be celebrated. The literacy team (including two MSU faculty members and one graduate assistant) did a self-evaluation in 1990–91, which revealed that students were much more articulate than in the previous year about what they had learned from literature, how it connected to people and events in their own lives, and how they learned the content. Students were requesting more books by African American authors and were writing about the stories and novels they had read. The social studies group developed a public issues unit to deal with the problems of violence that students were encountering in school and out. Students made connections between what they learned in class and what was going on in their own community, discussing tensions between personal liberty and the need for collective security. They debated the use of metal detectors, listened to police officers talk about search and seizure, and visited sites such as the county jail (MSU-33, 1995).

In addition to the subject-matter study groups, other groups emerged to deal with overcoming disengagement and developing constructive relationships. This involved fundamental changes in classroom norms:

> Teachers also struggled with "letting go," providing students with opportunities to investigate problems that might take them in many directions. . . . The teacher or the text as the sole source of knowledge had to give way to knowledge jointly constructed through student participation. Teachers had to learn how to conduct a genuine dialogue rather than relying heavily on lectures and demonstrations. As teachers and students adjusted to new ways of interacting . . . students took advantage of opportunities to decide what they wanted to study within a given topic and how they were to be assessed. (Sykes et al., 1995)

One such group was the learning community study group coordinated by Sharon Schwille, which consisted mostly of specialty teachers in such areas as home economics, art, and special education. This group sponsored an artist in residence who worked with students on a large mosaic for the building's entryway. Another of this group's projects found community quilters to help students design and put together quilts as a way to support learning community norms of interaction and culture.

In addition to these group projects MSU faculty member Sonya Gunnings-Moton and a graduate assistant did PDS work in the seventh and eighth grades to implement the advisor-advisee program, a Flint public schools mandated program with a one-hour class per week for teachers to serve as counselors on conflict resolution, problem-solving, decision-making, and career development. In 1990 the school also established an Alternative Education program to address academic and social needs of students who otherwise were going to be suspended from school. The objective of this one-semester experience was not to keep students out of the classroom but to return to it with a better sense of purpose and responsibility. It provided an integrated curriculum with experiential learning, follow-up counseling, short-term job experience, and home visits. Social work interns and school counselors provided counseling. The short-term job experience had high attendance rates, employer commendations, offers of summer jobs, and better student self-esteem as they brought home pay checks (MSU-9, May 1995, 11; MSU-22, March 1991, 21–22).

As teachers became involved, they learned that improving the curriculum was much more difficult and complex than they had imagined. They found out that "teaching for understanding" could occur only in classrooms characterized by trust, openness, and collaboration among students. It became clear that "cooperative learning, for example, could work only when norms had been established for listening, taking turns, respecting others' opinions, and modifying one's own views in light of new information" (Sykes et al., 1995, 38, 41, 44–47).

To work on these prerequisites for success, the leaders of the PDS planned a summer program taken by most of the teachers, in which the teachers would develop norms and be trained in constructive strategies for beginning the school year. Teachers learned to teach students nonviolent ways to handle disagreements. Incentives were offered for each team if they could avoid physical altercations for a week. When this program was introduced, there were fewer fights during the first two months of school than in the previous year (MSU-30, 1993, 54; MSU-29, 1993, 93; Sykes et al., 1995).

Evidence for success of these efforts included a 25 percent decline in the reported incidence of fighting and 16 percent decline in suspension rates, and a decline in student rates of retention in grade from 22 percent to 10 percent. Moreover, Holmes students expressed more positive attitudes toward school, more parental involvement in their schoolwork, and more engagement in youth activities than other middle school students in the district (Sykes et al., 1995, 66).

Nevertheless, other school statistics show that Holmes continued to face the hard problems of many urban schools serving low-income, minority communities. Seventh-grade students failed the state reading, math, and science tests at an "alarming" rate. Also, although the suspension rate declined in 1994, Holmes still had the second highest rate in the district. And finally, after daily absenteeism had dipped under 16 percent in 1991–92, it rose above 22 percent in 1993–94, the highest rate among the district's middle schools (Sykes et al., 1995, 67). Still, in the following year, it was down again to only 6 percent with the suspension rate dropping as well (MSU-32, 1995, 107).

As mentioned earlier, teachers at Holmes later in the PDS era criticized MSU for not making good use of the school for teacher education. According to a proposal submitted by Flint Schools in May 1995,

> Flint is an underutilized site. MSU's College of Education's lack of aggressive encouragement of students to do their internship in Flint, misinformed intern stereotypes, and a dismal MSU record of recruiting prospective teachers of color have combined to produce about 10 teacher educators a year for all Flint PDS schools. . . .
>
> Even so, Holmes teachers and [alternative program] students/interns have benefitted from the experience. During the years 1990–92 Holmes was the principal site for a group of Multiple Perspective (MP) [alternative program] students. Each year 7–9 students completed their entire field and student teaching experience at Holmes. . . . The fact that over 70 percent took teaching positions in Flint or other urban areas attests to the commitment and competence they developed. (MSU-9, 22–23)

The proposal goes on to say that the Post BA Flint Program that replaced MP provided an even richer experience for interns and mentor teachers. Two components were singled out as especially important: the cross-school study group led by Joyce Putnam, and the nine-week summer experience for interns.

Paradoxically in light of such mixed and inconclusive results, the PDS work at Holmes was relatively well funded. During the years 1988 to 1995, from a total PDS annual budget of about $3.5 million, Holmes received about $200,000 annually, before being cut to $164,000 in 1994–95. When fully funded, this 5–6 percent increase in the school's discretionary funding paid for consultants, graduate student assistantships, permanent substitutes to free up regular teachers, MSU travel to and from the school, support for the study groups, teacher stipends for summer and other work, and supplies. On top of this were the contributions in kind from MSU faculty, many of whom worked several days a week at Holmes. Unfortunately, this level of financial and in-kind support raised donor and constituency expectations to a level that proved nearly impossible to meet and sustain (Sykes et al., 1995, 36).

Overall, like the revolution in general, the PDS at Holmes was both a great success and a disturbing failure. It was a great success in the ability of MSU faculty and Holmes teachers to put into practice some impressive examples of innovative student-centered teaching (Putnam & Schwille, 2020; Sykes et al., 1995) and in other ways:

> With support from MSU colleagues and co-workers, [teachers] introduced cooperative learning into many classrooms and refined this practice over time. Within the subject area teams, teachers tried out or developed new curricular materials, teaching strategies, and approaches to assessment. In some cases they dramatically altered the character of classroom community, re-socializing students to more active roles while shifting their own stance from director to facilitator. Teachers teamed with each other to integrate special and regular education students and to construct an interdisciplinary curriculum. They also worked on connecting student learning to the surrounding community and tried out new ways of involving parents in school life and student learning. (Sykes et al., 1995, 62)
>
> The teacher participants . . . were open to new ideas, willing to experiment, and ready to inquire about their new initiatives. The willingness of university personnel to work side-by-side with teachers in their classrooms and to teach middle school students themselves was a significant factor in this work. . . . . What helped validate the exper-

tise of university faculty in the eyes of the teachers was not the credential they carried but the willingness they brought to try out their ideas with students rather than merely advocating approaches for others to try. The joint work helped create status equality between professors and teachers without undercutting the expert authority that each brought to inform experimentation. (40)

At least in self-report, these claims of success have carried over into the present (Putnam & Schwille, 2020). Every district informant interviewed (not just in Holmes but in three other Flint PDSs as well) some twenty-plus years after the fact reported that PDS involvement had changed the way they thought about and worked on their teaching or administrative duties. Informants remembered that university people had listened to and valued what the teachers had to say, giving the teachers a sense of importance and power.

In contrast, the PDS work at Holmes can be considered a failure in the sense that it could not get the desired commitment to school-wide reform and willing participation by all teachers, not just the voluntary few. Sykes and his fellow authors, even though three of them had worked at Holmes and deserve much credit for what they accomplished, are severe in criticizing this state of affairs. In their view, these PDS efforts were fragile and dependent on idiosyncratic factors and never had the full-hearted commitment of most teachers. In part this was because teacher turnover was a huge problem for the Holmes PDS. For example, from 1991 through the fall of 1995, there were fifteen teacher changes in mathematics classrooms (Sykes et al., 1995, 29, 47).

Those teachers who were highly involved were unable to influence the cultural and organizational dynamics that prevented more widespread participation. The new sources of authority cultivated by the PDS, namely professional expertise and standards, were not strong enough, when they conflicted with bureaucratic controls, to deal with and resolve the many issues that arose. Without more administrative pressure and schoolwide leadership on behalf of the PDS, the participating teachers had little choice but to give in to the constraints with which they were faced (Sykes et al., 1995, 53). However, in the midst of the iconic problems of a rust-belt city, the Holmes record is indicative of how important the school was to MSU during the revolutionary era.[1]

Holt High School in Holt

Holt High School, the only high school among the original PDSs, was not only one of the most accomplished, but also the best documented in publications. Part of the reason for this success was the leadership of Tom Davis, then principal of the high school. On January 9, 1992, in the midst of the revolutionary era, he gave a powerful testimonial to the importance of the school's PDS experience:

> In the fall of 1989 Holt High School and Michigan State University entered into a partnership to reinvent schools for the 21st century. . . . The details of the partnership were not well defined in the beginning (and still evolving in this third year) but the underpinning elements were well articulated based on a vision by Dr. Judith Lanier and the Holmes Group of university leaders throughout the United States. The vision embraces the notion that research and theory connecting with practice and craft knowledge has greater potential to reinvent schools than either in isolation.

Although the implementation of this vision at Holt High School took a lot of work and was described by faculty as draining and exhausting, these feelings were overcome, according to Davis by a "strong sense of empowerment." Davis described what was being done as follows:

---

1. Among the MSU faculty who trekked up to Flint, spending an hour driving to and from Holmes in icy as well as good weather, some of them every week in some cases for years, were Chris Wheeler, Joyce Putnam, Jacquie Nickerson, Sharon Schwille, Mark Connelly, Sandy Wilcox, Susan Peters, David Wong, and Bruce Cheney.

There are currently 29 Michigan State University employees to complement our existing staff of 60 teachers in various proportions of FTEs and university status. Some MSU employees are assigned to teach semester classes to reassign a Holt teacher to work on a specific project. Some participate in co-teaching assignments in classrooms where a study is being enacted, some collaborate with Holt faculty and assist with projects, and some assist with evaluation and documentation. The entire HHS faculty participates in one or more projects or a study group with time provided during school hours. The principal and three Holt teachers have also had an opportunity to co-teach teacher preparation classes on campus at the university and twelve teachers have served as mentors for teacher education students. . . .

We believe that our participation as a Professional Development School for the past three years has caused change in the fundamental practice and craft of the teachers (assessment practices changing, teaching less content in [more] depth [in order to achieve more] conceptual understanding, inclusion of all students in high expectation classes, students learning in teams and groups, teachers facilitating instead of lecture/demonstration, and teachers reflecting about and conducting research on their own craft). (January 9, 1992, unpublished document)

In short, Holt was a PDS with great strengths in teaching, put to good use through close collaboration with MSU faculty and students. In 1990–91 the PDS activities at Holt High School already included eleven cross-disciplinary groups and four subject-matter projects in literacy, mathematics, social studies, and science. Approximately 50 percent of the Holt High School faculty participated. Teacher committees addressed school-wide organizational concerns and were responsible for making major changes in the schedule for each day and the year as a whole, including the innovative Wednesday morning schedule that became one of the best-known changes at Holt, allowing for one morning each week for professional development. All teacher contractual time outside class hours was moved to Wednesday morning, with other days lengthened in compensation. Students came to school at 11:30 a.m. on Wednesday, giving teachers reallocated time from 7:30 to 11:30 for PDS work (MSU-22, March 1991, 26).

In 1990–91 an at-risk PDS group was formed to find ways to support all students so that those at risk would feel connected to school without being labeled and singled out, including orientation for new tenth-grade students and plans for fast intervention to attendance problems (26). Another group searched for ways to involve students in the community by giving credit for community service, piloting student placements in the community, and devising ways to assess these experiences (26–27).

Still another cooperative learning circle and an inquiry group worked on improving instruction. The circle was a design lab where participants collaborated in designing group work tasks to address teachers' instructional problems. In the inquiry group, Holt and MSU faculty worked together to learn from their own and others' practices with emphasis on specific classroom problems. All this led to presentations and reports on what they had learned (27). The impressive achievements of Holt's mathematics department have been discussed elsewhere. Holt High was heavily involved in teacher education as well (MSU-35, 1996, 191, 202).

Elliott Elementary School in Holt

Elliott Elementary School in Holt School District was a hotbed of PDS activity throughout the PDS era. It even had a precursor project in the IRT that lasted for four years before the PDS officially started. The eminent anthropologist of education Frederick Erickson, an expert in analyzing interactions between people of different backgrounds, had collaborated with two other MSU faculty members, Doug Campbell and Richard Navarro, in starting work on how to get teachers' voices heard in the educational reform movements then getting under way. This was an ethnographic research project in which "researchers would learn from the teachers' reflections on practice, and the teachers would have an opportunity to think about their practice and to make their implicit knowledge very explicit." The original research group consisted of three first-grade teachers, the principal, and seven university researchers. This allowed the group to divide into teams of two researchers working with each teacher, and one of these teams included the principal as well. The teachers had a half day a week to work on this project (MSU-1, 1988, 3).

Lengthy conversations among the Elliott teachers and with participating MSU staff were the principal mode of investigation for this project. Whereas the teachers were originally most motivated by concerns about classroom management, personal stress, and other frustrations, they were beginning to see that changes in their teaching practice could emerge from a conception of teaching and learning in which they would share responsibilities with students. At the same time, the teachers were starting to see themselves as effective teachers and professionals with greater control over their work lives than they had ever experienced or thought possible.

In a response to this project, Andy Porter reflected the views of the educational research establishment in a revealing rejoinder (June 12, 1986) addressed to Doug Campbell and Richard Navarro about a newsletter article about the Elliott project, saying that he had become

> increasingly convinced that you have fallen into some specialized uses of language which may make your work obscure to many audiences with which you would like to communicate. There are three types of problems that occurred repeatedly. One had to do with methodology. Your use of terms such as stories and conversations makes your methods sound casual and lacking analysis, which is not true. The term bottom-up carries a great deal of particularized meaning to a relatively small group of researchers interested in policy, but does not have those meanings for wider audiences, including even researchers. Another area where I found your use of language trouble-

some concerned descriptions of the results of your work. Terms such as empowered and transformative may have developed special meanings for you but these need to be made explicit for readers beyond your research team (and close colleagues elsewhere). Similarly, traditional models of teaching may have meaning to you, but will generally be without meaning (or worse, take on particularized meanings which vary from reader to reader).

In fact, the work of Florio-Ruane (e.g., 1986), Erickson (e.g., 2004), and even the iconic psychologist Brophy (e.g., Brophy, Alleman & Knighton, 2009) as it developed then and later did give the terms used, such as "conversation" and "stories," research currency and legitimacy.

When Doug Campbell presented on this project at a 1988 American Educational Research Association symposium, he called attention to difficulties inherent in the ethnographers' intent to be egalitarian, nonjudgmental, and nondirective. He explained:

One of the important lessons I have learned from working with Kathy in her classroom is that it was rather naïve to have assumed that any of us could have been truly non-directive and non-judgmental; worse yet, it was probably patronizing to have comported ourselves as such to the teachers, as if all we needed to do was to announce ourselves as non-intervening, rather than remaining ever watchful for ways in which we were enacting the inherent contradictions of our ideals. (MSU-1, 1988, 3–4)

What this meant for the history of the PDSs is that four years were spent trying to change the relationship between researchers and teachers in ways that were consistent with and contributed to the beginnings of the Elliott PDS founded in 1988–89. Nevertheless, the PDS work at Elliott, productive and meritorious as it would become, did not always benefit sufficiently from this earlier project to run as smoothly as one might have hoped, even though by the end of the PDS era Elliott was again in the forefront of the retrospective effort to document the overall impact and value of the PDS experience. In substantive terms, Elliott was a particularly good example of a PDS that evolved from primarily subject-matter work, emphasizing teaching for conceptual understanding, to later projects that dealt with school-wide issues such as student behavior problems and parental involvement.

One subject-matter project, Literacy in Science and Social Studies, was particularly active. Its team included three Elliott teachers (Elaine Hoekwater, Carol Ligett, and Barbara Lindquist), two MSU faculty (Rosaen and Roth), and three MSU graduate assistants. Three half-time coteachers had also been hired to teach in the project teachers' classrooms to free up time for the regular classroom teachers. This allowed the PDS teachers to spend half their day in regular classroom teaching and the other half time on research and study for the project. This project was especially ambitious in attempting to create two new roles (teacher as researcher and researcher as teacher), which required the use of writing in the teaching and learning of science and social studies. Writing workshops and dialogue journals between teacher and students served to enhance conceptually oriented science teaching as well as content learning in other areas (Rosaen & Lindquist, 1992; Roth & Rosaen, 1995).

During this period of initial success, there were problems at Elliott but they were not brought into the open until later. At the end of 1991, the first signs of the conflict surfaced when four teachers resigned all at once from the mathematics study group, saying they felt it was interfering with their regular teaching and not good for their students. Then the following year, 1992–93, still more hostility broke out, pitting teachers against one another as well as for and against the MSU faculty. At the time the annual reports dealt with this conflict in vague terms, revealing little other than to say that one of the study groups was being discontinued, with one of its members changing schools and the two others quitting the PDS. It was only later that enough could be said publicly to better understand the nature of the conflict. At that time, a 1995 proposal explained:

In combination with differences in personality and interaction style within Elliott staff and between Elliott and
MSU staffs, problems that were not addressed in a timely
manner had accumulated and festered to such an extent
that in 1992–93 severe conflict and hostility between
various factions burst into open in a highly stressful and
disruptive fashion. With the help of Sharon Hobson of
the Michigan Partnership for New Education (MPNE),
several Elliott and MSU PDS participants saw the need
to address head-on the specific issues that were dividing
people and to develop and institutionalize more effective
norms of and strategies for communication, problem
solving, conflict resolution and decision making. (MSU-
2, May 1995, 26–27)

By 1994–95, as documented in Elliott's annual report (MSU-
3, October 1995), there were six projects indicating that the
PDS had emerged from this period of conflict in relatively good
shape: two subject-matter improvement projects, a computer
technology project, a Home–School Connections project, a project aimed at a nurturing climate for everyone at Elliott (teachers,
students, support staff, families, MSU partners), and a teacher-education project. In the 1995–98 proposal for continuation
of the MSU PDSs (MSU-2, May 1995), subject-matter improvement remained very strong at Elliott as evidenced by reported
achievements in fifth-grade science, writing, and social studies.
Mathematics also built a strong record at Elliott (MSU-22, March
1991, 14).

Michigan Educational Assessment Program (MEAP) results
showed improvement in mathematics between 1992–93 and
1994–95. The percentage of Elliott students scoring in the highest category of achievement on the fourth-grade MEAP test of
mathematics rose from 36.8 percent in 1992–93 to 62.7 percent
in 1994–95. Moreover, of the eighteen students who had been
in classrooms taught by the math study group teachers since the
first grade, sixteen scored satisfactorily on the fourth-grade math
MEAP (MSU-14, March 1996).

In short, in spite of disputes and the tendency toward much self-criticism and agonizing over the changes of direction, Elliott was indisputably one of the more successful PDSs. By 1995, in addition to the four MSU faculty assigned to Elliott (Campbell, Rosaen, Roth, and Schram), twenty-one MSU graduate students had worked on projects at the school. In addition Elliott played a large role in MSU teacher education (MSU-2, May 1995, 20). The importance of Elliott in PDS work was emphasized by Dean Ames, who, though relentless in her criticism of schools that had not managed to be "real PDSs," included Elliott as one of the PDSs that she judged had done the most to deserve continued support (email from Cheryl Rosaen to Doug Campbell, May 13, 1999).

Spartan Village Elementary in East Lansing

Although, according to the 1990–91 PDS report (MSU-23, November 1991), Spartan Village Elementary School was to work on restructured leadership, professional growth time, and restructured collaborative classrooms, Spartan Village was still the epitome of the subject-matter approach that consisted of one classroom teacher and one MSU specialist in the subject matter working together on the subject-matter teaching and learning in that classroom.

Projects for 1990–91 were grouped in two sets. One set included seven collaborative classroom teams working on the improvement of teaching and learning: three in science, two in math, and two in literacy. The second set was intended to include the entire staff in restructured team teaching, but since time could not be freed up for this, it was postponed. Instead the number of collaborative classroom teams was increased to eleven, each with a classroom teacher and MSU participant to work on a specific subject matter (MSU-22, March 1991, 43).

In the case of mathematics, this made three teams and the beginnings of a fourth. In a third/fourth-grade class teacher Sylvia Rundquist and MSU faculty member Deborah Ball were focusing on how students think and learn. Ball took responsibility for the daily teaching while Rundquist observed. They met weekly to discuss the lessons, student response, and Rundquist's suggestions. As a result, that winter Rundquist was one of the teachers in the required introductory TE course at the university; she provided background on the classroom she shared with Ball and answered questions about the videotapes of Ball's teaching that were viewed in the course. As for the fifth-grade teacher Thom Dye, although he had resumed responsibility for math teaching, he and Magdalene Lampert still conferred regularly about his teaching as well as her reflections on the seven years she had taught math in his classroom. MSU graduate assistant Ruth Heaton brought another perspective. She, too, observed Dye's teaching and discussed his instructional decisions with him and Lampert, based on her having taught his students the previous year when they were fourth graders in another teacher's room (44).

In a first-grade science project, teacher Kathy Moss and one graduate assistant worked on teaching for understanding in science, using the state of Michigan science objectives. In fall 1990 they developed and taught one unit on terrariums and insects and another on plants. After the terrarium unit, these students made a presentation to the third/fourth graders on how to build terrariums, what observations they had made, and what theories about insects they developed—challenging tasks for first graders. In the unit on plants, before growing plants for observation, the students formulated criteria for identifying a plant as a plant (45).

In another science project, first-grade teacher Roberta Gardner and fourth-grade teacher Jackie Frese worked with MSU professor Ed Smith. They used a part-function framework to explain how things work, first by investigating what an object does, and then examining how each of its parts helps the object work. This team also explored developmental differences between first and fourth graders by pairing first and fourth graders to teach one another. Thus, both first and fourth graders had a chance to teach about how a particular object (such as a flashlight) works (46).

In literacy, four classroom teams were busy doing the initial work on their projects. Graduate assistant Dirck Roosevelt worked with third-grade teacher Alyjah Byrd. They focused on the meaning and purposes of student writing in Byrd's classroom, investigating what the writing revealed about student thinking and interests as well as strengths and weaknesses as writers, and how curricular goals and analytic schemes compared to what actually went on. Roosevelt also worked with fifth-grade teacher Thom Dye, making use of journals with students just beginning to learn English (46–47).

Averill Elementary School in Lansing

Another urban school, Averill in Lansing had started PDS work under exceptionally favorable conditions. It had a generally receptive and capable teaching staff, an extraordinary principal, Bruce Rochowiak, who knew how to support and facilitate this initiative, and not least, a long history of work on MSU teacher-education programs and special projects. With this history, Averill was able to develop its own innovative take on teacher education, reduce dependence on university colleagues, and achieve more equality between university and school in teacher education than in some other PDSs. All the teachers at Averill served as teacher educators in 1995–96 (MSU-35, 1996, 6, 19–26; Feiman-Nemser & Beasley, 2007).

Averill was a school of three hundred students, 63 percent of whom were from minority families by 1996. In 1990–91 it had been part of the PDS movement for two and a half years. All fourteen of the school's teachers were participating in PDS work, along with nine MSU faculty members and graduate students. Its main theme was "developing a learning community school," that is, "a collaborative commitment to create a school culture where all members (students, teachers, aides, principal, support staff, teacher education students, and university faculty) are vital players in an educational community that fosters an understanding of diversity and promotes equitable enriching learning experiences for everyone" (MSU-22, March 1991, 4–5).

Despite a long history of involvement in MSU teacher education (e.g., with the Multiple Perspectives program), traditional norms of teacher education still prevailed at the school. It had always been university personnel, not K–12 teachers, who designed the field assignments for student teachers and evaluated their performance, while Averill faculty were mostly limited to making their children and space available, with little input into what student teachers did. Frustration with this traditional division of labor came to motivate much of Averill's PDS work (Feiman-Nemser & Beasley, 2007).

To change these school–university relationships, Averill teachers analyzed aspects of the school's culture they had taken for granted. They identified existing and potentially dysfunctional norms and patterns of communication, including those that had never been made so explicit. Linda Forrest, a professor of counseling psychology at MSU, led these discussions uncovering many unwritten rules, such as not challenging other teachers' ideas or asking what they mean, not discussing substantive issues in the lunchroom, valuing harmony above all, and fearing that innovation by individual teachers could result in isolation. These meetings revealed the importance of developing different norms, such as tolerance for experimentation and, in particular, opportunities to share work, to confront differences in beliefs and practices, to talk systematically and candidly about curriculum, grouping, and instructional practice. Overall, this effort was one of the few instances in which Judy Lanier was successful in getting good faculty participation in the PDSs from a professor not otherwise engaged in teacher education—Linda Forrest in this case (Averill/MSU PDS staff meeting minutes, February 26, 1991; Forzani, 2011, 234).

These early discussions led to the realization at Averill that becoming a PDS meant more than just organizing a narrowly defined set of projects. "As it looked toward 1990, the team and its strategic planning committee set itself the task of developing long range goals embodying the idea that Averill itself is a PDS rather than a collection of projects which may not all actually support . . . overall goals" (MSU-20, November 1990, 29).

In one project important to these overall goals, classrooms were videotaped and students interviewed to answer questions about *learning communities*: What does a learning-community classroom look like? What is the teacher role in a learning-community classroom? How is that different from a traditional classroom? What values, beliefs, and practices interfere with or help teachers develop a learning community? (MSU-22, March 1991, 7–8).

Several other Averill projects dealt with learning to teach, as might be expected in a school in which Sharon Feiman-Nemser, one of the masterminds of MSU teacher-education reform, was playing a key role. In the Multiple Perspectives program twenty juniors and twelve seniors were in the school two times per week. One of the PDS projects included several Averill teachers and teacher candidates who were learning to study teaching together. One Averill teacher (Kathy Beasley), one MSU field instructor (Judy Murdoch), one MSU faculty member (Sharon Feiman-Nemser), and one teacher candidate (Deb Corbin) formed another team drawing on all the diverse roles involved in MSU teacher-education field experience. They met once a week to discuss teaching practice and the nature of field experience in a teacher-education program. Using journals and other data they collected, one of their main purposes was to rethink the role of the experienced teacher in the learning of novice teachers. In another related but broader project two MSU staff members met monthly with fourteen field instructors to discuss clinical practices and ways to help teacher-education students learn to teach. At the same time, a new group was formed from different PDSs in Lansing and Flint to examine clinical studies, drawing together teachers from Averill, Holmes, and Otto, plus field instructors and Joyce Putnam, the MSU PDS coordinator for the Lansing and Flint school districts (8–9).

To provide time for teachers to do this PDS work, two specialist teachers taught science in different classrooms five afternoons a week, providing each of the classroom teachers a half day of real-located PDS time. They taught the same content to the different classes but at different levels of difficulty. In addition, MSU students in their first year of teacher education taught reading to second and third graders for an hour two times a week, giving teachers an additional two hours a week of reallocated time. Similarly, second-year teacher-education students provided reallocated time to their cooperating teachers (10).

Conclusion

This chapter has been a window to shed light on what five of the seven original MSU PDSs were able to accomplish, showing how much they differed from one another while still pursuing the common goals of creating a new kind of school for school and university personnel to transform teaching and learning, conduct research on the grassroots problems experienced by the school, and play a greatly increased role in improving MSU's teacher-preparation program. None of this would have happened if the K–12 teachers, MSU doctoral students, and MSU faculty had not devoted extraordinary amounts of time as well as their talents to roles and responsibilities they had not had to carry out before. The result, although short-lived, was revolutionary enough to justify continued study of how such efforts could be sustained. An external panel to evaluate the PDSs concluded in 1995 that each of these PDS sites was exceptional in making holistic improvements and developing positive attitudes among university as well as K–12 teacher and student participants.

CHAPTER FOURTEEN

Amphibious Professors Learn to Be at Home in Both Higher Education and K–12

One role emerged during the revolutionary era that also served to refute the claim that the PDSs would not be able to do enough important research. The role was that of an "amphibious" university professor. Introduced by Jay Featherstone, this term is an apt way to describe the work of MSU faculty members who were given university load time to teach K–12 pupils daily in one of the PDSs. Making university educators responsible and accountable for K–12 learning was the most revolutionary development by far. An associated change was to recruit and assign K–12 teachers to university teaching duties in teacher-education courses. In short, one of the most far-reaching attempts at revolution during this period was to take preexisting roles of K–12 teacher, teacher educator, and university researcher and in one way or another blend them together as much as possible.

In the past the traditional differentiation of these roles led to dysfunctional status distinctions that fed the notion that persons in one or another of these traditional roles had little to learn from persons in the other roles and no need to collaborate with them on a continuing, more or less egalitarian basis. For much of the twentieth century, ever since teacher education was incorporated into universities or colleges of education at higher education levels, it was common to criticize their programs for the teaching done by persons deemed unqualified because they lacked K–12 experience. Nevertheless, at least in large universities that produced the lion's share of new teachers, this criticism was mostly disregarded. Hence, when MSU began to place superbly qualified new faculty with K–12 experience as well as sterling university credentials to

teach part-time in K–12 on a daily basis, this undeniably constituted some of the most radical changes of that era (cf. Forzani,
2011, 139–40).

The work of those extraordinary individuals is most profitably
examined in judging whether the PDSs were producing enough
research of high quality and importance not only to justify merit-
based salary raises and positive tenure/promotion decisions, but
also to help make judgments about whether the whole PDS enterprise was a legitimate use of higher-education resources. PDSs in
the eyes of influential university faculty and administrators were
alleged to be lacking in this respect (Forzani, 2011, 309), and this
shortcoming was used to call for the gradual abolition of PDSs at
MSU and the return to orthodoxy. Traditional university policy on
promotion with its insistence on a continuing stream of peer-reviewed publications was applied in this situation even though an
argument could be and was made that it did not fit. The needed
long-term commitment to PDSs was abandoned before it could be
brought to fruition.

Nevertheless, even at this point of uneven and partial implementation, the publications produced by the amphibious professors (not to speak of PDS publications in general) can be seen to be
of very high quality and markedly original. And most important,
these publications could not have been produced had their authors
not occupied amphibious roles.

To do all this, these amphibious faculty members had to overcome the unprecedented, difficult, and daily challenges inherent
in this new role. These faculty have written about what they had to
face and how they met these challenges. Deborah Ball, later dean of
education at the University of Michigan, Ann Arbor, aptly summarized the motivations of these amphibious professors: "Although I
fell in love with teaching at the university level, I also realized that
for my own learning I would have to continue to teach elementary
school. My own classroom was a site for my learning about the
practice of mathematics teaching that was as essential to my work
with teachers as my study of mathematics was to my teaching of
children" (Ball, 1998, 21).

Disentangling the Distinctive
Promise, Complexity, and Tensions
of Amphibious Teaching

In perhaps the best account of how revolutionary this amphibious teaching was, Magdalene Lampert wrote of her job at MSU:

> Currently I am a teacher in a public school who also has responsibilities for the education of both prospective and practicing teachers. I am also an educational researcher who spends an hour each day teaching a heterogeneous group of twenty-five students in an ordinary classroom, experimenting with innovative content and instructional forms and carefully monitoring the effects they have on students' learning. I am a university faculty member who is regularly engaged in local and national discussions of policy and practice. I am a scholar who writes about teaching in a way that connects what one can learn from practice with various research traditions. I am a teacher/colleague to a diverse group of elementary teachers who think of me as a specialist in mathematics education. (1991, 672)

Lampert adds that she would not have gotten involved in educational research or teacher education "if I could not have found a way to connect them directly with teaching in the schools" (671). Becoming a teacher who experiments with innovative practices and then works with prospective and practicing teachers to examine the impact of these practices allowed her to become a teacher educator who "does not need to preach about innovation" (671).

Lampert discusses each of the three jobs she blended in her role at MSU and Spartan Village Elementary School. She starts by discussing her work as a K–12 teacher:

> What I do as a teacher is directed toward getting all my fifth-graders to be truly engaged in every lesson. I want

> them to love mathematics, and I want them to do much
> better than average on the standardized achievement
> test that is administered at the end of the year. I try to
> be sensitive to individual differences and to the nonaca-
> demic influences on students' capacities to participate in
> a lesson. . . . I try to be available to parents whenever they
> have a concern, and I take on the challenge of trying to
> explain why math doesn't look the way it did when they
> went to school. In order to be a good teacher, I must be
> committed to the idea that all my fifth-graders can learn
> to understand mathematics. (673–74)

As a teacher educator, she served as a practicing teacher who regularly welcomed teacher-education majors to observe her teach and
then discuss what they observed. Other student teachers in the
Spartan Village PDS were sent by their mentors to observe some
of her lessons and to discuss them with her. And in two university
courses that others taught, videotapes of Lampert's teaching were
used to illustrate inquiry-oriented instruction so that the students
could compare that approach with what's commonly called "teaching as telling." Students were also assigned articles that Lampert
says were written "from a teacher's perspective" (672–73).

One of the main problems with this amphibious teaching,
according to Lampert, was that there were no agreed-upon ways
to evaluate work in such a boundary-blurring role. The rules for
evaluation of MSU university faculty work were not designed
for her. She noted that no one on the evaluation committees was
doing the work she did. These committees annually judge each
faculty member's work as the basis for merit raises and promotion. In fact, for the most part, before the revolution most faculty
members did not bother to go out in K–12 schools regularly at all,
even as observers, and during the revolution there were still many
professors outside the department of teacher education who were
not directly involved in K–12 schools (672).

Lampert continued with further examination of the role
conflicts inherent in her position:

The problem of how boundary-blurring work is to be regarded is not only a problem of formal evaluations imposed by institutions with potentially conflicting interests. It is also a problem of how one thinks about oneself. What it takes in a school setting to feel that one is a good teacher is very different from what it takes in a university setting to feel that one is a good faculty member. . . . The tensions for one who tries to work responsibly in both settings can be likened to those of the newly professionalized woman who is also a mother and homemaker, attempting to do well by the standards of both the workplace and the home—and having to play both roles better than those who hold either one or the other, just to prove that a dual role is possible. (673)

Being a teacher educator in an amphibious position, in Lampert's view, added a whole set of additional responsibilities that were difficult to fill:

I try to get my teacher education students and the experienced teachers with whom I work to realize that teaching mathematics for understanding is a very complicated business . . . that one needs to have ideals but also to be aware of the realities of classroom life. I try hard to communicate that I don't know all the "answers" and that becoming a good teacher is not a matter of knowing how to do it "right." . . . I want them to appreciate the fact that a knowledge of the subject matter of mathematics could enable them to be more responsive to children's way of thinking. . . . I want them to spend time in the classroom, seeing what teaching for understanding looks like and trying to do it, but I also want them to spend more time studying the subject matter themselves. (674)

Added to that is the third job, that of teacher-researcher, which is if anything even more difficult and fraught with dilemmas:

From this perspective, every lesson that I teach is not only an effort to get a group of fifth-graders to understand mathematics, but also a 45-minute long clinical interview conducted with 25 students at once. Most lessons are so rich with data and insights into how children think about a particular mathematical topic that they would provide enough material for me to chew on for at least a week. But I have to go in and teach another lesson the next day. (674)

The requirement to publish research makes the teacher-researcher role still more challenging, causing Lampert a good deal of anxiety:

I worry that my paper will not be accepted because it is written in the first person or because I do not have enough data in the form of test scores to document the outcomes of lessons. In order to be "good" as a scholar, I need to put distance between myself and my lessons, consider alternative actions and explanations, and expose my judgments to other researchers for analysis. I need to withhold my faith that students *will* learn—a faith that is essential to my work as a teacher—and try to determine whether they actually *are* learning. I need to explain the variations in their performance in a very different language from the one I would use with my teaching colleagues. (674)

The overall demands on the amphibious professor can be overwhelming: "The fundamental strain is that it takes a different sort of 'me' to be good at each of these jobs, and the 'me' in one job is often in conflict with the 'me' in another" (674). Since there have always been tensions between research and practice, between teaching as a profession and formal teacher education, and between researchers and teacher educators, reorganization in the form of PDSs or otherwise is not enough, in Lampert's view, to resolve them. After reorganization, in her experience, these tensions simply moved to the level of individuals in the boundary-blurring roles. To the extent that this transfer had already taken place during the revolutionary era at MSU, far too little had been done to provide the special support that the amphibious faculty needed to cope with all these demands. This made it very difficult to find individuals qualified and willing to fill these roles as is clear from the following discussions of their teaching.[1]

Lampert and Why Just Getting the Right Answer is Far from Enough

In one of her publications as an amphibious professor, Lampert examines the discipline of mathematics as experienced by mathematicians as compared with how it is taught in schools. What typically happens in school is a matter of certainty from the start. "In school, the truth is given in the teacher's explanations and the answer book; there is no zig-zag between conjectures and arguments for their validity, and one could hardly imagine hearing the words *maybe* or *perhaps* in a lesson" (1990, 32). But then the education-reform movement challenged this state of affairs. It called for schools, teachers, and students to do mathematics by "making conjectures, abstracting mathematical properties, explaining their reasoning, validating their assertions, and discussing and questioning their own thinking and the thinking of others" (33).

In one lesson on exponents, Lampert gave the class problems to do without explaining how to get answers. She also made it clear that she expected them to go beyond presenting a solution to being able to answer questions about their mathematical assumptions and the mathematical legitimacy of their approach. For comparison, Lampert discusses various "nonmathematical ways of knowing mathematics in school," such as relying on the teachers as the authority. Another nonmathematical response is to treat rules, formulas, and facts as if they were arguments. Students fail to recognize that using a rule is different from explaining why it works or why it is appropriate to use for a particular case. Still

---

1. This discussion may leave the impression of wide, more or less complete consensus on this amphibious role, but this was far from the case. See, for example, the conflicting views of two MSU amphibious professors that were published in *Educational Researcher* (Wilson, 1995; Wong, 1995a, 1995b).

another nonmathematical behavior is simply to remain silent. To Lampert, silence is such situations can mean a number of things: Sometimes the student simply lacks the verbal capability to explain his or her reasoning. Or maybe the student just lacks the courage to speak up and is uncomfortable being the focus of attention. And sometimes even, the student doesn't want to admit that he or she copied the answer from another student.

Roth and Student Understanding
of the Nature of Science

While the amphibious professors were mostly specialized in the teaching of one subject, Kathleen Roth was noted for her work in two subjects, both science and social studies. Her "Talking to Understand Science" is a good introduction to her approach (Roth, 2002, but see also Roth, 1989b). As a teacher and a researcher she was preoccupied by the question of what it means to really understand science and to teach for that understanding. Roth drew from both the conceptual change and social constructivist traditions as well as from her own research to analyze what matters in shaping the talk that takes place in a science classroom.

> In the 1980's, my first experience as a researcher had a profound effect on my thinking about science teaching practice. In particular, I became aware of a problem with the kinds of talk going on in science classrooms. In textbook-focused classrooms, the talk was dominated by teacher telling with teacher-student dialogue limited to the traditional, didactic pattern: teacher initiation ("What kinds of rocks are formed as the result of volcanic activity?"), followed by student response ("igneous"), followed by teacher evaluation ("right"). In hands-on, inquiry-oriented classrooms, student talk was much more prominent. Students were actively engaged in talking about their ideas, their observations, and their personal explanations of natural phenomena they observed. The teacher asked

> more open-ended questions and encouraged students to generate their own hypotheses and theories. In both types of classrooms, however, only a small minority of students developed meaningful understandings of science concepts or about the nature of science. (Roth, 2002, 197)

Roth admits that she had previously been excited about the "rich discourse" she encountered during the 1980s in the inquiry-oriented classrooms. If she had written only about those classes, in the absence of studies of student understanding, she could have produced "glowing reports," assuming that those classrooms had become true scientific communities. But when she examined the evidence from such classrooms, she found that the students still lacked understanding of scientific concepts or of the nature of science. It did not surprise Roth that students were not learning in classrooms when they just listened and only occasionally gave short answers to factual questions. But she was very surprised that in classes where students were actively engaged in and talking about observations and predictions, organizing data, and developing explanations for their observations, etc., those students did not understand the concepts either. In both types of classrooms students tended to develop notions that were erroneous when viewed in light of scientific evidence. In fact, Roth had had students who gave the same answers after taking a unit on how light helps people see as they had given on their pretest. The answers they gave had nothing to do with what they had been expected to learn. "Science" for them was textbook information that had nothing to do with explaining what they encountered in everyday life (3).

To do better, Roth had to dig more deeply for herself into what it means for elementary students to understand science:

> My study of my own students' learning at the end of my first year as a teacher-researcher was the first stimulus to broaden my definition of what students need a chance to talk about in science classrooms. From that research, it was clear that my students were not understanding that questioning, the use of evidence, and argumenta-

tion are core characteristics of the scientific enterprise. Modeling these scientific processes in the classroom was not enough. There must also be explicit talk about the nature of science and scientific inquiry, ways of talking and acting in science, explicit talk about the language, values, and practices of science. Students need the chance to talk about *why* evidence is so important, and about *why* all evidence is not equal, about *why* scientists debate ideas and measure things and graph things, etc. (45)

To address these issues, Roth developed explicit curriculum strands about the nature of science and scientific inquiry to add to each unit she taught. At the beginning of the year, she had students draw pictures of scientists at work, and then talk about their images and stereotypes of scientists. After this, they had opportunities to get to know real scientists throughout the year—scientists in the community, scientists in books and videos, and scientists to whom they wrote (45).

Initially, the students did not understand why Roth wanted evidence and student debate about the nature of science. They thought it was just a personality quirk of hers to raise such issues. But Roth did not give up. She added even more explicit attention to the nature of science and the ways in which their classroom was or was not like a scientific community. Finally, with comparisons of student interview data at the beginning and end of the school year, she was able to show that this explicit talk was effective in changing and enriching student understanding of how science works (15).

Nevertheless, after that first year as a teacher-researcher, her views on what was best to talk about in science class continued to change dramatically. At the beginning she had focused on conceptual learning, ignoring criticism of this sort of teaching for being too focused on narrow views of student learning. She did this in part because she did not want to "waste" time. Although fascinated by students' ideas about science, she was not open to personal stories that could take the class off track (44).

Earlier, Roth analyzed student thinking about science carefully, but without taking into account possible gender, racial, and ethnic influences on the classroom. Only gradually over time did she become more open to talking to students about their cultural values and identities. She learned how important it was to consider their personal values, their cultural or racial identities, their interests, their self-image and self-confidence, their frustrations and worries. Roth had been trying to be color blind, to ignore stereotypes, to treat all students the same, but it didn't work. She found that, if she did not get to know these students in a more personal, meaningful way, she had difficulty connecting with them in. science (50).

> I now welcome talk in science that might at first seem unrelated to the science. And I encourage students to talk and write about their feelings and values and worries and concerns. Daily journal writing entries and end-of-lesson reflection talk are just as likely to be about these topics as about the science concepts: "How are you feeling about yourself as a science learner?" "Would you like to be a scientist like Mary Seeley? Why or why not?" "In what ways are you acting like a scientist in our science class? Does that feel comfortable to you?" "What would you like to ask our visiting scientist about what it's really like to be a scientist? What do you want to ask her about herself and her life outside of work?" "What did you do over the weekend?" "Do you ever think about science outside of school?" "What things are really important to you?" (52)

In these ways Roth was working to create a more welcoming understanding of science in the classroom. She made it acceptable to talk in the class about ways in which science was uncomfortable for students. Having learned that young girls are often passionate about animal rights, she took that into account, making sure the students were aware of different ways to do science and that science does not always involve hurting or killing animals. When some students wanted to dissect a frog, Roth took advantage of this by holding a series of discussions about animal rights and the use of animals in research. Students were encouraged to develop and clarify their own values and positions on this issue, while at the same time coming to grips with differences in what other students thought. In the end, students decided that they should have a choice between doing a frog dissection in the classroom or a virtual dissection online (52).

Roth also engaged with her students in sensitive discussions about gender. When the girls and boys in her class did not want to work together, she had the class discuss the advantages and disadvantages of mixed-gender groups. They then did an experiment comparing their experience in same-gender groups versus mixed-gender groups, talking about how they felt about both situations. The girls were very vocal about boys trying to dominate or take over the equipment. Having had this experience, the class tried to come up with strategies for working out these differences within groups (52–53).

In Roth's class, students were also introduced to cases where ageism, sexism, and racism had affected the history of science. Having read about scientists who had experienced discrimination, they asked visitors to their classroom about whether they had had experiences of this sort. The class was very taken by the case of a Native American scientist who had to dissect plants in her studies, even though this violated her cultural and religious beliefs. This led the class to consider whether scientists have to give up part of their previous identities if they were to become scientists. As a result of these discussions, the students became more sophisticated in dealing with the questions of whose ideas count most in science (53).

As Roth helped students judge what sort of scientific community they had in their classroom, she found that they gained a better understanding about how science works. She no longer worried about the criticism that she, as the teacher, was doing too much of the selecting and directing of the science that students were studying. Instead, she began to think of herself as a principal investigator whose job is to create a research team among her students—students who would become interested in and understand the value of her plans. But at the same time, her role was also to welcome new ideas, new questions, and new research strategies from her students. And she knew that her team had to learn to talk in a new way—"talk that challenges, talk that supports, and talk that enables the group to consider and resolve different points of view on a given issue" (55–56).

Throughout, although more tolerant of discussions that might be considered distracting, Roth kept her focus on student understanding. She continued to worry about what individual students had learned. She wanted to know what conceptual knowledge, what knowledge about the nature of science, and what ways of thinking and acting each student took away at the end of the school year (59).

Wilson as Gutsy Traveler in Real Classrooms

Suzanne Wilson was another amphibious professor whose practice merits examination and discussion. The record is different in that her amphibious experience is described not just in terms of how she experienced it herself, but also as she was seen by K–12 teachers with whom she collaborated. In 1993 she coauthored an article with the two K–12 teachers with whom she taught: Carol Yerkes and Carol Miller. Wilson explains that she had taken this assignment in an effort to combine her research interests in the subject-matter knowledge required for teaching elementary school social studies and her practice as a teacher educator. She decided to teach part-time in a local elementary school. She approached Yerkes, who taught at Kendon Elementary School in Lansing, a new PDS, to ask if she could teach social studies every afternoon in Yerkes's class. Initially, Yerkes did not see this request as having anything to do with her own learning as a teacher but instead simply as a possible time of relief from the demands of her own teaching. When Wilson entered the scene, Miller and Yerkes were already team teaching. After a year in which Wilson and Yerkes started to collaborate and Miller was not so much involved, the three teachers decided to explore the integration of social studies, science, and language arts. They created a new curriculum and began teaching forty-five to sixty minutes four days a week in each of two third-grade classrooms. For example, when teaching a unit on Detroit, Wilson taught geography and map reading, Yerkes taught the history of Native Americans in Michigan, while Miller focused on the history of salt and salt mining in the region (Wilson, Miller & Yerkes, 1993).

As they describe it, each of the three was naive about their collaboration at first. For example, Wilson originally conceived of her work in Yerkes's room as a way to enhance her own learning to teach. Saddled with "feelings of ignorance and incompetence" because she had never taught in elementary school before, just in high school and at the university, she didn't even think about what Yerkes and Miller might learn from her (89).

The two other teachers told a different story. They had this to say about the challenges of working with Wilson, making it clear how special and unusual it was to team teach with an amphibious professor during the MSU revolution:

> Suzanne will do anything and try anything and is not afraid to fall flat on her face. It helps to know that we can do the same thing. If she can do this, we can do it, too" (100).Working with a college professor is exhilarating, exasperating, refreshing, frustrating, and rewarding. When we started working with Suzanne, we didn't know what we were getting into! It's always easy to sit back and explore new ideas by yourself because—as an individual teacher within the classroom setting—you are your own judge. But in a collaborative effort, there are strong feelings that you are being judged by others. To successfully build a team, we needed open communication, trust building, and time to be together. (84)
>
> What we saw in Suzanne was a college professor willing to take risks, willing to leave her comfortable world at Michigan State University and venture into an unknown atmosphere, trying to see if what she was teaching in her world was related to ours. It was easy for her to tell other teachers how to teach, but did this really fly in the classroom? We saw her not as a researcher, but as a gutsy traveler willing to experience the real classrooms. (100)

Conclusion

Later, in recognition of their exceptional contributions, three members of the amphibious group were all elected to the prestigious National Academy of Education: Deborah Ball, Magdalene Lampert, and Suzanne Wilson. The story of all these amphibious professors and their unique contributions to the study of teaching and teacher education makes me wonder after all these years how a revolutionary practice with such a record of achievement and promise could be abandoned by MSU for reasons of funding and disagreements over what are the most appropriate roles for scholars in schools of education. It was a self-inflicted and self-defeating setback and signal that the revolution had suffered a core failure. If there was a Spartan tragedy, surely the loss of amphibious professors was a huge part of it.

CHAPTER FIFTEEN

Pivotal Discoveries in Student Thinking and Learning

Some of the most important developments in educational research as it developed in the last half of the twentieth century can be found in discoveries of how much can be learned from investigating how students think and thereby revealing how unanticipated, creative, and contrary to researcher assumptions and paradigms this thinking could be. This movement developed and became important in the MSU context. The revolutionary idea here was that unlocking student thinking did not just lead to new insights that would enlighten the readers of books and articles, but was necessary to improvement of teaching and teacher education. This work was well under way outside MSU before it was incorporated in the unfinished MSU revolution. Lee Shulman, for example, took note of this when he wrote:

> Mathematics educators like Bob Davis and Max Beberman have told their teaching students for years: when a child makes a mistake, don't ask "Why did he do something so stupid?" Get inside the student's head and ask, "What would make that a *reasonable* thing for him and her to say?" (1990/2004, 413)

In growing awareness of these outside developments during the revolutionary era, understanding and responding to student thinking became central to the MSU reform agenda, following a broader shift in research on teaching (and other areas of psychological research) from looking only at behaviors to giving a central role to the cognitive processes of teachers and students.

In their article synthesizing what was known about learning

288

to teach, Feiman-Nemser and Remillard stress the importance of teachers being knowledgeable about student thinking:

> In order to build bridges between students and subject matter, teachers need to know how their students think about what they are learning. . . . Like most people, teachers often assume that students who share their language and culture, experience it as they do. . . . One of the central tasks of teacher education is to help teacher candidates overcome this "presumption of shared identity" in order to learn to attend to the thinking and actions of others. (1995, 8)

In a fascinating memoir about her career, Magdalene Lampert describes the influences that led her to place so much emphasis on paying attention to and understanding student thinking. Her experience at Prospect School in Vermont, the school founded by Pat Carini, was a major factor in learning to do this:

> The founders of Prospect [School] drew on ideas about curriculum and pedagogy that were being enacted in British Infant Schools and earlier had been part of the Progressive Movement in the U.S. In these schools, teachers organized around the idea that children think differently from adults and teachers need to observe and listen to children's attempts to investigate ideas through play as a basis for figuring out how to teach them. . . . [At] Prospect I saw . . . that they [children] could represent their ideas with paint and clay and blocks and talk, and that they had lots to do and say even before they "learned" what the teacher was there to teach. (1998, 4)

Others at MSU (e.g., Dirck Roosevelt, David Carroll, and Susan Donnelly) also acknowledged their debt to Prospect and similar connections: "We were in effect trying to create on the university level the ethos of small schools like Prospect and Commonwealth and the progressive public school experiments that were such a dramatic piece of educational reform in the 1970s and 1980s—examples such as . . . Central Park East . . . and the many public and private high schools in Theodore Sizer's Coalition of Essential Schools" (Carroll et al., 2007a, 18).

The Importance of Understanding
Student Thinking in Team One

When describing her initial experiences teaching mathematics methods in MSU's Team One, Helen Featherstone (2007) complains that despite her efforts to create assignments that would give prospective teachers insight into what children were thinking, most of these prospective teachers did not take an interest in how children explained their ideas. They did not even seem to think that this was a worthwhile pursuit. Sitting down to revise her course, Featherstone asked herself: How can I help students learn to listen to children's ideas and to enjoy and celebrate them? How can I help students feel that teaching that takes account of student thinking is possible in the schools where they plan to teach?

To help answer these questions, Featherstone drew on her Team One colleague, Dirck Roosevelt. In the journal quoted in her article, she recounts what she made of his advice:

> The most important thing Dirck said today, the most profoundly helpful to my efforts to figure out where I go wrong, where I might do better at this TE thing, was that one thing he had learned . . . when . . . he did not feel at all like teaching, he found it helpful to remind himself that he really was curious about how these students thought about things. . . . The realization that I had been almost without curiosity about my teacher education students' thinking came as a particular shock because I had, from the first time I taught TE-401, explicitly emphasized both with the students and in my own thinking, that a major

goal of the math methods course was to help students to learn the skills and pleasures of listening to and exploring children's mathematical ideas. (H. Featherstone, 2007, 77–78)

Writing later about the visit her TE students had made to a second/third-grade classroom, Featherstone was relieved and took particular satisfaction in having discovered that her students were astonished by the interest the pupils had shown and what they had to say: "More than three quarters of the students wrote with appreciation about the learning community that appeared to exist in the classroom, the respect students showed their classmates, and the interest and attention with which they listened to one another's ideas" (81). Overall, Team One was in fact the MSU TE program that most emphasized understanding of student thinking. It required students to do a classic in-depth child study, which took the form of a one-semester "guided inquiry into the strengths, educational needs, and worldview of an individual child." In describing the first course students took after admission to the program, Roosevelt emphasizes this course was aimed "to keep the attention of prospective teachers and teacher educators on 'real children' and to educate that attention" (2007, 116).

Child study as carried out in this course was based on the work of Pat Carini, director of the Prospect School, where several faculty taught before coming to MSU. Carini's written guidelines for child study became a core text for the TE 301 course. One guideline, for example, read:

> Thinking of a child's *Physical Presence and Gesture*, be attentive to what stands out to you immediately. . . . Think about where the child seems most at ease and how you can tell that is so; then take it other side round and think of where the child seems least comfortable or most constrained. . . . [Attend to] the voice, its inflection, volume and rhythm; characteristic phrases and ways of speaking; the expressiveness of the eyes, hands, and mouth. (Roosevelt, 2007, 123–24)

In the Team One child study, students were required to make at least one data-collection visit per week to a school after they had selected a child "whose particular strengths and interests, manner of connecting and communicating, modes of thinking and learning [the investigator must] take special care to learn" (122). During the course, the whole class was called upon to discuss not only the requirements for the project but also specific thoughts and actions of the children selected for study. Roosevelt has revealed how this child study typically changed over time for its participants:

> Students' initial curiosity, interest, or good will rises, as they find themselves noticing more and more about the study child, to enthusiasm and an air of knowledgeability, followed by a lull and perhaps a feeling of impatience, when they may think (and indeed say) that there is nothing new for them to see in the child—followed in turn by uncertainty, and renewed energy and attention, as they are pushed to make sense of their (continuing) observations as windows into the child's patterns and tendencies of *thinking* and *learning*. . . . A good deal of articulated structure is helpful if developments of this sort are to occur . . . because that articulated structure sends the message "this is real work." (2007, 122)

The Struggle to Make Student Thinking Public and a Matter of Discussion

At MSU one of the main proponents of focusing on student thinking was Sandra Crespo, who wrote "listening to students' mathematical thinking is one of the trademarks of reform-minded visions of mathematics teaching." This position led her to ask what, when, where, and how something might be done to help prospective teachers learn to attend to student thinking. In an early effort, she reported on her study of a letter exchange between prospective teachers and fourth-grade students designed so that the prospective teachers could gain experience in investigating student think-ing in mathematics (Crespo, 2000, 155).[1]

Her report described the interpretations of the teacher-ed-ucation students, what they paid attention to and what they ignored in what the fourth graders had to say, and how all this influenced their judgments about the mathematical ability and understanding of the fourth graders. The exchange took place over the course of an eleven-week term. Both the TE students and the fourth graders worked in groups of four, but most of the TE students corresponded with only one fourth grader. The letters dealt successively with a pair of word problems. The first, well known as the "horse problem," was inserted in the first letter sent to the fourth graders. The problem read: "A man bought a horse for $50. He sold it for $60. Then he bought the horse for $70. He sold it again for $80. What is the financial outcome of these transactions?" The problem caused uncertainty, confu-sion, and consternation among TE students, but it also generated much interest and lively discussion. The students came up with approaches and solutions (from gaining $30 to losing $20) to the problem, with reasonable sounding supporting arguments. Students struggled to explain why solutions other than their own were wrong. This lack of consensus and understanding left the TE students eager to find out what the fourth graders had to say. And yet, even when they got a response, they still focused, not on student thinking, but instead mostly on the correctness of the response. Very few asked themselves why the same prob-lem had produced different answers and whether the pupil had really understood the mathematics involved. Instead they more often made snap judgments about the abilities and attitudes of the fourth graders. Unfortunately, this was not the only instance in which the TE students made judgments about mathematics ability without regard to mathematics performance, but instead

1. Although this project took place before Crespo became an MSU faculty member, it was the beginning of a research agenda in which Crespo delved repeatedly into the importance of understanding student thinking for the improvement of teacher education.

based their conclusions simply and illogically on the fourth graders' ability to write and spell.

After a few weeks, the TE students wrote again to ask questions about two other topics: area and perimeter, area and volume.
Again, the prospective teachers began by exploring the mathematics topic themselves, once again becoming curious about what the
fourth graders would think and understand. The following is the
way one of the TE students put it in her letter:

> Our teacher told us that you were going to learn about
> area and perimeter this week. How is it going? Are you
> having trouble? Pretend that I have no clue about what
> area and perimeter mean. Can you explain what they
> mean in your own words? What is *area*? What is *perime-
> ter*? Try to explain these words to me. (170)

The fourth grader's response led the TE student to do a more
thorough analysis of the fourth grader's work than she had done
when considering the horse problem. Other TE students also
came up with more thoughtful and less conclusive interpretations
and judgments than in the first exchange. When they met the
fourth graders face to face, they ended up with some contradictory data—a result that led them to be more cautious, questioning
their earlier claims about their correspondent's mathematical attitudes and abilities.

To explain the difference between interpretations of the first
and second letters, Crespo concluded that familiarity with the task
made the difference. Because they were familiar with the horse
problem, in spite of disagreement about how to solve it, they were
overconfident and superficial in their response. But when the
problems were set in less familiar terms as in the case of area and
perimeter, the students had to think more for themselves. One
student went so far as to ask her fourth grader to find the rectan-
gular shape with maximum area for a given perimeter. Then when
the fourth grader argued that a square would produce the maximum area, the TE student had to do more study herself to be able
to respond with sufficient confidence (174, 177–78).

The revolutionary research attention to children's thinking also carried over to studies of how and why experienced teachers changed their practice. One publication that is particularly relevant here focused on a study of how a teacher learned to facilitate children's discussion and thereby take their ideas into account (Peterson, 1991). Throughout school year 1989–90, the author, Penelope Peterson, studied changes in the mathematics teaching of Keisha Coleman (pseudonym), a third-grade teacher at the Spartan Village PDS. Peterson was one of the last of Judy Lanier's prominent faculty recruits, coming to MSU in 1988 from the University of Wisconsin. She was already important in the literature and in the Invisible College for Research on Teaching (organized by Jere Brophy), for example, having written with Chris Clark one of the main reviews of research on teacher thinking (Clark & Peterson, 1986). Her move took place after Andy Porter was pulled away in 1988 from his job at MSU as one of Judy Lanier's most important deputies to become the director of the Wisconsin Center for Education Research. Unhappy, in payback Judy Lanier got even by persuading Peterson to leave her chaired professorship in Madison for MSU. From then until she left to become the dean of the School of Education at Northwestern, Peterson was one of the key leaders in the College of Education at MSU. She continued to do her own research on teaching, including the study of Keisha Coleman.

In this research, one lesson she observed was particularly eye-opening. It illustrated the ways in which Keisha's teaching had changed since Peterson had come to her classroom. Keisha had conclusively moved away from "teaching as telling," because, as she put it, she had learned that she could teach something one day and then two weeks later, the students couldn't remember a thing. Keisha no longer "told" students the answer or the mathematical procedure, nor did she even indicate whether an answer was correct or incorrect. With guidance and questioning from the teacher, students had to figure out solutions to mathematical problems for themselves. Students did the explaining, talking about how they had solved problems, and then clarified what they were trying to say. As a result, student thinking became visible, and students were able to learn from one another.

Investigating Student Understanding of History

Teacher thinking and student thinking are two sides of the same coin in the sense that if one asks what teachers think about and respond to, the answer is, among other things, what students say. The corollary of this point is to do research to enlighten teachers about aspects of student thinking to which they may have been oblivious. In the IRT, this line of thought led to investigating student misconceptions of science, mathematics, and other subjects and to figure out what teachers can do about these misconceptions. The term *misconception* itself became a matter of controversy about whether the term was appropriate to use in characterizing misunderstanding. Instead it was argued that it was better to consider student thinking about phenomena simply as naive conceptions worthy of study in their own right, and not just whether they could be categorized as consistent or inconsistent with the findings of science. Not using the term *misconception* thus opened the door wider to exploration of the variability and originality of student thinking. Specific examples can be drawn from faculty and doctoral student research conducted variously in the PDSs or the MSU research centers.

At MSU, empirical subject-matter research on elementary social studies teaching was one area in which much emphasis was put on studying children's thinking—in this case their thinking about history. In starting to do this research, Jere Brophy took note of the fact that research on misconceptions had proved particularly fruitful in mathematics and science, and that in his opinion, the potential benefit of this sort of research was at least as great in social studies. (Brophy, 1990, 402–4; Brophy & Alleman, 2003). Therefore, Brophy himself organized a major program of research on student understanding of history. Using a before-and-after design, a number of studies investigated what fifth graders knew about history before and after instruction about the following topics, among others: (1) the study of history in general (Brophy, VanSledright & Bredin, 1991), (2) Native Americans (VanSledright, Brophy & Bredin, 1992), (3) the "discovery" of America (Brophy, VanSledright & Bredin, 1992a), and (4) the English colonies in America (Brophy, VanSledright & Bredin, 1992b).

Although the studies found that students learned a great deal from these units, the study of instruction about Native Americans also revealed many examples of ignorance, naiveté, and misconceptions, even in the postunit interviews. Accurate understanding had to do mostly with facts and concrete details whereas students lacked understanding of important abstractions, such as the terms "hunting and gathering societies" and "nomadic societies."

Students also had not yet learned much about colonies or why European nations would even want to establish colonies. They thought of slaves, pilgrims, and others acting on their own initiative. Students also had difficulty, even following the units, answering questions about encounters between the Europeans and Native Americans. Ironically, this difficulty had more to do with lack of knowledge about the Europeans of that time than ignorance of Native Americans. Their understanding of the Europeans was not only extremely limited, but also tended to be negative. Some students pictured the Europeans as greedy, immoral people who practiced slavery, took other people's valuables, and killed those who tried to stop them. It should be noted, however, that the study does not permit generalization of this finding.

Conclusion

Given these intellectual and reformer roots, the attention given to student and teacher thinking became an important part of MSU teacher-education programs. The first course that teacher-education students took in their program (Exploring Teaching or TE 101) was an attempt to loosen the grip of unexamined beliefs and thinking about teaching that students had acquired from years of watching teachers and growing up in schools in which teacher-directed and knowledge-transmission teaching was the norm. A book edited by Sharon Feiman-Nemser and Helen Featherstone (1992) was devoted to the development of this course. The course addressed what became known as the apprenticeship-of-observation phase of learning to teach, the origin of much resistance to goals that tried to overcome what was learned during this phase.

It laid the groundwork for acceptance of more student-centered teaching and active-student learning.

On the PDS side, the Gary Sykes chapter on the reforms undertaken at Holt High School called attention to the importance of the assessment innovations pioneered by mathematics teacher Mike Lehman in making "both teaching and learning" open to observation and discussion as an alternative to the isolation and inwardness that had typically been the case earlier.

> The whole community now could witness "performances in meaning" in mathematics. Such demonstrations might reveal that students understood very little beneath their problem-bound grasp of procedural knowledge. Or the community might discover students' increasing conceptual reach along with their capacity to apply mathematical knowledge to new and novel problems. Such performances, and the preparation for them in countless classes, might open up windows to student thoughts and feelings that teachers previously lacked. And if student performances of meaning began uncovering pleasant surprises concerning what lower-track students were capable of, that would inevitably raise questions about the teaching. What kind of teaching could produce such performances among students who were traditionally written off? So might a widening circle of teachers—and not just math teachers—be intrigued into some reconsideration of their beliefs about student capabilities. (2008, 343)

Discoveries in student thinking had thus proved themselves essential to revolutionary change in teaching and teacher education.

The New Frontier of What It Takes to Mentor Novice Teachers

At most universities graduate students who supervise prospective teachers during field experience, as well as cooperating teachers in classrooms with prospective teachers, have had too little preparation for this work and too few regular opportunities thereafter to discuss this work and to receive feedback and guidance on how to improve it. It has too often been assumed that teachers with good reputations for their practice (as well as doctoral students in education) are inherently able to mentor novice teachers. It was not recognized how big the difference is between knowing how to teach something and helping others learn how to teach it (Feiman-Nemser and Beasley, 2007, 145). However, according to Patricia Norman, a former doctoral student, MSU was different. The revolution was a period of pioneering research and practice at MSU in how to mentor novice teachers. As Norman described it: "What sets MSU apart from other large schools of education is that doctoral students encounter both formal and informal opportunities to develop their practice as field-based teacher educators. As a novice teacher liaison, I received sustained support in conceptualizing my role and developing my practice, including opportunities to see models and profit from on-site coaching" (2007, 161). To be sure, the mentoring movement had become national in scope during the revolutionary period and was not at all confined to MSU. But MSU discoveries, publications, and documented practices greatly advanced the state of the art and constituted a knowledge base that is, I think, still not put into practice across the country and world nearly as much as it could and should be.

Development of a more reflective and educated mentor role for teacher educators had a long history at MSU, starting before

World War II, flourishing in the programs of the 1960s and 1970s, and becoming even stronger in the four alternative programs of the 1980s. Gradually terms that no longer fit were retired; "supervising teacher" was replaced by "collaborating teacher," and the term "field instructor" was introduced to emphasize that university personnel working with students during their practicum were there to "teach," not "supervise." But even in those years the knowledge base of mentoring was undeveloped; mentoring was not a significant subject of educational research. Moreover, when mentoring research began to develop nationally, the focus was not on the intentions, expertise, and outcomes of competent mentors, but instead on how to organize mentoring programs, again assuming that effective teachers needed no special preparation for this role. It was only after creation of the federally funded National Center for Research on Teacher Learning, when research on mentoring began to flourish at MSU, that much new knowledge on what it takes to mentor well came to light, proving how invalid it was to assume that effective teachers would make good mentors without organized and guided opportunities to learn this role.

Faculty member Sharon Feiman-Nemser became the intellectual leader and the grassroots mastermind in this revolutionary effort to understand and improve the mentoring of novice and prospective teachers. She was an inspiring teacher as well as a researcher of mentoring who brought new perspectives to the field. To make her point about what was lacking in the state of the mentoring art, she went back to ancient times, pointing out that the term *mentoring* originated in Homer's poem the *Odyssey*, in which Odysseus left Troy to fight in the Trojan Wars and entrusted his son and household to his old friend and advisor Mentor. Already the origin of this term was problematic in that Homer had little to say about what those responsibilities for raising the son Telemachus entailed. Thousands of years later this same problem still plagued the field of learning to teach. The term *mentoring* was used without much understanding of and ability to fulfill what it called for in practice.

According to Feiman-Nemser, educators had learned little from the way the term mentoring had been used in developmental psychology, higher education, or business where it was talked about well before becoming part of the language of educational reform in the 1980s. And then, when extended to preservice teacher education in the 1990s, it acquired a wide array of different definitions and specifications that still lacked clarity and agreement. When finally applied to improvement in the induction of teachers, the term in the United States was more often than not reduced "to a narrow view of mentoring as a form of temporary support to help novices cope with the demands of their first year of teaching" (Feiman-Nemser, 2001/2012b, 272; see also Feiman-Nemser, 2010; Feiman-Nemser & Norman, 2005/2012).

In responding to this undeveloped and unsatisfactory state of affairs, Feiman-Nemser advocated what she called "educative mentoring," which

> rests on an explicit vision of good teaching and an understanding of teacher learning. Mentors who share this orientation attend to beginning teachers' present concerns, questions, and purposes without losing sight of long-term goals for teacher development. They interact with novices in ways that foster an inquiring stance. They cultivate skills and habits that enable novices to learn in and from their practice. They use their knowledge and expertise to assess the direction novices are heading to create opportunities and conditions that support meaningful teacher learning in the service of student learning. (Feiman-Nemser, 2001/2012b, 254; see also Feiman-Nemser, 1998/2012)

Continuing, she went on to say that mentors need "bifocal vision": "keeping one eye on the immediate needs of the novice teacher and one eye on the ultimate goal of meaningful and effective learning for all students" (Feiman-Nemser, 2001/2012b, 254).

Educative Mentoring Requires
Special Knowledge and Skill

In addressing this situation, MSU research examined the skills
and knowledge that mentors need to give constructive feedback
and guidance to novice teachers. It was research that could be
used later for the professional development of cooperating teachers and field instructors. Sharon Schwille's detailed 1997 account
of just one conference with a student teacher shows how much
knowledge and skill it takes to mentor well—knowledge and skill
that even today cannot be taken for granted in the repertoire
that supervisors of student teachers bring to many teacher-education programs. In Schwille's analysis, she reports in detail on
what shaped her thinking and talk during the conference. As she
described it, she did not come to the conference with a precon-
ceived structure or approach to follow. Instead she drew upon the
cues she received during the conference to make judgments and
discuss the instructional methods that she thought could guide
her TE student in her learning. Her aim was to help the teacher
candidate connect principles of teaching and the MSU program
philosophy to the candidate's work with children. In doing this,
Schwille drew upon many forms of teaching, including improvisa-
tion, all the while building a trusting relationship with the preservice teacher to support their work together.

In the guided practice episode Schwille describes, the student
Louise (pseudonym) was a senior getting field experience to
prepare her for the extended term of student teaching that would
follow later in the same fifth-grade classroom. The conference
took place about three weeks into the term. Since the conference
did not immediately follow observation of her teaching, it was
not limited to providing feedback and reflection on a particular
teaching episode. Schwille describes how she saw her role in the
conference:

> I was not simply acting as the program missionary, indoc-
> trinating her with the program goals, but as her personal
> teacher calling upon what I knew about her and what we

were experiencing in the situation at the time. I was also willing to take risks with her, such as attempting to engage her in role plays, because I knew that if that instructional strategy failed, I would have more time with her to try another option. (65)

As the conference began, Louise talked about the writing corner she wanted to establish in her classroom. She was concerned about the skepticism her cooperating teacher had expressed about this idea. Schwille took this as a sign that Louise felt insecure in trying to establish herself in the classroom as a legitimate, respected participant in the teaching situation. She wanted to be known for good ideas that would help students learn. Schwille asked Louise to explain her reasons for keeping folders in the corner, encouraging her to think more deeply about her purposes. At the same time, the conference offered a model for how to organize thoughts in a form making them easier to articulate. This sort of modeling was important in helping Louise extend her thinking.

In the second part of the conversation Schwille suggested a role play for Louise to present her ideas. "I'll be the cooperating teacher. You talk to me." And even though Louise did not pick up on this cue, the interaction gave her a script that she could use in discussing her ideas with her cooperating teacher. At another point in the conference Schwille tried another role play, and this time it worked. Louise played the teacher, and Schwille a parent.

Later toward the end of the conference, Louise and her field instructor returned to discussion of the writing corner:

> In my view, Louise knew that her desire to have the children feel like the reading and writing corner belonged to them could be heightened by their bringing their own books and by making decisions about the materials needed for the writing corner. It was not apparent to me whether she recognized this as a program goal. I could have questioned her about the dispositions the program hoped to instill and pushed her to identify the one I wanted to highlight. Instead I chose to reinforce her

thinking by saying, "I want to tell you why I think that's neat," and then told her which program goal her strategy fostered. Several factors influenced my decision, not the least of which was time. I knew we needed to finish up, and the most expedient way to get my point across was to tell it. (65–66)

Writing about this conference gave Schwille a chance to clarify the influences on her practice and to consider the complexities of this kind of work. Several factors, operating simultaneously, that she considered particularly important included her role as a field instructor in a particular teacher-education program, her interpretation and enactment of that role, the goals of the program, her own views on what constitutes good teaching, her relationships with teacher candidates, and how these factors came together in a particular situation with a particular teacher candidate.

Years later in 2008, Sharon Schwille took a different tack on mentoring when she synthesized research on what teachers actually do in mentoring student teachers. This article broke mentoring down into moves and interventions *inside* and *outside* the classroom. Mentoring inside the action is an extreme contrast with the more conventional images of mentors who turn their classrooms over to their novices and do not intervene in what is happening. In those cases, the mentors expect novices to "learn from experience." However, a number of other articles by MSU researchers (e.g. Buchmann & Schwille, 1983; Floden, Buchmann & Schwille, 1987; Buchmann, 1989) make clear that experience without guidance and reflection is misleading.

Schwille discusses three "inside" forms of mentoring: coaching and stepping in, coteaching, and demonstration teaching. When "coaching and stepping in" mentors position themselves in the classroom while their novice is teaching, they can offer advice as needed and at the same time be available when the novice asks for advice, either in an explicit question or just in a look or glance that calls for a response. At times, the mentor "steps in" to teach or "steps out" so that the novice can resume the lesson. The mentor and novice can often be heard talking over the heads of students in the class when the mentor coaches from alongside or the novice asks questions. All the inside forms of mentoring "help novices learn how to think on their feet, figure out in the moment how to extend and probe students' thinking, modify the lesson content or activities based on immediate assessment, or adjust the environment in order to move toward learning goals" (2008, 144, 157).

Interactive tasks of teaching, such as facilitating student discussions in a way that leads to conceptual understanding, may look easy to someone who has not developed the required skill, but actually guiding and managing such a discussion calls for complex thinking or what Schon (1987) called "reflection-in-action." A mentor who remains close to a novice during teaching can share what each is thinking, what needs attention, and how to deal with the problems that arise. This guided reflection-in-action offers novices the possibility of learning ways to think and act that are closely linked to pupils' understandings at the moment.

At other times, the mentor and novice do coteaching. Either mentor or novice starts the lesson while the other takes over at some point. Deciding who will take the lead in each segment of the lesson becomes part of the planning that takes place before the lesson. On still other occasions, mentoring takes the form of demonstration teaching. This differs from the osmosis approach in which the novice is supposed to notice and pick up on practices on his or her own. Demonstrations instead are prepared for by talking about what to look for and what questions to ask about the mentor's thinking and decision-making. A mentor might, for example, invite students to observe her reform-minded mathematics teaching for a week, meeting before each lesson to discuss what the mentor hopes to accomplish and imagines how the lesson should progress. The group would meet after to each class to debrief and look ahead to the next day (Schwille, 2008, 148).

Mentoring outside the action typically consists of mentors engaging in lengthier (twenty to sixty minutes), more formal talk with their novices when the K–12 students are not present. Such outside mentoring interventions can take place in brief interactions that have been called "mentoring on the move" at times when neither is actively engaged with their students. By having brief talks with their novices throughout the day mentors can show that these are based on classroom realities and on what the novice has actually been doing or thinking.

Another form of mentoring outside the action is lesson coplanning, which "goes beyond the mentor reading and commenting on plans written by the novice. . . . It means that the mentor and the novice work together to design learning activities that lead to either the mentor or the novice or both teaching." Typically teacher educators have assumed that novices can learn to plan by working independently. Although in such instances the cooperating teacher may serve as a critic and may suggest changes in the plans, it has not been common to sit down with the novice to think through the planning together, helping the novice make a habit of this way to plan (152–53). Some mentors and novices also analyze videotapes together, using the recordings to prompt recall about decisions made in practice, to demonstrate specific kinds of teaching, and to compare what mentors and novices notice about teaching practice.

Working with different novices calls on different forms of mentoring expertise.

> You take the people you work with at the level where they are, and that's what you work with. [Some] are just so well prepared. They are so self-confident, and others are not confident. They don't know what they're doing. Of the [novices] I'm working with right now, I have one who is so high I don't feel he needs a whole lot of guidance in teaching. He's very serious about what he does. He's very reflective. He is as good as some teachers that have been teaching for ten years. . . . I have another novice who is barely holding on by her fingernails. She's really at a loss on how to do some of these things. . . . That's a part of the knack of being a mentor—figuring out where they are. (161)

Research on this sort of mentoring, according to the references cited, provides tools for the professional development of mentors, both beginning and experienced. It can help new mentors learn the skills they need, and also make it possible for experienced mentors to improve. Research helps mentors understand the complexity of their work and what it takes to do it well. Mentors can gain a sense of what is involved at a conceptual level as well as what constitutes the details or fine points of the practice. Research becomes useful as a basis for developing published cases of mentoring practice for professional development (Schwille, 2008).

Major Differences among Cooperating Teachers in Mentoring and Its Effects

Research on mentoring as actually practiced by cooperating teachers working with teacher-education students has illuminated both commonalities and differences in these experiences. Rozelle and Wilson (2012), for example, reported on their research on changes in six interns in science classes over the course of a whole school year. These TE students had two different ways of dealing with the internship. In the beginning, all the students tried to follow closely their teachers' scripts for teaching. When observing these teachers, they took detailed notes in order to be able to replicate not only the overall lesson structure and activities, but other characteristics of the teacher as well, including specific examples used, personal anecdotes, and even jokes. But it was not possible to keep doing this during "lead teaching" when the intern became the teacher in two or three classes instead of just one. At that point the interns no longer had the chance to observe the teacher teaching the lesson they were about to teach. Nevertheless, forced to work more independently, they still tried to follow the same pattern they had observed.

But at this point the six interns no longer all took the same approach. Four of them (termed "reproducers" by the authors) were successful in following the pattern established by the cooperating teacher, both in teaching methods and in relationships with students. This gave them a feeling of success and won them positive feedback. By the end of the year these interns described their experience in ways that sounded much like their cooperating teacher. For example, in the case of an intern who at the beginning of the year had emphasized respecting and caring for students, her language shifted from "care" and "respect" toward "routines" and "expectations," words she had heard from the teacher throughout the year. The other two interns (deemed "strugglers" in the article) at first tried to imitate their teacher, but there was less coherence in their teaching and a poor fit between what they did and what they aspired to. At the end of the year they stuck to visions of good teaching that were at odds with what they had tried or observed.

In the case of all six interns, they had started the year with differing views about teaching and differing experiences before the internship. Nevertheless, the main influence on all of them during the internship was the cooperating teacher, whether or not they were able to replicate what that teacher did. The authors of the article suggest that this may be a consequence of the MSU policy to assign interns to spend the whole fifth year with only one cooperating teacher. Programs that assign interns to more than one teacher's class could reduce the influence of a particular teacher.

In another study of MSU teacher-education interns, Jian Wang (1998) examined the influence of each collaborating teacher's teaching on the mathematics practice of his or her student. The teaching practices of these four interns turned out to be different from one another as was their experience and response to the mentoring they received (or failed to receive) from their cooperating teacher. Their university coursework called for a constructivist approach to the teaching of mathematics, but in their internships the students did not all take this approach.

Each of the four collaborating teachers Wang studied had different conceptions of mathematics content, teaching, and learning. Just one was constructivist. That one was very actively engaged in the teaching of his intern. Only one of the three others was likewise engaged. The two remaining cooperating teachers held back, because they felt unable to take on the role favored by the university. Still in the end, all four of these interns developed a view of practice like that of their cooperating teacher whether or not the teacher took a position consistent with the university program.

In yet other studies, Martial Dembele (1995, 1999) examined two mentors at opposing extremes of mentoring practice. His 1995 dissertation compared two teachers in the same PDS and how they mentored MSU intern teachers. One teacher was systematic in implementing her own curriculum for learning to teach with the intern while the other believed in a more conventional sink or swim approach for interns to learn from their mistakes. The systematic mentor (pseudonym Nancy) taught science in a secondary PDS. With a habit of thinking and planning carefully for working with novices, she developed her own curriculum for mentoring. Since she had the ability to scaffold specific teaching tasks, the participation of her novices evolved from peripheral to full participation in every central task of teaching, including preparing for instruction, managing instruction, writing tests, and grading them. For each practice, she went through a cycle of modelling, coaching, and then gradually fading away.

At the beginning of the year Nancy modeled teaching when she taught her first-hour class. The novice observed her and then taught the same content to a different group of students the second hour. After several weeks Nancy also turned her third-hour class over to the novice. Together Nancy and the novice always spent time analyzing the classes the novice had observed. Nancy realized from early experience as a mentor that the novice was not seeing what she saw.

Coplanning was important to Nancy's practice of mentoring. Again it was a matter of modelling, coaching, and fading. Nancy was acutely aware of the lack of needed content knowledge among her novices and accepted that it was part of her responsibilities to deal with this (in contrast to the traditional practice of assuming that novices had enough mastery of content knowledge to allow the classroom mentor to concentrate solely on the organization and pedagogy of the lesson). During the lesson preparation periods, Nancy taught content as well as working out a plan for other aspects of the lesson.

At the opposite extreme in Dembele's study was Ken (pseudonym), a social studies teacher in the same PDS, whose approach to mentoring was improvisational and lacking in structure. He believed that experience was primary, just being with children and practicing as much as possible. Whereas Nancy thought that mentors had to model all aspects of teaching, including how to plan for instruction, how to write and grade tests, and how to analyze teaching practice, Ken modeled only the management of his classroom instruction. In allowing his novice to take over all aspects of teaching her assigned lessons, he saw his role as limited to giving feedback and critiquing performance. Thus, his view of what mentoring could achieve was limited. At times he could foresee that his novice was about to make a major blunder, but he would not warn the student teacher. Instead, he held back in the belief that learning from mistakes was part of the process and beneficial. Ken also viewed his own teaching as artistry and relied heavily on charisma to enhance his performance skills. Ideally, from this perspective, mentoring would be about sharing artistry, but in Ken's opinion, he couldn't do that because teaching was in large part a genetic talent. Ken admired Nancy's systematic practice of mentoring but felt that it was the subject matter of science that made it possible. In his view, it was not feasible in social studies.

Averill PDS Takes the Lead in
Developing Educative Mentoring

One major motivation for MSU research on mentoring and efforts to improve mentoring for learning to teach was the discovery of practicing teachers who were effective with K–12 students but were convinced that they had little to offer the teacher-education students who came into their classrooms. Forzani asserts that in the early years of the five-year program, practicing teachers in the program turned out to be uncomfortable discussing their teaching in public and dealing with critical feedback. In a demonstration of how much needed to be done in this respect, excellent teachers confessed how difficult and dissatisfying their previous work with student teachers had been (2011, 189).

Sharon Feiman-Nemser addressed this problem. She did her PDS work at Averill Elementary School in Lansing, the school with one of the longest histories of collaboration with MSU on teacher education. Feiman-Nemser and Averill teacher Kathy Beasley convincingly portrayed one such example of teacher discomfort with TE field experience in the book on Team One.

> In the summer of 1990, Kathy approached Sharon at a PDS Institute, having heard that Sharon was doing research on student teaching, and asked if she could help her with a problem. Every year, Kathy said, she dreaded the time her student teacher would take over the classroom. Stepping aside, Kathy would watch helplessly as everything she had worked so hard to establish during the year slowly fell apart. While Kathy tried to give her student teacher helpful advice, she always felt deep frustration for herself and a sense of loss for her student. (2007, 140–41)

At the time, Kathy believed her role in helping the student learn to teach was minor, limited to providing a classroom where the student teacher could try things out, with the classroom teacher answering questions, and pointing out what the student was doing wrong in her teaching.

One reason for Kathy's feeling unprepared to help her student teacher learn to teach was that she never had had much chance or encouragement to talk about her knowledge of teaching and to explain her practices. She was inclined to overestimate what the student teacher could learn from simply watching her teach over the duration of several semesters spent wholly or in part in her classroom. Feiman-Nemser worked hard to convince Kathy that she had much knowledge to share with student teachers. Through her interaction with Feiman-Nemser, Kathy became more aware of the tacit and situated nature of teacher knowledge and confident that she could find ways to communicate it to teacher-education students (143–47).

Feiman-Nemser and Beasley wrote about what it took to "invent" a new teacher-educator role for cooperating teachers at Averill, building on an earlier forum in which teachers at the school had talked about new ways of thinking about and working with student teachers. Instead of just trying to do what MSU told them to do, the Averill Teacher Education Circle (TEC) developed its own curriculum for learning to teach in which it was able "to set the standards, frame the expectations, craft the assignments, and evaluate the learning" (158).

In a bold step, the TEC decided to design and operate their own student-teaching program based on what they had learned about the role of experienced teachers in mentoring novices. During a year of experimentation, they had to decide what to teach the student teachers as well as how to guide, support, and assess this learning. "In the past," they recalled, "such decisions had been made at the university, and cooperating teachers often found themselves in the position of helping student teachers do something that did not make sense to them." Now they had an opportunity to decide such matters for themselves. When the new five-year program took shape, this early work laid the foundation for the internship in which the roles of university supervisor and cooperating teacher were redefined. The TEC model was extended to other schools, and new forums were created to investigate this form of field-based teacher education (158–60).

In short, the five-year program at MSU was always viewed not just as the initial means of preparing K–12 teachers but also as an important learning experience for others with responsibilities in the program. In Team One it provided an environment in which "interns, collaborating teachers and university liaisons were all constructing new practices. Interns were students of teaching. Collaborating teachers were students of mentoring. University liaisons were students of field-based teacher education" (Norman, 2007, 161, 179).

In addition to this innovative work with cooperating teachers, Sharon Feiman-Nemser began to offer a university practicum to help doctoral students and retired teachers learn to work with student interns and cooperating teachers. The team also set up a cross-school group of liaisons from different Team One schools who developed a complex method of using artifacts to discuss the nature of mentoring (Carroll, 2007). Once Team One reached full scale, it needed one hundred mentors a year for eighteen to twenty schools. Each school also had to have a university liaison (Feiman-Nemser & Beasley, 2007, 160).

In writing about their experiences years later, Sharon Feiman-Nemser and Kathy Beasley offered a frank appraisal of how much progress was made during this long period of intensive learning and development: "Rereading our journals and the comments we made on them fifteen years ago, we are sometimes struck by the naiveté of our former selves. Having worked with and developed these ideas for more than a decade, we are surprised to see how unsophisticated we sounded before we developed them" (140).

MSU International Research Produces New Understandings of Mentoring

One of the most productive avenues in producing new knowledge about mentoring was international.[1] When MSU's National Center for Research on Teacher Learning was launched, Lynn Paine joined principal investigator Sharon Feiman-Nemser in an international comparative mentoring study of how novice teachers learn to teach in the company of experienced teachers who are reformers in their schools and classrooms. Data for this study were collected in the United States, the UK, and China. Logs, observations, and interviews revealed striking differences between the sites in China and those in England and the United States. Chinese participants in the project, when observing videos of American mentors working with their mentees, were surprised to find that the mentors did not seem to be doing or saying anything of note to show more competence at teaching than their mentee. The Chinese observers were "puzzled that so much time was spent on emotional support and so little direct engagement in working on the actual challenges/content of teaching" (Schwille, 2017, 64).

Americans in the study were equally amazed when they observed videos of a Chinese mentor, a "star" teacher. The mentor watched the mentee teach a first-grade lesson in beginning subtraction, using an image of a bird cage from which she extracted birds to show visually the mathematical operation of

1. This section was previously published in my book Schwille (2017).

subtraction. Although the Chinese mentor, after watching this lesson, complimented the student on some aspects of the lesson, she was not satisfied. To the surprise of the U.S. researchers, she proceeded to teach the very same lesson to the mentee alone. In short, mentoring in China meant critiquing the mentee's teaching and demonstrating how to teach better.

A later book (Britton, Paine & Raizen, 2003) reported on a study of teacher induction in five countries that all had well-established national programs of induction: France, Japan, China (Shanghai region), New Zealand, and Switzerland (three cantons). With a focus on studying teachers' opportunities to learn to teach mathematics in lower secondary school, the induction programs varied dramatically in goals, purposes, structures, logic, and scope. They were generally designed to address what beginning teachers lacked, and what they were perceived to be lacking varied from country to country. In preservice programs that required a great deal of field experience in elementary or secondary schools as well as instruction in pedagogy or didactics, these components tended not to be emphasized in the induction that followed completion of such programs. But other preservice programs provided very little field experience, concentrating instead on subject-matter learning, not on how it should be taught. Induction programs in such instances tried to compensate by emphasizing the pedagogical aspects that had been missing from the preservice programs. For example, in France, where novice teachers already possessed extremely high levels of subject-matter knowledge, mathematics pedagogy was considered central to their induction learning.

Likewise in Japan, where educators began developing special in-service programs for beginning teachers in the 1960s, the novices were considered well prepared in terms of content knowledge, but not in how to deal with students or with pressures from parents or society at large. More generally, since the prior education of these Japanese novices was considered too theoretical without needed practical experience, the subsequent induction programs were designed to redress this imbalance.

Induction in Switzerland had the broadest mandate, concentrating on developing the whole person, with extensive opportunities for counseling, cooperation, and reflective practice. Induction there was also distinctive in giving novice teachers a strong voice in deciding what they would learn and do during induction. Induction in the Swiss settings included "formal and informal practice groups, individual and group counseling, classroom observations and follow-on discussions, review of personal and professional status and progress, specially designed courses and help booklets" (Schwille, 2017, 66).

In the Shanghai region of China, the induction program systematically organized various activities and services to introduce novices to a special language of teaching as well as to distinctive ways of thinking and norms of practice. This meant that induction in Shanghai was the most comprehensive, extensive, and systematic of the programs studied, as well as the one with the most nearly unique features.

One of the unique features of the Shanghai system was a competition centering on "talk lessons":

> The event [that one successful competitor] participated in, typical of these competitions, had three elements: a "talk" lesson in which teachers have ten minutes to talk through how and why they would teach a topic they have chosen; a multimedia section, with five minutes for contestants to use and describe how they would use technology to help pupil thinking; finally, a five minute section demonstrating "blackboard skills," something this teacher (as well as many others we interviewed) stressed as very important. (Britton, Paine & Raizen, 2003, 42)

Each talk lesson was then evaluated by a jury in terms of reasons for choosing the lesson, how the topic is organized, appropriateness of the approach, and effectiveness of the language used and the teacher's demeanor.

Overall, this five-nation study thus gave various answers to the question, Should induction programs focus directly on teaching the novice to teach better? To some, the answer to this question might seem obvious, but earlier research on induction and mentoring by

Feiman-Nemser, Paine, and colleagues suggested that emphasis in the United States was on providing emotional support for the stresses of beginning teachers and on helping each teacher find his or her own approach to teaching; there was virtually no direct teaching of how to teach. In China, it was the opposite; the mentors of novice teachers were more likely to assume the role of master teacher and coach, providing more direct guidance to the novice on what he or she needed to know and do in order to teach well.

Conclusion

Nothing more need be said to indicate the importance of this international MSU research on mentoring and induction in challenging the U.S. teaching profession to rethink existing practices and norms of teaching and to reach higher standards of performance, whether by emulating to some degree what had been documented in other countries or by finding alternative, equivalent ways of enhancing the learning of novice teachers.

Mentoring research and development was, in fact, one of the most undeniable achievements of the revolution at MSU. It showed comprehensively and in detail how to mentor novice and practicing teachers effectively, what mentoring requires in terms of preparation, and how all this can be put into practice. Little of this had been thoroughly understood before or even available in any form. Unfortunately, there is still little to show that current mentoring practice has taken all this into account as thoroughly and widely as it should. Indeed a major review of research on methods courses and field experiences in the United States reported on studies of supervision in PDSs as follows: "There is a curious decrease in research on the nature of supervision [since last summarized in 1996]. The content and nature of supervisory conferences, relations between feedback and subsequent performance, and the struggle among role groups are examples of research topics that seem to have been lost" (Clift & Brady, 2005, 329). A major part of the MSU revolution was to create a new institution, the professional development school, that among other things could give teachers the preparation, time, and remuneration to implement comprehensively and in depth this state of the art in mentoring. But when the most revolutionary aspects of MSU practice petered out and the PDSs were abandoned, this possibility was no longer a realistic hope for the university's future.

CHAPTER SEVENTEEN

The False Dichotomy between Pedagogy and Subject Matter

There is a false dichotomy between pedagogy and subject matter in learning to teach, resulting in two competing and contradictory claims. One is that the formal study of pedagogy is a useless waste of time and has no place in the preparation of teachers. According to this claim, study of subject-matter content is sufficient for the preservice preparation of teachers. The other claim is that formal study of pedagogy (for example, the methodology of how to teach reading) does have an important place in the preservice preparation of teachers and that this can be done independently of learning more about subject-matter content.

Earlier programs of teacher education at MSU took the latter point of view. They were divided between courses to learn subject matter and courses to learn teaching methods. Some of the latter were specific to a subject-matter area, such as methods of teaching mathematics or methods of teaching science, but acquiring more advanced knowledge of subject matter was not the main goal of such courses. There were also generic methods courses that were not specific to subject matter and whose methods were meant to be applied across disciplines. In the MSU College of Education, at least for elementary-education majors, more emphasis was put on these generic methods than on in-depth issues of subject matter. Prospective secondary-school teachers, in contrast, were not given the same specific subject-matter methods courses as the elementary majors (although methods courses could be offered by the subject-matter department as was done in the MSU English Department for future secondary English teachers).

Shulman's Way of Overcoming Fallacy

Within this context, once again it was Lee Shulman who reconceptualized the relationship between subject matter and pedagogy in a meaningful and relevant way. After leaving MSU, he introduced a term for the idea that knowing how to teach a particular discipline is itself a kind of subject-matter knowledge. He called it *pedagogical content knowledge* (PCK) and originally described it as follows:

> Within the category of pedagogical content knowledge I include, for the most regularly taught topics in one's subject area, the most useful forms of representation of these ideas, the most powerful analogies, illustrations, examples, explanations, and demonstrations—in a word, the ways of representing and formulating the subject that make it comprehensible to others. Since there are no single most powerful forms of representation, the teacher must have at hand a veritable armamentarium of alternative forms of representation, some of which derive from research whereas others originate in the wisdom of practice. (Shulman, 1986/2004, 203)

Shulman's ideas came back to influence MSU in a major way through his continuing contacts with his former institution. These ideas became the basis for the argument that I espouse here that the dichotomy between content and pedagogy is in fact a false one and that practice would be better served if one were to assume that for purposes of practical learning opportunities and experiences, pedagogy at its best and most effective embodies in-depth subject-matter understanding. Shulman made still stronger claims in a 1990 article, which amounted to declaring the dichotomy between content and pedagogy to be a false one:

> Aristotle was right: the deepest understanding one can have of any field is an understanding of its pedagogy,

because pedagogical understanding is predicated on the kind of multiple readings, the kind of contingent understandings that reflect the deep objectives of a liberal education. Deep knowledge is never enough for rich pedagogy. Advanced skill in the processes of teaching will not suffice either. To reach the highest level of competence as an educator . . . demands a melding of knowledge and process. (415)

Overcoming Fallacy as the Focus of Ball's Career

In following this line of thought, it is possible to see Deborah Ball's whole career—first at MSU and then at the University of Michigan—as devoted in large part to investigating and helping teachers overcome the pedagogy-content dichotomy. She has characterized the integrated knowledge needed by teachers as "knowledge for teaching." In discussing this approach (Ball, 2000), she analyzes three problems to be solved if teachers are to combine and use both content and pedagogy effectively in teaching. The first problem is to figure out what subject-matter content matters for teaching. The second focuses on how subject matters have to be understood to be used in teaching. And the third centers on how to use this knowledge in practice to solve these three problems; it is not enough to start with a description of the content to be taught. Instead scholars must start by analyzing what teachers actually do in order to determine what part subject matter plays in this practice.

Coming to grips with the second problem requires recognizing that just learning more subject matter—more mathematics, science, history, etc.—does not by itself improve the ability to teach. As Ball puts it: "Paradoxically, expert personal knowledge of subject-matter is often ironically inadequate for teaching. Because teachers must be able to work with content for students in its growing, unfinished state, they must be able to do something perverse: work backward from mature and compressed understanding of the content to unpack its constituent elements" (245).

As Shulman said in defining PCK, teachers need knowledge of what students find difficult and which representations of subject matter make it easier to teach an idea or procedure. Teachers must also consider the advantages and disadvantages that representations bring to teaching particular concepts. "Knowing that subtraction is a particularly difficult idea for students to master is not something that can be seen from knowing the 'big ideas' of the discipline. . . . It is quite clearly mathematical, yet formulated around the need to make ideas accessible to others" (Ball, 2000, 245).

But knowing about pedagogical content knowledge in the abstract and how it is supposed to integrate content and pedagogy are not enough. Ball suggests that prospective teachers engage in "content-based design work," developing an assignment or segment of instruction based on their analysis of what their students have done. This approach enables teacher-education students to learn new content as shaped by the setting in which they use it. In these ways, prospective teachers can acquire "a sense of the trajectory of a topic over time or how to develop its intellectual core in students' minds and capacities so that they eventually reach mature and compressed understandings and skills" (246).

Strategies to Circumvent the Dichotomy
Embedded in University Organization

Ball asserted that solving the three problems—what subject-matter knowledge is important for teaching, how that knowledge is useful for teaching, and how it fits into practice—will help close the gap John Dewey described between content and pedagogy. But a quick look at the curriculum of most teacher-preparation programs would show that methods courses are still separated from disciplinary courses, so that "bridging these strangely divided practices will be no small feat" (Ball, 2000, 246–47). At MSU as in other major universities, the different colleges are not organized in a way that would facilitate a transformation of subject-matter knowledge to include both pedagogy and content. The arts and sciences colleges have remained dominant in determining what subject matter to teach future teachers as well as to the students in other fields who need some of the same subject matter to fill out their majors.

At MSU this failure to recognize the unique needs of prospective teachers for more rigorous content integrated with pedagogy was not just for lack of trying. College of Education faculty had tried to convince colleagues in the other colleges to admit education students to their most advanced courses and to develop better curricula to enable prospective teachers to understand the basic structure of a discipline and what it took to do work in that field (Forzani, 2011, 214–17). But little of this was done. In the book on Team One (Carroll et al., 2007b) Jay Featherstone for one strongly criticized what the MSU arts and science departments were doing to prepare both secondary and elementary teachers:

> Both groups often got a jumble of courses, more a reflection of scheduling than substance or coherence. We on Team One had hoped that the MSU reforms would make it possible to craft what we called "liberal arts for professionals." . . . We had talked of sponsoring book clubs, science clubs, art groups, and the like, to promote a spirit of curiosity and continuous amateur learning, but we found this hard to do with MSU undergraduates. . . .
>
> [Team One's] grand vision remained far from reality. It was not uncommon for our students to confess that teacher education was the first MSU class in which discussion was the norm and they were actually required to write, or even to think, and in some cases attend class regularly. (J. Featherstone, 2007, 206)

One of the Team One faculty members even suggested that the MSU teacher-education program should address this problem by knuckling down and accepting courses for credit only if they were of limited size, with real discussions, with papers to write, leading to feedback and opportunities to rewrite, courses that grapple with the large ideas of a discipline and at some point to do (rather than just study) the subject in an intellectually respectable form—but this idea got nowhere. It did not prove possible to require a "real" subject-matter major for all education students.

Nevertheless, the mathematics and science courses that prospective teachers took did improve, even from Featherstone's critical point of view. And in the language arts, the combination of child study in TE 301 with readings in children's literature (such as Vivian Paley's "The Girl with the Brown Crayon") served as a "model for creating curriculum units that would elicit children's thinking about literature and build on it in imaginative ways" (207–8).

The effect of these improvements could be seen by the fifth year of the program. Featherstone reported that "evidence of [the wonderful work done by interns] could be found in the portfolios our graduating interns presented every year. . . . Members of Team One . . . often presented curriculum units that had real intellectual depth as well as playfulness and imagination. Many were interdisciplinary. They reminded us of how far we had come but also, in their unevenness, of how much work remained in the area of subject-matter knowledge, pedagogy, and child study" (209).

Transforming Pedagogy and Content at Holt High School

Elsewhere at MSU, other ways to deal with the gap between pedagogy and content were explored. Some of the best work took place, not on the main campus in East Lansing, but in the PDSs. Holt High School was among the most advanced in this respect. Overall, the Holt PDS brought to the revolutionary enterprise an unmatched mix of talent, expertise, and experience, drawing on both the high school faculty and on faculty and doctoral students at MSU. The challenge was great. For example, decisions to teach algebra to all students and to adopt a functions approach to that subject were highly contentious. And the MSU faculty was there to facilitate, not dictate (Radin, ca. 1992, 6). Instead, the Holt faculty stepped up to the plate and took decisions on their own, such as when they decided to eliminate their pre-algebra class and put all their students in algebra 1.

Within this collaborative environment, it was amphibious professor Dan Chazan, together with his coteacher Sandy Bethell (aka Callis), who has given us the most illuminating, in-depth demonstration of how content knowledge alone falls far short of preparing people to teach (Chazan, 2000; Chazan, Callis & Lehman, 2008). When Chazan began to work in the Holt High School PDS, he focused on figuring out how to improve the learning of algebra by all students, in particular succeeding with students who for one reason or another have had difficulties in learning this subject. According to Chazan: "The argument that we have been exploring is that algebra provides a new insight into our world; but in order for this argument to be credible, students must be able to see algebra in the world around them. As teachers we must then develop an understanding of algebra that will help us appreciate the algebraic thinking already done by our students, their working class parents, and other members of their community" (1996, 458)

When Chazan started to teach at Holt, he found that teachers, students, and even the general public thought of algebra as largely a matter of learning symbolic algebraic manipulation. The students practiced manipulation at home, and when back in school, this work was discussed and graded, allowing the teacher to decide whether the solution is correct or incorrect. Thus a typical lesson included review of homework on the previous manipulation, teacher presentation of a new skill, teacher-guided practice of the new skill in class, and finally a new homework assignment (6).

But Chazan discovered, in spite of these commonalities in practice, there was no intellectual consensus on what the content of elementary algebra should actually be. Drawing on his beliefs about what knowledge of algebra is important for teaching, what makes learning algebra difficult for students, and what teaching practice could be, Chazan sought a different blend of content and pedagogy:

> I believe that the current algebra curriculum is deeply flawed and must be challenged—that the way we teach algebra makes it the difficult subject that, some argue,

is impossible for many students to study successfully. Sandy and I have been exploring an alternative view of the central objects of study in algebra, one that suggests a wealth of connections between algebra and calculations with quantities that are performed repeatedly in everyday work situations. One benefit of this view of algebra is that it helps us bridge our students' interests and the curriculum; it also helps us identify strengths that our low achieving students exhibit, in addition to their easily identified academic weaknesses. (458–59) . . .

We wanted our students playing an active role in constructing knowledge. In class, we spent a large amount of time exploring a small number of problems, instead of a small amount of time on each of a large number of exercises. We sought to understand what the problems were asking and why that might be important or useful to know. Students worked on problems . . . and then we (teachers and students) discussed their results as a whole group. In these discussions, Sandy and I tried to get our students to articulate their ideas. We tried to take students' ideas seriously and help them develop and extend their ideas. (464)

Conclusion

The experience and analysis that Chazan and his three algebra 2 colleagues used to examine what knowledge it takes to teach for understanding in algebra takes us back to the Shulman claim that this sort of knowledge is an example of the most advanced knowledge of subject matter, one that addresses all aspects of guiding learners to the desired level of understanding, taking into account the characteristics and history of the students and the settings in which they live. Sykes explains:

The knowledge which teachers had to master centrally involved their subject matter along with the pedagogy of the subject. The reform's knowledge focus directed teachers to the "right stuff," rather than diverting their time and attention to subsidiary matters. Perhaps equally important, though, the reform was grounded deeply in knowledge of subject matter *and* pedagogy, not pedagogy alone. This seems an obvious point, but many instructional reforms—group work, for example, or activity-based teaching—have been introduced in content-free ways, leading to predictable shortcomings. When teachers merely change their grouping arrangements or merely begin to use manipulatives in math class, they do not reach deeply into the nature of learning. The outer form of teaching may change, but its internal dynamics remain relatively unaffected. (2008, 345)

Nevertheless, at MSU as well as elsewhere the effort not only to identify and analyze the special knowledge required to teach diverse subject matters, but also to ensure that beginning and experienced teachers have opportunities and incentives to achieve sufficient mastery of this knowledge was bound to remain limited as long as faculties of arts and science have the main responsibility for teaching subject matter to prospective and in-service teachers, but without commitment to the programmatic changes required if this effort was to be successful. The efforts of the Carnegie-led project Teachers for a New Era that took on this problem was successful mainly in demonstrating that far more would be needed.

CHAPTER EIGHTEEN

Using Instructional Materials and Technology to Advance the Revolution in Learning to Teach

Undeveloped in most of the history of formal teacher education was evidence-based learning of how to use instructional materials to best advantage in order to produce or facilitate student learning. Here, as in other areas, the governing assumption was that teachers could use these materials with little formal preparation or mentoring. Moreover, as evidence mounted that educational achievement in the nation left much to be desired, the response to this neglect of preparation and professional development was to double down on use of materials in two contradictory and counterproductive ways. One was to assume that trained teachers had sufficient subject-matter knowledge to free themselves from slavishly following their textbooks and other instructional materials and to selectively choose and adapt materials in deciding what to teach. Much of the early work on the unfinished revolution at MSU and elsewhere supported the belief that K–12 textbooks should have little or at least much less place in K–12 teaching (MSU-27, 1986, 17, I25). Ball and Feiman-Nemser (1988) found that teacher-education students in two MSU programs were led to think that following teachers' guides and textbooks was not good teaching.

In opposition to the idea that teachers should free themselves as much as possible from straightforward following of textbooks, another major and even more radical trend emerged in the attempt to develop and use materials that did not depend on teacher knowledge to be effective. It was the era of so-called "teacher-proof" curricula (MSU-27, 1986, 2). In science education, MSU faculty member Christina Schwarz and colleagues (2008) explained that both the teacher-proof and no-use approaches were problematic, but that there was little research to help new teachers take a more reasonable, middle-of-the-road approach. Since neither of these approaches had called for much guided preparation in how to use the materials, formal teacher preparation was left free to avoid teaching the use of materials as a part of the curriculum.

In face of these conflicting pressures, how teachers use curriculum materials gradually became the subject of research in the revolutionary era. The belief in teachers being able to teach with very little or no use of textbooks was gradually superseded by efforts to help teachers use textbooks wisely and well. In the IRT, the question of how teachers use textbooks in deciding what to teach in fourth-grade mathematics was intensively investigated by a team that included five faculty members (Andy Porter, Bill Schmidt, Bob Floden, Don Freeman, and Jack Schwille), one doctoral student (first Theresa Kuhs and then Gabriella Belli), and one teacher collaborator (first Lucy Bates and then Linda Alford). This research found that teachers used textbooks in various, often questionable ways (see, for example, Schwille et al., 1983; Porter et al., 1988).

Both teacher-proof and no-use approaches having failed to improve pupil learning, a better solution was needed. Once again it was Lee Shulman who brought this problem to the attention of teacher educators and others:

> If we are regularly remiss in not teaching pedagogical [content] knowledge to our students in teacher educa-tion programs, we are even more delinquent with respect to the third category of content knowledge, *curricular knowledge*: . . . [knowledge about] the variety of instruc-tional materials available . . . and the set of characteristics that serve as both indications and contraindications for the use of particular curriculum or program materials in particular circumstances. (Shulman, 1986/2004, 203–4)

This neglect of curricular knowledge is not surprising, given that at MSU and elsewhere teacher education gave use of textbooks or other prescriptive materials little place in the curriculum for fear that these resources would infringe on the autonomy thought necessary for the most effective teaching.

What Ball Learned from Materials

In the 1980s Sharon Feiman-Nemser and Deborah Ball began to tackle this problem. Ball used her own experience in learning to teach to show the importance of learning from materials. She recounts compelling examples from her teaching of both science and mathematics.

> [In my first year of teaching] I was handed three grade levels' worth of Science Curriculum Improvement Study (SCIS) materials. . . . I could not have been less prepared for this assignment. In college, as a French major, minoring in English, I had not studied any science other than the requirements for my teaching certificate. . . .
>
> My own lack of pedagogical or content resources left me reliant on the curriculum materials. . . . Since I knew so little about science or how to teach it, I had no alternative but to design my lessons drawing heavily from the curriculum materials and to work with my students on those lessons. I read the teachers' guides closely and tried to follow the suggestions. (1998, 12)

After a few years of teaching, Ball shifted from early grades to grade 5 and found that she needed support to be able to teach mathematics at that level. "I asked around and soon was fortuitously introduced to the Comprehensive School Mathematics Program (CSMP) by Perry Lanier, a professor at MSU. . . . I began experimenting with the curriculum in my classroom and the next year, teaching first grade, I used the materials as the primary mathematics curriculum." She found that following this curriculum led to a dramatic change in her teaching. "Adherence to the CSMP curriculum developers' plans produced a classroom full of talk about mathematics. I was astonished at the serious intellectual work in which my 6-year-olds could engage" (Ball, 1998, 15; see also H. Featherstone, 1990).

Limitations and Possibilities in Teacher Learning from Materials

According to Ball, this was the beginning of her career-long commitment to and investigation of mathematics education. In 1988 Ball and Feiman-Nemser took on the issue of what to do in teacher education to prepare teacher-education students to use textbooks. They examined two programs that took the position that following a textbook was an undesirable way to teach and that textbooks therefore should be used only as a resource. Instructors in both programs acted as if their students knew their subject matters well enough for them to make their own curriculum decisions.

In a related paper Schram, Feiman-Nemser, and Ball (1990) compared twelve beginning teachers with nine experienced teachers in how they taught subtraction with regrouping and the use of textbooks in this process. They gave each of the participants in this study two excerpts on this topic from different textbooks and asked the teachers how they would teach it with or without textbooks. Not surprisingly, the experienced teachers had more to say about how to teach the topic. The responses of beginning teachers were more diffuse and fragmented. But the beginning and experienced teachers did not differ in their understanding of multidigit subtraction. The experienced teachers did not have more to say about the conceptual foundations of regrouping or the borrowing algorithm than the beginners did. Even though the experienced teachers had more elaborate scripts, the scripts were not necessarily good ones.

This study suggested that experience led to subject-specific knowledge of what children are learning, but not better knowledge of the subject matter itself. For example, they did not learn what they needed to know to make well-justified choices in the use of manipulatives. Use of manipulatives was a major weakness for the experienced teachers as for the beginners. Both the experienced teachers and the beginners seemed to believe that use of manipulatives is inherently worthwhile, that if children simply examine and manipulate concrete objects they will understand. The textbooks did not help. For example, a recent textbook simply advised teachers to "use base ten materials" without sufficiently explaining how to do this.

In science education, Schwarz and colleagues (2008) carried out an intervention to assess whether teacher-education students were capable of analyzing curriculum materials on their own, according to criteria developed by the American Association for the Advancement of Science (AAAS). The results were mixed. The students found it difficult to understand what was meant by some of the criteria. In addition, they tended to use their own personal criteria instead of the AAAS reform-based criteria in assessing the strengths and weaknesses of the materials they examined. They were apt to assume that a "good" teacher would just naturally know what materials are good and what ones are not.

Ball and Cohen (1996), for their part, writing about the use of commercially published curriculum materials that dominate teaching practice in the United States, asserted that "hostility to texts, and the idealized image of the individual professional" had worked against a more constructive role for curriculum materials (6). They proposed instead that "materials could be designed to place teachers in the center of curriculum construction and make teachers' learning central to efforts to improve education, without requiring heroic assumptions about each teacher's capacities as an original designer of curriculum" (7). They discussed several changes to accomplish this shift. First, teachers' guides could be written to help teachers learn how to listen to and interpret what students have to say, and to anticipate what the students may think or do in response to certain activities. Second, they could help teachers learn content by, for example, discussing alternative representations of the ideas to be learned and the connections among them. Third, they could provide probes and questions to be used in exploring student ideas, questions, responses, and writing. Their fourth suggestion was to discuss the strengths and weaknesses of lesson suggestions proposed in the materials.

Use of Technology for Reform under
Carole Ames Leadership

The use of computer-based technology in teacher education followed a path similar to the one taken by hard-copy curriculum materials, going from insufficient attention and rigorous study early on to becoming a priority area of innovation and research. One of the weaknesses of the Lanier era at MSU had been limited technology use in the college and K–12. Lanier remained highly focused on the improvement of face-to-face teaching and was suspicious of any effort she perceived as bypassing or giving short shrift to teachers. When Carole Ames became dean in 1992, on the other hand, she was instrumental in extending the revolution in learning to teach to include a priority on technology. She insisted not only on keeping hardware and software in the college up-to-date, but also on preparing and rewarding faculty for use of technology in their classrooms. Because her emphasis was on teacher's use of technology, in both higher education and K–12, rather than doing research and development on hardware or software, her approach did not conflict with Lanier's emphasis on improvement of teaching practice. She brought the same priority concerning use of technology in teaching to the graduate and undergraduate students in the college as she did to the faculty.

One notable success was a course led by technology faculty to develop competence in use of technology for teaching among other faculty and graduate students. Faculty in the course did a special project for use of technology in one of their own courses. Incentives for faculty to take this course included financial support and the assistance of graduate students in technology who were also taking the course (they got graduate credit). Ultimately, this course was so successful in responding to the need for such preparation in use of technology that it resulted in the book *Faculty Development by Design: Integrating Technology in Higher Education*, edited by faculty members Punya Mishra, Matthew Koehler, and Yong Zhao in 2007. Still another of the dean's consequential efforts to advance the use of technology in the college was her establishment of the Office of Teaching and Technology to be run by Yong Zhao. Zhao was hired to continue innovation in educational technology, but soon turned to work in international education as well. With an incomparable record of grants and publications in his early career, by 2005 he had become the youngest University Distinguished Professor in MSU history (see the profile of Zhao in J. Schwille, 2017).

Technology and the Transformation of Teacher Knowledge

Gradually, the use of technology to improve teaching practice brought about a further transformation of teacher knowledge through theoretical work known initially by the acronyms TPCK and later TPACK. TPACK brings together three knowledge domains (content, pedagogy, and technology) in a situated form of knowledge, which includes teachers' integrated understanding of the complex relationships between content, pedagogy, technology, and the surrounding educational context (students, school, social networks, parental input, infrastructure, etc.). Herring, Koehler, and Mishra (2016) treat the TPACK framework as an extension of Shulman's seminal work on pedagogical content knowledge (PCK) although Shulman himself did not come to terms with technology and its relationship to content and pedagogy.

Leaders in this aspect of the revolution at MSU were Punya Mishra and Matthew Koehler, faculty members who played a key role in the development of technology throughout the college. Mishra, in his 1998 dissertation at the University of Illinois, had already started to work with the three constructs—technology, pedagogy, and content—that became the basis for the TPACK framework. The dissertation was a qualitative study, focusing on multiple ways to represent the periodic table of elements in chemistry and the learning that occurred as four students worked their way through multimedia hypertext (Mishra & Yadav, 2006; also Mishra website post, https://punyamishra.com/, February 29, 2009).

From such beginnings, technology knowledge (TK) earned its place as another essential category of teachers' knowledge. This expansion of PCK to TPCK has proved to be a powerful way to study and understand teacher cognition in the technology of teaching and learning and the knowledge needed to teach with technology. For example, this knowledge has enabled teachers to find ways of transforming content in forms difficult to support by traditional means into forms that are more readily understood. These include interactive representations, dynamic transformations of data, dynamic processing of data, multiple simultaneous representations of data, and multimodal representations of data. This knowledge when applied to the use of computers in classrooms makes it possible in turn to use teaching tactics and learner-centered strategies difficult or impossible to implement by other means, including the manipulation and application of ideas not experienced in real life. TPCK has been shown to be a distinct body of knowledge that goes beyond mere integration or accumulation of the constituent components toward transformation of these contributing knowledge bases into something new and different. Therefore instruction targeted not just on the individual components but on integration of these components is needed. For example, Ioannou and Angeli (2013) found that encouraging computer science teachers to think about technology integration as a transformation process forced them to reflect deeply about their content domain, considering students' intrinsic difficulties in understanding abstract computer science concepts and how the use of technology could alleviate these learning difficulties (see also Valinides & Angeli, 2015).

Making Revolutionary Use of
Hypermedia in Teacher Education

Gradually various members of the faculty became more expert in technology as well as use of video for teacher education. Rosaen, Hobson, and Khan (2003) discuss professional development for prospective teachers, collaborating teachers, and teacher educators in learning better use of technology. Then in a later article, Rosaen and colleagues reported on an investigation of three fifth-year interns to find out whether and in what ways "using video help[s] interns reflect on their discussion-based teaching in a more complex manner than when they use memory-based written reflection" (2008, 347). The authors concluded that requiring interns to use video records for reflection helped them write more specific comments than they could when just writing from memory and shift their comments from a focus on classroom management to a focus on instruction. They were also able to focus more on the children and less on themselves.

But a much more revolutionary and innovative use of technology for learning to teach got under way when amphibious professors Magdalene Lampert and Deborah Ball each videotaped an entire year of their teaching at Spartan Village Elementary School in East Lansing. In the 1998 book coauthored with Ball, Lampert recalls how this came to be:

> Some years ago, Sharon Schwille, an experienced teacher and a colleague in the teacher education program at MSU, sensed my frustration in trying to answer those recurring questions about establishing a classroom culture and covering the curriculum. She boldly suggested that I should start to videotape on the first day of school and tape everything I did for a whole year. . . . [As a result,] I began to imagine what daily videos could add to my journal records and how they could be used for the study of teaching. (Lampert and Ball, 1998, 39)

The idea was for Lampert and Ball to investigate ways in which "our teaching might serve as a medium for others' learning" (23). With support from the National Science Foundation, they created "a multimedia, computer-supported learning environment that would make instances of practice available for study by prospective teachers." Rather than recording lessons to be copied by other teachers, they documented "an entire year's worth of teaching and learning by collecting a variety of records that could be studied by ourselves and others. . . . [The records served as] a rich and unique collection of materials that we could use to develop a different approach to teacher education" (47).

Over the next several years, Lampert and Ball worked with a group of graduate students to create teacher-preparation courses that used these records as a centerpiece.

Across these courses, we worked with our graduate assistants as more experienced partners in teacher education
and research on teaching, inventing new pedagogies as
we used new technologies, and piloting them in courses.
Together we evolved problems, tasks, and structures for
interacting with teacher education students, and these
moved around back and forth among us. (92–94; see also
Forzani, 2011, 88–89)

In the afterword to the book, David Cohen makes clear the
profound significance of this enterprise as far as teacher education
is concerned. He argues that this work shows how the practice of
teaching could in ways never before possible be brought into the
university classroom and used as an unprecedented resource for
initial learning to teach (1998, 186).

In other action research on use of hypermedia, Rosaen, Schram,
and Herbel-Eisenmann (2002) report on the use of these materials
in a senior-level course. Focusing on thirteen teacher-education
students, they examined what understandings of reform-based
teaching in mathematics the students gained from the hypermedia
environment created from Ball's recordings of practice. Immersion
in that environment helped the students begin to rethink and
reimagine what it means, in elementary school, to teach and learn
mathematics, and the role that discussion can play in that process.

The study revealed that the hypermedia environment enabled
students to engage in conversations that were very different from
those they were accustomed to. Through this process of inquiry,
they became familiar with "framing problems and questions;
generating conjectures; seeking evidence; formulating questions;
making arguments, playing out their ideas; and revising their
thinking." In recording this thinking and talking, the students
were able to "think on paper," that is, document their intellectual
progress as well as revisit and revise their ideas (325–26).

The authors concede that not all their students have responded
in the same way as this class. Some came into the course willing to
share their thinking because they had already taken such risks in the
past. Others had had no such experience and waited to see if they

could trust the instructors enough to take such risks. Some even had prior experience with open-ended, self-paced projects with loosely defined tasks. Others found this sort of experience difficult, confusing, and frustrating. But overall, most students started the course without a history of success in mathematics learning and therefore lacking in confidence in their ability to learn. Students also differed in their ability to collaborate. Some had the interpersonal and organizational skills to work well in groups. Others were not prepared and disliked belonging to such groups. Nevertheless, in the class studied, all four groups of students working with the materials developed an attitude of inquiry.

Conclusion

Learning how to operate computers and become accustomed to software, like learning to read at a competent level, is no longer an issue for most teacher-education programs. But using textbooks and technology to learn to teach at basic and more advanced levels is still a challenge. As in other areas, the assumption that novice teachers can pick up what they need to know by themselves is not viable. The revolution in teacher education no longer takes for granted the ability of prospective teachers to learn to cope and figure out things for themselves. In the case of textbooks and technology, the revolution has demonstrated the need and the possibility of designing textbooks, other materials, and technology environments to facilitate and enhance teacher learning at the beginning and throughout teacher careers.

CHAPTER NINETEEN

Rethinking the Revolution
Down in Ann Arbor

A s the restoration of orthodoxy continued at MSU, the revolution in teacher education took a new turn, not in East Lansing but at the University of Michigan, Ann Arbor, a university with which MSU relations had never run smooth. But, in this case, reform in Ann Arbor was strongly tied to the earlier history at MSU. The main link was through Deborah Ball, who became a faculty member and dean at U of M, but only after being a faculty leader at MSU and before that a doctoral student. Having received all three of her degrees from MSU, she confessed in a later talk at MSU how delightful it was as dean to hand out diplomas resplendent in MSU's green doctoral robe, surrounding by a sea of maize and blue.

A Different Approach Emerges
under Ball's Leadership

Over her years in Ann Arbor, Ball had become convinced that practice was neglected in MSU teacher education, meaning that there were no specific standards for what teacher-education students had to learn and be able to do at the end of their program. Her doctoral student Francesca Forzani made this criticism a central point in her dissertation study of teacher-education reform at MSU. For example, in discussing the 1988 task-force report that had been the basis for developing the five-year program at MSU, Forzani took a very critical position. According to her, the task-force members were unable to articulate the specific practices and skills that prospective teachers should be required to master in preservice programs. They did not spell out what novices should be able to do before being licensed to teach. It was an indication, Forzani asserted, of the undeveloped state of the field. Teacher educators were not asking questions that are fundamental to any field of professional education. It was difficult to know whether the task-force members even envisaged a curriculum focused on core practices of teaching. They seemed to realize the need to attend more closely to practice but were not able to explain what that meant. They were at the beginning of a development that has taken place since that time (Forzani, 2011, 207).

While Ball later laid out a set of high-leverage practices beginning teachers must learn, her 1998 book with Lampert is different. It is a rich source of insights into how learning to teach involves constructing knowledge in practice and appreciating the situated nature of this knowledge. Teachers have "to make and test conjectures, invent new ideas and approaches, collect and interpret data, and analyze, construct, and challenge arguments in the course of their work" (Lampert & Ball, 1998, 36). This represents a continuation of the philosophy that the development of teacher judgment, not the learning of specific practices, is uppermost in setting priorities for initial teacher preparation. But shortly thereafter Ball took a different position.

Instead of (or more accurately together with) the judgment-based approach dominant at MSU, Ball and Forzani launched the development of a practice-based curriculum, believing that MSU's reforms were less successful than envisaged because the new TE curriculum at MSU was not based on specific teaching practices that beginners needed to learn. By 2009, Ball and Forzani called for making the learning of specific practices the core of teachers' initial preparation (Ball & Forzani, 2009). They used this approach in Teaching Works, a University of Michigan project in which teaching practices considered "high leverage" were selected and developed as the basis for learning and assessment in preservice teacher education. Under their leadership, the teacher-education program at U of M was revamped around these practices, and other institutions around the country were recruited to collaborate in this reform (University of Michigan, 2018; Davis & Boerst, 2014).

Agreeing on the definition of core tasks of teaching is difficult, and in the past practitioners and experts have come to no consensus. Nevertheless, Ball and Forzani (2009) say that to prepare teachers well demands agreement on a flexible repertoire of strategies and techniques shown to make a substantial difference (considered "high leverage") and that can be put into practice with the good judgment called for by a specific situation. They contrast this position with the belief that teaching is highly improvisational and context dependent. They find fault with this latter point of view because it suggests that the complexities of teaching with all its diversity of practices, techniques, and judgments cannot be adequately codified and taught. Instead they agree with Lampert and Graziani's discussion of the tension between flexibility and rigidity in teaching practice:

> How can novices be prepared for the interactively challenging work of ambitious teaching if it constantly needs to be invented from scratch and be tailored to particular students? If professional education for teaching is to make ambitious teaching more common . . . we would need to assume, first, that this kind of teaching involves stable and learnable practices and that we could specify the kind of skills and knowledge needed to do it, . . . that teacher educators could teach these skills and knowledge, and that novices could learn them. (2009, 492)

To develop a practice-based curriculum, Ball and Forzani advocated breaking practice down into parts that can be improved through targeted instruction. Given time constraints, the broad scope of teaching practice, and the challenges of working with novices, they set out to identify those practices that would offer the most leverage to new teachers. In short, it would be a teacher-education program worthy of their motto: "Great teachers aren't born, they're taught" (University of Michigan, 2018).

Once these high-leverage practices were identified, the challenge was to develop ways of teaching them. Grossman, Compton, and their colleagues argued for the use of what they called representations, decompositions, and approximations in teaching such practices. Representations refer to written case studies and video records. Decompositions have to do with dissecting the elements of a larger practice. Approximations are "opportunities for novices to engage in practices that are more or less proximal to the practices of a profession"; they allow for "instructive failure," that is, they provide opportunities to make mistakes in an environment that is relatively safe with low stakes. These approximations can help novices focus attention on specific aspects of their work, while ignoring other aspects (2009, 2068–73, 2076–83).

Example of How to Teach Practice

Ball and Forzani provide examples of this approximations to practice approach. One such example is about helping students learn to read a story aloud to young pupils. In this case, a student teacher was required to practice reading a story aloud about a group of children going on a fishing trip. The instructor sat right in front of the student teacher in order to pay close attention and to stop the student as needed to provide feedback and coaching. The other students watched from nearby where they could ask questions or make suggestions as they wished. After reminding the audience that they had already begun to read this story the day before, the student began to read haltingly. And immediately, the instructor interrupted to say that just telling the children where they had left off was not enough. She also had to say something about what was happening at that point in the book or ask the children themselves what was going on in the story. At a certain point, the student teacher stopped to ask whether she should discuss technical terms used in fishing like "reel." The instructor agreed that this would be good. Then later, when the student teacher wrote the word "wound" on the board, thinking it would be difficult for the children, the instructor told her to be careful in how she pronounced and wrote the word to avoid confusion.

This example shows how specific and elaborated the Ann Arbor approach had become. In feedback and coaching, the instructor referred to specific moves and techniques and explained why they were needed. She paid attention to many aspects that would have gone unnoticed by many adults who had not had this training. Although nonteaching adults read aloud to children, this sort of professional practice is different. It is neither intuitive nor natural. The example makes clear that reading a story aloud in a classroom is not simple at all and therefore merits professional preparation as part of teacher education.

The New Practice-Based Curriculum
at the University of Michigan

Shifting from a theory- and knowledge-based teacher-education curriculum to one focused on practice is difficult and complex. It demands not only a precise, common language for talking about instruction, but also much work to identify specific pedagogical moves for teaching different subjects and grade levels. It also calls for not the abandonment, but a reworking of the foundations components in teacher education. Instead of offering broad survey courses, disconnected from situations faced by teachers, the practice-based approach focuses on what will most benefit teachers in practice. Teachers would benefit, for example, from knowing how testing came to be so central and important to American schooling and about the influence of educational and social inequalities. These and other such questions are authentic, on-the-ground matters that impinge heavily on teachers' practice.

Davis and Boerst (2014) have described in some detail this new practice-based teacher-education program for elementary schoolteachers at the University of Michigan. Students enter this program as juniors and spend three semesters in professional coursework, plus six to nine hours each week in a clinical practicum. At the same time, they complete their subject-matter preparation. Then in the fourth semester, students have an extended student-teaching experience (although one that is much shorter than the year-long internship at MSU).

The high-leverage practices on which the program was based are the following:

- Explaining core content
- Posing questions about content
- Choosing and using representations, examples, and models of content
- Leading whole-class discussions of content
- Working with individual students to elicit, probe, and develop their thinking about content
- Setting up and managing small-group work
- Engaging students in rehearsing an organizational or managerial routine
- Establishing norms and routines for classroom discourse and work that are central to the content
- Recognizing and identifying common patterns of student thinking in a content domain
- Composing, selecting, adapting quizzes, tests, and other methods of assessing student learning of a chunk of instruction
- Selecting and using specific methods to assess students' learning on an ongoing basis within and between lessons
- Identifying and implementing an instructional strategy or intervention in response to common patterns of student thinking
- Choosing, appraising, and modifying tasks, texts, and materials for a specific learning goal
- Enacting a task to support a specific learning goal
- Designing a sequence of lessons on a core topic
- Enacting a sequence of lessons on a core topic
- Conducting a meeting about a student with a parent or guardian
- Writing correct, comprehensible, and professional messages to colleagues, parents, and others
- Analyzing and improving specific elements of one's own teaching. (Davis & Boerst, 2014, appendix A, 21–22; also Ball et al., 2009)

Assessment in the program starts on the very first day of the internship with baseline assessments that do not require working with students—for example, interpreting a video of a student reading aloud—and those that do demand working with students, such as explaining core mathematics content and giving directions for work to a student. As the internship goes on, assessments turn to more complex practices with higher expectations for performance. This could include video clips with classroom-management situations as well as simulations that require the intern to analyze a student's thinking about mathematics. Then, at the end of the internship, interns prepare a portfolio of correspondence to demonstrate their capability to communicate with the families of students. They also must provide evidence of teaching lessons based on formative data they have collected from children.

Resulting Differences between MSU and the University of Michigan

Forzani's dissertation provides an ideal basis for comparing the revolution as it took place at MSU with the turn it took at the University of Michigan. The thesis is the extraordinarily well-documented and well-written history of national teacher-education reform that focused on the work of both the Holmes Group and MSU, as well as providing excellent introductory chapters on how these efforts fit into the history of teacher education in the United States.

But I do have reservations about this work. In Forzani's earlier writing, the work of identifying and analyzing practices as the basis for curriculum development is mainly done by experts and explained to practitioners in terms of what needed to be done. The thesis has little discussion of the tension between, on the one hand, bringing outsiders in to work on reform with major parts of an agenda already developed and, on the other, the belief that to have effective collaboration between schools of education and K–12 schools, it is necessary to enter with a clean slate, gain the trust of K–12 teachers, and recognize that K–12 teachers have knowledge that is potentially as important to reform as that of university experts. Forzani's use of the words "intervention" and "interveners" in her thesis to describe desirable relationships between higher education and K–12 is in this sense problematic and contrary to the philosophy that inspired the PDSs during the revolutionary era.

At one point Ball and Cohen (1999) took this technocratic approach to an extreme. They even argued that interveners might treat the work of implementation as a teaching task, one in which a large part of their job is to help teachers learn about the program and how to offer it effectively. Their position was reformers ought to be able to "specify" and "develop" a program and thus improve practitioner capabilities. By "specify," they mean the "explicitness with which an intervention is articulated and mapped—to the plans for action, including what the intervener chooses to treat explicitly and . . . the plans or educational blueprints for intervention, including plans for a curriculum for enactors' learning, plans to collect and use evidence on enactment, and much more." They assert that "the more fully reformers design, specify, and develop a reform program, the more likely that they will achieve success" (Ball & Cohen, 1999; Forzani, 2011, 105–6).

Forzani contends that Judy Lanier and the MSU faculty were seriously lacking in the knowledge actually necessary to carry out the reform that was needed (Forzani, 2011, 207, 219, 224, 230). She asserts that Lanier may not have understood how great the gap was between the teacher education in the four alternative programs of the 1980s and the kind of teacher education that was called for (221). In reaching this conclusion, Forzani makes assumptions about what MSU was attempting to do that, to me, are not justified. For example, she asserts that the faculty leaders who spearheaded the work at MSU were convinced that teacher education needed to be "developed into a more powerful intervention—one of their chief goals was to improve professional education so as to produce more effective classroom teachers. In this sense, their project was to develop more practice-focused teacher education" (293). With this in mind, Forzani reached the conclusion that the new five-year program had "moved only a few

steps closer to practice," and "intended outcomes were still not
defined in terms of specific knowledge or specific practices that
students should be able to do" (275). But my understanding is that
there was never any strongly expressed intention at MSU during
the revolutionary era to achieve such a practice-based form of
teacher education.

The Hyperrationalistic Nature
of Forzani's Analysis

Forzani's analysis at this point became highly technocratic in its
rationalistic and experimental approach to instructional design
and organizational development. Such an approach in my view is
not consistent with what MSU was trying to do. Forzani spells out
what I would call a "hyperrationalistic" approach as follows:[1]

> This conception of the work of reform in teacher educa-
> tion suggests that those who take on the tasks of design
> and analysis necessary to improving teacher education
> face time consuming and resource intensive work, and
> more so the more comprehensively they pursue change. To
> summarize, evidence from reform in other fields suggests
> that the search for more effective curricula, materials, and
> pedagogies, for example, might require that courses and
> other learning experiences for teachers be redesigned and
> reenacted in multiple iterations. The creation of effective
> "field experiences" for student teachers, to name another
> example, might depend on labor intensive efforts to
> build relationships with schools and practicing teachers;
> to train teacher educators, including faculty members,
> doctoral students, and practicing teachers; to partici-
> pate in a design experiment; and even to create alterna-
> tive environments for the delivery of teacher education.

1. The term "hyperrationalistic" was coined and applied by Wise (1979) in his critique of
the educational reform efforts current at that time.

It could require experimentation with several different ways of structuring and sequencing student teachers' participation in K–12 classrooms. In these areas of the work and in each of the others, designers would need to document and study each trial. They would also need to attempt to sort through the impact of different elements of a particular intervention, and attend in particular to how different elements of teacher education interacted with each other in influencing outcomes of interest; increased comprehensiveness of an intervention would increase the complexity of this work just as it made it more productive. Care would need to be taken to maintain the coherence and continuity of the work associated with an intervention over several years. The process would be expensive and would demand sustained organization, commitment, and interest by multiple parties. (2011, 111–12)

Forzani admitted that this agenda might be overly ambitious and impossible to carry out in such a comprehensive manner. She conceded that it conflicts with emphasis on and rewards for faculty members' individual autonomy and specialization. The loose coupling that characterizes educational institutions, together with the priority universities give to basic research and research publication over teaching and curriculum development is, she admitted, a big obstacle to what she proposed. Moreover, the preparation of the teacher educators heretofore has given little attention to developing the competence in experimental design required for such an approach.

In my view, the technocratic aspects of Forzani's thesis failed to take sufficiently into account the fact that technocratic solutions have been much advocated and tried in the history of American education without, in the end, having much to show for it. For example, the classic book by Callahan (1962) criticized the Taylor efficiency movement in education in the early parts of the twentieth century; the book by Arthur Wise, *Legislated Learning* (1979), focused on hyperrationalized attempts at reform that came later, such as those associated with the behaviorist era of programmed instruction, and the competency-based teacher-education (CBTE) reforms. These failures do much to explain the reliance on developing judgment as opposed to teaching practice in the MSU revolution. In his commentary on the success of mathematics education reform at the Holt High PDS, Sykes suggests that a more rationalistic approach would have been inappropriate, conflicting with the priority given to formation of a professional community:

> If practice can be codified in routines, standard procedures, or technologies, then bureaucratic forms of organization may be efficient. But if practice involves non-routine judgement, information use, and decision-making, the professional form of organization is optimal as it supplies access to expert sources of knowledge that help to mediate complex tasks and problems. . . . A new technology—the graphing calculator—played an important role in the story, but the work on curriculum, instruction, and assessment involved teachers in complex practices that placed heavy demands on skills of interpretation, judgment, and problem-solving. Such work . . . required participation in a professional community of the kind that formed at Holt. (2008, 349)

The University of Michigan work on the tasks of teaching may be better characterized as the development of professional standards than of bureaucratic procedures. However, it remains to be seen how much teacher judgment is developed when the practice-based approach is applied in teacher education or whether this arm of the revolution eventually moves in a more bureaucratically scripted direction.

In the meantime, it is worth noting that Forzani was relatively positive in discussing the history of CBTE and microteaching (unlike the way they were typically portrayed in the revolutionary environment at MSU), characterizing them as unfinished attempts to base teacher education on a curriculum of practice. She praises the CBTE movement for its advances over earlier attempts at practice-focused teacher education (2011, 80–81).

In fact, Forzani notes that the era of CBTE

> also witnessed the development of some of the first genuine pedagogies of teacher education. Though the researchers who designed and studied microteaching have been repeatedly criticized for their lack of explanatory theory, the strategy represents one of the first attempts to engage novice teachers systematically in an intermediate activity between observing teaching and practicing it in a full classroom of real students. It is based on the assumption that students . . . learn best when they have opportunities to engage in scaled-down versions of the activity first. (81)

In contrast, Sharon Feiman-Nemser expresses an opposing perspective that in my view continued to be the dominant one at MSU during the revolutionary era. As far as I can tell, the revolutionary vanguard at MSU was not knowingly or unknowingly in search of a practice-based curriculum to the extent that Forzani tends to assume. Instead, Feiman-Nemser takes her direction from John Dewey's 1904 essay "On the Relation of Theory and Practice."

> For me, Dewey's essay was a raft in the sea of CBTE. It offered a view of teachers as practical intellectuals, students of subject-matter and children's thinking who learn from experience, including their own experience as learners. It underscored the place of dispositions—habits of mind and heart—in teaching and learning to teach. It offered a vision of liberal/professional teacher education that contrasted sharply with the narrow technical views of teaching and teacher training associated with CBTE. (2012, 12)

Rehabilitating the Term *Teacher Training*

This philosophy of teacher education expressed by Feiman-Nemser had begun to sink roots at MSU still earlier when the IRT was established with its emphasis on teacher thinking and decision-making in reaction against CBTE and related efforts. Training prospective teachers on specific teaching practices was considered inappropriate because the value and use of any practice was thought to depend mainly on situational factors and the judgment of the teacher about what practices to use and how to adapt it to circumstances. Teacher education was seen as the development of this judgment. The very term *teacher training* was largely taboo at MSU during the revolutionary period.

In spite of (or perhaps because of) her experience at MSU, Deborah Ball came to think that although the term *training* seemed to "connote mindless and atomized repetition and, hence, to 'deskill' the professional work on teaching," the term should be rehabilitated as "fully worthy of the intricate demands of teaching." She further explains that "the intricacy of this work demands a disciplined approach to preparing teachers and a determined rejection of approaches that permit a good general education, reflective field experiences or unstructured mentoring to suffice as professional training" (Ball and Forzani, 2009, 498).

However, Forzani by no means dismisses all of the innovation in teacher education based on viewing teachers as practical intellectuals. In her view, MSU was offering knowledge-based as opposed to practice-based teacher education. By relying on cases, hypermedia, and portfolios and giving insight into the complexities of teaching, this approach Forzani viewed as a worthy adjunct to the development of a practice-based curriculum that she insisted was also needed.

Another indication that MSU continued to be inhospitable to Forzani's position can be found in David Labaree's statement in preparation for the agenda-setting leadership retreat for the college early in the Ames era in May 1994. He was one of the faculty members recruited to the Department of Teacher Education in the belief that expertise in disciplines even without K–12 classroom teaching experience was needed to enrich the knowledge base of teacher education. In May 1994 he emailed Gary Sykes to make his views on practice clear:

> I think it is both counterproductive and inappropriate for us to adopt the rhetoric of practice. Focusing our efforts as teacher educators and researchers around classroom practice ignores the larger social and political context which we know exerts such a strong impact on teaching and learning in classrooms. Such a focus also effectively writes us out of a job. After all, if practice is the key, then the K–12 classroom is the only place to learn to teach. So prospective teachers can learn subject-matter in the core colleges, and can learn teaching practice in the schools. Under these circumstances, who needs an ed school?

In contrast to the views of Labaree, Sykes, and the other faculty members at MSU who held this position, Ball and Forzani pushed ahead and extended the revolutionary agenda of not taking anything for granted by devising an explicit and formal curriculum based on training and assessment of practices for learning to teach. But contrary to what Labaree says, their emphasis on learning from practice was in no way just the responsibility of K–12 teachers, nor was it to take place entirely within K–12 schools. To explain what they meant by a curriculum based on practice, they first described the work of teaching as follows.

> By work of teaching, we mean the core tasks that teachers must execute to help pupils learn. These include activities carried on both inside and beyond the classroom, such as leading a discussion of solutions to a mathematics problem, proving students' answers, reviewing material for a science test, listening and assessing students' oral reading, explaining an interpretation of a poem, talking with parents, evaluating students' papers, planning and creating and maintaining an orderly and supportive environment for learning. . . . Skillful teaching requires appropriately using and integrating specific moves and activities in

particular cases and contexts, based on knowledge and understanding of one's pupils and on the application of professional judgment. . . . Professional training should be designed to help teachers learn to enact these tasks skillfully. Such training would involve seeing examples of each task, learning to dissect and analyze the work, watching demonstrations, and then practicing under close supervision and with detailed coaching aimed at fostering improvement. (Ball and Forzani, 2009, 497–98)

It can be seen that the emphasis on teacher judgment was not abandoned, but rather embodied in the study of specific practices. In other words, this conception of training integrates the learning of practices with the application of judgment and the intellectual capabilities already emphasized at MSU.

Conclusion

However one views this emphasis on interveners offering specific guidance to practitioners, a decisive turn in the revolution in learning to teach had taken place in Ann Arbor, and one that greatly reduced the ambitious approach taken earlier by MSU in giving priority to the development of teacher judgment. It was developed in the framework of a hyperrationalistic analysis of needed education. Although this approach had proved disappointing when treated as a panacea, it remains to be seen how successful it will be in the more limited form it has taken in Ann Arbor. In my view the attempt to do this in an incremental and systematic way cannot be bad and is not completely contrary to the philosophy of the revolutionary era. In fact, I think it is unfortunate that MSU did not take up the University of Michigan's invitation to collaborate more fully in this initiative and thereby be better able to judge whether the criticism of the revolution as neglecting practice is warranted or not. In any case, without unduly prejudging the case, I am eager to find out what can be learned from the Ann Arbor chapter in the revolutionary saga of learning to teach.

Conclusion

This book could be characterized as a "revisionist" account of the MSU revolution. But in what sense is it revisionist? How does the revolution portrayed here differ from earlier accounts and the fading personal memories of what was attempted and accomplished? How does it attempt to set the record straight? There are various ways that I have attempted to do this. First, the book argues that the attempt to reform teaching and teacher education at MSU should be remembered as qualitatively different from many other attempts to change teaching and teacher education. For a time it was not just a collection of projects, but rather a *crusade* that mobilized more resources, talent, ambition, grit, and ceaseless work than any other school of education had been able to put together. Revisionism is a way to fight against the natural tendency of events, even great events, to fade from collective memory, to appear less consequential than they were, when not countered by institutional prompts of some kind. Such prompts are no longer salient enough at MSU to keep what was important about the revolution readily accessible for inspiration, reflection, and continued debate.

The book is also revisionist in its insistence on judging the revolution to be both a great success and a great failure in contrast to the natural tendency for interested parties to discount one side or the other. Even so, in my view the success can be counted as definitive in terms of achievements that could not be taken away whereas, given the unfinished nature of the revolution, failure was provisional with an unknown future. My analysis attempts to bring this two-sided legacy into the present where, instead of being forgotten or fading into obscurity, it can be seen as relevant and instructive as far as the future of teaching and teacher education is concerned, not just history that can be easily dismissed.

Reviewing the legacies the revolution left behind means taking into account both its successes and its failures, both enduring lessons and the tentative, even imaginative lessons of what might have been. This book approaches this difficult task in three parts. Part 1 is a narrative account of the forces that were mobilized to bring about the revolution and how ambitious and monumental they became—overly ambitious in the minds of many. Parts 2 and 3 deal with what it was that was so revolutionary about all this.

Part of what might be seen as failure was simply lack of time to move the reforms onward. Thus revisionism means keeping in mind that the revolution in teacher education at MSU was never intended as a fast or easy fix, or even one that would be brought to fruition in the medium term. It was intended for the long run with all its attendant complexities, difficulties, and uncertainties. Unfortunately, a long-term time frame was not to be. The revolution was cut short. The PDSs, for example, lasted not even a decade before they were shut down or transformed into much less ambitious enterprises. It is therefore not possible to draw any firm conclusions about how successful they might have been in the long run or what their impact and accomplishments might have been.

The book is also revisionist in that it makes little use of the high-blown rhetoric of the Holmes Group and its supporters in describing what the reforms were supposed to accomplish. This rhetoric served its purpose as motivation and inspiration, but it was vague and open to various interpretations and even fostered intentional attempts at seeming compliance without really challenging the status quo. At MSU the stirring words of the Holmes Group manifestoes (or at least the first two) did have more meaning for those caught up in the revolution, and it is this meaning that can be inferred not only from what was said or written at MSU at the time, but also from what was actually attempted and done. Revisionism in this book resides in the attempt to bring to life actual experience and accomplishments, in what the Holmes Group reforms produced on the ground at the university and in affiliated K–12 schools.

At the heart of the revolution was its insistence on treating teacher education, however low status it had been, respectfully as of great importance to the future of schooling and the nation at large. Teaching was to be understood not as a low-level occupation that anyone could do, but as a formidable intellectual challenge that could consume whole lifetimes without running short of matters requiring investigation in the endless journey of learning to teach. "Teaching is impossible," Lee Shulman tells us (1983/2004, 151). Teaching according to the revolution meant developing professional judgment to the point of being able to guide students toward success in learning regardless of the difficulties and attitudes they bring to the classroom—a level of judgment in teaching that few could hope to master at more than a modest level.

Perhaps this goal was indeed overly ambitious for preservice students and inappropriate in that it did not take into account the need for the graduates of initial teacher preparation to have mastered certain basic practices. This was the take on the revolution developed by Deborah Ball (MSU PhD and former MSU faculty member) and her associates at the University of Michigan, Ann Arbor. The jury is still out on this, awaiting more results from work on the Ann Arbor agenda, work that continues to assume, as the whole revolution did, that the ability to teach can be taught. It may come easily or naturally to some people but, for the most part, it is neither natural nor innate.

Learning to teach from this perspective would no longer be primarily an individual matter in which it is taken for granted that sufficiently talented and motivated persons could find their own way without much guidance or without close collaboration with others. Instead collaboration was at the heart of the revolution as new forms of collaboration were introduced at the university and in K–12 schools. But the revolution was not able to institutionalize all these forms of collaboration in order that they become the new taken-for-granted norms. Old forms of organization and a host of disincentives were never overcome. Nevertheless, experiments in collaboration left sufficient artifacts and evidence to show that belief in their importance was not unwarranted and that they might be revived in full at some point.

Much relevant evidence was assembled and left behind by the PDSs after they were shut down before being able to demonstrate their full potential. From a perspective of collective amnesia, the PDSs are easily misunderstood. They were not supposed to be just sites for teacher education, not laboratory schools, not sandboxes in which university professors could freely engage in K–12 schooling without the constraints that such experimentation normally entails. Instead the PDSs were to emerge from regular K–12 schools, including those with all the problems of the most difficult inner-city and rural environments, without excluding better-off schools that felt no need to commit to the sort of university collaboration that had so often gone wrong in the past. In the PDSs, K–12 teachers were supposed to enjoy equal status with university faculty in doing research on teaching and learning in the school and in preparing novice teachers to practice. This was the vision, but as already said, it did not come to pass, and as with many reforms in the history of education, it was abandoned or watered down before the concept was adequately tested. The PDSs at MSU could not be sustained primarily because the donors and the state government did not have the commitment and will to stay the course, even though they had been warned that the PDS agenda was long-term and could not be realized in just a few years. Nevertheless, as this book has repeatedly documented, at their peak the PDSs did have accomplishments of enduring value. They were able to do this because for some years about a quarter of the MSU permanent faculty in the College of Education spent a quarter or more of their work time out in K–12 PDSs engaged with K–12 colleagues in the grueling and often thankless work of school reform.

There was no ivory tower for any of those folks and especially not for the few who carried this work to extremes, adopting the role of "amphibious" professors. The latter were the MSU faculty members who proved capable of building national reputations for outstanding research and other achievements while teaching on a daily basis in K–12 schools. Their work broke new ground in the teaching and learning of mathematics, science, and other subjects. Their PDS publications made unique contributions to educational research.

As part of this work, the revolution continued to bring to light much of what was not known or not considered in the improvement of teaching and teacher education, for example, in expanding knowledge of student thinking and how this knowledge could improve teaching and learning, thus extending one of the richest and most fruitful areas of inquiry in educational research. For example, the ability of students in grades 1–3 to engage in real intellectual discussion of subject matter was demonstrated. Lower-track high school algebra students showed that they could engage in real-life problem-solving using algebra to the satisfaction not only of teachers, but of members of the outside community as well. Again there is a question of how well these capabilities have been maintained since the end of the revolutionary era. We lack data on whether these capabilities continue to be demonstrated at the same level of achievement on a widespread level in schools affiliated with or influenced by MSU, but there are reasons to doubt they are.

One area of discovery and innovation developed almost from scratch and in depth by the revolution was in understanding what it takes to mentor novice teachers. MSU doctoral students, other MSU staff members, and K–12 teachers have benefited from learning how to mentor MSU teacher-education students, and especially the fifth-year interns. Research on this learning led in turn to publications that have shown what it takes to mentor well, demolishing the old assumption that effective teachers can be counted on to be effective mentors. However, here again major obstacles have continued to restrict our ability to realize the full potential of what is now known about mentoring. At MSU and elsewhere, lack of sufficient support for the formal preparation and continued professional development of mentors in terms of time, financial compensation, and other rewards continues to outweigh the benefits that can be achieved without this support.

If there is one area in which the revolution made demands that were far beyond the state of the art with results that could not be sustained, it was in the area of subject-matter teaching and learning. The fallacy of the dichotomy between pedagogy and content was recognized and investigated, but it could not be overcome on a systematic basis as long as universities include subject-matter colleges that do not take responsibility in collaboration with education researchers to offer the advanced subject matter and enhanced pedagogy needed by prospective teachers.

It was further recognized during the revolution that teacher education had been remiss in not offering special preparation in the use of materials—another case of assuming that individual teachers would learn what they need largely on their own as they gain experience. Likewise, when use of technology in the form of computers and other affordances began to be omnipresent in American life (although initially not in schools), this was another challenge with which teacher education was slow to come to grips. As far as materials were concerned, limited work was done to demonstrate that teacher-education programs need to give explicit attention and guidance to use of materials, but the most revolutionary development was in technology where the work of Lampert and Ball brilliantly used videos on a year of their teaching with associated digital technology to make it possible for students to learn new practices not just during their regular K–12 field experience, but in university or PDS classrooms where this experience can be examined and reexamined and discussed in various ways by a succession of student cohorts. In addition, work on the knowledge required to use technology effectively in teaching by Punya Mishra, Matthew Koehler, and others led to extending needed teacher knowledge beyond the pedagogical content knowledge of Shulman or "knowledge for teaching" of Ball to include use of technology as an additional basic category of teacher knowledge—as signaled by the acronym TPACK.

Finally, as noted above, the issue of whether the revolution had failed to develop the skill and expertise to carry out practices that students need to develop before taking on teaching jobs is still being vigorously pursued by colleagues in Ann Arbor. Likewise, colleagues remaining at MSU are moving teacher education forward in their research even though they do not have as much college-level support and priority as in the past. In short, this last chapter of the revolutionary era is yet to be finished. In fact, this whole book is manifestly about unfinished work that deserves further exploration, testing, and study. Much more could have been accomplished had there been the will and resources to do so. Hopefully, the reading of this book will create new opportunities to continue this work by putting the legacies of the unfinished revolution back on the table and supporting those still committed to the revolutionary agenda.

Technical Terms Used
in Parts 2 and 3

Opportunities to Learn to Teach
through Situated Knowledge

The conventional view among teacher educators is that learning to teach is a two-step process of first acquiring knowledge and then applying or transferring it to practice, whereas the lay public, in contrast, has tended to assume that learning to teach occurs through trial and error. Both of these views, according to Feiman-Nemser and Remillard (1995), have proved incorrect. The belief that knowledge and skills exist independently of the context in which they were acquired and that therefore knowledge and skills can first be learned and then applied in real-world situations has been shown to be misguided.

According to cognitive psychologists, all knowledge should be seen as situated and growing out of the contexts in which it is used. The theory of situated cognition calls for embedding teacher learning in authentic activities. Research indicates that people learn better when solving real problems, using available clues, tools, and social support. Traditional apprenticeships are an example of this kind of learning. Apprentices develop flexible skills and conditional knowledge when they work on genuine tasks under the guidance of a master (Feiman-Nemser & Remillard, 1995, 24).

Learning can best be understood as the interaction between the learner and a learning opportunity. Learning opportunities have been further defined in terms of the contexts of learning, such as programs, settings, and interventions, as well as the social interactions within these contexts that promote learning. To understand what, how, and why teachers learn from a particular opportunity, it is necessary to investigate both how the opportunity was experienced and what it meant to the teachers. Designing learning opportunities calls for clarifying "what we want teachers to learn, what kind of intellectual work that will entail, where teachers are in relation to the desired outcome, and what kinds of resources and activities are likely to help teachers move in the desired direction." The position of Feiman-Nemser and Remillard is that no single theory or model of learning can do all this.

Conceptual Change

By and large, research on how teachers learn has tended to focus on how teachers' beliefs, perceptions, attitudes, orientations, understandings, knowledge, and skills change over time. When teacher educators have tried to change the beliefs of their students, they have often failed. Students tend to finish teacher preparation with the same beliefs they had when they entered, beliefs that limit the ideas and actions they are willing to entertain. These beliefs are resistant to change while at the same time they serve as filters through which students interpret new and potentially conflicting information.

In light of the difficulty of changing teacher beliefs, researchers have turned to conceptual change models in order to explain what it takes for people to change their minds. This transformation turned out to be much more difficult than it was once thought to be. The once prevalent idea of a student as an empty container for the teacher to fill with knowledge was found to be wrong. New knowledge is always shaped by a learner's prior knowledge and established ways of making sense. From this constructivist perspective, what the learner already knows drives what he/she pays attention to and how new knowledge is understood (Roth,1989b).

Conceptual change theory suggests that changing a teacher's beliefs requires the teacher to recognize discrepancies between their earlier beliefs and new visions of teaching and learning. Change is more likely if the alternatives are vivid, concrete, and detailed enough to be plausible. From this perspective, several conditions have been found necessary to bring about conceptual change among prospective or practicing teachers. First, teachers need opportunities to consider whether new practices as well as the values and beliefs with which these practices are associated are better than the more conventional approaches with which the teachers are more familiar. Second, they must be able to see examples of these practices in action, preferably under realistic conditions. Third, teachers must at some point experience such practices firsthand. Lastly, but by no means least, for teachers to incorporate these ideas and practices into their own teaching, they need intensive, ongoing, and on-the-spot support and guidance (22–24).

Cognitive Apprenticeship

Field experience in teacher education has much that is like an apprenticeship, such as authentic activity, social interaction, collaborative learning, and the presence of a person experienced and considered competent in teaching. The term "cognitive" indicates that the same conditions or opportunities that support the development of physical skills can also support the development of cognitive skills. This view of cognitive apprenticeship is applicable to student teaching, internships, and other mentored learning situations where the teacher's learning is situated in the context of practice. Ideally, the novice learns how to think and act like a teacher by observing and engaging in teaching alongside an experienced practitioner. The mentor can model ways of thinking and acting, coach the novice on how to carry out particular tasks, and gradually withdraw support as the novice learns to teach on his or her own (Feiman-Nemser & Remillard, 1995, 24–25).

Assisted Performance, Zone of Proximal Development, and Scaffolding

The Russian psychologist Lev Vygotsky introduced the theory of assisted performance in a zone of proximal development (ZPD) to account for how learning occurs through social interaction with someone more capable. The ZPD is the gap between what an individual can do independently and what he or she can do with assistance. Assistance from and cooperative activity with a teacher, expert, or more capable peer enables the learner to perform at levels beyond his or her level of independent performance. This assistance has come to be known as scaffolding. Knowledge and skills that initially exist only in the interaction between the novice and the more capable other person eventually get internalized by the learner. Vygotsky's work was primarily concerned with children, but contemporary proponents have applied these ideas to teacher education.

Anne-Marie Palincsar was an MSU faculty member when she wrote a 1986 article on what scaffolding means when applied to the learning of adults. She explains that scaffolding involves selecting a learning task that the learner has begun to develop; modifying the task if necessary to make it simpler and easier to learn; identifying features of the task that need to be emphasized during instruction; organizing the task for instruction; using modeling, questioning, and explanation to make all relevant aspects of the task explicit; finding ways to elicit and sustain student interest in the task; and coming up with approximations to the task where needed. As the learner becomes more proficient, scaffolding is gradually withdrawn, allowing the learner to perform in less structured contexts with less aid. In scaffolding, talk between mentor and learner is crucial. "It is this dialogue, occurring with initial instruction regarding the strategy, that enables learners to participate in strategic activity even though they may not fully understand the activity and would most certainly not be able to exercise the strategy independently" (74–75; see also Hogan & Pressley, 1997; Roehler & Cantlon, 1997; the latter chapter was based on data collected from third–fifth graders in an MSU affiliated school).

References

A sterisks in the following reference list identify those authors or editors who were affiliated with MSU during the revolutionary era as either faculty, students, or K–12 teachers/administrators. Many of these references were written later, after the revolution had waned and when the authors/editors had taken other positions. Nevertheless, I believe these references owe their development in some sense to the MSU revolution. My reason for flagging these affiliations is to provide evidence that revolutionary involvement in K–12 schools and reform of K–12 teaching did not undermine publication and scholarship to the extent that has · sometimes been alleged.

*Alleman, J. (2009). Remembering Jere Brophy. *Educational Psychology Review, 21*, article 291, retrieved from http://doi.org/10.1007/S10648-009-9115-x.

*Alleman, J., & *Brophy, J. (2001–3). *Social studies excursions, K–3*. 3 vols. Portsmouth, NH: Heinemann.

*Alleman, J., & *Brophy, J. (1991). *Is curriculum integration a boon or a threat to social studies?* MSU Institute for Research on Teaching research series no. 204. East Lansing: Michigan State University.

*Almeida, T., & *Callis, S. (2008). Elementary mathematics + a culture of questioning = complex mathematics. In D. Chazan*, S. Callis*, & M. Lehman* (Eds.), *Embracing reason: Egalitarian ideals and the teaching of high school mathematics* (238–40). New York: Routledge.

*Almeida, T., & *Carmody, S. (2008). Our contrasting preservice field experiences. In D. Chazan*, S. Callis*, & M. Lehman* (Eds.), *Embracing reason: Egalitarian ideals and the teaching of high school mathematics* (168–70). New York: Routledge.

*Anderson, C. W. (1991). Policy implications of research on science teaching and teachers' knowledge. In M. Kennedy (Ed.), *Teaching academic subjects to diverse learners* (5–30). New York: Teachers College Press.

*Ball, D. (2000). Bridging practices: Intertwining content and pedagogy in teaching and learning to teach. *Journal of Teacher Education, 51* (3), 241–47.

Ball, D. (1998) Where did these ideas come from? Ball's story. In M. Lampert
& D. Ball*, *Teaching, multimedia, and mathematics: Investigations of real practice* (10–22). New York: Teachers College Press.

*Ball, D. (1988). Unlearning to teach mathematics. *For the Learning of Mathematics, 8* (1), 40–48.

*Ball, D., & *Cohen, D. (1999). Developing practice, developing practitioners: Toward a practice-based theory of professional education. In L. Darling-Hammond & G. Sykes (Eds.). *Teaching in the learning professions: Handbook of policy and practice* (3–22). San Francisco: Jossey-Bass.

*Ball, D., & *Cohen, D. (1996). Reform by the book: What is—or might be—the role of curriculum materials in teacher learning and instructional reform? *Educational Researcher, 25* (9), 6–8.

*Ball, D., & *Feiman-Nemser, S. (1988). Using textbooks and teachers' guides: A dilemma for beginning teachers and teacher educators. *Curriculum Inquiry, 18* (4), 401–23.

*Ball, D., & Forzani, F. (2009). The work of teaching and the challenge for teacher education. *Journal of Teacher Education, 60* (5), 497–511.

*Ball, D., Sleep, L., Boerst, T., & Bass, H. (2009). Combining the development of practice and the practice of development in teacher education. *Elementary School Journal, 109* (5), 458–74.

*Barnes, H. (1989). *Teacher education at MSU: A century of "FIRSTS."* Unpublished document, Michigan State University, College of Education, East Lansing.

*Book, C. (1996). Professional development schools. In J. Sikula, T. Buttery, & E. Guyton (Eds.), *Handbook of research on teacher education: A project of the Association of Teacher Educators* (2nd ed., 194–210). New York: Macmillan.

*Britton, E., Paine, L., & Raizen, S. (2003). *Comprehensive teacher induction.* New York: Springer.

*Brophy, J. (1990). Teaching social studies for conceptual understanding and higher order applications. *Elementary School Journal, 90* (4), 351–417.

*Brophy, J., & *Alleman, J. (2006). *Children's thinking about cultural universals.* Mahwah, NJ: Lawrence Erlbaum.

*Brophy, J., & *Alleman, J. (2003). Primary grade students' knowledge and thinking about the supply of utilities (water, heat, and light) to modern homes. *Cognition and Instruction, 21* (1), 79–112.

*Brophy, J., & *Alleman, J. (1993). Elementary social studies should be driven by major social education goals. *Social Education, 57* (1), 27–32.

*Brophy, J., *Alleman, J., & *Knighton, B. (2009). *Inside the social studies classroom.* New York: Routledge.

*Brophy, J., & *VanSledright, B. (1997). *Teaching and learning history in elementary school.* New York: Teachers College Press.

*Brophy, J., & *VanSledright, B. (1993). *Exemplary elementary teachers' beliefs about social studies curriculum and instruction.* MSU Elementary Subjects Center series no. 93. East Lansing: Michigan State University.

*Brophy, J., *VanSledright, B., & *Bredin, N. (1992a). *Fifth graders' ideas about European exploration of the New World expressed before and after studying this topic within a U.S. history course.* MSU Elementary Subjects Center series no. 78. East Lansing: Michigan State University.

*Brophy, J., *VanSledright, B., & *Bredin, N. (1992b). *Fifth graders' ideas about the English colonies in America expressed before and after studying them within a U.S. history course.* MSU Elementary Subjects Center series no. 80. East Lansing: Michigan State University.

*Brophy, J., *VanSledright, B., & *Bredin, N. (1991). *Fifth graders' ideas about history expressed before and after their introduction to this subject.* MSU Elementary Subjects Center series no. 50. East Lansing: Michigan State University.

*Buchmann, M. (1989, April). *Breaking from experience in teacher education: When is it necessary, how is it possible?* Paper presented at the annual meeting of the American Educational Research Association, San Francisco.

*Buchmann, M., & *Schwille, J. (1983). Education: The overcoming of experience. *American Journal of Education, 92* (1), 30–51.

Callahan, R. E. (1962). *Education and the cult of efficiency.* Chicago: University of Chicago Press.

*Callis, S., *Chazan, D., *Hodges, K., & *Schnepp, M. (2008). Starting a functions-based approach to algebra. In D. Chazan*, S. Callis*, & M. Lehman* (Eds.), *Embracing reason: Egalitarian ideals and the teaching of high school mathematics* (29–41). New York: Routledge.

*Campbell, D. (1988). Collaboration and contradiction in a research and staff development project. *Teachers College Record, 90* (1), 99–121.

*Campbell, D., *Peters, S., *Putnam, J., *VanStratt, T., & *Wright, A. (2000, April). *A ten-year retrospective: Challenges and lessons learned from Michigan State University partnerships with professional development schools.* Paper presented at the annual meeting of the American Educational Research Association, New Orleans.

Carini, P. (2007). Keeping real children at the center of teaching: Overview of the child study project, student handout. In D. Carroll*, H. Featherstone*, J. Featherstone*, S. Feiman-Nemser*, & D. Roosevelt* (Eds.), *Transforming teacher education: Reflections from the field* (135–37). Cambridge, MA: Harvard Education Press.

Carroll, D. (2007). Helping teachers become teacher educators. In D. Carroll, H. Featherstone*, J. Featherstone*, S. Feiman-Nemser*, & D. Roosevelt* (Eds.), *Transforming teacher education: Reflections from the field* (181–201). Cambridge, MA: Harvard Education Press.

*Carroll, D., with *Donnelly, S. (2007). Caring for students while gatekeeping for the profession: The student coordinator role. In D. Carroll*, H. Featherstone*, J. Featherstone*, S. Feiman-Nemser*, & D. Roosevelt* (Eds.), *Transforming teacher education: Reflections from the field* (33–50). Cambridge, MA: Harvard Education Press.

*Carroll, D., *Featherstone, H., *Featherstone, J., & *Feiman-Nemser, S. (2007a). From boutique to superstore: History and context of the program. In D. Carroll*, H. Featherstone*, J. Featherstone*, S. Feiman-Nemser*, & D. Roosevelt* (Eds.), *Transforming teacher education: Reflections from the field* (9-31). Cambridge, MA: Harvard Education Press.

*Carroll, D., *Featherstone, H., *Featherstone, J., *Feiman-Nemser, S., & *Roosevelt, D. (Eds.). (2007b). *Transforming teacher education: Reflections from the field.* Cambridge, MA: Harvard Education Press

Carver, C. (2010). The university's role in supporting new teachers: Glimpsing the future by examining the past. In J. Wang, S. Odell, & R. Clift (Eds.), *Past, present, and future research on teacher induction* (169-84). Lanham, MD: Roman & Littlefield.

Case, C., *Lanier, J., & Miskel, C. (1986). The Holmes Group report: Impetus for gaining professional status for teachers. *Journal of Teacher Education, 37* (4), 36-43.

*Chazan, D. (2000). *Beyond formulas in mathematics and teaching: Dynamics of the high school algebra classroom.* New York: Teachers College Press.

*Chazan, D. (1996). Algebra for all students? The algebra policy debate. *Journal of Mathematical Behavior, 15* (4), 455-77.

*Chazan, D., & *Callis, S. (2008). Finding mathematics in the world around us. In D. Chazan*, S. Callis*, & M. Lehman* (Eds.), *Embracing reason: Egalitarian ideals and the teaching of high school mathematics* (79-85). New York: Routledge.

*Chazan, D., *Callis, S., & *Lehman, M. (Eds.) (2008). *Embracing reason: Egalitarian ideals and the teaching of high school mathematics.* New York: Routledge.

*Clark, C., & *Peterson, P. (1986). Teachers' thought processes. In M. Wittrock (Ed.), *Handbook of research on teaching* (3rd ed., 255-96). New York: Macmillan.

Clift, R., & Brady, P. (2005). Research on methods courses and field experiences. In M. Cochran-Smith & K. Zeichner (Eds.), *Studying teacher education: The report of the AERA panel on research and teacher education* (309-424) Mahwah, NJ: Erlbaum.

Cohen, D. (1998). Experience and education: Learning to teach. In M. Lampert & D. Ball*, *Teaching, multimedia, and mathematics: Investigations of real practice* (167-87). New York: Teachers College Press.

*Crespo, S. (2000). Seeing more than right and wrong answers: Prospective teachers' interpretations of students' mathematical work. *Journal of Mathematics Teacher Education, 3* (2), 155-81.

*Crespo, S., & Nicol, C. (2006). Challenging preservice teachers' mathematical understanding: The case of division by zero. *School Science and Mathematics, 106* (2), 84-97.

Darner, R. (2019). How can educators confront science denial? *Educational Researcher, 48* (4), 229-40.

Davis, E., & Boerst, T. (2014, March). *Designing elementary teacher education to prepare well-started beginners*. Teaching Works Working Papers. University of Michigan School of Education.

*Dembele, M. (1999, April). *What does it take for good teaching to lead to thoughtful mentoring? A case exploring the connections between teaching and mentoring*. Paper presented at the annual meeting of the American Educational Research Association, Montreal.

*Dembele, M. (1995). *Mentors and mentoring: Frames for action, ways of acting, and consequences for novice teachers' learning*. Unpublished PhD dissertation, Michigan State University, East Lansing.

*Devaney, K. (1991). Corrigan says R&D is the key new idea in the PDS. *Holmes Group Forum, 6* (1), 17–19.

*Englert, C., *Raphael, T., *Fear, K., & *Anderson, L. (1988). Students' metacognitive knowledge about how to write informational texts. *Learning Disability Quarterly, 11* (1), 18–46.

*Erickson, F. (2017). Some lessons learned about teaching, research, and academic disputation. *Education Review, 24*. http://dx.doi.org/10.14507/er.v24.2290.

*Erickson, F. (2006). Studying side by side: Collaborative action ethnography in educational research. In G. Spindler & L. Hammond (Eds.), *Innovations in educational ethnography: Theory, methods, and results* (235–57). Mahwah, NJ: Erlbaum Associates.

*Erickson, F. (2004). *Talk and social theory: Ecologies of speaking and listening in everyday life*. Cambridge, MA: Blackwell.

Featherstone, H. (2007). Preparing teachers of elementary mathematics: Evangelism or education? In D. Carroll, H. Featherstone*, J. Featherstone*, S. Feiman-Nemser*, & D. Roosevelt* (Eds.), *Transforming teacher education: Reflections from the field* (69–92). Cambridge, MA: Harvard Education Press.

*Featherstone, H. (1990, Summer). A community of young mathematicians. *Changing Minds*. Published by the Michigan Educational Extension Service, 5–9.

Featherstone, J. (2007). Values and the big university education school. In D. Carroll, H. Featherstone*, J. Featherstone*, S. Feiman-Nemser*, & D. Roosevelt* (Eds.), *Transforming teacher education: Reflections from the field* (203–19). Cambridge, MA: Harvard Education Press.

*Featherstone, J., Featherstone, L., & Featherstone, C. (2003). *"Dear Josie," Witnessing the hopes and failures of democratic education*. New York: Teachers College Press.

*Feiman-Nemser, S. (2012). *Teachers as learners*. Cambridge, MA: Harvard Education Press.

Feiman-Nemser, S. (2010). Multiple meanings of new teacher induction. In J. Wang, S. Odell, & R. Clift (Eds.), *Past, present, and future research on teacher induction* (15–30). Lanham, MD: Rowman & Littlefield.

Feiman-Nemser, S. (2001/2012a). From preparation to practice: Designing a continuum to strengthen and sustain teaching. In S. Feiman-Nemser, *Teachers as learners* (105–50). Cambridge, MA: Harvard Education Press.

*Feiman-Nemser, S. (2001/2012b). Helping novices learn to teach: Lessons from an exemplary support teacher. *Journal of Teacher Education* 52: 17–30. In S. Feiman-Nemser*, *Teachers as learners* (253–75). Cambridge, MA: Harvard Education Press.

*Feiman-Nemser, S. (1998/2012). Linking mentoring and teacher learning. *Vilon* 9 (3): 5–13. In S. Feiman-Nemser*, *Teachers as learners* (235–51). Cambridge, MA: Harvard Education Press.

*Feiman-Nemser, S. (1990/2012). Teacher preparation: Structural and conceptual alternatives. P. Burden & W.R. Houston (Eds.), *Handbook of Research on Teacher Education*. New York: Macmillan. In S. Feiman-Nemser*, *Teachers as learners* (55–104). Cambridge, MA: Harvard Education Press.

*Feiman-Nemser, S. (1983/2012) Learning to teach. L. Shulman & G. Sykes (Eds.), *Handbook of Teaching and Policy*. San Francisco: Jossey-Bass. In S. Feiman-Nemser*, *Teachers as learners* (27–53). Cambridge, MA: Harvard Education Press.

*Feiman-Nemser, S., & *Beasley, K. (2007). Discovering and sharing knowledge: Inventing a new role for cooperating teachers. In D. Carroll*, H. Featherstone*, J. Featherstone*, S. Feiman-Nemser*, & D. Roosevelt* (Eds.), *Transforming teacher education: Reflections from the field* (139–60). Cambridge, MA: Harvard Education Press.

*Feiman-Nemser, S., & *Buchmann, M. (1987/2012). When is student teaching teacher education? *Teaching and Teacher Education, 3* (4), 255–73. In S. *Feiman-Nemser, *Teachers as learners* (203–34). Cambridge, MA: Harvard Education Press.

*Feiman-Nemser, S., & *Buchmann, M. (1986/2012). The first year of teacher preparation: The transition to pedagogical thinking. *Journal of Curriculum Studies, 18* (3), 239–56. In S. *Feiman-Nemser, *Teachers as learners* (181–201). Cambridge, MA: Harvard Education Press.

*Feiman-Nemser, S., & *Buchmann, M. (1985/2012). Pitfalls of experience in teacher education. *Teachers College Record, 87* (1), 53–65. In S. *Feiman-Nemser, *Teachers as learners* (167–80). Cambridge, MA: Harvard Education Press.

*Feiman-Nemser, S., & *Featherstone, H. (Eds.). (1992). *Exploring teaching: Reinventing an introductory course*. New York: Teachers College Press.

*Feiman-Nemser, S., & *Floden, R. (1986). The cultures of teaching. In M. Wittrock (Ed.), *Handbook of research on teaching* (3rd ed., 505–24). New York: Macmillan.

*Feiman-Nemser, S., & *Floden, R. (1981). A critique of developmental approaches to teacher education. *Action in Teacher Education, 3* (1), 35–38.

*Feiman-Nemser, S., & *Floden, R. (1980). *What's all this talk about teacher development?* MSU Institute for Research on Teaching research series 70. East Lansing: Michigan State University.

*Feiman-Nemser, S., & *Hartzler-Miller, C. (2007). Professional standards as interpretive space. In D. Carroll*, H. Featherstone*, J. Featherstone*, S. Feiman-Nemser*, & D. Roosevelt* (Eds.), *Transforming teacher education: Reflections from the field* (51–68). Cambridge, MA: Harvard Education Press.

*Feiman-Nemser, S., & *Norman, P. (2005/2012). Mind activity in teaching and mentoring. *Teaching and Teacher Education, 21* (6), 679–97. In S. *Feiman-Nemser, *Teachers as learners* (277–306). Cambridge, MA: Harvard Education Press.

*Feiman-Nemser, S., & *Remillard, J. (1995). *Perspectives on learning to teach.* Issue Paper 953. East Lansing: Michigan State University, National Center for Research on Teacher Learning.

*Fendler, L. (2004). Governance and accountability in the Michigan Partnership for New Education: Reconstructing democratic participation. In B. Franklin, M. Bloch, & T. Popkewitz (Eds.), *Partnerships and the state: The paradoxes of governing schools, children, and families* (187–209). New York: Macmillan.

*Floden, R. (2015). Learning what research says about teacher preparation. In M. Feuer, A. Berman, & R. Atkinson (Eds.), *Past as prologue, the National Academy of Education at 50: Members reflect* (279–84). Washington, DC: National Academy of Education.

*Floden, R., *Buchmann, M., & *Schwille, J. (1987). Breaking with everyday experience. *Teachers College Record, 88* (4), 485–506.

*Floden, R., & *Feiman-Nemser, S. (1981). *A developmental approach to the study of teacher change: What's to be gained?* MSU Institute for Research on Teaching research series 93. East Lansing: Michigan State University.

*Floden, R., *McDiarmid, W., & *Wiemers, N. (1990). *Learning about mathematics in elementary methods courses.* NCRTE research report 90-1, East Lansing: Michigan State University.

*Florio, S. (1978). *Learning how to go to school: An ethnography of interaction in a kindergarten/first grade classroom.* Unpublished EdD dissertation, Harvard University.

*Florio, S., & *Clark, C. (1982). The functions of writing in an elementary classroom. *Research in the Teaching of English, 16* (2), 115–30.

*Florio, S., & *Clark, C. (1980). *What is writing for? Writing in the first weeks of school in a second/third grade classroom.* Unpublished research report, MSU Institute for Research on Teaching.

*Florio-Ruane, S. (1990). Written Literacy Forum: An analysis of teacher-researcher collaboration. *Journal of Curriculum Studies, 22* (4), 313–28.

*Florio-Ruane, S. (1986). *Conversation and narrative in collaborative research.* Institute for Research on Teaching occasional paper 102. East Lansing: Michigan State University.

Forzani, F. (2011). *The work of reform in teacher education.* PhD dissertation, University of Michigan, Ann Arbor.

Fullan, M., Galuzzo, G., Morris, P., & Watson, N. (1998). *The rise and stall of teacher education reform.* Washington, DC: American Association of Colleges of Teacher Education.

Gage, N. (Ed.). (1975). *NIE conference on studies in teaching; panel 6: Teaching as clinical information processing.* Washington, DC: National Institute of Education.

Gormas-Simonson, J. (1998).*The centrality of a teacher's professional transformation in the development of mathematical power A case study of one high school mathematics teacher.* Unpublished PhD dissertation, Michigan State University.

Green, E. (2014). *Building a better teacher: How teaching works (and how to teach it to everyone).* New York: Horton.

Grossman, P., Compton, C., Ingre, D., Ronfeldt, M., Shahan, E., & Williamson, P. (2009). Teaching practices: Cross-professional perspective. *Teachers College Record, 111* (9), 2055–2100.

Hall, G. (1978, March). *Concerns-based in-service teacher training: An overview of the concepts, research, and practice.* Paper presented at Conference on School-focused In-service Training, Bournemouth, England.

Herring, M., *Koehler, M., & *Mishra, P. (2016). Introduction to the second edition of the TPACK handbook. In M. Herring, M. Koehler, & P. Mishra (Eds.), *Handbook of technological pedagogical content knowledge (TPACK) for educators* (11–18). New York: Routledge.

Hogan, K., & *Pressley, M. (Eds.). (1997). *Scaffolding student learning: Instructional approaches and issues.* Advances in learning & teaching. Cambridge, MA: Brookline Books.

Holmes Group. (1995). *Tomorrow's schools of education.* East Lansing: Holmes Group.

Holmes Group. (1990). *Tomorrow's schools.* East Lansing: Holmes Group.

Holmes Group. (1986). *Tomorrow's teachers.* East Lansing: Holmes Group.

Holmes Partnership. (2007). *Holmes Partnership trilogy: Tomorrow's teachers, tomorrow's schools, tomorrow's schools of education* (2nd ed.). New York: Peter Lang.

Holmes Partnership. (ca. 1997). *Origins of Holmes Partnership (1987–1997).* Retrieved from http://www1.udel.edu/holmes/origins.html.

*Huhn, C., with *Schnepp, M., *Callis, S., *Kueffner, L., *Johnson, W., & *Sandow, D. (2008). Questioning ourselves and the authorities. In D. Chazan*, S. Callis*, & M. Lehman* (Eds.), *Embracing reason: Egalitarian ideals and the teaching of high school mathematics* (258–75). New York: Routledge.

*Huhn, K., & *Schnepp, M. (2008). What is "mathematical power"? And related dilemmas of teaching. In D. Chazan*, S. Callis*, & M. Lehman* (Eds.),

Embracing reason: Egalitarian ideals and the teaching of high school mathematics (155–59). New York: Routledge.

*Inzunza, V. (2002). *Years of achievement: A short history of the College of Education at Michigan State University.* East Lansing: Michigan State University, College of Education.

Ioannou, I., & Angeli, C., (2013). *Teaching computer science in secondary education: A technological pedagogical content knowledge perspective.* Proceedings of the 8th Workshop in Primary and Secondary Computing Education, ACM, Aarhus, Denmark.

Jin, H., & *Anderson, C. W. (2012). A learning progression for energy in socio-ecological systems. *Journal of Research in Science Teaching, 49* (9), 1149–80.

Johnson, W. (2008). Lines and points: Aristotle vs. modern mathematics. In D. Chazan, S. Callis*, & M. Lehman* (Eds.), *Embracing reason: Egalitarian ideals and the teaching of high school mathematics* (281–94). New York: Routledge.

Johnston, M., Brosnan, P., Cramer, D., & Dove, T. (Eds.). (2000). *Collaborative reform and other improbable dreams: The challenges of professional development schools.* Albany, NY: State University of New York Press.

*Judge, H. (1982). *American graduate schools of education: A view from abroad.* New York: Ford Foundation.

*Judge, H., Johnson, S., & Carriendo, R. (1995). *Professional development schools at MSU: The report of the 1995 review.* Michigan State University, College of Education, East Lansing.

*Kelly, A., & *Huhn, C. (2008). Thoughts from latecomers. In D. Chazan*, S. Callis*, & M. Lehman* (Eds.), *Embracing reason: Egalitarian ideals and the teaching of high school mathematics* (200–202). New York: Routledge.

*Kennedy, M. (2005). *Inside teaching: How classroom life undermines reform.* Cambridge, MA: Harvard University Press.

*Kennedy, M. (1998). *Learning to teach writing: Does teacher education make a difference?* New York: Teachers College Press.

*Kennedy, M. (1991, Spring). *An agenda for research on teacher learning.* NCRTL special report. East Lansing: Michigan State University, National Center for Research on Teacher Learning.

*Labaree, D. (1995). A disabling vision: Rhetoric and reality in tomorrow's schools of education. *Teachers College Record, 97* (2), 166–205.

*Labaree, D. (1992). Doing good, doing science: The Holmes Group reports and the rhetorics of educational reform. *Teachers College Record, 93* (4), 628–40.

*Lampert, M. (2001). *Teaching problems and the problems of teaching.* New Haven: Yale University Press.

Lampert, M. (1998). Where did these ideas come from? Lampert's story. In M. Lampert & D. Ball*, *Teaching, multimedia, and mathematics: Investigations of real practice* (1–9). New York: Teachers College Press.

*Lampert, M. (1991). Looking at restructuring from within a restructured role. *Phi Delta Kappan, 72* (9), 670–74.

*Lampert, M. (1990). When the problem is not the question and the solution is not the answer. *American Educational Research Journal, 27* (1), 29–63.

*Lampert, M. (1985). How do teachers manage to teach? Perspectives on problems in practice. *Harvard Educational Review, 55* (2), 178–94.

*Lampert, M., & *Ball, D. (1998). *Teaching, multimedia, and mathematics: Investigations of real practice.* New York: Teachers College Press.

*Lampert, M., & *Graziani, F. (2009). Instructional activities as a tool for teachers' and teacher educators' learning. *Elementary School Journal, 109* (5) 491–509.

*Lanier, J. (2007). Foreword to the Holmes Partnership trilogy: Tomorrow's teachers, tomorrow's schools, tomorrow's schools of education. In *Holmes Partnership trilogy: Tomorrow's teachers, tomorrow's schools, tomorrow's schools of education* (2nd ed.). (197–200) New York: Peter Lang.

*Lanier, J. (1989). *A leadership academy for tomorrow's schools.* Proposal submitted to the Rockefeller Foundation. East Lansing: MSU College of Education.

*Lanier, J., with Little, J. (1986). Research on teacher education. In M. Wittrock (Ed.), *Handbook of research on teaching* (3rd ed., 527–69). New York: Macmillan.

Lehman, M. (2008a). Being treated (and treating ourselves) as professionals. In D. Chazan, S. Callis*, & M. Lehman* (Eds.), *Embracing reason: Egalitarian ideals and the teaching of high school mathematics* (195–200). New York: Routledge.

Lehman, M. (2008b). Mathematics performance assessment. In D. Chazan, S. Callis*, & M. Lehman* (Eds.), *Embracing reason: Egalitarian ideals and the teaching of high school mathematics* (15–25). New York: Routledge.

*Lehman, M. (1991). *Assessing mathematics: A continuing process.* East Lansing: Michigan State University, National Center for Research on Teacher Learning.

[*Lehman, M. *Wilson J., & *Geist, P.] (ca. 1990–91). *Algebra II study.* Unpublished draft paper from PDS group at Holt High School, Holt MI.

*Lensmire, T. (2000). *Powerful writing, responsible teaching.* New York: Teachers College Press.

*Lensmire, T. (1991). *Intention, risk, and writing in a third grade writing workshop.* Unpublished PhD dissertation, Michigan State University, East Lansing.

*Little, T. (1984). *Course design within the context of a thematic teacher education program: A case study.* MSU College of Education program evaluation series 6. East Lansing: Michigan State University.

*Little, T., *Gillett, J., *Gray, M., *Lamb, P., & *Brice, L. (1995). *A handbook for teaching global studies: The Holt High School experience.* Holt, MI: MSU-Holt High School Professional Development School.

Lortie, D. (1975). *Schoolteacher: A sociological study*. Chicago: University of Chicago Press.

*McDiarmid, W. (1989). *What do prospective teachers learn in their liberal arts courses?* Issue paper 89-8. East Lansing: Michigan State University, National Council for Research on Teacher Education.

*McDiarmid, W., & Caprino, K. (2018). *Lessons from the Teachers for a New Era project: Evidence and accountability in teacher education*. New York: Routledge.

*McDiarmid, W., & *Vinten-Johansen, P. (2000). A catwalk across the great divide: Redesigning the history teaching methods course. In P. Stearns, P. Seixas, & S. Wineburg (Eds.), *Knowing, teaching, and learning history* (156–77). New York: New York University Press.

*Mishra, P., *Koehler, M., & *Zhao, Y. (Eds.). (2007). *Faculty development by design: Integrating technology in higher education*. Charlotte, NC: Information Age Publishing.

*Mishra, P., & *Yadav, A. (2006). Using hypermedia for learning complex concepts in chemistry: A qualitative study on the relationship between prior knowledge, beliefs and motivation. *Education and Information Technologies, 11* (1), 33–69.

Mohan, L., Chen, J., & *Anderson, C. W. (2009). Developing a multiyear learning progression for carbon cycling in socio-ecological systems. *Journal of Research in Science Teaching, 46* (6), 675–98.

National Council for Social Studies (1993). Vision of powerful teaching and learning in social studies: Building social understanding and civic efficiency. *Social Education, 57* (5), 213–23.

*Nevins-Stanulis, R., & *Floden, R. (2009). Intensive mentoring as a way to help beginning teachers develop balanced instruction. *Journal of Teacher Education, 60* (2), 112–22.

Norman, P. (2007). Learning the practice of field-based teacher education. In D. Carroll, H. Featherstone*, J. Featherstone*, S. Feiman-Nemser*, & D. Roosevelt* (Eds.), *Transforming teacher education: Reflections from the field* (161–79). Cambridge, MA: Harvard Education Press.

*Palincsar, A. (1986). The role of dialogue in providing scaffolded instruction. *Educational Psychology, 21* (1 & 2), 73–98.

*Pallas, A. (1995). *Interpretive notes on results of survey of PDS teachers [and] summary of survey comparisons*. MSU College of Education unpublished documents prepared as part of 1995 evaluation of the PDSs.

*Parker, J., de los Santos, E., & *Anderson, C. W. (2015). Learning progressions and climate change. *American Biology Teacher, 77* (4), 232–38.

*Peterson, P. (1991). *Revising their thinking: Keisha Coleman and her third-grade mathematics class*. MSU Elementary Subjects Center series no. 49. East Lansing: Michigan State University.

*Porter, A. (1987). Teacher collaboration: New partnerships to attack old problems. *Phi Delta Kappan, 69* (2), 147–52.

*Porter, A., *Floden, R., *Freeman, D., *Schmidt, W., & *Schwille, J. (1988). Content determinants in elementary school mathematics. *Perspectives on research on effective mathematics teaching, 1,* 96–113.

*Putnam, J., & *Schwille, S. (2020). A retrospective account of intensive school-university collaboration: Misconceptions revealed, mistakes made, and lessons learned. *School-university Partnerships: The Journal of the National Association of Professional Development Schools, 13* (2), 47–58.

*Radin, D. (ca. 1992). *Mathematics education through collegial discourse, self-enquiry and mutual classroom observation and with minimal outside guidance.* Unpublished MSU PDS paper from Holt High School.

*Raphael, T., *Englert, C., & *Kirschner, B. (1988). *Acquisition of expository writing skills.* University of Illinois, Center for the Study of Reading technical report no. 421.

*Raphael, T., & *Kirschner, B. (1985). *Effects of instruction in compare/contrast text structure on sixth-grade students' reading comprehension and writing products.* MSU Institute for Research on Teaching research series no. 161. East Lansing: Michigan State University.

*Raphael, T., *Kirschner, B., & *Englert, C. (1988). Expository writing programs: Making connections between reading and writing. *Reading Teacher, 41,* 790–95.

Roehler, L., & Cantlon, D. (1997). Scaffolding: A powerful tool in social constructivist classrooms. In K. Hogan & M. Pressley (Eds.). *Scaffolding student learning: Instructional approaches and issues.* Advances in learning & teaching. Cambridge, MA: Brookline Books.

Roosevelt, D. (2007). Keeping real children at the center of teacher education: Child study and the construction of local knowledge in teaching. In D. Carroll, H. Featherstone*, J. Featherstone*, S. Feiman-Nemser*, & D. Roosevelt* (Eds.), *Transforming teacher education: Reflections from the field* (113–37). Cambridge, MA: Harvard Education Press.

*Rosaen, C., *Hobson, S., & *Khan, G. (2003). Making connections: Collaborative approaches to preparing today's and tomorrow's teachers to use technology. *Journal of Technology and Teacher Education, 11,* 281–306.

*Rosaen, C., & *Hoekwater, E. (1990). Collaboration: Empowering educators to take charge. *Contemporary Education, 61,* 144–51.

*Rosaen, C., & *Lindquist, B. (1992). *Collaborative teaching and research: Asking "what does it mean?"* Michigan State University, Center for the Teaching and Learning of Elementary Subjects.

*Rosaen, C., *Lundeberg, M., *Cooper, M., *Fritzen, A., & *Terpstra, M. (2008). Noticing noticing: How does investigation of video records change how teachers reflect on their experiences? *Journal of Teacher Education, 59* (4), 347–60.

*Rosaen, C., *Schram, P., & *Herbel-Eisenmann, B. (2002). Using hypermedia technology to explore connections among mathematics, language, and literacy in teacher education. *Contemporary Issues in Technology and Teacher Education, 2* (3), 297–326.

Rosenthal, B. (2008). Preservice teachers as curriculum makers. In D. Chazan, S. Callis*, & M. Lehman* (Eds.), *Embracing reason: Egalitarian ideals and the teaching of high school mathematics* (64–75). New York: Routledge.

Roth, K. (2002). Talking to understand science. In J. Brophy (Ed.), *Advances in research on teaching* (6:197–262). Greenwich, CT: JAI Press.

*Roth, K. (1994, Spring). Second thoughts about interdisciplinary studies. *American Educator*, 44–48.

*Roth, K. (1989a). Science education: It's not enough to do or relate. *American Educator, 13* (4), 16–22, 46–48.

*Roth, K. (1989b). *Conceptual understanding and higher level thinking in the elementary science curriculum: Three perspectives.* East Lansing: Michigan State University, Center for the Learning and Teaching of Elementary Subjects.

*Roth, K., & *Anderson, C. W. (1987). *The power plant: Teachers' guide to photosynthesis.* MSU Institute for Research on Teaching occasional paper no. 112. East Lansing: Michigan State University.

*Roth, K., *Anderson, C. W., & *Smith, E. (1987). Curriculum materials, teacher talk, and student learning: Case studies in fifth grade science teaching. *Journal of Curriculum Studies, 19* (6), 627–28.

*Roth, K., & *Garnier, H. (2007). What science teaching looks like: An international perspective. *Educational Leadership, 64* (4), 16–23.

*Roth, K., & *Rosaen, C. (1995) Similarities and contrasts between writing during a writing workshop and writing in science: Examining the teachers' role. *Advances in Research on Teaching, 5*, 291–354.

*Roth, K., *Smith, E., & *Anderson, C. W. (1983, April). *Students' conception of photosynthesis and food for plants.* Paper presented at the annual meeting of the American Educational Research Association, Montreal.

*Rozelle, J., & *Wilson, S. (2012). Opening the black box of field experiences: How cooperating teachers' beliefs and practices shape student teachers' beliefs and practices. *Teaching and teacher education, 28* (8), 1196–205.

*Schmidt, W., *Houang, R., *Cogan, L., & *Solario, M. (2020). *Schooling across the globe: What we have learned from 60 years of mathematics and science international assessments.* Cambridge: Cambridge University Press.

*Schmidt, W., McKnight, C., & Raizen, S. (1997). *A splintered vision: An investigation of U.S. science and mathematics instruction.* Dordrecht: Kluwer.

*Schmidt, W., et al. (2002). *Characterizing pedagogical flow: An investigation of mathematics and science teaching in six countries.* New York: Kluwer Academic Publishers.

*Schmidt, W., et al. (2001). *Why schools matter: A cross-national comparison of curricula and learning.* San Francisco: Jossey-Bass.

Schnepp, M. (2008). Theory is practical! In D. Chazan, S. Callis*, & M. Lehman* (Eds.), *Embracing reason: Egalitarian ideals and the teaching of high school mathematics* (316–30). New York: Routledge.

Schon, D. (1987). *Educating the reflective practitioner: Toward a new design for teaching and learning in the professions.* San Francisco: Jossey-Bass.

*Schram, P., *Feiman-Nemser, S., & *Ball, D. (1990). *Thinking about teaching subtraction with regrouping: A comparison of beginning and experienced teachers' responses to textbooks.* NCRTE research report no. 89-5. East Lansing: Michigan State University.

*Schram, P., *Wilcox, S., *Lanier, P., & *Lappan, G. (1988). *Changing mathematical conceptions of preservice teachers: A content and pedagogical intervention.* NCRTE research report no. 1988-4. East Lansing: Michigan State University.

*Schwarz, C., Gunckel, K., *Smith, E., Covitt, B., Bae, M., Enfield, M., & Tsurusaki, B. (2008). Helping elementary preservice teachers learn to use curriculum materials for effective science teaching. *Science Education, 92,* 345–77.

*Schwille, J. (2017). *Internationalizing a school of education: Integration and infusion in practice.* East Lansing: Michigan State University Press.

Schwille, J., Porter, A., Belli, G., Floden, R., Freeman, D., Knappen, L., Kuhs, T., & Schmidt, W. (1983). Teachers as policy brokers in the content of elementary school mathematics. In L. Shulman & G. Sykes* (Eds.), *Handbook of teaching and policy* (370–91). New York: Longman.

*Schwille, S. (2016). *Never give up: An experienced teacher overcomes obstacles to change.* Charlotte, NC: Information Age Publishing.

*Schwille, S. (2008). The professional practice of mentoring. *American Journal of Education, 115* (1), 139–67.

Schwille, S. (1997). Louise and me: An analysis of a field instructor's practice. In S. Feiman-Nemser & C. Rosaen* (Eds.), *Guiding teacher learning: Insider studies of classroom work with prospective and practicing teachers* (53–72). Washington, DC: American Association of Colleges of Teacher Education (AACTE).

Scrupski, A. (1999). Change in teacher education: How Holmes was hijacked. *Academic Questions, 12,* 36–49.

Shils, E. (Ed.). (1991). *Remembering the University of Chicago: Teachers, scientists, and scholars.* Chicago: University of Chicago Press.

*Shulman, L. (2004). *The wisdom of practice: Essays on teaching, learning, and learning to teach.* Ed. S. Wilson*. San Francisco: Jossey-Bass.

*Shulman, L. (1998/2004). Theory, practice and the education of professionals. *Elementary School Journal, 98* (5), 511–26. In L. *Shulman, *The Wisdom of Practice: Essays on Teaching, Learning, and Learning to Teach* (483–500). San Francisco, CA: Jossey-Bass.

*Shulman, L. (1997/2004). *Communities of learners and communities of teachers.* Monographs from the Mandel Foundation 3. Jerusalem: Mandel Foundation.

In L. *Shulman, *The Wisdom of Practice: Essays on Teaching, Learning, and Learning to Teach* (483–500). San Francisco, CA: Jossey-Bass.

Shulman, L. (1993/2004). Calm seas, auspicious gales. In M. Buchmann & R. Floden* (Eds.), *Detachment and concern: Conversations in the philosophy of teaching and teacher education.* New York: Teachers College Press. In L. *Shulman, *The Wisdom of Practice: Essays on Teaching, Learning, and Learning to Teach* (433–52). San Francisco, CA: Jossey-Bass.

*Shulman, L. (1992/2004). Research on teaching: A historical and personal perspective. In F. Oser, A. Dick, & J.-L. Patry (Eds.), *Effective and responsible teaching: The new synthesis* (14–29). San Francisco: Jossey-Bass. In L. *Shulman, *The Wisdom of Practice: Essays on Teaching, Learning, and Learning to Teach* (363–81). San Francisco, CA: Jossey-Bass.

*Shulman, L. (1991/2004). Joseph Jackson Schwab (1909–1988). In E. Shils (Ed.), *Remembering the University of Chicago: Teachers, scientists, and scholars* (452–68). Chicago: University of Chicago Press. In L. *Shulman, *The Wisdom of Practice: Essays on Teaching, Learning, and Learning to Teach* (417–34). San Francisco, CA: Jossey-Bass.

*Shulman, L. (1990/2004). *Aristotle had it right: On knowledge and pedagogy.* East Lansing: Holmes Group. In L. *Shulman, *The Wisdom of Practice: Essays on Teaching, Learning, and Learning to Teach* (399–415). San Francisco, CA: Jossey-Bass.

*Shulman, L. (1988/2004). Teaching alone, learning together: Needed agendas for new reforms. In T. Sergiovanni & J. Moore (Eds.), *Schooling for tomorrow* (166–87). Boston: Allyn and Bacon. In L. *Shulman, *The Wisdom of Practice: Essays on Teaching, Learning, and Learning to Teach* (309–33). San Francisco, CA: Jossey-Bass.

*Shulman, L. (1987/2004a). The wisdom of practice: Managing complexity in medicine and teaching. In D. Berliner & B. Rosenshine (Eds.). *Talks to teachers: A festschrift for N. L. Gage* (369–87). New York: Random House. In L. *Shulman, *The Wisdom of Practice: Essays on Teaching, Learning, and Learning to Teach* (249–73). San Francisco, CA: Jossey-Bass.

*Shulman, L. (1987/2004b). Knowledge and teaching: Foundations of the new reform. *Harvard Educational Review, 57* (1), 1–22. In L. *Shulman, *The Wisdom of Practice: Essays on Teaching, Learning, and Learning to Teach* (217–48). San Francisco, CA: Jossey-Bass.

*Shulman, L. (1986/2004). Those who understand: Knowledge growth in teaching. *Educational Researcher, 15* (2), 4–14. In L. *Shulman, *The Wisdom of Practice: Essays on Teaching, Learning, and Learning to Teach* (187–215). San Francisco, CA: Jossey-Bass.

Shulman, L. (1983/2004). Autonomy and obligation: The remote control of teaching. In L. Shulman & G. Sykes* (Eds.), *Handbook of teaching and policy* (484–504). New York: Longman. In L. *Shulman, *The Wisdom of Practice: Essays on Teaching, Learning, and Learning to Teach* (131–62). San Francisco, CA: Jossey-Bass.

*Shulman, L. (1974). The psychology of school subjects: A premature obituary? *Journal of Research in Science Teaching, 11* (4), 319–39.

*Shulman, L., & *Elstein, A. (1975). Studies of problem solving, judgment and decision-making: Implications for educational research. *Review of Research in Education, 3*, 3–42.

*Shulman, L., & *Lanier, J. (1977). Institute for Research on Teaching: An overview. *Journal of Teacher Education, 28* (4), 44–49.

Simonson, J. (2008a). One teacher's transformation in teaching. In D. Chazan, S. Callis*, & M. Lehman* (Eds.), *Embracing reason: Egalitarian ideals and the teaching of high school mathematics* (89–105). New York: Routledge.

Simonson, J., (2008b). One transformed teacher's viewpoint. In D. Chazan, S. Callis*, & M. Lehman* (Eds.), *Embracing reason: Egalitarian ideals and the teaching of high school mathematics* (225–38). New York: Routledge.

*Simonson, J., & *Rosenthal, B. (2008). Field experience really was the best teacher! In D. Chazan*, S. Callis*, & M. Lehman* (Eds.), *Embracing reason: Egalitarian ideals and the teaching of high school mathematics* (162–68). New York: Routledge.

*Stanulis, R., *Burrill, G., & *Ames, K. (2007). Fitting in and learning to teach: Tensions in developing a vision for a university-based induction program for beginning teachers. *Teacher Education Quarterly, 34* (3), 135–47.

Sykes, G. (2008). A quiet revolution? Reflecting on mathematics reform at Holt High School. In D. Chazan, S. Callis*, & M. Lehman* (Eds.), *Embracing reason: Egalitarian ideals and the teaching of high school mathematics* (337–51). New York: Routledge.

*Sykes, G., *Bird, T., & *Kennedy, M. (2010). Teacher education: Its problems and some prospects. *Journal of Teacher Education, 61* (5), 464–76.

*Sykes, G., *Wheeler, C., *Scott, A., & *Wilcox, S. (1995). *Professional community among teachers: How does it form? An inquiry and a case study*. Unpublished MSU PDS paper, East Lansing.

*Thompson, C. (1990). On the development of professional development schools: Interview with Charles Thompson. *NCRTE Colloquy, 3* (2), 5–13.

*Thompson, C. (1989). *The Michigan Educational Extension Service: A summary*. East Lansing: Michigan State University, College of Education.

*Thompson, C. (1988, April 19). *Statement to the Senate Appropriations Committee on K–12 and Department of Education in support of the proposed Educational Extension Service*. East Lansing: Michigan State University.

University of Michigan. (2018). *Teaching Works annual report 2017–18*. Ann Arbor: School of Education. See also University of Michigan. (n.d.). *Teaching Works*. Retrieved from www.teachingworks.org/.

USDE (U.S. Department of Education). (1983). *Nation at risk*. Washington, DC: U.S. Department of Education, National Commission on Excellence in Education.

Valinides, N., & Angeli, C. (2015). *Technological pedagogical content knowledge: Exploring, developing, and assessing TPCK*. New York: Springer.

*VanSledright, B., *Brophy, J., & *Bredin, N. (1992). *Fifth graders' ideas about Native Americans expressed before and after studying them within a U.S. history course.* MSU Elementary Subject Center series no. 77. East Lansing: Michigan State University.

*Vinten-Johansen, P., & *McDiarmid, W. (1997). *Stalking the schoolwork module: Teaching prospective teachers to write historical narratives.* MSU Research Report.

*Wang, J. (1998). *Learning to teach mathematics: Preservice teachers, their collaborating teachers and instructional contexts.* Unpublished PhD dissertation, Michigan State University, East Lansing.

*Wilcox, S., *Schram, P., *Lappan, G., & *Lanier, P. (1991). The role of a learning community in changing preservice teachers' knowledge and beliefs about mathematics education. *For the Learning of Mathematics, 11* (3), 31–39.

*Wilcox, S., & *Wagner, P. (1994). Sense making in middle school mathematics. In C. Thornton & N. Bley (Eds.), *Windows of opportunity: Mathematics for students with special needs* (367–76). Reston, VA: National Council of Teachers of Mathematics.

*Wilson, S. (2012). Doing better: Musings on teacher education, accountability, and evidence. In M. LaCelle-Peterson & D. Rigden (Eds.), *Inquiry, evidence, and excellence: The promise and practice of quality assurance. A festschrift in honor of Frank B. Murray* (39–57). Washington, DC: Teacher Education Accreditation Council.

*Wilson, S. (1995). Not tension but intention: A response to Wong's analysis of the researcher/teacher. *Educational Researcher, 24* (8), 19–22.

Wilson, S. (1992). Thinking about teaching, teaching about teaching. In S. Feiman-Nemser & H. Featherstone* (Eds.), *Exploring teaching: Reinventing an introductory course* (129–45). New York: Teachers College Press.

*Wilson, S., with *Miller, C., & *Yerkes, C. (1993). Deeply rooted change: A tale of learning to teach adventurously. In D. Cohen*, M. McLaughlin, & J. Talbert (Eds.), *Teaching for understanding: Challenges for policy and practice* (84–129). San Francisco: Jossey-Bass.

Wise, A. (1979). *Legislated learning: The bureaucratization of the American classroom.* Berkeley: University of California Press.

*Wong, D. (1995a). Challenges confronting the researcher/teacher: Conflicts of purpose and conduct. *Educational Researcher, 24* (3), 22–28.

*Wong, D. (1995b). Challenges confronting the researcher/teacher: A rejoinder to Wilson. *Educational Researcher, 24* (8), 22–23.

Wood, A., & *Stanulis, R. (2010). Components of 1997–2008 teacher induction programs: Reflections on comprehensive systems. In J. Wang*, S. Odell, & R. Clift (Eds.), *Past, present, and future research on teacher induction* (135–49). Lanham, MD: Rowman & Littlefield.

Yager, R., & Yager, S. (1985). Changes in perceptions of science for third, seventh and eleventh grade students. *Journal of Research in Science Teaching, 22* (4), 347–58.

MSU and PDS Source Documents

Note: Of the great volume of MSU and PDS reports consulted for the years 1971–2001, only those cited in the text are listed below. In the text they are cited by number, e.g., MSU-1, MSU-2, MSU-3, etc.

1. Elliott-MSU Elementary Professional Development School (1988). Transcript of AERA panel session on teachers' conceptual change in practice project (aka teacher development and organizational change or TDOC) at Elliott Elementary School.

2. ———(May 1995). MSU/Elliott Elementary PDS continuation proposal for 1995–98. MSU and Holt Public Schools.

3. ———(October 1995). 1994–95 end of year report. MSU and Holt Public Schools.

4. ———(July 1996). 1996–97 workplan. MSU and Holt Public Schools.

5. ———(July 1997). End of year report for 1996–97 and workplan for 1997–98. MSU and Holt Public Schools.

6. ———(September 1998). End of year report for 1997–98 and workplan for 1998–99. MSU and Holt Public Schools.

7. ———(July 1999). End of year report for 1998–99 and workplan for 1999–2000. MSU and Holt Public Schools.

8. Holmes Group (1988). Summaries of six national seminars on K–12 school design for invited experts and held in East Lansing as part of the preparation for *Tomorrow's Schools*.

9. Holmes Middle School PDS (May 1995). Proposal to MSU and MPNE.

10. ———(June 1997). End of year report 1996–97 and proposal 1997–98, 2 vols.

11. Holt High PDS (1998). End of year report for 1997–98. MSU and Holt Public Schools.

12. Michigan State University, College of Education (1971–75). J. Lanier (aka J. Henderson), edited course materials for MSU ED 200, Individual and the School.

13. ———(24 February 1987, revised 16 June 1987). Professional Development School (proposal).

14. ———(March 1996). Collateral evidence submitted in support of the report of the 1995 [PDS] review.

15. ———(Fall 1997). *New Educator* college magazine.

16. ———(July 2000). Organization, leadership, and culture: What was learned from the first generation of professional development schools at Michigan State University. Unpublished draft.

17. Michigan State University, College of Education, and Lansing School District joint planning committee (ca. 1976–77). Towards excellence in

elementary education: A program for improving the professional growth opportunities for elementary teaching personnel.

18. Michigan State University, College of Education, Educational Extension Service (October 1989). First year (1988–89) report and second year (1989–90) plan.

19. —— (March 1990). Progress report.

20. —— (November 1990). Second year (1989–90) report.

21. —— (September 1990). Third year (1990–91) plan.

22. —— (March 1991). Progress report.

23. —— (November 1991) with Michigan Partnership for New Education, School and University Alliance. Third year (1990–91) report, 2 vols.

24. Michigan State University, Department of Teacher Education (1988). Report of the task force for reform of teacher education at Michigan State University.

25. Michigan State University, Institute for Research on Teaching (IRT) (1976). Technical proposal in response to RFP-NIE-R-76-0001.

26. —— (1981). Technical proposal in response to RFP NIE-R-81-0003.

27. —— (1986). Final report.

28. Michigan State University, Michigan Partnership for New Education (MPNE) (1991). School and university alliance, a program of MPNE (draft).

29. —— (1993). 1992–93 report of School and University Alliance and Educational Extension Service.

30. —— (1993). 1993–94 plan, 2 vols.

31. —— (1994). 1994–95 plan, 2 vols.

32. —— (1995). 1993–94 report.

33. —— (1995). 1994–95 report, 2 vols.

34. —— (1995). 1995–96 plan, 2 vols.

35. —— (1996). 1995–96 report, vol 2.

36. Michigan State University, National Center for Research on Teacher Education (NCRTE) (1990). Final report.

37. Michigan State University, National Center for Research on Teacher Learning (NCRTL) (1991). Findings from the Teacher Education and Learning to Teach (TELT) Study.

38. —— (1992). Surprising findings on how teachers learn to teach. Pamphlet.

39. Michigan State University, Department of Teacher Education (2000). Fostering school-university partnerships for teacher preparation (draft plan ed. T. Bird), Oct. 17, 2000.

40. Michigan State University, PDS Steering Committee (2000). A proposal for a professional development network (ed. T. Bird & S. Melnick, March 2000 version, then revised in May).

Index

AAAS (American Association for the Advancement of Science), 331

Academic Learning Program, 20–21, 37n1, 129

advisor-advisee program in, 255

AFL-CIO, 71, 97

Alford, Linda, 240, 328

algebra 1 course, 135, 136, 140, 323

Alleman, Jan: on Brophy, 248–49; *Children's Thinking about Cultural Universals*, 163–65; and collaboration, 150, 161–62, 247–50; as creative, 247; and cultural universals, 161, 163–66; on curriculum, 152, 166; on goals, 150, 166; on social studies teaching, 160–62; on social studies textbooks, 151, 175; and subject matter integration, 153, 160; and utopian visions, 165

Almeida, Tom, 142

Alternative Education program, 255

American Association for the Advancement of Science, 331

American Association of Colleges of Teachers Education, 105

American Association of School Administrators, 105

American Educational Research Association, 13, 264

American Educator (journal), 153

American Federation of Teachers, 153

Ames, Carole: agenda of, 80, 106–8; and budget cuts, 86–87; and Elliott school, 267; faculty quality focus of, 109–10; MPNE opposed by, 87, 98; as MSU dean, 79–80, 83, 86–87, 98, 101, 106–10, 267, 332; and PDSs, 79–81, 83–88, 101–2; relationship with Lanier, 79–80, 83–85, 106, 108; skills of, 107, 110; successes of, 106–10; technology for

reform by, 332–33; at University of Illinois, 79, 106

"amphibious" professors, 120, 140, 280, 324, 335; Ball as, 274; definition of, 62, 77, 247, 273–74; demands on, 278; and Jay Featherstone, 273–74; and K–12 learning, 273, 275–79, 285, 356–57; and Lampert, 77, 131, 275–79; loss of, 287; and PDS, 77, 274, 356; as revolutionary, 275; team teaching by, 285–86; Wilson as, 285–87. *See also* Chazan, Dan; Roth, Kathleen; and Wong, David

"amphibious" teaching, 275–78, 285–86; and PDS, 77, 274, 356

Anderson, Charles W. (Andy), 26n1, 45, 168–69, 178, 181, 182, 185

Angeli, C., 334

Ann Arbor, MI. *See* Ball, Deborah; Cohen, David; and Forzani, Francesca

Aristotle: 146, 148–49, 216, 233, 319–20; and Johnson's "Lines and Points," 147; *Metaphysics*, 147

Australia, science teaching in, 171, 172

Averill Elementary School (Lansing): faculty at, 269, 271; innovation at, 269–70; and Lanier, 270; leadership academy at, 73; and learning community, 270–71; and mentoring, 310–13; and MP programs, 67, 269, 271; as MPNE venue, 72; as PDS, 56, 63, 67–68, 72, 102, 252, 269–71; principal at, 269; science in, 271; student culture at, 269–70; teaching staff at, 269, 271

Averill Teacher Education Circle (TEC), 311–12

Ball, Deborah: as amphibious teacher, 77, 274; career of, 229, 320, 355; and Cohen, 331, 345; on commercial curriculum